A Concise Companion to
Psychoanalysis, Literature, and Culture

Concise Companions to Literature and Culture
General Editor: David Bradshaw, University of Oxford

This series offers accessible, innovative approaches to major areas of literary study. Each volume provides an indispensable companion for anyone wishing to gain an authoritative understanding of a given period or movement's intellectual character and contexts.

Published

Modernism	Edited by David Bradshaw
Feminist Theory	Edited by Mary Eagleton
The Restoration and Eighteenth Century	Edited by Cynthia Wall
Postwar American Literature and Culture	Edited by Josephine G. Hendin
The Victorian Novel	Edited by Francis O'Gorman
Twentieth-Century American Poetry	Edited by Stephen Fredman
Chaucer	Edited by Corinne Saunders
Shakespeare on Screen	Edited by Diana E. Henderson
Contemporary British Fiction	Edited by James F. English
English Renaissance Literature	Edited by Donna B. Hamilton
Milton	Edited by Angelica Duran
Shakespeare and the Text	Edited by Andrew Murphy
Contemporary British and Irish Drama	Edited by Nadine Holdsworth and Mary Luckhurst
American Fiction 1900–1950	Edited by Peter Stoneley and Cindy Weinstein
The Romantic Age	Edited by Jon Klancher
Postwar British and Irish Poetry	Edited by Nigel Alderman and C. D. Blanton
Middle English Literature	Edited by Marilyn Corrie
Terror and the Postcolonial	Edited by Elleke Boehmer and Stephen Morton
Postcolonial Literature	Edited by Shirley Chew and David Richards
Realism	Edited by Matthew Beaumont
Psychoanalysis, Literature, and Culture	Edited by Laura Marcus and Ankhi Mukherjee

A Concise Companion to

Psychoanalysis, Literature, and Culture

Edited by Laura Marcus
and Ankhi Mukherjee

WILEY Blackwell

This edition first published 2014

Registered Office
John Wiley & Sons, Ltd, The Atrium, Southern Gate, Chichester, West Sussex, PO19 8SQ, UK

Editorial Offices
350 Main Street, Malden, MA 02148-5020, USA
9600 Garsington Road, Oxford, OX4 2DQ, UK
The Atrium, Southern Gate, Chichester, West Sussex, PO19 8SQ, UK

For details of our global editorial offices, for customer services, and for information about how to apply for permission to reuse the copyright material in this book please see our website at www.wiley.com/wiley-blackwell.

Library of Congress Cataloging-in-Publication Data

A concise companion to psychoanalysis, literature, and culture / edited by Laura Marcus and Ankhi Mukherjee.
pages cm
Includes bibliographical references and index.
ISBN 978-1-4051-8860-9 (cloth)
1. Psychoanalysis and literature. 2. Psychoanalysis and culture. I. Marcus, Laura. II. Mukherjee, Ankhi.
PN56.P92C666 2014
150.19′5–dc23

2014001165

A catalogue record for this book is available from the British Library.

Cover image: Juan Gris, *Bowl and Book* (detail), oil on canvas. © The Art Gallery Collection/Alamy

Set in 10/12.5pt Meridien by SPi Publisher Services, Pondicherry, India

1 2014

Contents

Notes on Contributors

Isobel Armstrong is a fellow of the British Academy, Senior Research Fellow of the Institute of English Studies, and Professor Emeritus of what is now the Geoffrey Tillotson Chair. During her time at Birkbeck, continuing the powerful tradition of nineteenth-century studies established by Geoffrey Tillotson, Barbara Hardy, and Michael Slater, she founded the London Seminar for Nineteenth-Century Studies and the Centre for Nineteenth-Century Studies (of whose committee she is still a member). She has published widely on nineteenth-century studies (in particular *Victorian Poetry: Poetry, Poetics and Politics*, 1996) and theory (see *The Radical Aesthetic*, 2000). Her latest book, *Victorian Glassworlds: Glass Culture and the Imagination* (2008), won the Modern Language Association's James Russell Lowell Prize in 2009. She gave the British Academy Warton Lecture on Poetry in 2011. She is working on a study of the nineteenth-century novel and the democratic imagination. During retirement she has taught at Harvard and Johns Hopkins universities and spoken at international conferences. She is a published poet.

Carolyn Burdett is Senior Lecturer in English and Victorian Studies in the Department of English at Birkbeck, University of London. Her research interests have focused on the literature, culture, and politics of the period 1880–1920. She has written a monograph titled *Olive Schreiner and the Progress of Feminism: Evolution, Gender, Empire* (2001). She co-edited a special issue on 'Eugenics Old and New' for the journal *New Formations* in 2007 and has also co-edited a collection of essays on

The Victorian Supernatural (2004). She is currently researching a book about the emergence of the term "empathy" at the beginning of the twentieth century, with particular focus on how cultural forms in the nineteenth century helped to shape the ways emotional life was conceived and discussed.

Tim Dean is Professor of English at the State University of New York at Buffalo. He is the author of *Gary Snyder and the American Unconscious* (1991), *Beyond Sexuality* (2000), *Unlimited Intimacy: Reflections on the Subculture of Barebacking* (2009), and *What Is Psychoanalytic Thinking?* (forthcoming).

Maud Ellmann is Randy L. and Melvin R. Berlin Professor of the Development of the Novel in English in the Department of English at the University of Chicago. Her research and teaching interests focus on British and European modernism and critical theory, particularly psychoanalysis and feminism. Her monographs include *The Poetics of Impersonality: T.S. Eliot and Ezra Pound; The Hunger Artists: Starving, Writing, and Imprisonment;* and *The Nets of Modernism*. Her recent journal articles have been on Irish fiction in English, the British psychoanalyst Marion Milner, the author of several luminous and idiosyncratic works on creativity, and the burgeoning new field of animal studies. Currently she is working on several projects, including World War II writing in Britain, the British novelist and poet Sylvia Townsend Warner, and fantasies of bodily disintegration in modernism, ranging from Melanie Klein to Samuel Beckett.

Stephen Frosh is Pro-Vice-Master and Professor in the Department of Psychosocial Studies at Birkbeck College, University of London. He is the author of many books and papers on psychosocial studies and on psychoanalysis, including *Psychoanalysis Outside the Clinic* (2010), *Hate and the Jewish Science: Anti-Semitism, Nazism and Psychoanalysis* (2005), *For and Against Psychoanalysis* (2006), *After Words* (2002), and *The Politics of Psychoanalysis* (1999). His most recent books are *Hauntings: Psychoanalysis and Ghostly Transmissions* (2013), *A Brief Introduction to Psychoanalytic Theory* (2012), and *Feelings* (2011).

Patricia Gherovici PhD is a licensed psychoanalyst and analytic supervisor practicing in Philadelphia and New York. She is an award-winning author, who has published nationally and internationally. Most recently she wrote the foreword to *Erotic Anger: A User's Manual* (2001) and contributed to *The Dreams of Interpretation: A Century Down* *the Royal Road* (2007). Her book *The Puerto Rican Syndrome* (2003) won the Gradiva Award and the Boyer Prize of the American Anthropological Association. Her latest book is *Please Select Your Gender: From the Invention of Hysteria to the Democratizing of Transgenderism* (2010).

Martin Hägglund is Professor of Comparative Literature and Humanities at Yale University. He is the author of *Dying for Time: Proust, Woolf, Nabokov* (2012); *Radical Atheism: Derrida and the Time of Life* (2008); and *Kronofobi: Essäer om tid och ändlighet* (2002).

Ranjana Khanna is Margaret Taylor Smith Director of Women's Studies and Professor of English, Women's Studies, and the Literature Program at Duke University. She works on anglophone and francophone postcolonial theory and literature, art, and film, psychoanalysis, and feminist theory. She is the author of *Dark Continents: Psychoanalysis and Colonialism* (2003) and *Algeria Cuts: Women and Representation 1830 to the Present* (2008). She has published in journals including *Differences, Signs, Third Text, Diacritics, Screen, Art History, positions, SAQ, Feminist Theory,* and *Public Culture*. Her current books in progress are titled *Asylum: The Concept and the Practice* and *Technologies of Unbelonging.*

Anna Kornbluh is Assistant Professor of English at the University of Illinois, Chicago, where her research centers on Victorian literature, critical theory, and cinema. She is the author of *Realizing Capital*, and is currently at work on *The Order of Forms* (a prehistory of structuralism), and *Marxism* (for the Bloomsbury Film Theory in Practice series).

Catherine Liu is Professor of Film and Media Studies and Visual Studies at the University of California Irvine. She is the author of *American Idyll: Anti-Elitism as Cultural Critique* (2011) and *Copying Machines: Taking Notes for the Automaton*. Kaya Press recently reissued her 1997 novel *Oriental Girls Desire Romance*. She has published on higher education theory and policy, the Frankfurt School, psychoanalysis, and historical materialism. She is at work on a book titled *Higher Education and Austerity: A Look at MOOCs.*

Laura Marcus is Goldsmiths' Professor of English Literature at the University of Oxford and a Fellow of the British Academy. She was previously Regius Professor of Rhetoric and Literature at the University of Edinburgh. Her research and teaching interests are in nineteenth-, twentieth-, and twenty-first-century literature and culture, with a particular focus on modernism, Virginia Woolf and Bloomsbury culture, life writing, literature and film, the history of psychoanalysis, and contemporary fiction. She is the author of several books, including *The*

Tenth Muse: Writing about Cinema in the Modernist Period (2007) (winner of the James Russell Lowell prize of the Modern Languages Association) and the forthcoming books *Dreams of Modernity: Literature, Psychoanalysis, Cinema* (2014) and *Autobiography: A Very Short Introduction* (2014).

Todd McGowan teaches theory and film at the University of Vermont. He is the author of *Enjoying What We Don't Have: The Political Project of Psychoanalysis* (2013), *Rupture: On the Emergence of the Political* (with Paul Eisenstein; 2012), *Out of Time: Desire in Atemporal Cinema* (2011), and other works.

Ankhi Mukherjee is CUF Lecturer (Associate Professor) in the Faculty of English Language and Literature at the University of Oxford and a Fellow of Wadham College. Her key areas of specialism are Victorian literature and culture, modern British and anglophone literature, postcolonial studies, critical theory, and intellectual history. She has published widely in international peer-reviewed journals such as *PMLA, Modern Language Quarterly, Paragraph, Parallax*, and *Contemporary Literature*. Her first book, *Aesthetic Hysteria: The Great Neurosis in Victorian Melodrama and Contemporary Fiction*, was published in 2007. Her second monograph, *What Is a Classic? Postcolonial Rewriting and Invention of the Canon*, was published in 2013 by Stanford University Press in its prestigious Cultural Memory in the Present series.

Jean-Michel Rabaté is Professor of English and Comparative Literature at the University of Pennsylvania, a curator of the Slought Foundation, an editor of the *Journal of Modern Literature*, and a Fellow of the American Academy of Arts and Sciences. He has authored or edited more than thirty books and collections on modernism, psychoanalysis, and philosophy. His forthcoming books are *An Introduction to Literature and Psychoanalysis, A Companion to 1922*, and *Crimes of the Future*.

Frances L. Restuccia is an English Professor at Boston College, where she teaches contemporary theory, modernism, the world novel, and film theory. Her publications include *James Joyce and the Law of the Father* (1989); *Melancholics in Love: Representing Women's Depression and Domestic Abuse* (2000); *Amorous Acts: Lacanian Ethics in Modernism, Film, and Queer Theory* (2006); and *The Blue Box: Kristevan/Lacanian Readings of Contemporary Film* (2012). She has published numerous articles in journals such as *Raritan, Contemporary Literature, Novel, Genre, Genders, American Imago, Lacanian Ink, Film-Philosophy*, and *Semplokē*. A chapter titled "Sebastian's Skull: Establishing 'the Society of the Icon'" is part of the recently published volume *Kristeva's Fiction* (2013), and an essay on

Don Quixote, love, and messianism in Agamben appeared in *Philosophy Today* (2012). She is co-chair of the Psychoanalytic Practices seminar at Harvard's Humanities Center.

Laurence A. Rickels is Professor at the Academy of Fine Arts, Karlsruhe (Staatliche Akademie der Bildenden Künste Karlsruhe). He is also the Sigmund Freud Chair at the European Graduate School. Since 1990 he has been teaching at the University of California, Santa Barbara. He teaches in the Comparative Literature Department as well as the Germanic, Slavic, and Semitic Studies Department, and has also been affiliated to Art, Film and Media Studies departments. He divides his time his time between California and Europe, notably Germany and Switzerland. His interests are in the intersections between psychoanalysis, technology, and Nazis. Strongly influenced by psychoanalytic theory, Professor Rickels' work is formed in the interrelationships of psychoanalysis, the Frankfurt School of critical theory, and deconstruction. His numerous works include *Aberrations of Mourning: Writing on German Crypts* (1988); *Der unbetrauerbare Tod* (1990); *The Case of California* (1991); *The Vampire Lectures* (1999); *Nazi Psychoanalysis* (2002); *Ulrike Ottinger: The Autobiography of Art Cinema* (2008); *The Devil Notebooks* (2008); and *I Think I Am: Philip K. Dick* (2010).

Nicholas Royle is Professor of English at the University of Sussex. He has published many essays and is the author of numerous books, including *Veering: A Theory of Literature* (2011); *In Memory of Jacques Derrida* (2009); *An Introduction to Literature, Criticism and Theory* (with Andrew Bennett; 4th edn. 2009); *How to Read Shakespeare* (2005); *The Uncanny* (2003); *After Derrida* (1995); and *Telepathy and Literature: Essays on the Reading Mind* (1990). He is also an editor of the *Oxford Literary Review*. Besides critical and theoretical writings, Professor Royle has also published numerous works of short fiction and a novel, *Quilt* (2010).

Naomi Segal is Professorial Fellow at Birkbeck, University of London. She has published twelve books, most recently *Consensuality* (2009), *Indeterminate Bodies* (2003), *Le Désir à l'œuvre* (2000), and *André Gide: Pederasty & Pedagogy* (1998).

Daniel Steuer worked at various British and Irish universities between 1989 and 2013. His research interests include literature and philosophy, and social and political theory, and he has published on figures including Goethe, Büchner, Musil, Bernhard, Wittgenstein, Sebald, and Adorno. He is co-editor of *Wittgenstein Reading* (2013), a volume of essays investigating the influence of literary authors on Wittgenstein.

Pamela Thurschwell is a Senior Lecturer in English at the University of Sussex and the author of *Literature, Technology and Magical Thinking, 1880–1920* (2001) and *Sigmund Freud* (2000; 2nd edition, 2009) and the co-editor, with Leah Price, of *Literary Secretaries/Secretarial Culture* (2005), and with Nicola Bown and Carolyn Burdett of *The Victorian Supernatural* (2004). She is currently working on a study on modern adolescence and anachronism.

Andrew Webber is Professor of Modern German and Comparative Culture in the University of Cambridge and a Fellow of Churchill College. He has published widely on relationships between psychoanalysis, literature, and other cultural forms. His works include *The Doppelgänger: Double Visions in German Literature* (1996); a translation of the "Schreber case" for the new Penguin edition of the works of Freud; and *The European Avant-Garde 1900–1940* (2004). His most recent work has been concerned with urban space, and in particular Berlin. From 2004 to 2007 he held a Major Research Fellowship from the Leverhulme Trust to work on the city, and the resulting book, *Berlin in the Twentieth Century: A Cultural Topography*, was published by Cambridge University Press in 2008.

Robert J.C. Young is a postcolonial theorist, cultural critic, and historian. He has taught at the universities of Southampton and Oxford and is currently the Silver Professor of English and Comparative Literature in the Department of English at New York University. His publications include *The Idea of English Ethnicity* (2008); *Postcolonialism: A Very Short Introduction* (2003); *Postcolonialism: An Historical Introduction* (2001); *Torn Halves: Political Conflict in Literary and Cultural Theory* (1996); *Colonial Desire: Hybridity in Culture, Theory and Race* (1995); and *White Mythologies: Writing History and the West* (1990). He is the general editor of *Interventions: International Journal of Postcolonial Studies*

Nicolette Zeeman teaches at King's College, Cambridge, and in the English Faculty of the University of Cambridge. She is the author of *Piers Plowman and the Medieval Discourse of Desire* (2006), and has written on *Piers Plowman*, Chaucer, song, scholasticism, devotional literature, medieval literary theory, and ideas of image use and idolatry. An interest in psychoanalysis has shaped her work on *Piers Plowman*, Chaucer, and a forthcoming essay on the will in spiritual writing. She is currently finishing a study titled *Arts of Disruption: Conflict and Contradiction in Medieval Allegory*, and editing, with Jean Michel Massing, a volume on the chapel of King's College.

Acknowledgments

We would like to profusely thank our commissioning editors at Wiley Blackwell: Emma Bennett, who championed the book idea, and Ben Thatcher, who guided it to completion. We are grateful to Alys Moody, then a graduate student in the English Faculty at Oxford, for her careful preparation of the essays to requisite style specifications over summer 2013. We are also thankful to Janet Moth for her meticulous copyediting, and to Bridget Jennings and Joanna Pyke for their assistance. In curating a collection of essays on the history, theory, and futures of psychoanalysis, we revisited the formative force of this discourse (and its diverse reckonings) in our scholarly lives. For this, and for the laughter-filled hours of a strong collaboration and friendship, we thank our contributors and each other.

Laura Marcus
Ankhi Mukherjee

Introduction: Psychoanalysis at the Margins

Laura Marcus

The essays in this volume represent the variety of new ways of taking up the legacy of psychoanalytic thought and theory, reaching forward to us from the close of the nineteenth century. The continuities between then and now are revealed in the focus on sexualities, on the form of the case history, on the place of vision and the specular, and on the role of language as manifestation of unconscious processes. There are also marked discontinuities, however, not only from the original texts of psychoanalysis but from many of their later twentieth-century reformulations. Most notable, perhaps, is the near-total absence of any direct discussion of the Oedipal, the "complex" which for Freud founded human identity, sexual organization, and his new science. The Oedipal and Oedipalization were central topics, to take one example, in Maud Ellmann's excellent collection of essays, *Psychoanalytic Literary Criticism* (1994). Two decades later, our contributors continue to be preoccupied with questions of sexuality and psychic life, but their frameworks are substantially those of queer and postcolonial theory, cultural criticism, translation in its many senses, models of time and temporality, and the human–animal interface.

In Part I of the volume, "Histories," Stephen Frosh offers the fullest account of the place of psychoanalysis in the twentieth century – a

A Concise Companion to Psychoanalysis, Literature, and Culture, First Edition.
Edited by Laura Marcus and Ankhi Mukherjee.

long twentieth century, since the processes he describes seem to persist into the second decade of the current century. He mentions in passing the neglect of psychoanalytic theory by psychologists and stresses the conjunction of "the slow and rather dull work of clinicians" and "a more flamboyant and speculative use of psychoanalysis as a key to cultural knowledge."

> whatever one might think of the validity or efficacy of psychoanalysis, it has come to define a very widespread form of cultural experience and to be indispensable to ways of living in, as well as understanding, that cultural form. ... the human subject reflexively deploys psychoanalytic understanding in the construction of selfhood; psychoanalysis itself is reflexively embodied in the cultural processes to which it has partially given rise.

The other paradox Frosh identifies is the place of rationality in psychoanalytic theory: committed to scientific rationalism while "enacting the irrational otherness it is striving to theorize." He mentions in particular the uneasy relationship between psychoanalysis and telepathy, parapsychology, and so on – the topic which is at the center of Carolyn Burdett's chapter discussed below – but his main focus is on a similarly tense relationship, with reflection on colonial and gender relations. In both cases, what initially looks like a disaster area, shaped by Freud's analysis of the "primitive" on the one hand and the masculinist and heteronormative associations of the explanatory models he developed on the other, contributes to some of the most powerful and influential work in postcolonial and feminist theory.

Andrew Webber's analysis of the "case study" – a term which he points out was not used by Freud – is one of several chapters which bring out the notorious difficulties of Freud translation. The case study is, however, "the foundational mode of representation for psychoanalysis ... a form of study that psychoanalysis adapts from established conventions of medical and other scientific or disciplinary writing, but also adapts to its own purposes." Freud does use the term *Krankengeschichte* which, as Webber points out, "modulates between the historical account of the analysand's illness and that of the treatment of the illness in question." As Webber shows in detail in Freud's discussion of Wilhelm Jensen's novella "Gradiva," the relations between *Fall* (case), and *Anfall, Unfall, Zufall,* and so forth inevitably get lost in translation.

Burdett, as noted above, addresses the question of the occult and paranormal which "were not the marginal interests of cranks but rather phenomena studied and investigated by figures otherwise engaged in uncontentiously respectable scientific pursuits and intellectual enquiries." Freud, she suggests, despite Ernest Jones' attempts to play down this area of his interests, was one of these, and the early reception of Freudian theory in the English-speaking world was mediated by Frederic Myers, who had been one of the founders of the Society for Psychical Research. Gothic novels, the New Woman, and the Oscar Wilde affair all formed part of the background to more specifically psychological reflection on the nature of desire.

Both Laurence Rickels and Daniel Steuer engage in their essays with Adorno's thought – in Rickels' case as a prologue (to borrow the title of Adorno's essay on television, which he discusses in some detail) to an analysis of psychoanalytic theories of adolescence, notably by Winnicott. The end of conscription and mass warfare, together with improved techniques of contraception, meant for Winnicott that "Adolescence now has to contain itself . . . in a way it has never done before."

Steuer engages with the broader issue of the relationship of psychoanalysis, as mediated by Freud and Cavell, to theorization of the political as well as of literary production. Both Adorno and Cavell, he suggests, uphold a radical conception of psychoanalysis as a "threshold science," transcending the opposition between positivism and a more speculative approach, foregrounding Adorno's central theme of "natural history" (*Naturgeschichte*) and deploying "a specifically psychoanalytic sensitivity."

> Freud confronts case histories and other anthropological material with metapsychological constructions; in Adorno, philosophical reflection is endlessly answerable to cultural artifacts, be they philosophy, music, or literature; and in Cavell the reporting on the process of readings is itself the message.

As Adorno put it, addressing a reproach frequently made to psychoanalysis, "The critique of the superego ought to become the critique of the society which produced it; if it falls silent before this, then it becomes subservient to the prevailing social norm."

In turning to the question of literature, we encounter one of the key problems and paradoxes of psychoanalytic criticism and theory. Literature is threaded through psychoanalytic thought and theory. On the occasion of his seventieth birthday Freud was greeted as the "discoverer of the unconscious," but he corrected the speaker: "The poets and philosophers before me discovered the unconscious. What I discovered was the scientific method by which the unconscious can be studied" (quoted in Trilling 1981, 95). He drew his fundamental concepts from literary works, among them Sophocles' *Oedipus Rex*, Shakespeare's *Hamlet, The Merchant of Venice*, and *King Lear*, E.T. Hoffman's *The Sand Man*, Jensen's "Gradiva." Yet the "application" of psychoanalytic theories to literary texts in the work of Freud's followers has frequently been seen as the least satisfactory dimension of psychoanalytic thought, in large part due to an unease with the "treatment" of the writer or the work as if he, she, or it were the patient on the analytic couch.

Nonetheless, there is a persistent desire, as Peter Brooks has pointed out, for "a convergence of psychoanalysis and literary criticism." For Brooks, this dream stems from an apprehension of a structural homology between literature and psychic life:

> We sense that there ought to be, that there must be, some correspondence between literary and psychic process, that aesthetic structure and form, including literary tropes, must somehow coincide with the psychic structures and operations they both evoke and appeal to.
>
> (Brooks 1987, 4)

The wish for this convergence of psychoanalysis and literary criticism was continuous across the twentieth century, though it was conceived in very different ways. The earliest modes of psychoanalytic literary criticism were primarily focused on author and character, following on from Freud's analyses of the literary work as a symptom of the artist, and of the work of art as a kind of dream-text. This gave way to a greater focus on the reader, with the development in the middle decades of the twentieth century of psychoanalytic reader-response criticism, exploring subjective responses and the forms of identification readers make with literary texts. The latter decades of the century saw a shift of focus to texts and textual processes, including transference, narrative transmission, and the subversion of authority. The work of psychoanalytic, deconstructive, and feminist critics following Jacques Lacan was described thus by Shoshana Felman, writing in the 1980s:

> The history of reading has accustomed us to the assumption ... that reading is finding meaning ... Lacan's analysis of the signifier opens up a radically new assumption, an assumption that is nonetheless nothing but an insightful logical and methodological consequence of Freud's discovery: that what *can* be read (and perhaps what *should* be read) is not

> just meaning, but the lack of meaning; that significance lies not just in consciousness, but, specifically, in its disruption; that the signifier can be analyzed in its effects without its signified being known; that the lack of meaning – the discontinuity in conscious understanding – can and should be interpreted as such, without necessarily being transformed into meaning ... Thus, for Lacan, what is analytical par excellence is not (as is the case for [Marie] Bonaparte) the *readable* but the *unreadable*, and the *effects* of the unreadable. What calls for analysis is the insistence of the unreadable in the text.
>
> (Felman 1988, 149)

The essays in Part II of the volume, "Literatures," both take up and transform a number of these preoccupations. Jean-Michel Rabaté opens with a key question: "Should one apply psychoanalysis to literature? Can one do this without having it unravel?" He argues rather that psychoanalysis must learn from literature, which becomes, in his readings, an "ambassador." The lines of connection in Rabaté's essay begin with Holbein's painting *The Ambassadors*, whose use of anamorphosis to conceal and simultaneously reveal the image of the skull (and of a relationship between death and writing), was explored extensively by Lacan. The furnishings represented in Holbein's painting appear to have been a model for Freud's study and consulting-room, in which the antique rug, the couch, and the antique statues acted as "dream-catching machines." The theme of "the ambassadors" is pursued by Rabaté through Henry James' novel of that title, which presents us, "like all novels and paintings," with the model of "a knowledge about ourselves that we had without knowing it." Rabaté's models of weaving and unweaving function as a counter and corrective to an outmoded conception of "applying" psychoanalysis to literature: the continuous "unfolding" of images is the appropriate way of proceeding, and it is one which "transgresses its limits as soon as they appear." The most significant and the most difficult question for psychoanalytic theory is, then, that of how "process" is to become "method."

Nicholas Royle, writing on "Freud's Double," finds "the double" to be at the heart of the literary, relationships between literature and psychoanalysis, and the interweavings of literature and life. The figure of the double, inextricably linked to Freud's understandings of "the uncanny," points to death and existence beyond this world; to the mirror-world of language itself; to the very strangeness of being in the world. Royle extends the argument for a suspension of, or resistance to, meaning, arguing that Freud's writing should be seen as "a kind of event, a work of strange energies that are not ... within his control or restricted to 'what Freud meant'." He finds in Freud a form of "writing double" that is also constitutive of literature in all its strangeness; it takes us inside the movement of consciousness and thought while simultaneously placing us in a position outside, or "extimate" to, it.

Dreams, "the royal road to the unconscious," have been the most significant of all phenomena for psychoanalysis. They share with Royle's model of literary doubleness or duplicity the quality of being both part of and external to us, appearing at once to rise up from our perceptions, memories, and desires and to be unbidden visitors. Nicolette Zeeman explores the place of dreams and dreaming in medieval literature and culture, noting the continuities between medieval writers' focus on the visual dimension of dreams, the role of interpretation and "retelling," and the complex origins of dreams with those of psychoanalytic theory, and in particular the models of dreams explored by Freud and Lacan. Zeeman also points to the relationship between representations of desire in medieval writings (such as those of Chaucer and of Guillaume de Lorris, author of the *Roman de la rose*) and Lacan's account of "courtly love."

"Courtly love" is also addressed, in a very different context, in Tim Dean's discussion of Thom Gunn's poem sequence "Troubadour," written in part in the voice of the serial killer Jeffrey Dahmer. These suggest that, Dean proposes, "although [Dahmer's] desires were beyond-the-pale abhorrent, his desires may be recognizably familiar when read in light of the Western lyric tradition." Bringing together Lacan's writings on desire with those of Michel Foucault, Dean explores the significance of queer theory for psychoanalytic literary criticism and understandings of literary subjectivity. Returning to "Troubadour," he shows that "rather than 'othering' Dahmer as monstrous, Gunn brings Dahmer closer by allowing him to inhabit the lyric 'I' and then couching his voice in the idioms of a distinguished poetic tradition." In this way, Gunn suggests that "Dahmer's desire, far from monstrous, may be familiar. It is precisely the excessiveness of his desire that makes him human; or, to put it another way, the inhuman dimension of Dahmer's desire is not his alone." For Dean, Gunn's way of proceeding is "at once psychoanalytic and profoundly ethical."

Pam Thurschwell also takes up the importance of queer theory for psychoanalysis in her account of adolescence as a category and "case." Recent writings on queer temporality, such as those of Lee Edelman, have argued for an identification of homosexuality with the death drive, in a refusal of teleologies and futurities which are tied to the figure of the child, as the product and emblem of "heteronormative" and procreative sexualities. For Thurschwell, the overlooked category of "the adolescent" represents a more intransigent and more interesting refusal of "development" and an alternative version of atemporality. This was recognized by Freud, who, for all his trouble with adolescents (paramount among them "Dora," the subject of one of his fullest case histories), recognized their right "to linger at certain stages of development." Adolescent "resistance" is represented in striking ways not only in psychoanalytic writings, including case histories (those of Freud and of his child-analyst daughter Anna), but in the literary text which Thurschwell explores in detail: Willa Cather's 1905 story "Paul's Case," published in the same year as Freud's "Fragment of a Case of Analysis" ("Dora").

The essays in Part III of the volume, "Visual Cultures," explore a wide range of contemporary images and visual narratives through the lens of psychoanalytic theory. The approaches included here point to the profound influence of the psychoanalytic feminist theories inaugurated in the 1970s (paramount among them Laura Mulvey's manifesto "Visual Pleasure and Narrative Cinema," with its formulations of a gendered "gaze theory") while marking the new turns taken by more recent psychoanalytically inflected approaches to visual culture. Frances Restuccia gives a close account of Pedro Almodóvar's film *Volver*, using an account of "intimacy" and "intimate revolt" drawn from the writings of Julia Kristeva to explore the film's arousal of the senses as well as its psychological dynamics (which revolve around incest, trauma, and mothering.) Where Laura Mulvey created a polarization between the subversive, anti-narrative representations of the filmic avant-garde and Hollywood "narrative cinema" (with what she defined as its rigid visual and psychical structures of male regard and female spectacle), Restuccia argues that *Volver* "sets up a clash between delicate psychic life and the commodification of that life in the society of the spectacle."

Spectacle as commodity in late capitalism is the subject of Catherine Liu's essay, "Pychoanalysis, Popular and Unpopular," in which Liu addresses the rise and fall of psychoanalysis in US popular culture, with the initial enthusiasm in Hollywood and New York in the 1920s and 1930s waning in the 1970s and 1980s, just as it became more solidly established in the academy and notably in film studies, in North America as in Europe. "Psychoanalytic terms like 'id' were common currency in the Hollywood of the 1950s: long before 1970s film theorists embraced sexual difference, the gaze, and fetishism as keys to understanding film form, spectatorship, and the ideological apparatus." In the longer term, however, "psychoanalysis appeared exotic and foreign while self-help and mind-cure were allied to American traditions and folk cures. . . . popular representations of psychic life would be reshaped and rearranged by post-war self-help movements, and the rise of new forms of popular culture and an advice industry that married self-hypnosis, self-help, the power of positive thinking, and business motivation." This is linked, she suggests, to the focus on identity in the thought and politics of advanced capitalism, where feminism and film theory developed in tandem and often formed important alliances, adopting and developing psychoanalytic theory. "Feminist filmmakers and activists looked for new ways of working and intervening in the art world, in the film industry, and in academia."

Ankhi Mukherjee pursues the question of psychoanalysis as represented in popular culture, focusing on prime-time TV and, in particular, the series *In Treatment* (2008) which depicts, in Mukherjee's words, "three neurotics who represent different facets of the great American excluded," seeking treatment from the analyst Paul (Gabriel Byrne). The chapter explores not only the ways in which popular cultural representation and reception engage with the practices and processes of psychoanalysis and the figure of the analyst but also the forms of (gendered) fantasy and dreaming involved in the production and consumption of the televisual.

Patricia Gherovici's essay, which focuses on transsexuality and transsexual memoirs, takes a different critical turn in relation to "visual culture." The visibility of transsexual symptoms (as an embodying of unconscious phenomena) becomes of less significance in Gherovici's account than acts of writing, exemplified in transsexual memoirs. These frequently represent "the experience of slipping in and out of the body" (a slipping away which Gherovici also finds in Joyce's representations of his fictional alter ego Stephen Dedalus and which she explores in part through Lacan's readings of Joyce's texts). The conundrum (the title adopted by the writer Jan Morris in her autobiographical account of transsexualism and sex change) of sexual difference confounds the binary of sex and gender (the first conventionally understood as biologically given [body] and the second as culturally constructed [symbol and representation]). Transsexual memoirs reveal the crucial place of writing in the procedures of bodily transformation: "Writing a sex change memoir aims not just at passing from one side to the other; it has the function of tying together body and text ... the writing of the memoir can bring the author home to the body transformed."

Todd McGowan's "The Desert of the Real" returns us to the cinema, and the forms of "imaginary plenitude" offered to the cinema spectator.

For McGowan, this experience of "plenitude" is to be understood as "a secondary response to an originary excess." He revisits and revises the work of earlier psychoanalytic film theorists (including Christian Metz and Laura Mulvey) in order to produce a focus on the category of "the Real" (as theorized in the work of Lacan and Slavoj Žižek). "Contra Metz," McGowan argues, "the task of the psychoanalytic theorist does not involve detailing the symbolic structure that underlies the cinema's illusory imaginary plenitude. It involves instead distinguishing between this plenitude and the excessive disruptions of it." The model of spectatorship derived from this account is explored through two recent films, *Black Swan* (Darren Aronofsky, 2010) and *127 Hours* (Danny Boyle, 2010), which, in their very different ways, "take a bite out of us."

The final part of the book, "Transformations," addresses the ways in which psychoanalysis interacts with and transforms other discourses. One aspect of this is what Anna Kornbluh describes as "the radical questioning by which psychoanalysis transcends psychology," and it is also in play in Martin Hägglund's model of chronolibido and Ranjana Khanna's analysis of hospitality and asylum. Another, which is the topic of Kornbluh's essay, is what Freud himself called his tortured relation to economic motifs:

> Along with the "topographic," which maps regions of the psyche (conscious, unconscious, preconscious, and later, id, ego, superego), and the "dynamic," which models repression (regulating the expression of psychic ideas in and across the different topographic regions), the "economic" is the third of Freud's metapsychological hypotheses, metaphorizing the "distribution" of psychic resources.

The last of these, Kornbluh suggests, is primary, but it needs to be disentangled, for English-speaking readers, from Strachey's bizarre translation of *Besetzung* as "cathexis" and, sometimes, "investment." Like a number of authors in this collection, Kornbluh emphasizes that Freud himself, when writing in English or translating his own work, used much freer and more informal formulations such as "colored" or "toned," whereas Strachey repeatedly renders informal notions such as "psychic household" in the language of economics.

For Hägglund, "chronolibido" involves a mediation between what he calls chronophilia and chronophobia. "It is because one is attached to a temporal being (chronophilia) that one fears losing it (chronophobia)." Platonic thought offers the idea of life after death (one of the Greek elements which Christianity seems to have bolted on to Judaism), while Epicureans urged one instead to accept the idea of death as the end and thus "to eliminate chronophobia." Hägglund pursues this theme through the work of Lacan.

Several chapters in this last part of the book also address the issue of "resistance" to psychoanalysis. Maud Ellmann takes up Freud's suggestion that his emphasis on animal instincts had led to attacks on psychoanalysis as an "assault on the dignity of the human race." As she shows, animals are central to psychoanalysis at all kinds of levels, whether Anna Freud's scary Alsatian, which aroused an all too real castration anxiety in an American client, Freud's Little Hans's horse, or the Rat Man's rats. Psychoanalytic theory, she suggests, following Deleuze and Guattari, "tends to overlook the multiplicity of species that crops up in patients' discourse by identifying every animal with the Oedipal scenario." Moving through a discussion of animal dreams, which are increasingly open to scientific investigation, Ellmann ends with some reflections on the upright gait of humans (and occasionally of fantasy animals like the Wolf Man's wolf). The wolf in the illustration rises from the page, while the writer (at least the hand-writer) is tied to the horizontal and "pitted, pockmarked, spotted page."

Khanna addresses Levinas' analysis of insomnia based initially on his work in a World War II prison camp. As Khanna summarizes it, "The institutions of asylum, rendered through the lens of 'insomnia,' raise questions concerning art, conceptual thinking, subject constitution, and theories of being, space, and ethical relation." On the question raised by Frosh about the relation of psychoanalysis to rationalism, Levinas' critique of the "fables" of psychoanalysis, quoted by Khanna in her chapter, could perhaps be read in a more optimistic light: "Psychoanalysis is, in its philosophical essence, the end point of rationalism: it places the same demands on reflection that reflection placed on naively thinking thought."

Robert Young raises perhaps the most radical doubt: "to what extent does psychoanalysis offer real understanding or explanation as opposed to a translation into its own specialized idiom ...?" He suggests, however, that the model of psychoanalytic translation is peculiarly fruitful as "a possible way of reading the invisible, the subaltern, those whose forms of public representation distort their fundamental being, where the invisibility or repression of subalterns in official discourses and documents from the past require a detranslation exercise to make them visible in their own terms." While Freud does not describe this sort of process as cultural *translation*, his concept of cultural change or transformation (*kulturelle Wandlung*) might be seen to point in this direction.

Isobel Armstrong, reflecting on a Master's course she taught for some years at Birkbeck College in London, takes up psychoanalysis in a pedagogical context. Exploring the attitudes, often very negative, of her women students to Freud's writings on female sexuality, she discusses the psychoanalytic texts that she would now put before students, which would include the work of object-relations theorists, including that of Wilfred Bion, D.W. Winnicott and Christopher Bollas, and would represent the shift in recent psychoanalytic literary criticism from the phallus-centered work of previous decades towards questions of affect, intersubjectivity, and the maternal.

Naomi Segal's chapter, "Touching and Not Touching," takes up the topics of intersubjectivity and intrasubjectivity in its focus on those dimensions of the human sensorium which lie outside "the five senses," as they are conventionally understood. Segal examines the multiple dimensions of "touch," in the context of contemporary theoretical understandings of the senses as a multiplicity. She opens up the significance of touch in psychoanalytic theory, including Didier Anzieu's concept of the "skin-ego," and explores an understanding of the self as, in her words, "a complex structure of surfaces." The final section of the chapter looks at the ways in which human relations based on touch are played out, or resisted, in works of literature.

Some of these essays are solidly located in a psychoanalytic framework. Others, like those by Frosh and Young, place psychoanalysis in a broader cultural or intercultural context. To attempt to efface the differences between them would be as wrong as the process which Ellmann, in her essay on the psychoanalytic animal, calls the "suppression of zoological diversity." Together, they illustrate the continuing vitality of the streams of thought inspired by Freud and his followers.

References

Brooks, Peter. 1987. "The Idea of a Psychoanalytic Literary Criticism." In *Discourse in Psychoanalysis and Literature,* ed. Shlomith Rimmon-Kenan. London and New York: Methuen.

Ellmann, Maud. 1994. *Psychoanalytic Literary Criticism.* London: Longman.

Felman, Shoshana. 1988. "On Reading Poetry: Reflections on the Limits and Possibilities of Psychoanalytic Approaches." In *The Purloined Poe: Lacan, Derrida and Psychoanalytic Reading,* ed. John P. Muller and William J. Richardson. Baltimore: Johns Hopkins University Press.

Trilling, Lionel. 1981. "Freud and Literature." In *Freud: A Collection of Critical Essays.* Englewood Cliffs, N.J.: Prentice Hall.

Part I

Histories

Chapter 1

The Freudian Century

Stephen Frosh

Psychoanalytic culture

The idea that western culture is saturated by psychoanalysis may seem excessive, given how controversial psychoanalysis continues to be, and how often we are faced with the assertion that "Freud is dead." Certainly its clinical manifestations are constantly under threat from ostensibly more efficient short-term therapies and supposedly more effective "evidence-based" approaches, or from simple market forces that work against the slowness and expense that characterize psychoanalytic forms of treatment. Whilst psychoanalytic training in some parts of the world (notably Latin America) is thriving, in Anglo-American settings there is much more concern over its future, and in the UK there have been several psychoanalytic psychotherapy training programs that have failed to recruit sufficient students to sustain themselves. In the universities, too, clinical psychoanalysis is a small area; and in the social sciences the longstanding struggle over the place of psychoanalysis in research continues. There may in fact be a small resurgence here, with the emergence of a psychoanalytically informed new "discipline" of psychosocial studies and with regular attempts to find ways to draw on, or incorporate, psychoanalytic ideas into

A Concise Companion to Psychoanalysis, Literature, and Culture, First Edition.
Edited by Laura Marcus and Ankhi Mukherjee.

qualitative research methodologies (see, for example, Frosh and Saville-Young 2011) and to fight for its place in sociology and psychology (see, for example, Roseneil 2006). But in the social sciences it is still the case that psychoanalysis is a minority position, facing all the accusations of "subjectivity" and unscientific speculativeness that it has always faced (Frosh 2006).

There are, however, various ripostes to this. The first is that whatever one might think of the validity or efficacy of psychoanalysis, it has come to define a very widespread form of cultural experience and to be indispensable to ways of living in, as well as understanding, that cultural form. This has its ironies, given the roots of psychoanalysis in the clinic; but it also reveals what has happened to psychoanalysis in terms of influence – that it has created a way of thinking and a mode of reflexive self-consciousness that has become a taken-for-granted element of much cultural experience. This argument relies on the idea that humans are constituted as self-reflexive subjects in culture – as *social* subjects – continually making sense of themselves through the application of discourses that surround them. Put more simply, culture constantly throws up modes of self-understanding that are then drawn on by subjects in a self-referential way, strengthening some of these cultural discourses and weakening others. In the case of psychoanalysis, the early idea of the dynamic unconscious was extraordinarily seminal for twentieth-century self-understanding, in that it named and explained the widespread experience of how something dangerous and exciting might break through from "below" to upset the balance of the supposedly rational, yet actually repressive, surface (Frosh 1991). This might sometimes be life-enhancing, as with the new forms of art, music, and literature that emerged in the early years of the twentieth century; but sometimes it might manifest destructively, for instance in the outbursts of vicious irrationality expressed in the plethora of wars and in the rise of Nazism in the heart of European "civilization." In the light of these cultural phenomena, can western subjects understand themselves without recourse to notions such as the "unconscious," "repression," or "defenses"? Of course the answer to this must be "yes," but these notions have nevertheless been amongst the most potent and widespread of those available for self-explanation in the past hundred years.

An obvious caveat applies here, which is about the geographical and political limitations of the claim that the last century was "Freudian" and that culture is saturated by psychoanalysis. Psychoanalysis grew up in the crucible of Europe; it had very specific origins in the scientific culture of the late nineteenth century alongside the then-current fascination with various branches of occultism; and it was laced in its original location with the complexities of Jewish emancipation and hence also with antisemitism (Frosh 2005). It was relatively quickly exported to Britain, where its early history was rather different, being closely connected to the widespread interest in psychical research and also linked from near the start to feminism and the arts (Frosh 2003); and of course it found quite considerable acceptance in America. But whilst there was interest in psychoanalysis in various other places before World War II, it was only with the "diaspora" of European psychoanalysts that it really took off in South America and elsewhere. One increasingly important issue that arises from this narrative of dissemination is the connection between psychoanalysis and colonialism. This is not a statement about how psychoanalysis gradually "colonized" societies around the world; it is, rather, a comment on the connection between psychoanalytic culture and theories and practices that draw on, and sustain, oppressive social structures – despite the many psychoanalytic radicals who have populated the psychoanalytic movement, and the longstanding investment of psychoanalytic social critics in social change (Frosh 1999; Jacoby 1975, 1983). For example, psychoanalysis has a complex history of reproduction of colonial tropes such as the "primitive," meaning both foundational (basic) states and "crude" sexual and destructive impulses akin to those of the "savage" of the nineteenth-century European imagination (Brickman 2003). This association is found in Freud's own use of the "ontology recapitulates phylogeny" model to match the development of the European infant with that of the "savage," but it continues in relatively everyday clinical use as an uninterrogated marker of the difference between the "civilized" and "primitive" mind. This places psychoanalysis as a discourse of colonialism, meaning both that it may not be "applicable" to non-European cultures, and more strongly that where it does apply, it may be as a *subjugating* discourse rather than an emancipatory or therapeutic one.

In this context, it is perhaps surprising to discover that psychoanalysis is proving to be a useful ground for postcolonial studies. This is because, speaking as it may from the heart of colonialism, it nevertheless offers a range of expressive ideas that can be used to unpick both the colonial mind and its legacy in the postcolonial world. Much of the work here draws on the famous intervention of Frantz Fanon (1967), which deploys psychoanalytic ideas to examine the psychological effects of colonialism and in so doing draws a picture of a whole social world infiltrated by Freudian (and Lacanian) categories. More recently, this has been taken up energetically by a wide range of authors interested for example in the "melancholic" aspects of the postcolonial state, meaning by that a cultural situation in which there is haunting of the present by a felt loss of a treasured past, which has been so comprehensively occluded as to make even mourning it impossible. The consequence of this is the creation of postcolonial societies still in thrall to colonialism; and the articulation of this is in psychoanalytic terms. Ranjana Khanna (2004), for example, advances this general thesis by using Freud's idea of melancholia, outlined in "Mourning and Melancholia" (Freud 1953–74, 14:237–58), in conjunction with a social analysis of postcolonial states, as in the following passage:

> Whereas Freud wrote of the work of mourning as the work of assimilating the lost object, the work of melancholia has a critical relation to the lost and to the buried. It manifests, sometimes in paralysis, stasis, or demetaphorization, loss, and it thus calls upon the inassimilable remainder. It does not merely call for inclusion, assimilation, reparation, or retribution. It calls for a response to the critical work of incorporation, and the ethical demand that such incorporation makes on the future. In the context of newly formed colonized nation-states, the critical response to nation-statehood arises from the secret embedded in nation-state formation: that the concept of nation-statehood was constituted through the colonial relation, and needs to be radically reshaped if it is to survive without colonies, or without a concealed (colonial) other.
>
> (Khanna 2004, 25)

The shift from a psychological to a social frame is very obvious and deliberate here, and evidences the way in which the psychoanalytic paradigm is being used to advance thinking at a cultural level. One might expect this to feed back subsequently into critical thought in literature and the humanities, given the importance of postcolonial ideas there, and indeed this has happened. For example, Edward Said's (2003) analysis of Freud's 1939 text *Moses and Monotheism* (1953–74, 23:138) under the expressive title of *Freud and the Non-European* is perhaps characteristic of one postcolonial use of psychoanalysis. Rather than draw on psychoanalysis as a privileged discipline for comprehending the psyche from the point of view of the "European," he attends instead to the fractures within psychoanalysis itself as revealing openings through which a broader understanding might emerge. This has two forms: first, the lacunae of western thought are brought out into the open, manifested in the contradictions of psychoanalytic theory. Secondly, at a "meta" level there are ways that psychoanalysis performs that might be deployed counter-hegemonically (and even against psychoanalysis itself) in these "non-European" settings. For Said, pursuing a view of psychoanalysis as a disruptive discipline, *Moses and Monotheism* dramatizes an opposition to be found in Freud's writing to a notion that identity might be formed once and for all, coherent and complete, at either the individual or cultural level. This is constituted in "Freud's profound exemplification of the insight that even for the most definable, the most identifiable, the most stubborn communal identity – for him, this was the Jewish identity – there are inherent limits that prevent it from being fully incorporated into one, and only one, Identity" (Said 2003, 53). Making Moses an Egyptian, as Freud did in his book, has the effect of asserting a brokenness within Jewish communal identity: at its source is an outsider, so claims for national or racial purity must always break down, in the specific case of Jews and in the general case of all cultures. What this does therefore is make a general point that can be applied everywhere (that identities are always broken); and it also specifically disputes claims for the fixedness and superiority of European colonial culture. There is no one identity, it is always open to the other; and so the European is infected from the start with the disruptive presence of the colonized, and psychoanalysis shows how this occurs.

This account of how psychoanalysis both shares in colonial practices and offers some routes out of it is paralleled elsewhere, most notably in the debates over sexual difference that stemmed initially from feminist criticism of psychoanalytic assumptions. For Freud (1953–74, 23:252), sexual difference ("the wish for a penis and the masculine protest") was the "bedrock" of psychoanalysis, beyond which it could not go, and this took the specific form of the refutation of femininity and the pursuit of masculinity. This was contested from very early on, in the work of psychoanalytic writers of the 1920s and 1930s, and the general sexual normativeness of psychoanalysis has continued to be the object of critique, both from feminists and from gay and lesbian writers (see Frosh 1999, 2006). However, especially since the publication in 1974 of Juliet Mitchell's book, *Psychoanalysis and Feminism*, psychoanalysis has also been drawn upon by many theorists in a search for theoretical leverage on gender and sexuality. This does not mean that Mitchell's promotion of psychoanalysis as a sexually progressive discipline has gone unchallenged. Indeed, psychoanalysis's conservatism in this area is well documented: in theory and in clinical work it has rarely supplied convincing recruits to the radicalization of gender politics or to the ranks of sexual revolution, despite a great deal of interest in this in its early years (Makari 2010). More importantly, however, there is now a sense of banality about many of the psychoanalytic claims concerning gender and sexual difference. Virginia Goldner (2003), in a paper exploring the relationships between contemporary psychoanalytic thinking on gender and on sexuality, points out how gender is now commonly discussed in an ironic tone, to accentuate the way in which its taken-for-granted status has been thoroughly undermined. With the exception, she claims, of "a band of Euro-Lacanians and a few surviving True Believers, Freud's theoretical contrivances on behalf of the penile phallus are now taken as prima facie evidence of his ambivalent homophobia, casual misogyny, and traditional family values." The issue of "penis envy" no longer has much resonance outside stand-up comic routines, and even the object-relational idea that girls, because of their close ties with their mothers, struggle with issues of autonomy and separation whilst boys trip up over intimacy can now be seen both as a truism and as a tautology, describing a socially induced state of affairs without grasping hold of the complexities of the psychological mechanisms at its root. What has replaced all this has been, as Goldner lists it, the work of "Contemporary feminists, gay and lesbian scholars, queer theorists, and generations of psychoanalysts looking for better ideas about sex and gender," which has produced what she describes as "theories that refuse to sit still, retaining the density of the analytic perspective while digging up the ideological infrastructure of normativity, objectivism and biologism" (2003, 113–14).

More than is the case for postcolonial theory, gender theory has thus had a striking impact on psychoanalysis itself, querying its allegiance to a normative model of heterosexuality, disputing the homophobia that seems to be close to the heart of its musings on homosexuality, and demanding that it renew itself in the context of contemporary understanding of sexuality, sexual orientation, and gender politics. This has been received positively in some psychoanalytic circles, even though in the dogged work of the clinic there is perhaps less evidence of novel thinking. However, the influx of feminists into psychoanalysis (for instance, Julia Kristeva, Juliet Mitchell, Nancy Chodorow, and Jessica Benjamin are all psychoanalysts) has meant that there is a way of speaking to psychoanalysis from within, whatever the difficulties of holding on to one's radicalism without being co-opted, and this has resulted in some genuinely transgressive thinking. This is now extending into arenas such as mothering (Baraitser 2009), historically the bastion of the most regressive psychoanalytic theorizing, though also an area hard fought over by feminist writers. Perhaps here more than anywhere there is evidence of a reciprocal relationship between psychoanalysis and the surrounding intellectual culture; and this is despite the fact that it also contains some of the most conservative elements of the psychoanalytic approach.

An occult interlude

Just as the apparent rationalism of colonialism (i.e., assumptions that "civilized" white society is in sole possession of reason) is consolidated in power by a brutality that indexes its own "irrational" underside, so psychoanalysis itself is located in a set of contradictions around rationality and irrationality. As it moves to promote scientific explanation to the forefront of its concerns – bringing order to the disordered unconscious, in crude terms – so it also undermines its own display of reason by enacting the irrational otherness it is striving to theorize. Freud's emphasis was always on the scientific status of psychoanalysis and on the necessity of drawing on science to give it credibility. This made psychoanalysis a fundamentally rationalist discipline, adhering very firmly to the idea that whilst irrationality might be intrinsic to the human subject, the intellectual task of psychoanalysis was to make sense of it and the therapeutic task was to bring it under the control of the ego – not to live out the passion, but to modulate it so that it could be incorporated into regular social life. In Freud's famous statement about the aim of therapy, "Where id was, there ego shall be. It is a work of culture – not unlike the draining of the Zuider Zee" (1953–74, 22:80), one can see that the project of psychoanalysis is to take the unfettered "natural" and make it "cultural," its energies useable in the interests of building civilization.

Yet alongside this rationalist project, or perhaps as an underside to it, there is a different set of origins, associations, and practices. This is not to be read as a statement of psychoanalysis's failings in this sphere, though the debate on its scientific status has usually been couched that way, as if its claims to knowledge depend on adherence to a narrowly defined version of the scientific model (see, for example, Grünbaum 1984). Ernst Gellner's designation of psychoanalysis as a "mystical experience" is part of this critique, as this label is meant to be denigratory; but it also expresses a clear truth of the psychoanalytic heritage that has more mixed effects. "Psychoanalysis does indeed consist of the penetration of a Special Realm," he writes, "discontinuous from the ordinary world though dominating it, and accessible only to forms of exploration distinct from those prevalent in the ordinary world: success is heralded by intense emotion, and a deep transformation of the knower himself. All this it shares with older forms of mysticism" (1992, 43). Psychoanalysis is a transformative discipline; once one is "in" it one sees the world from its perspective. Knowledge brings about personal change, and conversely change is dependent on knowledge in the form of a newly totalizing "insight." The notion of psychoanalysis as "ideological" rather than "scientific" is connected with this, and has framed many debates in the course of psychoanalytic history. However, one might legitimately argue that in pursuing scientific rationalism but enacting mystical irrationalism, psychoanalysis is not only caught up in some iconic juxtapositions but is also expressive of a pervasive issue in the "Freudian century." The dream of progress remains, but is undermined – or perhaps underpinned – by a "regressive" longing for what cannot be understood, a mystical gap that has been filled in various ways, including (on its negative pole) violence, nationalist mythologies, and religious fundamentalism.

Psychoanalysis would always be likely to be marked by its contact with the irrational; it could never contest and try to control it without being influenced by it, any more than it could speak about sexuality without being sexualized – another pivot of twentieth-century life. But some of the sense of non-rational strangeness that characterizes psychoanalysis arises from the specific historical circumstances in which it was formed, for example from its emergence from the stigmatized and marginalized position of European Jewry that placed it outside the mainstream and could rapidly infiltrate both its assumptions and the way it was looked on by others (Diller 1991; Frosh 2005). In addition, the nineteenth-century interest in the occult that was also part of the heritage of psychoanalysis has continued to resonate and has possibly been resurgent in the early years of the twenty-first century. Telepathy is a good example here. As has been shown convincingly by many writers (see, for example, Luckhurst 2002), psychoanalysis emerged in conjunction with a set of questions about "communication at a distance" that included thought-transference and was very clearly embedded in what might be termed "superstitious" thinking. Royle offers some historical context:

> The word "telepathy" was invented and first used by Frederic Myers in 1882 ... Freud's definition, which involves bringing together the concepts of telepathy and thought-transference ... is very close to Myers's:

> telepathy and thought-transference, says Freud, concern the idea "that mental processes in one person – ideas, emotional states, conative impulses – can be transferred to another person without employing the familiar methods of communication by means of words and signs." (1995, 368)

Eliza Slavet also points to the mystical background in which much of psychoanalysis is mired. Whilst Freud created a practice of speech that seemed to strive towards clarity and discrimination, she writes, "he suggests that pre- or extra-linguistic forms of transmission, such as heredity or telepathy, are always in the background, silently and subtly controlling the more palpable transmissions such as writing and talking. Precisely because they are ungraspable, heredity and telepathy may be more potent; unlike that which is sensorially apprehended or physically graspable, such phenomena 'seize' the psyche, compelling the imagination to conjure mysteries beyond belief" (2009, 133). For other contemporary commentators, what is most revealing in the material on telepathy is how it dramatizes the apparent contradiction between a "private" unconscious located within the individual and a communicative intent that can never be foiled, and that provides the basis for what has become the elaborated theory of transference. Campbell and Pile comment, "Telepathy reveals the paradox at the heart of the Freudian unconscious, because it shows how our unconscious worlds are always simultaneously outside and inside; communicated and secret: shared and yet always enigmatic" (2010, 408). What is emphasized here is how telepathy brings to the fore the social aspect of the unconscious, how it leaks all the time and dissipates itself interpersonally and intersubjectively, that is, as a cultural phenomenon.

One of the issues that is important here, and that has reappeared in recent work on haunting (see Frosh 2012), is the way psychoanalysis both emerges from and gives leverage on the irrational in personal psychology and in culture. This is not solely expressive, as it is visible in the project of some of the most mainstream psychoanalysts wrestling with the potential disruptiveness of unconscious life. Although such analysts have tended to be apolitical, one could even argue that ego psychology, pilloried by Lacanians and leftists for its "adaptational" attitude in American culture after World War II, was in some ways a principled attempt to come to terms with the eruption of bestiality and irrationalism seen in Nazism. However, other branches of psychoanalysis draw on the irrational more openly – for example

Bion's (1992) notion of "O" is widely though not universally understood in this way, and one might even argue that the Lacanian Real, being outside symbolization, has its own non-rational or "spiritual" trajectory (Parker 2011). More generally, psychoanalysis shows a kind of Mephistophelian capacity to dip itself into the irrational as well as to theorize – or perhaps one should say that it is this "satanic" impulse that gives it the capacity to do the theorizing in the first place. Sharing both in the murk of the occult and in the scientific *Weltanschauung* emphasized by Freud himself, and laced with a Jewish sensibility that made thinking "against the grain" or "from the margins" possible, psychoanalysis has never been purified of its hybrid associations. This too is part of the Freudian century. Beginning with the prospect of scientific advance and the triumph of reason over unreason; sharing in the modernist optimism that despite the continued presence of the irrational it would be possible to make progress towards a fuller, more liberated existence; then marred by the explosion of destructive barbarism that showed itself to be the irreducible underside of "civilization" – something that colonized peoples would always have known, of course – psychoanalysis at least offered western culture a theory that used the tools of reason but respected the force and reality of the brutal, self- and other-destructive elements of the human subject. Whatever its protestations, psychoanalysis has always moved in this mire; it may strive to conquer madness, but it always allows it to speak.

Psychoanalysis, the humanities, and losing meaning

Another response to the thought that psychoanalysis might be withering away is to consider how extensively it has been deployed in intellectual circles. Despite the ups and downs of fashion, psychoanalysis continues to hold a significant place in the humanities, understood broadly and rather tendentiously as those disciplines focusing on the *elaboration* of meaning through analytical and critical thinking rather than on its *reduction* to empirical principles. For the purposes of this chapter, this is the relevant field of application rather than, for example, the influence of psychoanalysis on psychotherapy (which has been profound) or psychology (where it has been marginalized). From the start, there was involvement of social and literary people with psychoanalysis, with several members of Freud's early "Wednesday Society" having that as their main focus, so much so that his influence spread more through what Makari (2010, 166) calls "humanist applications of Freudian theories" than through scientific interest. Makari notes, "The publication of the Three Essays [on the Theory of Sexuality] made Freud a hero of the Viennese coffeehouse scene. It placed him at the center of a network of artists, writers, journalists, feminists, and reformers" (2010, 151). The social, cultural, and psychological were not fully distinct domains for Freud. Anthropology, religion, art, and politics were areas in which the unconscious could be observed at work, and consequently had things to say to psychoanalysis and, even more significantly, things to learn from it. As early as 1912, Otto Rank and Hanns Sachs had founded a journal, *Imago*, which was "concerned with the application of psycho-analysis to non-medical fields of knowledge" (Freud 1953–74, 20:269). *Imago* was entertaining from the start, and involved some of the early psychoanalysts in exciting cultural speculations of a kind that, as widely read bourgeois, they immensely enjoyed. This tradition continues, and indeed is one ground on which contemporary interest in "literature and psychoanalysis" is based.

Much of the early work was in essence crude psychobiography. For example, Freud's (1953–74, 11:57–138) own famous mis-analysis of Leonardo da Vinci presented the artist's creativity as deriving from his repressed homosexuality, itself linked to the speculative history of his relationship with his mother. In retrospect, it is predictable that this reductionism, focusing analysis on "personality" or "character," should be the psychoanalytic tendency. Partly this is because psychoanalysis was an element in a psychological revolution that, far from displacing the human subject as the center of all things (as Freud thought, with his famous assertion that he had shown how the ego was not "master in its own house" [1953–74, 16:285]), rather developed or invented the *individual* as the locus of scientific and literary concern. That the individual psyche should be seen as the source of artistic meaning is therefore predictable from the character and conditions of emergence of psychoanalysis itself. It was a reflection of, and a way of expressing, the pressure towards individualization and the construction of an autonomous human subject, however self-contradictory this task should eventually turn out to be. Moreover, the push in psychoanalytic literary and art criticism to find roots for creativity in the artist's developmental history is a reflection not just of the specifics of psychoanalytic theory, but of its structure: the discipline was founded on the premise that meaning is made retrospectively, that looking backwards to childhood is necessary if one is to understand what happened "next."

The primacy given to a view of *history* in formulating explanations for human action is symptomatic of a pervasive modernist consciousness in which ideas of progression have central significance. In its most widespread and "classical" form, the developmental thrust of psychoanalysis promotes a backward-looking approach, mining the past to uncover a linear sequence that is taken to be explanatory of the here and now. Yet clearly this is not the only way to develop notions of causality: *circular* explanations, in the sense of recurrent, repetitive time, are also rife in Freud. They are, for example, key to the notion of the death drive as summarizing a universal tendency to repetition, and the unconscious has *timelessness* as one of its chief characteristics (see *Beyond the Pleasure Principle* [Freud 1953–74, 18:1–64]). So the reductive, linear approach is not only problematic from the point of view of art, which sees it as neglecting the specifics (formal properties and so on) of art traditions themselves; it is also very partial from the point of view of *psychoanalysis*. Whilst biography matters enormously, it only takes its meaning retrospectively, hence it cannot be used unproblematically as a formula for interpreting the present (with a patient) or the produced work (in art). Yet it is also important to note how the now-fashionable concept of retrospection, or *Nachträglichkeit*, promotes a kind of melancholic consciousness that has some possibilities for emancipatory practice in an unexpected way. In constantly restructuring the past in the light of the present, it makes it possible to think of something new that might break through; that is, whilst the past might "determine" the present to a greater or lesser extent, and this might seem to ensure that nothing can ever change, the fact that the past is continually "re-invented" means that it is always a *new* past that operates. Said's (2003) notion of the *contrapuntal* is relevant here: reading or hearing different lines of thought against one another, keeping them in tension without it being a case of restoring the past in the present or harking back to a better time. Out-of-time reading of this kind leads to a radical form of "reading against the grain" that operates in two directions – to unsettle the present and to reopen the past in the light of present concerns, exploring how it changes as one reads it differently. Said comments:

> Thus later history reopens and challenges what seems to have been the finality of an earlier figure of thought, bringing it into contact with cultural, political and epistemological formations undreamed of by – albeit affiliated by historical circumstances with – its author.
>
> (2003, 25)

One can go back to the texts and stories, the reconstructed memories and cultural myths, and make use of them for purposes for which they were not intended, to shake up and challenge the present, to offer new ways through. This reflects a certain kind of psychoanalytic as well as historical consciousness: just as the individual experiences her or his history in analysis as a process of reinvention rather than recovery, so in the cultural sphere the past is in a dialogue with the present, midwifed into existence through the operations of the cultural critic, both formative and re-produced.

If this kind of liberatory attitude towards the past, in some ways redolent of postmodernism, has made it possible to rethink how psychoanalysis can help the humanities to reinvent themselves, there have also been some other countervailing tendencies to the potential reductiveness of psychoanalysis. For example, the poststructuralist interest in the way in which knowledge is constructed in the relation between the material itself and the reader or viewer has made a profound difference to the reception of psychoanalysis in art and literary criticism, and to a lesser extent in the social sciences. It has, for example, rendered obsolete the solely biographical approach (however inviting it may be, because individualism still exists) and has promoted examinations which explore the manifold ways in which meanings might be attributed to art works – that is, what they *produce*, rather than what they *reveal*. Psychoanalysis has come up with its own parallel method, especially amongst those who have drawn on Lacanian theory, which is concerned with "chains of signifiers" and representational practices that refuse (or intentionally fail) to pin down meaning but instead focus on opening it up. This has to do again with retroaction: Lacan (1979) holds that sense is always made post hoc, being produced by the interpreter re-reading the subject's discourse in order to even it out, to find anchor points for it and consequently to make it safe and orderly, however complexly and aesthetically this may be done. Sense-making is consequently to be understood as a *defensive* process that makes life livable by attaching meaning to it; as it unfolds, however, the chain of signifiers has no particular meaning, it just moves on, throwing out shards from which retroactive sense is then made. The role of psychoanalysis is to stay connected to the signifying process itself; it aims not to make narrative sense in which the unconscious is drawn on as an "explanation," but rather to *disrupt* sense, to examine the building blocks out of which sense is being produced as a kind of epiphenomenon. From a slightly different psychoanalytic tradition, Jean Laplanche expresses this clearly in distinguishing between an "analytic" and a "narrative" vector:

> The fact that we are confronted with a possibly "normal" and in any case inevitable defence, that the narration must be correlated with the therapeutic aspect of the treatment, in no way changes the metapsychological understanding that sees in it the guarantee and seal of repression. That is to say, that the properly "analytic" vector, that of de-translation and the questioning of narrative structures and the ideas connected to them, remains opposed in every treatment to the reconstructive, synthesising narrative vector.
>
> (2003, 29)

This opposition between therapy and psychoanalysis is an influential one, especially in more radical uses of Lacan (Parker 2011), and it has a long history, for example in Philip Rieff's (1966) separation of the "analytic attitude" from the therapeutic or "ecstatic" one. What it does here is provide grounds for opposing the use of psychoanalysis as an "expert" discourse that can make sense of a literary or art work – or, indeed, of a person. Sense-making of this kind is a way of taking refuge in the role of the "subject who knows," what Lacanians refer to as the discourse of the Master (Lacan 2007); this is an understandable tendency, called into being by the relentless probing of the one who *wants to know* – the discourse of the Hysteric, manifested both in the patient and in the student or other consumer of knowledge. Vacating this position, in psychoanalysis as well as in psychoanalytically influenced work in the humanities, is in line with some other interpretive practices that avoid positing any specific "truth" of the work of art to be uncovered; instead, interpretive strategies continuously seek to fix meaning for only long enough for it to have an impact, and then to move on, disrupting the meaning that has just been found. Such an approach reduces the risk of psychoanalysis presenting itself as a master discourse that can uncover the truth, and sustains at least some element of its subversiveness.

On implication

This antagonism to psychoanalysis as "expert discourse" also fuels Shoshana Felman's (1982) famous intervention in the conjunction of psychoanalysis and literature, which has marked psychoanalytic criticism for the past thirty years. Felman points out that psychoanalysis's approach to literature has been one of attempted mastery, with literature being called on to take a subservient or "slave" position, in which interpretation is the key to unlock what literature has to say, in which, that is, psychoanalysis knows literature better than literature knows itself, so that psychoanalysis "occupies the place of a *subject*, literature that of an *object*" (Felman 1982, 5). Maud Ellmann explains the problem well, in terms that echo the earliest criticisms of psychoanalysis as reading *into* others what it claims to find there – of really being a manifestation of the imagination of psychoanalytic theorists:

> the stories psychoanalyse their own interpreters: the scenes of sexual possession discovered in the texts tell us less about the authors than about the critics, and less about eroticism than about the will to power over literary ambiguity. Only by attending to the rhetoric of texts, to the echoes and recesses of the words themselves, can we recognise the otherness of literature, its recalcitrance as well as its susceptibility to theorisation. Without this vigilance to language, psychoanalysis is doomed to rediscover its own myths grotesquely multiplied throughout the course of literature.
>
> (1994, 3)

Ellmann emphasizes the importance of attention to "the rhetoric of texts," which can be thought of as parallel to the clinical imperative to stick closely to the word of the patient. Lacan writes, "You must start from the text, start by treating it, as Freud does and as he recommends, as Holy Writ. The author, the scribe, is only a pen-pusher, and he comes second. ... Similarly, when it comes to our patients, please give more attention to the text than to the psychology of the author – the entire orientation of my teaching is that" (1988, 153). Psychoanalysis is reframed here as a *non-psychological* disciplinary practice: in this Lacanian version of hermeneutics it is decidedly antagonistic to interpretation but instead tries to stay attuned to the specific contours of the other, whether that be the speech of the patient or literary writing. In this way, psychoanalysis steps back from claims to know what is happening "beneath" the surface, belying its traditional stance as "depth psychology" at least in its non-clinical manifestations (Lacanians might extend this to a wariness about interpretation within the clinic too [Parker 2011]). Felman (1982) takes up the issue of "application" more generally, albeit remaining within the sphere of literary studies, developing an idea that addresses the broad question of how psychoanalysis can speak to other disciplines as equals – not one mastering the other, either as psychoanalysis speaking the truth of literature or literature exposing the narrative assumptions of psychoanalysis, even though both disciplines do have something to say to the other from these places. For Felman, the issue is one of exposing the fictional nature of authority (hence exposing the unconscious underside of psychoanalysis) and the dubious authority to be claimed by fiction (hence exposing the unconscious traces within literature itself). Each is entwined in the other, and through this intense face-off, something unexpected can be called on that keeps open the possibility of surprise and refutes the claims of either literary studies or psychoanalysis to have an answer to the question of meaning. Felman writes,

> In view of this shift of emphasis, the traditional method of *application* of psychoanalysis to literature would here be in principle ruled out. The notion of *application* would be replaced by the radically different notion of *implication*: bringing analytical questions to bear upon literary questions, *involving* psychoanalysis in the scene of literary analysis, the interpreter's role would here be, not to *apply* to the text an acquired science, a preconceived knowledge, but to act as a go-between, to *generate implications* between literature and psychoanalysis – to explore, bring to light and articulate the various (indirect) ways in which the two domains do indeed *implicate each other*, each one finding itself enlightened, informed, but also affected, displaced by the other.
>
> (1982, 8–9; emphasis original)

What Felman pushes for is recognition of this mutual implication and the teasing out of its effects – what each discipline does to the other, how the strategies of reading involved in textual and clinical work draw on one another and produce new ideas. It is this question of *reading* that is perhaps central: not just the masterful analyst reading the patient's discourse for its unconscious significance or the sophisticated literary critic reading the text for its nuances and resonances, but the awareness present in both disciplines that reading is a process of involvement that draws the reader in – it is a productive process that changes the reader/analyst as much as it explores any text.

This argument concerning implication is highly productive for the elaboration of meanings that characterizes much of the humanities and for the avoidance of any "last word" that would close down the creativity of the arts by stating with conviction what they are unequivocally about. Such refusal of knowledge also references a tension that has been present in psychoanalysis from its earliest beginnings. This is often coded as a tension between psychoanalysis as "causal/scientific" versus "hermeneutic," and it will be clear that the emphasis in this chapter has been primarily on the latter. But it also links with a more general point that characterizes the implication of psychoanalysis in the cultural order. Psychoanalysis set itself up as a scheme for explaining psychological phenomena, especially neurotic ones, and for remedying those that could be touched by the talking cure. Rapidly, the attention of literary and artistic practitioners and critics, and of social reformers, was drawn to it, and it has been characteristic of its entire history that alongside the slow and rather dull work of clinicians there has been a more flamboyant and speculative use of psychoanalysis as a key to cultural knowledge. This has certainly contributed to the saturation of western culture by psychoanalytic tropes – the unconscious, defenses, repression, sublimation, and the like – and to an understanding of psychosocial surfaces as opaque, hiding something meaningful beneath them. It has also, however, pushed psychoanalysis into a position of "expert discipline" or "master discourse" to be *applied* as if it can provide the key to true understanding of social and cultural materials. This is not, however, the creative use of psychoanalysis that one might hope for; it is rather a way of closing down debate, as well as being an enactment of the conformist elements in psychoanalysis that have at various times dominated its forays into social commentary – not just in the much-maligned case of ego psychology, but also in religious spheres and in some egregious examples of compromise with oppressive state structures (Frosh 2005; Harris and Botticelli 2010). With the gradual emergence of feminist, poststructuralist, and postcolonial perspectives challenging the certainty of knowledge, psychoanalysis has something else to offer: a disruptive awareness of how pasts are constantly reinvented in the present, and an interrogatory attitude towards its own implication in the material it interprets. If it makes sense to think of there having been a "Freudian century," it perhaps traces this immersion of culture in psychoanalytic ideas and the subsequent discovery of how psychoanalysis, like many other forms of colonial knowledge, has its underside and standpoints, and how as it disrupts the surfaces of other disciplines – in this case, literature – its own premises are also called into question. This can be run together into the idea of reflexivity: the human subject reflexively deploys psychoanalytic understanding in the construction of selfhood; psychoanalysis itself is reflexively embroiled in the cultural processes to which it has partially given rise.

References

Baraitser, Lisa. 2009. *Maternal Encounters: The Ethics of Interruption*. London: Routledge.

Bion, Wilfred. 1992. *Cogitations*. London: Karnac.

Brickman, Celia. 2003. *Aboriginal Populations in the Mind*. New York: Columbia University Press.

Campbell, Jan, and Steve Pile. 2010. "Telepathy and Its Vicissitudes: Freud, Thought Transference and the Hidden Lives of the (Repressed and Non-Repressed) Unconscious." *Subjectivity*, 3: 403–25.

Diller, Jerry V. 1991. *Freud's Jewish Identity: A Case Study in the Impact of Ethnicity*. London: Associated University Presses.

Ellmann, Maud. 1994. "Introduction." In *Psychoanalytic Literary Criticism*, ed. Maud Ellmann, 1–35. Harlow: Longman.

Fanon, Frantz. 1967. *Black Skin, White Masks*. London: Pluto.

Felman, Shoshana. 1982. "To Open the Question." In *Literature and Psychoanalysis: The Question of Reading: Otherwise*, ed. Shoshana Felman, 5–10. Baltimore: Johns Hopkins University Press.

Freud, Sigmund. 1953–74. *The Standard Edition of the Complete Psychological Works of Sigmund Freud*, 24 vols., ed. James Strachey, with the assistance of Anna Freud, Alix Strachey, and Alan Tyson, trans. James Strachey. London: Hogarth Press.

Frosh, Stephen. 1991. *Identity Crisis: Modernity, Psychoanalysis and the Self*. London: Macmillan.

Frosh, Stephen. 1999. *The Politics of Psychoanalysis: An Introduction to Freudian and Post-Freudian Theory*, 2nd ed. London: Palgrave.

Frosh, Stephen. 2003. "Psychoanalysis in Britain: The Rituals of Destruction." In *A Concise Companion to Modernism*, ed. David Bradshaw. Oxford: Blackwell.

Frosh, Stephen. 2005. *Hate and the Jewish Science: Anti-Semitism, Nazism and Psychoanalysis*. London: Palgrave

Frosh, Stephen. 2006. *For and Against Psychoanalysis*, 2nd ed. London: Routledge.

Frosh, Stephen. 2012. "Hauntings: Psychoanalysis and Ghostly Transmission." *American Imago*, 69, no. 2: 241–64.

Frosh, Stephen, and Lisa Saville-Young. 2011. "Using Psychoanalytic Methodology in Psychosocial Research: Researching Brothers." In *Understanding Social Research: Thinking Creatively about Method*, ed. Jennifer Mason and Andrea Dale, 49–61. London: Sage.

Gellner, Ernest. 1992. "Psychoanalysis, Social Role and Testability." In *Psychotherapy and Its Discontents*, ed. Windy Dryden and Colin Feltham, 41–51. Milton Keynes: Open University Press

Goldner, Virginia. 2003. "Ironic Gender/Authentic Sex." *Studies in Gender and Sexuality*, 4: 113–39.

Grünbaum, Adolf. 1984. *The Foundations of Psychoanalysis: A Philosophical Critique*. Berkeley: University of California Press.

Harris, Adrienne, and Steven Botticelli, eds. 2010. *First Do No Harm: The Paradoxical Encounters of Psychoanalysis, Warmaking, and Resistance*. New York: Routledge.

Jacoby, Russell. 1975. *Social Amnesia*. Sussex: Harvester.

Jacoby, Russell. 1983. *The Repression of Psychoanalysis*. New York: Basic Books.

Khanna, Ranjana. 2004. *Dark Continents: Psychoanalysis and Colonialism*. Durham, N.C.: Duke University Press.

Lacan, Jacques. 1979. *The Four Fundamental Concepts of Psychoanalysis*, ed. Jacques-Alain Miller, trans. Alan Sheridan. Harmondsworth: Penguin.

Lacan, Jacques. 1988. *The Seminar of Jacques Lacan*, Book II: *The Ego in Freud's Theory and in the Technique of Psychoanalysis*, ed. Jacques-Alain Miller, trans. Sylvana Tomaselli. Cambridge: Cambridge University Press.

Lacan, Jacques. 2007. *The Seminar of Jacques Lacan*, Book XVII: *The Other Side of Psychoanalysis*, ed. Jacques-Alain Miller, trans. Russell Grigg. New York: Norton.

Laplanche, Jean. 2003. "Narrativity and Hermeneutics: Some Propositions." Trans. John Fletcher. *New Formations*, 48: 26–29.

Luckhurst, Roger. 2002. *The Invention of Telepathy*. Oxford: Oxford University Press.

Makari, George. 2010. *Revolution in Mind*. London: Duckworth.

Mitchell, Juliet. 1974. *Psychoanalysis and Feminism*. Harmondsworth: Penguin.

Parker, Ian. 2011. *Lacanian Psychoanalysis: Revolutions in Subjectivity*. London: Routledge.

Rieff, Philip. 1966. *The Triumph of the Therapeutic: Uses of Faith After Freud*. Harmondsworth: Penguin.

Roseneil, Sasha. 2006. "The Ambivalences of Angel's 'Arrangement': A Psychosocial Lens on the Contemporary Condition of Personal Life." *The Sociological Review*, 54: 846–68.

Royle, Nicholas. 1995. "The Remains of Psychoanalysis I: Telepathy." In *Deconstruction: A Reader*, ed. Martin McQuillan, 361–69. Edinburgh: Edinburgh University Press.

Said, Edward. 2003. *Freud and the Non-European*. London: Verso.

Slavet, Eliza. 2009. *Racial Fever: Freud and the Jewish Question*. New York: Fordham University Press.

Chapter 2

The Case Study

Andrew Webber

Exemplary tales

If there is a particular basis for the relationship that has developed between the theories and practices of psychoanalysis and those of literature, it is the attention to language use, its creativities and its vicissitudes. In view of this, it seems appropriate to introduce this essay with a close consideration of some key terms, their status in language and between different language systems. There are two terms particularly at issue here, terms which are sometimes used more or less interchangeably but which could benefit from careful consideration and distinction. The first is the case study of the title, which puts emphasis upon a sustained, scientific act of scrutiny and interpretation of the case in hand. A case study, in this sense, is understood as having a model character, following a set of disciplinary conventions and testing out certain principles of interpretation, with the expectation that what it yields will also contribute to the understanding and management of future cases. The case study can be seen as the foundational mode of representation for psychoanalysis, establishing what is the case for this system of ideas about the human condition. It is a form of study that psychoanalysis adopts from established conventions of medical and

A Concise Companion to Psychoanalysis, Literature, and Culture, First Edition.
Edited by Laura Marcus and Ankhi Mukherjee.

other scientific or disciplinary writing, but also adapts to its own purposes. Curiously enough, however, and notwithstanding the currency of *Fall* (case) and *Studie* (study) in Freud's lexicon, *Fallstudie* – case study proper – is nowhere to be found. This essay is thus perhaps operating under something of a false license, but one that might prove productive.

The second key term here is one that, in its German form, *Krankengeschichte*, does indeed repeatedly appear in Freud's writings, from the *Studies on Hysteria* (1895) onwards: case history. This term has a rather ambiguous character. It modulates between the historical account of the analysand's illness and that of the treatment of the illness in question. The latter suggests at least a significant overlap with the case study, implying that the historical narrative is expected to be organized in such a way as to yield meaning. Case histories are, in other words, subject to certain historiographical principles and strategies, extending to acts of analysis and interpretation. In practice, psychoanalytic cases are presented in a varying combination of these modes; they provide, in different proportions, a narrative of the analysand's illness "in itself," a narrative of its treatment, and an apparatus of the study of both of these histories and their dynamic relationship. These elements may be presented in sequence, or they may be combined in a more integral fashion. The fact that the study, like the two levels of history embedded within it, is subject to a form of narrative organization, what we might call the meta-narrative of the case, means that psychoanalytic cases are complex constructs, with multiple narrative and hermeneutic frames. And Freud is a highly self-conscious manipulator of those frames in relation to one another.

If Freud, famously, compared his case histories to novellas, this might arguably be taken to be an implicit recognition on his part of this multilayered and interleafed narrative structure, given that this is also characteristic of the novella genre, with its multiple perspectives and conventions of framing. Freud's much-cited statement ("daß die Krankengeschichten, die ich schreibe, wie Novellen zu lesen sind" [Freud 1999, 1:227]) has been subject to misreading, its particularity lost in translation, with many anglophone critics following the Standard Edition in suggesting that what Freud says is "that the case histories I write should read like short stories" (Freud 1953–74, 2:160). There is every reason to be attentive in our reading of Freud here. Firstly, this means to insist upon the generic specificity of the comparison: that it relates the case histories to novellas rather than simply to short stories. Most immediately, this would imply the tradition of writing in the novella genre that was central to German literary culture in and around the nineteenth century, and to which Freud might be seen to be contributing, albeit from an unlikely angle. Secondly, we should note the emphasis on acts of writing and reading. What Freud does is to compare the *reading* of the case studies that he *writes* to that of novellas, thus recognizing the importance of those practices for the psychoanalytic project, its reception and cultural status. And thirdly, if we are indeed committing ourselves to a concern with reading here, we should note that "wie Novellen zu lesen sind" can be understood not just as a descriptive statement but as prescriptive: that they "should be read like novellas." This is to ask questions about normativity of reading, and what is truly at stake in the parallel or interactive reading of a scientific genre – the case history – and a literary one – the novella.

When Freud suggests that, as a medical writer trained in conventional neuropathological methods of diagnosis and prognosis, he finds it strange that his case histories read in this way, the implication seems to be that his critical agency and responsibility as writer are somewhat suspended here. The texts, as "biographies" of psychical disorders (Freud 1953–74, 2:161), lacking the serious "stamp of science," have some kind of compelling life of their own for the reader (including Freud as reader of his own texts). Freud suggests that this is determined less by his own predilections, whether for literature in general or for novellas in particular, but by the "nature of the subject" (1953–74, 2:160). In the case of hysteria, in particular, which is Freud's main focus here (the statement frames the case of "Fräulein Elisabeth von R." from the *Studies on Hysteria*), the distinguishing character of the subject is an intimate relationship between the history or "story of the patient's suffering" (1953–74, 2:161), and the symptoms of the illness. And it seems this is part of what aligns such narratives with the novella and accounts for the ability the two might share to touch the reader in a strange way with their hybrid character. As the case history may read strangely like a novella, so the novella can read strangely like a case history. One might think, most famously, of the strange case of Hoffmann's *The Sandman* (1814), the personal history of suffering retold and analyzed by Freud in *The Uncanny* (1919). Clinical reality and fictional fantasy are strangely, uncannily entwined in either case.

The extent to which Freud's comparison could be extended from the "case history" to the "case study," incorporating an explicit hermeneutic structure, an apparatus of study encasing the narrative, is an interesting question. Certainly, some novellas have that more pronounced interpretive character, though the genre as a whole tends to be thought of as handling elements of "study" with a light touch, sometimes to the point of elision of interpretive guidance. A leading German exponent of the genre in the nineteenth century, Theodor Storm, described his attachment to a method of "symptomatic treatment" rather than an explicit unfolding of psychological motivation (quoted in Webber 1996, 242), and this tendency to encode psychological insight in symbolically allusive forms is characteristic of much writing in this genre. The term symptomatic here suggests that the novella writer also sees the proximity of the genre to the medical, and perhaps in particular the psychiatric case. Indeed, Robert Musil saw novellas as an individual's "symptomatic actions," quite possibly borrowing the term of art from his contemporary, Freud (see Webber 1990, 137). This would seem to suggest that the genre has a rather immediate, performative character – enacting the psychical condition of the protagonist(s) in the given case. And it is to this that the inclination to set a narrative frame around it might respond, offering a certain form of containment, albeit one that may not be fully fitting. Particularly telling in this regard are the examples of the genre that feature doctor figures of one kind or another, for these rarely serve to provide secure diagnostic frames. We might think of the case of a novella by one of the writers most closely related to Freud, Arthur Schnitzler, the sometime doctor and author of narratives and dramas whom Freud famously saw as his literary doppelgänger. Schnitzler's *Traumnovelle* (*Dream Novella* [1926]) turns on the experiences of a doctor, called to treat cases that serve as functions of his own psychosexual condition. The text that is cited to frame the opening of that psychoanalytically disposed example of the genre is not in the objective voice of the medical case study, but a piece of fantasy literature as bedtime reading.

The enclosing frame that so often features in the construction of novellas by Storm, Schnitzler, and others is rarely one of elaborated, meta-narrative study. Indeed, when Freud establishes the comparison between how the two forms of writing might be read, it seems that this might draw less on the idea of the novella as a potentially sophisticated narrative construct than on its status as a – sometimes rather scurrilous or titillating – strange tale, an engaging narrative curiosity. The statement seems to identify a threat of literary misappropriation. At limit, this would be the kind of crudely exploitative reading that Freud seeks to expose in the introduction to the Dora case, in the danger that certain Viennese colleagues might seek to read it as a *roman-à-clef* (Freud 1953–74, 7:9), or perhaps rather a novella *à clef*. Such are the temptations that these literary-style texts may hold for potentially wayward readers, professional or otherwise.

The comparison with the novella raises fundamental narratological questions about the case history or the case study, and – given the inclination of this literary genre to purvey narrative novelties with uncertain framing strategies – concomitant epistemological uncertainties. At the heart of the parallel is a paradox that the two forms of writing may be said to share. The novella as "strange case" is of its essence devoted to the exceptional, the marginal or eccentric; and yet, from its origins, and if only as a strategy of generic legitimation, it also lays claim to exemplarity (think of the *Novelas ejemplares* [1613] of Cervantes). By illuminating the strange case, the genre aspires to a particular kind of normative function, reviewing norms from an apparently abnormal perspective and thereby repositioning them. The novella is thus cast between a subversive and a more exemplary function, and this same double character, making examples of what is exceptional or extravagant, is inherent in the logic of the psychoanalytic case study.

Two further significant ambiguities rest in the term *Krankengeschichte* ("case history"), as used by Freud, both of them tending to be concealed in its English version. The first is that this is the history of a sick person (*Kranke*), and the ownership of the narrative is thereby raised as an issue. The translation into "case" objectifies the narrative, removing it from its subject, and thereby exposes a fundamental ethical question for case histories: to whom do they belong? The case is written into the casebook, where it serves the purposes of the doctor as writer, a function of his or her authorship. The second ambiguity is that *Geschichte* in German means both story and history, and so in itself aligns the objective notion of the historical with a less reliable fictional status. The fact that this "story" is often full of symptomatic fictions, the analysand not just a protagonist within the text but typically the auto-fictional author of his or her own fantasy tales, makes for a collaborative form of narrative that is typically ambiguous in character.

If Freud compares the reading of his case histories to that of a literary genre, this would seem to push the *Geschichte* in question in the direction of the fictional. At the same time, it can be argued that the case history, like the novella, has a particular relationship to the historical that coincides with the aspiration of the two forms of writing to normative or exemplary status. On the face of it, both are lifted out of the grand narratives of history, standing as strange and contradictory developments at the margins. In the terms of August Wilhelm Schlegel, who helped provide a poetological frame for the historical re-emergence of the novella as a key genre in German literature around 1800, it provides a "counter-image" to history, telling stories "behind the back" of the dominant social order (see Webber 1996, 235–36). It is thereby seen to cast a particular light upon what is conventionally repressed from that order's historical accounts of itself. For the Romantic theorists August Wilhelm Schlegel and his brother Friedrich the novella is a genre that is characterized by subjectivity, its function not least to correct objectively constructed accounts of historical processes by the adoption of personal perspectives. Novellas are characteristically narratives of subjective extremity, describing cases in which what Musil calls the "symptomatic actions" of the subject exceed and scandalize social and psychological norms. For Freud's case histories, too, readable as a set of novella-like narrative curiosities, there is a strategic intention to illuminate more general patterns of experience through that of distinctly individual subjects – to derive a new understanding of history, against the grain, from its apparently idiosyncratic and exceptional cases.

In our commitment to be attentive to how things are or should be read, there is a further question to ask of our focal terms here. It is perhaps a coincidence that the German word for case is also the word for a fall; but it is one that cannot remain innocent in the discourse of psychoanalysis. The case, the *Fall*, is indeed generally characterized by falling of various kinds. By dint of his or her illness, its protagonist typically falls out of social frameworks and their conventions, and thereby lapses from the historical norm. This is perhaps most literally enacted in the case of Little Hans (1909), which is preoccupied with symptomatic acts of falling down, organized around the figure of the falling horse, with connotations inter alia of "falling" pregnant (Freud 1953–74, 10:128). Compulsive falling plays through many of the case histories, and this in the uncanny proximity of *Fall* to *Unfall* (accident), as to *Zufall* (coincidence/attack of illness). The case history is characteristically a tale of symptomatic coincidences and of domestic or other incidents, accidents, and attacks of illness. Hans' falling horse is such an accident, symptomatically experienced as an attack of illness, and cast between the public and the domestic. Another would be the *Unfall* of Herr K. that closes the case of Dora and is apparently responsible for her *Anfall* or hysterical attack (Freud 1999, 5:285), as though the two events fall together through semantic similarity. This indicates how the *Fall*, once extended beyond its neutral, scientific meaning, is ready to collapse into accidental or coincidental effects with psychopathological implications – into *Unfall, Anfall,* and *Zufall.*[1] We will see such effects at work in the detailed discussion of a particular case – that of "Gradiva" – below.

Particulars of the case

As shown by the foundational *Studies on Hysteria*, case studies tend to be gathered in casebooks. There is an abiding modulation between their individual character and needs and their collective attributes and affiliations. As we have said, case studies are exercises in modeling, setting up certain exemplary patterns that will help to inform other cases and the techniques required for their treatment. Like the *Novelas ejemplares*, or other more or less formal collections of novellas (think of Boccaccio's medieval classic, *The Decameron* [1370]), the case study thus tends towards the serial or cyclical in its narrative logic. As such, what might seem like highly individual case narratives are bound into collective structures, which push them towards a more communal, general level of experience. The case study or history, in psychoanalysis as in other systems of knowledge, exemplifies a primary epistemological tension for such systems: that between the individual and the general, the particular and the universal. It is a relationship that is fundamental to any systematic structure of cognition, hence its centrality for philosophical traditions of metaphysics, which are concerned with the possibility of universal categories of understanding. It raises the double question – ethical as much as epistemological – as to how universals can be derived from particulars without also becoming impossibly diversified, and how particulars can be used to illustrate universals without violence being done to their particularity.

For the purposes of the present argument, the question is what we might draw from this dialectically complicated relationship between particularity and universality in the special case of the psychoanalytic case study, and – by extension – its literary cognates. Our examples are drawn from the earlier part of Freud's work, where they perform a key strategic function of exemplification for the new system of ideas that he is constructing. As such they also illustrate in especially acute form a paradox that inheres in the case study per se: that it is cast between deductive and inductive functions. It creates the possibility for the emergence of new forms of understanding but is also instrumentalized in order to confirm forms of understanding that pre-exist it, supplementing other cases and the a priori assumptions that have arisen from them. As a form of knowledge construction and representation, psychoanalysis follows casuist principles, and indeed its critics would see its weaving between cases proper and paradigms, using the one to provide warrant for the other, as casuistry of a questionable kind.

It seems important, then, to consider how Freud's case histories manage this critical tension between the particular or the individual, and the communal, the general, or the universal. As we will see shortly, through the particularities of a case that expressly aligns the narratological models of novella and case study, *Delusion and Dreams in Wilhelm Jensen's "Gradiva"* (1907), the tension is fundamental to the textures of their narratives. As such, it has profound implications for the model of ontology – of identity and being – that psychoanalysis constructs in particular through its case studies, with their focus upon the symptomatic actions of misfit individuals who are fitted up as typological models. The Freudian case study constructs forms of ontological exemplarity and thereby lays itself open to charges of reductive or essentialist treatment. We need only think of a case that has been particularly subject to such charges, that of Dora, where the fragmentary individual case of hysteria is taken as the key to the psychosexual motor that drives all neuroses. Freud acknowledges here that the "single case" can never suffice to prove a general principle, but nonetheless uses this fragment of one to aver that sexuality provides the engine for "every single symptom" and "every single manifestation of a symptom." The single is thus ramified into the "every single," extrapolating a general psychical truth that Freud can only "repeat over and over again" through his representation of the singularities of his case histories (Freud 1953–74, 7:115).

The case study has to be recognizable at once as singular and generic, unique and repetitive in its logic, and this it shares with the novella. The nineteenth-century German theorist of the novella, Paul Heyse, called the singular feature that is supposed to provide a symbolic core for the novella the falcon, after one of the tales of the *Decameron* (see also Timms 1983); and this falcon embodies the duality in question here: peculiar to one novella, but transferable as an organizational feature to the generality of such narratives. In order to satisfy the dual requirements of novelty and exemplarity that apply as much to the novella as to the case study, this characteristic of generalizable singularity is fundamental. It enables the two genres of writing to be identifiable as such, as well as serving as a token of similarity between them. The fact that the "falcon" of many novellas is as likely to embody mysteries of identity as provide a structural emblem of recognition indicates that the generic prescription and the principle of exemplarity that goes with it is no simple matter. And the problems of identification that so often figure at the core of novellas are certainly also a feature that is shared with the case study.

We could see this question of identification through distinctive features as a derivation of the structure or figure that Freud applies to identification as a fundamental process of both individual and group psychology, and of the relationship between them: the *einziger Zug*, the singular feature or "single trait" (Freud 1953–74, 18:107). This feature is the basis at once for identifying somebody, marking their identity, and for identifying with them, whether on the part of the individual or the collective. In a recent essay, Samuel Weber (2009) has focused on this key trait of psychoanalytic thinking in conjunction with ways of thinking about literary genre developed by Walter Benjamin. Weber draws upon the singular trait as both a vehicle for identification, after Freud (in the essay "Group Psychology and the Analysis of the Ego" [1921]), and the characteristic structure of the comic character in Benjamin's essay of the same year, "Destiny and Character." As he points out, for Freud the *einziger Zug* is the basis for an intense, but partial, identification in the early formation of the individual, but also for the relation of partial identification between the group and the charismatic individual as leader. That is, we could say that the *einziger Zug* is a pivot between the individual and the mass, singularity and generality. This *Zug* is a fundamentally psychosomatic feature or trait, investing a physiognomic feature with psychonomic meaning, in a development of the Morellian method of identification. In Freud's development, physiognomic theory is complicated in its attention to the individual case as exemplification of the general law. The singular trait becomes a basis for an attachment which is impossible, because based on a failure to recognize properly the complexity of the relation between part and whole. The shine (*Glanz*) on the nose that introduces the essay on "Fetishism" (1927) would be a case in point, where fetishistic attachment is sustained by the effect of an environmental condition (light) upon a physiognomic feature (the nose) of the desired other; this is then extrapolated into an interlingual play of words (*Glanz*/glance) upon the play of light upon that feature (Freud 1953–74, 21:152). The fetishistic version of the attachment to the singular trait of the other also shows, in exceptional form, what is the case for identificatory attachments per se: they are complex, figuratively relayed, and fundamentally partial.

Lacan elaborates upon the *einziger Zug* – the *trait unaire* – in his 1962 seminar on "Identification." For Lacan, the *trait unaire* represents the impossibility that informs identification, its attachment less to an ideal unity than to singularity and so to the exceptional. As Weber glosses it, this trait is the marker of the network of signification, what for Derrida would become known as the trace. It suggests the same modality as attaches to the German *Zug* in its physiognomic sense, which may be a set feature or a transient effect of facial or bodily mobility. Weber goes on to apply this to the law in the cases of Kafka and of Genet's *Balcony*. He follows Benjamin in arguing that the officers of the law, "have to mediate between the structural generality of the law and the necessity of applying it to 'cases' that are always more or less singular, more or less exceptional" (Weber 2009, 396). For our purposes, the same question can be applied to the legislative order of psychoanalysis, where the treatment of cases is always a compromise between the instantiation of general laws and the characteristic singularity that marks them out as exceptional, as lying in part beyond that which they are used to exemplify.

The singular case of "Gradiva"

Let us consider, then, the function of a particular – or singular – case for the judgment system of psychoanalysis: that of "Gradiva." It is a case that brings together literary and psychic analysis, its burden being that the relationship between the protagonist Norbert Hanold and his lost and then recovered object of love, Zoë Bertgang, corresponds to that of analysand and analyst. For Freud, the "analysand" is enabled to love the "analyst" in this fictional case not merely in the transitional form of the transference, but as appropriate object for life. As such, it presents what he calls an "ideal" case (Freud 1953–74, 9:119), a paradigmatic example of analysis. Understood as a model for psychoanalytic treatment, this novella is thus indeed a fantasy narrative, in keeping with its generic subtitle ("A Pompeian Fantasy"). While Freud claims that the techniques of conventional psychiatric medicine must be eluded by a literary case history of this sort, psychoanalysis can at least claim it as an exceptional case to prove its rules. It can adopt surrogate means towards emulating the fictional model. By the same token, this singular Freudian case study, based on a literary protagonist rather than a living analysand, provides a paradigm case for the generic logic of the case study. And at the same time, the singular case history is made general by being bound up with the singular historical moment of the submersion of Pompeii (Freud 1953–74, 9:40), which stands here allegorically for the possibility of understanding human history at large in psychoanalytic terms as a process of repression (submersion) and retrieval (archeological work).

The "Gradiva" case is fundamentally concerned with questions of singularity and generality, and the tensions between these categories. Norbert Hanold, the young archeologist, has a fetishistic and melancholic attachment to a singular figure, that of the Gradiva relief, and to a particular *Zug* of that figure: the "single feature" (1953–74, 9:42) of the peculiar lifting of her foot as she walks. At the same time, the novella is saturated with features of seriality and generality that complicate the attachment to the singular "find" of the Gradiva figure, which apparently comes alive in the person of Zoë Bertgang. The archeological icon is embedded in a system of commodified reproduction of artifacts for the archeological tourist trade. And this tension between the original and its duplicated versions extends to the kinship between novella and case study. Freud finds himself engaged in a two-fold process of "reproduction" (1953–74, 9:43) of the features of Jensen's "case history," the first as unadulterated copy and the second adapted to the technical terms of the psychoanalytic discipline. As the novella makes claims to singularity but also inevitably reproduces generic conventions, so the case history – the psychoanalytic "novella" that frames it – is cast between new claims and derivative practices of narration and interpretation (see also Downing 2006, 87–166).

Beyond the economy of archeological commodities, Jensen's novella explores serial reproduction and categorical distinctions and confusions in various other forms.[2] The recuperative logic of the narrative is for the singular, deluded young man to be united with his singular object of desire, so that the exceptional case may be normalized and come to accord with the rule. Hanold, the single man marked out as different, is tormented by what he experiences as a universal orgy of reproductive indifference, as the single is displaced by the dual and the plural (Jensen 1993, 30). It is an orgy that extends to bestiality, in the form of the mating flies and birds that are associated with the migratory young lovers on their honeymoons. If the human becomes confused with aesthetic reproduction, through the protagonist's passion for a sculpted figure, on one side, it merges with animal reproduction on the other, and especially the rampant species of the common house fly, which embodies the threat to human singularity of creaturely indifference or commonality. Jensen's text plays elaborate games with the hybridization of species and with the shifting of the human species between unique character and mass experience. Thus the pairs of young lovers, the "inseparables" (1993, 24), that accompany Hanold's

Italian journey are perceived as indiscriminate and interchangeable in their coupling, so that the lovers' discourse of singularity ("My only Augustus"/"My sweet Gretchen" [1993, 25]) is exposed as a mass phenomenon. In Hanold's dream the discourse is repeated by those much-reproduced icons, the Apollo Belvedere and the Capitoline Venus (1993, 26); and Hanold imagines that the flies might in their turn reproduce the same terms in their acts of coupling (1993, 33). The young woman and man that Hanold at first takes for sister and brother (a singular couple, sharing a single distinctive, half-laughing *Zug* [1993, 81]),[3] are subsequently exposed as another iteration of Augustus and Gretchen, setting the scene for the hysterically abstinent Hanold also to become party to the common "mating impulse" (1993, 22).

The "Gradiva" case can be seen as a kind of hybridized coupling between the psychoanalytic case study and the fantasy novella. Jensen's text provides a model for psychoanalysis as a form of quasi-literary and literary critical practice. The resolution of the novella lies in the recognition that Gradiva and Zoë are not identical, but just compellingly similar. Zoë turns out to have a singular feature that the relief does not, a dimple which is associated by Hanold with the very flies that have represented the torment of coupling during his Italian journey. Thus this other singular trait becomes at once a mark of difference in the fantasy identification of sculpture and living woman and one of commonality with life in general (as embodied in the name, Zoë). The fetishistic, singular trait of the characteristically lifted foot is relativized by another feature, so that Gradiva (the art object) and Zoë (the living "analyst") are not after all identical "in allen Zügen" ("in every detail" [Freud 1953–74, 9:70]).

For the pair of literature and psychoanalysis also, the analogy would suggest, identification must be a process that adequately recognizes difference. An absolute identification would be distorting and life-threatening for the distinct forms and needs of each. While both novella and case study might seem to require organization around a distinctive feature, each also threatens the loss of transparency and distinction. The element of obscurity and refraction that Freud attributes to the medium of creative writing (1953–74, 9:41) implies a dangerously alluring object of emulation for the case studies of the psychoanalyst. And the identificatory danger is reciprocal. In the Dora case, the same sort of obscurity is identified in the case study, which has to efface its "poetic" outlines in order to represent psychological over-determination, in a way that a novella writer might wish to resist (1953–74, 7:59–60). One thinks of the obscure, refracted other self that is the doppelgänger figure as an uncanny embodiment of this double-bound relationship between psychoanalysis and literature, not just in the case of Freud and Schnitzler (see Webber 1996).

Freud introduces into the "Gradiva" case an uncanny miniature narrative of his own and with it a version of the specter of the doppelgänger. He relates the anecdote of a doctor who felt some responsibility for the loss of a patient of his to Basedow's disease, and who was then visited in his consultation room a few years later by a woman he took to be the deceased patient, only to discover that this was in fact her sister – her features similarly disfigured by the same disease.[4] The twist in the narrative is that the doctor "to whom this occurred was, however, none other than myself" (Freud 1953–74, 9:72). The susceptibility of the enlightened analyst to seeing ghosts in the clinic is disavowed by the displacement of his experience into the third person, only for this uncanny narrative alter ego to be recognized *après coup* as himself. He identifies here with the uncannily repetitive experience of the ghost-seer Hanold, who also – as Freud notes a page later – "diagnosed" (that is, misdiagnosed) the young lovers he saw in Pompeii as siblings (1953–74, 9:72). Thus, the analyst not only sees his double in the fantasy writer, but in his fantasizing protagonist – as if in counter-transferential identification with the "analysand." It seems that the relationship between the doubles of novella and case study can run the danger of misidentification or misdiagnosis.

This seeing double of himself through the refractive and obscure medium of the literary text extends to the act of writing for Freud. His analysis of the text turns upon the ambiguous language of dreams, the meanings that can be encoded in wordplay through the disfigurement that is the "characteristic feature" (*Zug*) of dreams (1953–74, 9:86). Zoë, in the role of analyst, employs double meanings of this kind as a feature of her work upon Hanold, not least through serial wordplay with terms sharing the root of *Fall*, as first *Zufall* (coincidence) and then *Anfall* (attack of illness) are coupled with *Einfall* (idea).[5] It is as though these games with language are in fact playing with the case (*Fall*) of the "analysand" and the forms of repetition, imitation, and contingency that are at the core of his pathology. When Freud comes to explore other examples of double talk in the text, he notes that he is unable to subject Hanold, the literary protagonist, to analysis through association of ideas (*Einfälle*[*n*]) but must substitute these by *Einfälle*, "associations" of his own (1953–74, 9:73). He thus also seems to participate in what Kofman calls Zoë's "double science" (1991, 113). His associations (*Einfälle*), by association with hers, might fall in with effects of coincidence and disorder. Whether analyzing patients or texts – or here a patient in a text – psychoanalysis can always be open to charges of false identification, of taking coincidence or association for identity and misdiagnosing attacks of illness in an associative manner. As with the sisters with Basedow's disease, the psychoanalyst may be subject to an uncanny misreading of features and their singular and general meanings.

At the end of his study of the "Gradiva" case, Freud appropriately raises the question of the authenticity of that which he has seen in what Rand and Torok have called this "mirror of psychoanalysis" (1997, 49). There are, he says, "zwei Fälle" (translated as "two possible explanations" [Freud 1953–74, 9:91), but strictly "two cases") that may apply in his treatment of the case. Either he has been tendentious in his reading, as has so often been the case in "the history of literature" (1953–74, 9:91), or he has recognized the fundamental truths of the text. The reader, he says, will have to seek to become "at one with himself" in judging between the two "cases."[6] What is more likely to emerge here, however, is a less self-identical position, one that is cast in tantalizing – potentially uncanny – transition between the one and the two or more, between secure identification with the features of Freud's reading and more obscure or refracted possibilities. This, it seems, is always liable to be the case in the singular and multiple relations between psychoanalysis, literature and literary criticism.

Notes

1 For similar play on tropes of falling in Freud, see Caruth (1996, 22).
2 See, for instance, the reference to Linnaean classification (Jensen 1993, 22).
3 The translation wrongly attributes this "expression" to the woman alone.
4 The scene is read by Derrida (1996, 89–90) as exemplifying the "archive fever" or "trouble" with record at the heart of the Freudian project.
5 This double play on words is elided in the translation (Jensen 1993, 97).
6 The Standard Edition translates this as "Let every reader now make up his mind" (Freud 1953–74, 9:91).

References

Caruth, Cathy. 1996. *Unclaimed Experience: Trauma, Narrative, and History*. Baltimore: Johns Hopkins University Press.

Derrida, Jacques. 1996. *Archive Fever: A Freudian Impression*. Chicago: University of Chicago Press.

Downing, Eric. 2006. *After Images: Photography, Archaeology and Psychoanalysis and the Tradition of Bildung*. Detroit: Wayne State University Press.

Freud, Sigmund. 1953–74. *The Standard Edition of the Complete Psychological Works of Sigmund Freud*, 24 vols., ed. James Strachey, with the assistance of Anna Freud, Alix Strachey, and Alan Tyson, trans. James Strachey. London: Hogarth Press.

Freud, Sigmund. 1999. *Gesammelte Werke*, 18 vols. Frankfurt am Main: Fischer.

Jensen, Wilhelm. 1993. *"Gradiva" by Wilhelm Jensen and "Delusion and Dream in Wilhelm Jensen's 'Gradiva'" by Sigmund Freud*, trans. Helen M. Downey. Los Angeles: Sun and Moon Press.

Kofman, Sarah. 1991. *Freud and Fiction*, trans. Sarah Wykes. Cambridge: Polity.

Lacan, Jacques. 1962. *The Seminar of Jacques Lacan*, Book IX: *Identification 1961–1962*, trans. Cormac Gallagher. http://www.valas.fr/IMG/pdf/THE-SEMINAR-OF-JACQUES-LACAN-IX_identification.pdf. Accessed November 30, 2013.

Rand, Nicholas, and Maria Torok. 1997. *Questions for Freud: The Secret History of Psychoanalysis*. Cambridge, MA: Harvard University Press.

Timms, Edward. 1983. "Novelle and Case History: Freud in Pursuit of the Falcon." *London German Studies*, 2: 115–34.

Webber, Andrew. 1990. *Sexuality and the Sense of Self in the Works of Georg Trakl and Robert Musil*. London: MHRA.

Webber, Andrew. 1996. *The Doppelgänger: Double Visions in German Literature*. Oxford: Clarendon Press.

Weber, Samuel. 2009. "Between Part and Whole: Benjamin and the Single Trait." *Paragraph*, 32, no. 3: 382–99.

Chapter 3

Modernity, the Occult, and Psychoanalysis

Carolyn Burdett

> Even ghost stories, the delight of Christmas Eve, have been ravaged and annexed by psychology.
>
> (Lang 1894, 47)

Death is a difficult idea for human beings. Freud admitted in his 1919 essay on "The Uncanny" that there is "scarcely any other matter ... upon which our thoughts and feelings have changed so little since the very earliest times." Death, he acknowledged, stubbornly retains its connection to a primitive past, remaining obscure and mysterious. Even "our great cities," thoroughly modern in other ways, are atavistic in this respect. Placards on the streets advertise lectures promising to reveal secrets of how to talk with the dead – for "almost all of us still think as savages do on this topic," including the men of science who are otherwise unimpeachable in their pursuit of evidence and rational truths (Freud 1985, 364–65). Like these men, Freud was intrigued by the strange transmissions associated with spiritualism and other types of occult phenomena, including thought-reading and telepathy.[1] Such mysterious types of communication did indeed seem startlingly similar to the distinctive forms of subjective sharing which characterize psychoanalytic technique. Psychoanalysis attends to what, for the

A Concise Companion to Psychoanalysis, Literature, and Culture, First Edition.
Edited by Laura Marcus and Ankhi Mukherjee.

individual, remains hidden, to what is undisclosed or undivulged even to him- or herself. Like the occult scenarios of trance, séance, or thought transference, psychical reality disturbs notions of memory, time, and distance and, like spiritualist mediums, or adepts and occultists, analysts must know how to receive and interpret messages deriving from the obscure realm that Freud called the unconscious.

Freud admitted that even a naive spooky tale could unnerve him with its uncanny effects (Freud 1985, 367). He was fascinated by patients' stories of prophetic dreams and inexplicable coincidences and liked to recount them. He was addicted to magical numbers and alternately entranced and disappointed when he witnessed mediums and clairvoyants. At various times his inner circle contained avowed occult enthusiasts, including Carl Jung and the Hungarian analyst Sandor Ferenczi. Ferenczi courted mediums, lectured on thought transference, and believed that occult communications were key to understanding how a fantasy could be shared or a child be invaded by an abusive parent (Thurschwell 2001). In Freud's various formal discussions of occult topics – which include comments in *The Psychopathology of Everyday Life*, a talk on "Psychoanalysis and Telepathy" that was never delivered, and essays on "Dreams and Occultism" and "Dreams and Telepathy" – both his attraction and his anxious repudiation are obvious as he alternates between professed disinterest in the topic and a hunger to know more.[2] The history of how psychoanalysis was (and was not) established as a reputable science has been told many times.[3] It is a story of exclusion and affiliation, tests of authority and loyalty, and painful scenes of betrayal. For both advocates and opponents, occult phenomena were persistently proximate to this history. Freud acknowledged that the occult was "a dangerous expedition" (Jones 1957, 415) capable of threatening psychoanalysis with associations of supernaturalism and "hocus-pocus" (1957, 423). In his biography of Freud, Ernest Jones devotes a chapter to this tricky topic, much of it devoted to damage limitation, explaining how he warned Freud of disaster should psychoanalysis become contaminated by occultism. Declaring his own thoroughgoing skepticism about such substitute religious yearnings for an afterlife, Jones tries hard to defuse the implications of Freud's interest, acknowledging that genius invariably carries with it a touch of aberrance. Nor was Freud ever a true believer like Jung or Ferenczi, Jones insists, but rather maintained an "exquisite oscillation between scepticism and credulity" (1957, 402).

Despite these efforts, the gatekeepers of psychoanalysis' reputation were never successful in definitively separating Freud or the history of psychoanalysis from the occult. This was not surprising for, despite Jones' effort to recast Freud's interest in the occult as the individual foible of genius, this was palpably not the case. Occult phenomena were strikingly present, and persistently so, in innovative approaches to the study of mind and conceptualizations of modern subjectivity throughout the nineteenth century. They were an integral part of the emergence of modern psychology, forming a shadowy accompaniment to the materialist models of mind which dominated late Victorian science. In particular, the occult was the road to the discovery of the unconscious in the nineteenth century, as the conviction grew in many quarters that consciousness was not a sufficient category by which to explain human motives, behavior, and experience (ffytche 2012; Nicholls and Liebscher 2010). In the 1880s, when Freud visited the Salpêtrière hospital in Paris to learn about the treatment of hysteria from Jean-Martin Charcot, he witnessed experiments with hypnosis which were part of a remarkably lively public and professional fascination with mysterious or abnormal states of mind. These included, alongside hypnotism, dreams and somnambulism, automatisms, magnetism, trance states, mediumism, table-rapping and -turning, spectral illusions, apparitions, hallucinations, ectoplasm, spirit photography, thought-reading, automatic writing, telepathy, catalepsy, forms of mental illness, and double or multiple personality states. These were not the marginal interests of cranks but rather phenomena studied and investigated by figures otherwise engaged in uncontentiously respectable scientific pursuits and intellectual inquiries. Reviewing Janet Oppenheim's now-classic examination of spiritualism in Victorian England, *The Other World* (1985), Richard Altick found that her research reveals "the extent to which spiritualism and psychical research drew the attention of men who were, in their various disciplines, helping to develop our modern concepts of mind and the physical universe" (Altick 1986, 18).

In scholarship of the last two decades, these diverse occult ideas and beliefs have begun to be better understood. In particular, the "psychical research" to which Altick makes reference, an initiative begun in the 1880s to investigate scientifically what are now called paranormal phenomena, has been retrieved from its marginalization as a pseudo-scientific surrogacy for lost religious faith. Instead, new contexts and motives for interest in quasi-magical things have been brought into view, providing more convincing accounts of psychical research. These include the contingencies of securing institutional authority for the emerging discipline of psychology and the close connections between new technologies, sensory experiences, and occult phenomena; widespread debate about degeneration and hitherto unknown forms of evolution, and related ideas about inheritance, memory, and the past; destabilized hierarchies associated with "nervy" modern women or the volatile urban masses, and issues of proximity and distance in relation to the far reaches of empire (Luckhurst 2002; Owen 2004; Thurschwell 2001).

The richest form for exploring this unsettled, sometimes anxious, apprehension of modernity at the *fin de siècle* proved to be the prolific resurgence of literary Gothicism. The "torrent of Gothic imaginings" that filled the pages of periodicals and publishing houses at the end of the century was extraordinarily diverse and varied, and include some of the most enduring icons of the culture, among them Dr. Jekyll and Mr. Hyde, Dorian Gray and Count Dracula (Luckhurst 2005, ix). These tales of divided personality, imperiled bourgeois men and sexually predatory women, haunted houses and alien invaders, produced the metaphors and narrative forms through which modern selves and societies could be imagined, feared, and desired. They variously drew from, contested, and contributed to the scientific tenor of late-century debate, transplanting what was largely marginal and borderline to mainstream scientific inquiry into the center of cultural life. Their narratives, in turn, helped to shape the unconscious as integral to the modern condition of being human.

In 1912 Freud published a version of what would develop into his major 1915 metapsychological paper on "The Unconscious." "A Note on the Unconscious in Psycho-Analysis" appeared in the *Proceedings of the Society for Psychical Research* (*PSPR*). Nearly twenty years previously, Freud's early psychoanalytic ideas had been introduced for the first time to an English readership in the same publication. Frederic W.H. Myers, a classics scholar and minor poet, and a founding member of the Society for Psychical Research (SPR), discussed part of what was to become Freud and Joseph Breuer's "Preliminary Communication" to the *Studies On Hysteria* in a paper on "The Mechanism of Hysteria" published in the *PSPR* of 1894 (Myers 1893–94; Keeley 2001). By then the SPR had been in existence for twelve years. It was founded by a group of prominent Cambridge intellectuals and scientists who were interested in – if not necessarily always convinced by – the claims of spiritualism.[4] Spiritualists, active since the mid-century, believed that human personality can survive bodily death and may subsequently seek to make contact with the still living. Waves of enthusiasm for séances occurred during the second half of the century, attracting celebrity mediums and their supporters as well as those dedicated to exposing mediumistic fraudulence and debunking naive wishful thinking about an afterlife (Oppenheim 1985). A small but significant body of men, however, saw spiritualism as affording an opportunity to re-establish on a robust scientific basis elements of what had been regarded as religious or supernatural belief. The chemical scientist William Crookes, for instance, believed spiritualism revealed a hitherto undetected "psychic force" capable of persisting after bodily death (Luckhurst 2002, 24–32; Noakes 2004).

Following hotly contested debates, scandals, trials, experiments, and copious discussion in books and the periodical press, in March 1882 the Society for Psychical Research was formally launched in London under the presidency of the Cambridge moral philosopher Henry Sidgwick. Its brief was to investigate the claims and practices of spiritualism using the methods of "exact and unimpassioned inquiry" associated with the established sciences (quoted in Ledger and Luckhurst 2000, 272). The SPR's committee included medically trained men like Edmund Gurney, the physicist Oliver Lodge, and the man who went on to theorize a comprehensive psychology, Frederic Myers. Its original aims quickly expanded to include investigation of trance states, hypnotism, ghosts and haunted houses, and the claims of theosophists such as Madame Blavatsky.

Freud and Myers were both convinced that human agency was not reducible to consciousness. Certainly the dominant philosophical traditions of the Enlightenment understood subjectivity primarily in relation to consciousness: Angus Nicholls and Martin Liebscher acknowledge that for Locke, consciousness is "the perception of what passes in a man's own mind," while for Hume, the self is a "bundle of perceptions." Nevertheless, ideas of unconscious aspects of mind were widely discussed during the eighteenth century. Indeed, the seventeenth-century German philosopher Leibniz had already distinguished what he termed *petites perceptions* which, while not different in kind from ordinary perceptions, occur at a low level of consciousness and do not entail reflexive thought. These he distinguished from the "apperceptions" of which a subject has conscious and reflexive awareness (Nicholls and Liebscher 2010, 4–6). This notion of an area of mind obscure and "under the threshold" of consciousness was influential in the many varied accounts of unconscious mental activity that circulated in the nineteenth century. These latter were associated with experiences of trance states, mental abnormalities, dreams, or creativity, and they were invariably accompanied by occult ideas such as mesmerism or religiously inflected notions of spirituality and mysticism.

In his influential account of mind, Myers emphasized the partial nature of everyday "empirical consciousness," insisting that he accorded "no primacy to my ordinary waking self." Instead, he conceived of psychical being as stratified, encompassing subliminal as well as ordinary conscious "supraliminal" selves (quoted in Ledger and Luckhurst 2000, 259). "Uprushes" of energy from the former were capable of penetrating through to everyday consciousness, and these provided a hint about the potential future spiritual "progeneration" to which Myers looked forward. The further evolutionary advance of civilized societies depended, he believed, on the psychic potential of hitherto unrecognized subliminal personality.

Like those of Freud, Myers' theories of psychic life emerged out of studying hypnosis and the treatment of hysteria taking place in French psychiatry. The idea of split, double, and multiple personalities, where a range of personas seemingly coexisted in an individual, especially attracted him. He drew from William James' ideas about the "stream of thought," which lent support to his contention that everyday consciousness was merely one element of a vastly extended consciousness, imagined by Myers as a spectrum, an image borrowed from technical innovations in the measurement of infra-red and ultra-violet light (Luckhurst 2002, 108–9). His ideas about "Multiplex Personality" borrowed from Continental case studies which seemed to substantiate the contention that "consciousness" could exist without an individual's immediate apprehension of it. William James, writing in 1890 of one of Pierre Janet's cases of multiple personality in which a woman has three identities, one of which knows nothing of the others, one of herself and one other, and one of all three, sees in it "the possibility of a new kind of 'Comedy of Errors,' to which it would take the skill of a Parisian *vaudevilliste* to do justice" (James 1890, 367; see also Hacking 1995).

Instead of a comedy of errors, however, at the beginning of 1886, the same year that Myers published his essay on "Multiplex Personality" in the *Nineteenth Century*, Robert Louis Stevenson's *Strange Case of Dr. Jekyll and Mr. Hyde* appeared. In February, Myers wrote to Stevenson, perhaps alerted by a review in *The Times* describing the story as a "flash of intuitive psychological research" (quoted in Luckhurst 2002, 191–92). Praising the story, Myers also urged Stevenson to correct some of its details in order to conform to current research into split personas. Studies of double and multiple personality, he insisted, ruled out the possibility of Jekyll and Hyde having the same handwriting, and the "community of memory" in alternating personalities needed careful treatment to be aligned with recent findings (Luckhurst 2002, 192).

Stevenson politely resisted Myers' requests, but his story nevertheless reverberated in relation to psychological accounts of mind in the period (Wilde's Vivian, in "The Decay of Lying," comments that it reads "dangerously like something out of the *Lancet*" [quoted in Mighall 2002, 145]). Robert Mighall cites Henry Jekyll's awed acknowledgment of what Hyde's creation means – "Think of it – I did not even exist" – as evidence of Stevenson's (and Jekyll's) exploitation of recent theories of memory and double personality which contended that memories of split personalities are independent, one disappearing when the other appears (Mighall 2002, 146–47). For Dr. Jekyll, however – like Myers – this layered and stratified personality is imagined as the norm rather than a pathological aberrance: "I hazard the guess that man will ultimately be known for a mere polity of multifarious, incongruous and independent denizens" (Stevenson 2002, 56). Insights being promulgated in pathology were extended to encompass the psychic qualities of all humans for psychical researchers as well as for Freudians.

Jekyll and Hyde tapped into proliferating discourses of degeneration in the period, in the midst of fertile traffic between evolutionary accounts of atavism, reversion, and parasitism; economic and social anxieties; and fear of cultural decline. This latter was most strongly associated with critiques of aestheticism and decadence, such as Max Nordau's overheated *Degeneration* of 1895, whose targets included Ibsen, Nietzsche, and Wagner, as well as the Pre-Raphaelites and Oscar Wilde (see Ledger and Luckhurst 2000, 1–24). Hyde's "ape-like" figure positions him within evolutionary discourse, while his unlocatable and indescribable deformity both evokes and troubles the practices of physiological classification employed by Cesare Lombroso and others in identifying criminal and other "types" (Pick 1989). The fascinating corporeality obsessively explored in Gothic fiction accounts in part at least for why degeneration has become such a major point of critical reference in literary and cultural studies of the *fin de siècle*. The transpositions which took place – from biology and embryology to notions of social behavior, individual morality, and the character of nations and races – perhaps make this inevitable. Thomas Henry Huxley's 1868 lecture on "The Physical Basis of Life," which domesticates the technical term "protoplasm" to allude to the cellular matter common to all life, appeared to herald a potentially terrifying leveling and dissolution of boundaries between humans, creatures, and matter itself: "What community of form, or structure, is there between the animalcule and the whale; or between the fungus and the fig tree?" (Huxley 1869, 130).

In Arthur Machen's "The Great God Pan" – described by Roger Luckhurst as "the quintessential text of the late Victorian Gothic" (Luckhurst 2005, xxix) – Helen Vaughan is born out of the illicit collusion of experimental neurology and primitive pagan forces. Her demise is firmly locatable within the degeneration paradigm, threatening as it does the disintegration of boundaries between sexes and species, and between science and the supernatural. At the end, there is "nothing but a substance as jelly" as Helen Vaughan becomes a form "too foul to be spoken of": the common physical basis of life also threatens the human order of communicative language (Luckhurst 2005, 228–29).

But degeneration is only one paradigm for the occult fiction of the period. Luckhurst emphasizes intersections with ideas emanating from psychical research which reconfigure degeneration as a disturbed but temporary interregnum heralding a new spirituality that both parallels and counters materialism. A character in Arthur Machen's *The Three Imposters* (1895), intellectually committed to materialism, is nevertheless forced to acknowledge that "matter is as really awful and unknown as spirit, that science itself but dallies on the threshold" (quoted in Hurley 1996, 31). Jekyll is a scientist, but his study has led to "the mystic and transcendental," seeing the body not as the corporeal basis of mind but rather a "trembling immateriality" which he might "shake and pluck back" (Stevenson 2002, 56). As with the physician Dr. Reymond in Machen's "The Great God Pan," who performs brain surgery to access "a sphere unknown," materialist science provides a new route to the transcendental in these stories, as it does in psychical research (quoted in Luckhurst 2005, 185). Myers believed that the "perturbation" of "our degenerates" may "mask an evolution which we or our children must needs traverse" to a higher stage of humanity (quoted in Groth 2011, 11). Even Edward Hyde's unspeakable, indescribable presence might, on this account, hint at as yet unimagined future possibilities for evolving humanity.

In an essay on dreaming from 1888, Stevenson reconfigures E.S. Dallas' 1866 advocacy in *The Gay Science* of a "Hidden Soul" – the "fairy in our thoughts … [an] unknown and tricksy worker" commonly called "Imagination" (Dallas 1866, 1:201). Stevenson's sleepless "Brownies" provide him with bits and pieces for his tales while "I, my conscious ego" is disabled in sleep. One of the qualities of this nighttime "unseen collaborator" is a lack of even "a rudiment of what we call a conscience." Stevenson's ironic admission that as a consequence he was saddled with "most of the morality, worse luck!" pinpoints the anxieties that accompanied psychological research into double and multiple personalities in relation to questions of moral and legal responsibility (Stevenson 2002, 141). These, in turn, resonated with debate about the function of mass culture and the unruly potential of the crowd. Occult tales of the *fin de siècle* gave myriad form to both fears and desires about the barely consolidated, already fragile, liberal individual with its compromised agency and uncertain self-control. Their narrative form consolidated the sense of boundaries to be policed: the thought-reading omnipotent narrator of nineteenth-century realism, with access to the innermost thoughts of his or her characters, was replaced by professedly neutral observers and recorders. Predominantly male, these Gothic narrators are homely or level-headed types, often pressed into documenting or editing the tales they present, and occasionally reluctant to divulge the full truth. "This part is not to be printed" asserts the narrator of Rudyard Kipling's "The Mark of the Beast" (1890), while Machen's narratives bristle with gaps and silences, and secrets whispered so that the reader cannot hear (Luckhurst 2005, 94, 186). In "The Great God Pan," the relay of narrative fragments, of sudden end stops, of letters written and erased begins itself to feel like a product of split selves or of memory running along separate channels, undermining the male, bourgeois narrators who profess to control and release the story.

Occult formulations flourished as a newly scientific psychology emphasized the physiological and material determinants of mind. Physiological reflexes and neural processes were manifestations of an evolved body-machine of fibers and nerves and cells. The physiologist William Carpenter conceived of latent thoughts occurring in the nerve substance in a process he called "unconscious cerebration" (in Bourne Taylor and Shuttleworth 1998, 99–101). But Carpenter was concerned to retain the concept of a guiding Will, writing in the 1870s that the relation between automatic physiological functions and volitional consciousness "may be compared to the independent locomotive power of a horse under the guidance and control of a skilful rider … the rate and direction of the movement are determined by the Will of the rider" (Bourne Taylor and Shuttleworth 1998, 96). Committed to a materialist analysis of mind, Carpenter saw the will as the essential mediating force that organized selection and directed attention. The will was crucial in countering ideas about automata which were current in the 1870s. The proposition advanced by influential naturalists such as Thomas Henry Huxley that humans were physiological machines and consciousness a mere epiphenomenal accompaniment to physiological reflex functions caused widespread disquiet amongst scientists and traditionalists alike (Dixon 2003, 135–79). For writers such as Carpenter, the will was a crucial guarantor of human freedom against a determinism that threatened to void moral existence.

As debate about political consensus, the function of the popular press, and mass culture intensified in the final decades of the nineteenth century, ideas about human suggestibility proliferated, threatening the notion of a sovereign ethical will as well as social order itself. Motifs of manipulation, invasion, and influence permeate the fiction of the period, from the alien enchanter Svengali in George du Maurier's *Trilby* (1894) to the aristocratic mesmerizer Count Dracula, plotting penetration into the heart of *fin-de-siècle* London. In Oscar Wilde's *The Picture of Dorian Gray* (1891), the artist Basil Hallward eventually pays with his life for allowing Dorian's personality to dominate him "soul, brain, and power" (Wilde 2000, 110): "psychologists tell us" that passions can so dominate that "men and women at such moments lose the freedom of their will. They move to their terrible end as automatons move" (2000, 181). In *Dorian Gray*, it remains unnervingly undecidable whether Dorian's "rose-red youth" and "rose-white boyhood" (2000, 21) are corrupted by the external influence of Lord Henry Wotton and the fascinating "poisonous" yellow book (2000, 121), which creates fancies over which Dorian "seemed, at times, to have almost entirely lost control" (2000, 123). Or is Dorian's character determined elsewhere, perhaps by the other kind of haunting that gripped Victorian imaginations, namely the biological inheritance suggested by his family history of money, beauty, power, and crime?

Pamela Thurschwell has noted the currency that notions of influence accumulated during the trial of Wilde in 1895 on charges of gross indecency. Both Wilde and *Dorian Gray* were made to stand in for an illicit and dangerously seductive sexuality. As his story was transformed into prime legal evidence, cited at length in court, Wilde's literary skill came to signal his corrupting influence: verbal wordplay, witty epigram, and the celebration of surface over depth "began to be understood as a code for his homosexuality" (Thurschwell 2001, 56). Freud originally hypothesized that something traumatic about sexuality is caused by an external act of sexual seduction, but later understood such disturbance as internal to the individual, taking place in their fantasy. In a similar fashion, occult texts like *Dorian Gray* raised questions about where desire comes from, who it belongs to, and whether it can be transferred to others. Cultural aestheticism, Thurschwell argues, became charged with sexual meanings associated with newly visible sexual acts and identities (Thurschwell 2001, 62, 39–40). Books contaminate and infect, but while Dorian "never sought to free himself" from the "poison" of Huysman's *A Rebours* (Wilde 2000, 123), replicating copies to stand in for his many moods, the criminal law attempted to cauterize *Dorian Gray* during the Wilde trials.

The composite figure of the New Woman at the end of the century was less easy to take to the dock. Occult stories conveyed a mixture of fascination and fear about the sexual allure associated with powerful women. Some of these women, such as the immortal queen Ayesha in Rider Haggard's *She* (1887), are disconcertingly articulate and well educated, as were the women asserting claims to emancipation in the period. In Machen's "The Great God Pan" – denounced on its appearance as "a nightmare incoherence of sex and the supposed horrible mysteries behind it" (quoted in Luckhurst 2005, xxix) – the narrative breaks and gaps leave unspeakable the terrible erotic potency of Helen Vaughan, who precipitates a contagion of male suicide in the midst of the respectable West End. In both of these examples, the potent woman is literally dis-composed, subject to a punitive devolutionary process that reveals her as frighteningly archaic at the same time as neutralizing her power. But the femme fatale figure is also prominent in the supernatural stories of Vernon Lee, where female beauty and seductive power are far more ambiguous. Here sexuality is not a reductive terminus for the stories' meaning but integral to how haunted characters from the present are made to participate in and repeat the past. In "Amour Dure" (1887), the scholar Spiridion Trepka weeps with disappointment on his first encounter with modern Italy at the gap between reality and his projected fantasy, which casts Italy and its inhabitants as aesthetic objects for his contemplation. Wedded to the romance of history, he cannot find romance in the women around him, occupying himself instead with the history of Medea da Carpi, a woman who used sex, intrigue, and assassination to make her way through sixteenth-century Italy. Increasingly pale, feverish, and prey to hallucinations or haunting, Trepka dies violently, the history he is writing unfinished, and the ambiguous nature of what has occurred unresolved (Lee 2006, 41–76). Diverse possibilities could be imagined in the literature of the supernatural.

If in 1895, the year of Wilde's trial, the occult seemed to function as a code for illegitimate or prohibited or dangerous sexuality, the relationship between the two terms could also turn about in surprising ways. In his autobiography, Carl Jung provocatively suggests that for Freud sexuality "was a sort of *numinosum*" or divinity, before proceeding to relate an occasion in 1910 when Freud begged him not to abandon "the sexual theory," insisting that sex must be a "dogma ... an unshakeable bulwark." Jung reports asking Freud in astonishment: "'A bulwark – against what?'" to which Freud replied, "'Against the black mud' – and here he hesitated for a moment, then added – 'of occultism'" (Jung 1983 [1961], 173). Without probing further into Jung's agenda here, it is worth recalling that in 1912 Freud used the *PSPR* to define "what the term 'unconscious' has come to mean in Psychoanalysis and in Psychoanalysis alone" (Freud 1984, 50). Competing accounts of the unconscious, especially Myers' ideas about subliminal consciousness, were perceived as alternatives from which psychoanalysis had aggressively to distinguish itself. This was not primarily because of fears about the taint of "hocus-pocus" supernaturalism, however, but, as Luckhurst has argued, a sign of psychoanalysis' marginality in relation to the tentative non-physiological conceptions of dynamic psychology emerging at the beginning of the twentieth century: "what, after all, could be more occulted at the time than the Freudian unconscious, this dynamic, structural thing, founded on the mechanisms of sexual repression?" (Luckhurst 2002, 275).

The "black mud" of the occult, though, is a reminder of other dark places – most obviously female sexuality, the "dark continent" for psychoanalysis, which haunted Gothic imaginings too. In analyzing a dream about the evisceration of his own pelvis, in which he magically travels through alien lands, Freud links the dream's occasion to a conversation with a woman assisting with his book on dreams to whom he recommended Rider Haggard's *She*: "A *strange* book, but full of hidden meaning." *She* had dictated his dream-script, Freud realizes: perilous journeying, undiscovered regions, and the dismal prospect of death instead of immortality at the journey's end. His interpretation associates the dissection of his pelvis with his self-analysis, and his hopes of immortality as the founder of psychoanalysis (Freud 1976, 586–87). But the turning inside out of his eviscerated pelvis is surely also an image of castration, a way to identify with both the corporeality and the intelligence of Haggard's immortal queen. Mysterious and irresistibly seductive, Ayesha is a linguist, a chemist, a geologist, an astronomer, and a practical eugenicist who also knows that materialism has limits, and that female beauty works because it is an idea. "How thinkest thou that I rule this people?" she asks the narrator, Horace Holly; "it is not by force ... my empire is of the imagination" (Haggard 1991, 175).

The black mud and the dark continent are also figures for the past. Darwin's evolutionary thinking had drawn its ideas of time from geological accounts which stretched the history of the world into hitherto unimaginably far-off pasts. The notion of the past as forged and shaped by random variations amongst individuals and species, coupled with the fossil evidence of mass extinctions, contributed to a version of modernity as a condition beset by loss. Memory became one important way in which losses might be retrieved and agency re-established. Samuel Butler, for instance, challenged the Darwinian account with a revised version of Lamarckian heritable experience – of experience (or habits) passed through time and culture in the form of unconscious memory. Unconsciousness in this account salvages the past and rescues it from the domain of degeneration. This is echoed in the fiction of lost worlds, of submerged, subterranean, extraterrestrial, or astral spaces "conjured up for occult colonization" (Ramaswamy 2004, 54). Lost and recoverable worlds in turn become metaphors of the psyche. When Freud writes about the "special characteristics" of the unconscious – which prominently include timelessness and the absence of contradiction, giving rise to the popular sense of nothing left behind or abandoned in the processes of unconscious life (1984, 190) – it is a description close to occult claims of an "imperishable" record of the extra-ordinary world beyond the senses from which what has been missing or has gone lost is recoverable. Technology helped to shape such ideas, as it did occult communications. Myers wrote in an autobiographical fragment: "I hold that all things thought and felt, as well as all things done, are somehow photographed imperishably upon the universe" (1921, 1). If history is the written record of victors, this alternative provides at least the possibility of a different past to be told. In its version of listening to hitherto excluded stories – beginning with the stories of women hysterics – psychoanalysis established its progressive potential.

"Was there anything so real as words?" Dorian Gray asks himself, oppressed by their vivid and cruel effects, agitated that he cannot escape them, and yet struck by "what a subtle magic was in them!" (Wilde 2000, 22). Freud would agree. In "The Question of Lay Analysis," he imagines an "impartial interlocutor" questioning psychoanalysis' claims to cure without instruments or medicines. Psychoanalysis is just "Words, words, words," the interlocutor complains; it is "a kind of magic; you talk and just blow away his complaint." Freud's response affirms the fundamental connection which links literature and psychoanalysis to the politics and poetics of modern human subjectivity:

> Quite right, it *would* be magic, if it worked more rapidly. Speed is the essence of magic; instant success, you might say. But analytic treatment takes months and even years, such slow magic can no longer be called miraculous. Incidentally, we should not despise the *word*. It is after all a powerful instrument, the means to let each other know about our feelings, the way to achieve influence over others. Words can have an unutterably positive effect, or inflict terrible injury. To be sure, in the very beginning was the deed, the word came later; in many circumstances it was a cultural step forward when the deed was reduced to the word. But the word was originally a form of magic, a magic act, and it has preserved much of its old force.
>
> (Freud 2002, 99)

By the slow magic of disclosing in words what Freud called psychic reality, psychoanalysis acknowledges as well as demystifies what feels like the occult within each of us. "Amour Dure – Dure Amour" – the refrain of the haunting Medea da Carpi in Lee's tale – is literature's contribution to the affective tasks which its occult tales bring into view.

Notes

1 "Occult" was widely used in the late nineteenth and early twentieth century to encompass diverse phenomena including telepathy, spiritualism, and psychical research. Recent scholars of the period have found it helpful to adopt this loose usage, specifying the more narrowly defined occult practices and beliefs associated, for instance, with theosophy or hermetic traditions.

2 Freud's major writings on occult topics are collected, with additional material, in Devereux (1974). For further discussion and interpretation, see Gyimesi (2009), Luckhurst (1999), McQuillan (2009), and Rosenthal (2010).

3 A recent and hostile account is Borch-Jacobsen and Shamdasani (2012).

4 A now substantial secondary literature on spiritualism includes Galvan (2010), Owen (1989), and Tromp (2006).

References

Altick, Richard. 1986. "Behind the Veil." Review of *The Other World: Spiritualism and Psychic Research In England 1850–1914*, by Janet Oppenheim. *London Review of Books*, 8, no. 4: 18–19.

Borch-Jacobsen, Mikkel, and Sonu Shamdasani. 2012. *The Freud Files: An Inquiry into the History of Psychoanalysis*. Cambridge: Cambridge University Press.

Bourne Taylor, Jenny, and Sally Shuttleworth, eds. 1998. *Embodied Selves: An Anthology of Psychological Texts 1830–1890*. Oxford: Clarendon Press.

Dallas, E.S. 1866. *The Gay Science*, 2 vols. London: Chapman & Hall.

Devereux, George, ed. 1974. *Psychoanalysis and the Occult*. London: Souvenir Press.

Dixon, Thomas, 2003. *From Passions to Emotions: The Creation of a Secular Psychological Category*. Cambridge: Cambridge University Press.

ffytche, Matt. 2012. *The Foundation of the Unconscious: Schelling, Freud and the Birth of the Modern Psyche*. Cambridge: Cambridge University Press.

Freud, Sigmund. 1976. *The Interpretation of Dreams*. Pelican Freud Library 4. Harmondsworth: Penguin.

Freud, Sigmund. 1984. *On Metapsychology: The Theory of Psychoanalysis*. Pelican Freud Library 11. Harmondsworth: Penguin.

Freud, Sigmund. 1985. "The Uncanny." In *Art and Literature*, 339–76. Pelican Freud Library 14. Harmondsworth: Penguin.

Freud, Sigmund. 2002. "The Question of Lay Analysis: Conversations with an Impartial Listener." In *Wild Analysis*, ed. Adam Phillips, 93–160. London: Penguin.

Galvan, Jill. 2010. *The Sympathetic Medium: Feminine Channeling, the Occult, and Communication Technologies, 1859–1919*. Ithaca, N.Y.: Cornell University Press.

Groth, Helen. 2011. "Subliminal Histories: Psychological Experimentation in the Poetry and Poetics of Frederic W. H. Myers." *19: Interdisciplinary Studies in the Long Nineteenth Century*, 12: 1–22. Accessed November 20, 2011. http://www.19.bbk.ac.uk/index.php/19/article/view/594/683.

Gyimesi, Júlia. 2009. "The Problem of Demarcation." *American Imago*, 66, no. 4: 457–70. DOI: 10.1353/aim.0.0064.

Hacking, Ian. 1995. *Rewriting the Soul: Multiple Personality and the Sciences of Memory*. Princeton: Princeton University Press.

Haggard, H. Rider. 1991. *She*, ed. Daniel Karlin. Oxford: Oxford University Press.

Hurley, Kelly. 1996. *The Gothic Body: Sexuality, Materialism, and Degeneration at the Fin de Siècle*. Cambridge: Cambridge University Press.

Huxley, Thomas Henry. 1869. "On the Physical Basis of Life." *Fortnightly Review*, n.s., 26: 129–45.

James, William. 1890. "The Hidden Self." *Scribner's Magazine*, 7, no. 3: 361–73.

Jones, Ernest. 1957. *The Last Phase, 1919–39*. Vol. 3 of *Sigmund Freud: His Life and Work*. London: Hogarth.

Jung, Carl Gustav. 1983 [1961]. *Memories, Dreams, Reflections*. London: Flamingo.

Keeley, James P. 2001. "Subliminal Promptings: Psychoanalytic Theory and the Society for Psychical Research." *American Imago*, 58, no. 4: 767–91. DOI: 10.1353/aim.2001.0021.

Lang, Andrew. 1894. "Ghosts up to Date." *Blackwood's Edinburgh Magazine*, 155: 47–55.

Ledger, Sally, and Roger Luckhurst, eds. 2000. *The Fin de Siècle: A Reader in Cultural History c.1880–1900*. Oxford: Oxford University Press.

Lee, Vernon. 2006. *Hauntings and Other Fantastic Tales*, ed. Catherine Maxwell and Patricia Pulham. Plymouth: Broadview.

Luckhurst, Roger. 1999. "'Something Tremendous, Something Elemental': On the Ghostly Origin of Psychoanalysis." In *Ghosts: Deconstruction, Psychoanalysis, History*, ed. Peter Buse and Andrew Stott, 50–71. Basingstoke: Macmillan.

Luckhurst, Roger. 2002. *The Invention of Telepathy*. Oxford: Oxford University Press.

Luckhurst, Roger, ed. 2005. *Late Victorian Gothic Tales*. Oxford: Oxford University Press.

McQuillan, Martin. 2009. "Tele-Techno-Theology." In *Deconstruction After 9/11*, 47–64. New York: Routledge.

Mighall, Robert. 2002. "Diagnosing Jekyll: The Scientific Context to Dr Jekyll's Experiment and Mr Hyde's Embodiment." In Robert Louis Stevenson, *The Strange Case of Dr Jekyll and Mr Hyde and Other Tales of Terror*, ed. Robert Mighall, 143–61. Harmondsworth: Penguin.

Myers, Frederic W.H. 1893–94. "Mechanism of Hysteria." *Proceedings of the Society for Psychical Research*, 9. London: Kegan Paul, Trench, Trübner.

Myers, Frederic W.H. 1921. *Collected Poems with Autobiographical and Critical Fragments*, ed. Eveleen Myers. London: Macmillan.

Nicholls, Angus and Martin Liebscher, eds. 2010. *Thinking the Unconscious: Nineteenth-Century German Thought*. Cambridge: Cambridge University Press.

Noakes, Richard. 2004. "Spiritualism, Science and the Supernatural in Mid-Victorian Britain." In *The Victorian Supernatural*, ed. Nicola Bown, Carolyn Burdett, and Pamela Thurschwell, 23–43. Cambridge: Cambridge University Press.

Oppenheim, Janet. 1985. *The Other World: Spiritualism and Psychical Research in England, 1850–1914*. Cambridge: Cambridge University Press.

Owen, Alex. 1989. *The Darkened Room: Women, Power, and Spiritualism in Late Victorian England*. London: Virago.

Owen, Alex. 2004. *The Place of Enchantment: British Occultism and the Culture of the Modern*. Chicago: University of Chicago Press.

Pick, Daniel. 1989. *Faces of Degeneration: A European Disorder c.1848–c.1918*. Cambridge: Cambridge University Press.

Ramaswamy, Sumathi. 2004. *The Lost Land of Lemuria: Fabulous Geographies, Catastrophic Histories.* Berkeley: University of California Press.

Rosenthal, Lecia. 2010. "Fictions of Possession: Psychoanalysis and the Occult." In *Freud and Fundamentalism,* ed. Stathis Gourgouris, 125–37. New York: Fordham University Press.

Stevenson, Robert Louis. 2002. *The Strange Case of Dr Jekyll and Mr Hyde and Other Tales of Terror,* ed. Robert Mighall. Harmondsworth: Penguin.

Thurschwell, Pamela. 2001. *Literature, Technology and Magical Thinking, 1880–1920.* Cambridge: Cambridge University Press.

Tromp, Marlene. 2006. *Altered States: Sex, Nation, Drugs and Self-Transformation in Victorian Spiritualism.* Albany: State University of New York Press.

Wilde, Oscar. 2000. *The Picture of Dorian Gray,* ed. Robert Mighall. Harmondsworth: Penguin.

Chapter 4

Back to Frankfurt School

Laurence A. Rickels

Prologue

In his *Fichus* lecture (2002), Jacques Derrida addressed his future debt to a Frankfurt School that was for him the coupling in theory of Theodor Adorno and Walter Benjamin. Among the two or three things he knew about their compatibility as a threesome was the investment in Freud's science. Although for Derrida this was in keeping with modern French philosophy, which was immersed in psychoanalysis, it was an investment that counted Adorno and Benjamin out of German philosophy (or academic discourse at large) as the other state of exception. Derrida's silent reading in this lecture, which he gave in receipt of the Adorno prize, addressed the highly influential tendency in global theory to divorce Benjamin from a Frankfurt School connection viewed as the imposition of a forced marriage. While these ideologues can still subsume the Marxism in Benjamin's mix of declared interests by means of onto-theology, for example, they prefer not to go near psychoanalysis. By the time Marxism was treated as publicly going out of business (while in effect going out for business in the academy as cultural studies) it was psychoanalysis that was being doubly disowned.

A Concise Companion to Psychoanalysis, Literature, and Culture, First Edition.
Edited by Laura Marcus and Ankhi Mukherjee.

Adorno's own belated inclusion of psychoanalysis did not so much supplement Marxism according to a logic of division of labor as displace it from the foreground or objective of understanding mass culture. Admittedly this is true to the extent that Adorno had already projected it onto Benjamin in their infamous exchange of letters. But in exchange Adorno developed in this correspondence, out of an allegiance to Benjamin's own earlier work, a strategy of loyalty typical of the good student or follower.

I have tried throughout my work to recover as couples therapy the Freud transference passing through the so-called Frankfurt School, even wagering an interpretation of the isolationism that besets Benjamin's reception as intrapsychically rehearsed in the sui-citational mode of manic denial that staggered Benjamin's relationship to Freud's thought. My reading of unmourning at the border to psychosis initially relied more heavily on Adorno's thought. It was through Freud's notion of endopsychic perception, on which I modeled my Freudian genealogies, and which relies on a self-reflexivity of relations between psychoanalysis and the staging within psychotic delusions of insights into our technological relation over undead bodies, that I sought to re-start Adorno's notion of a coextensivity between the psychic apparatus and the culture industry. Since Adorno grounded the reversal of psychoanalysis subtending this busy interchange in the anchor-personification of controlling interests, he just the same treated the psychoanalytic model as a timely fit that was also throwaway. Re-read via the endopsychic genealogy of psychoanalysis and mass culture that subsumes it as paranoid syndication, Adorno's reading can be reclaimed for the study of unmourning, restoring focus (for example) to Adorno's passing reference in his reading of television, as we will see, to that which lies buried in the consumer. And yet for a closer reading of the belief in ghosts as secular caption to the proximity between religious metaphysics and schizophrenia I more recently came to rely on Benjamin to pick up as allegory where Freud's almost phobic secularism leaves off.

For this essay I investigate in unlikely sites the Freudian influence, which cannot always be reconstructed as contact sport, but instead must be assessed for the endopsychic genealogy passing through it. First I will consider the Freudian genealogy of mutations in psychic relationality commenced during World War I as laid out in Benjamin's "The Storyteller" ("Der Erzähler"), one out of three media essays giving advance notice of the *Arcades Project*. By World War II the borderline along which psychic reality was resettling between neurosis and psychosis was in place in science fiction as in psychoanalytic theory.

But then the World War II era, as open season for the realization of future projections, brought the colonization of psychosis for the survival of the species before a new limit to psychoanalytic understanding, that of psychopathic violence, and a new prospect or problem, that of its integration. I turn to Adorno's postwar essays on television, in which we watch among the ruins of sublimation no longer the psychotic sublime but our own channeling of violence as the new "station identification," to issue the update and continuity shot of Benjamin's reading of media innovation in terms of inoculation. I leave it to D.W. Winnicott, however, as Freud's delegate in a new era, to continue the work of the Frankfurt couple in his recasting of psychoanalysis around the newly introduced and excluded object of treatment, the so-called antisocial tendency, which in adolescence renders the psychopath and the teen, short of criminal evidence, indistinguishable.

Visualization studies

Prior to the inevitability of a greater visualization brought to us by digital media, Freud introduced the book of analogues for unconscious thought. What is impossible can, in the unconscious, be visualized at the limit. To analogize and visualize the nature of unconscious thought Freud asks us to see the history of a city in the light of remembrance. When gazing upon Rome, we see not only the Colosseum, for example, but also, at the same time, the edifices it replaced (Freud 1961a, 69–71). Outside of this instructive assignment, Freud already advised elsewhere that the analogy carries forward grief misplaced in time. The hysteric, in this version, is like a modern citizen of London who, overcome with sorrow before Charing Cross train station, still recognizes its original address as a station in the crossing of Queen Eleanor's funeral procession (Freud 1957, 16–17). Stuck in grief, one can see better the alternate realities that fold out of loss.

On the terms and turf of psychoanalysis the tracks of visualization open wide before two primal questions: Where do babies come from? and Where do the dead go, where are they kept? Each opening track of research or response is multiplied and skewed through blockages, displacements, and repressions. The first question, however, is early on taken into the light by Oedipalization and Christianity. Prior to the leap of faith that recognition of the reality of reproduction requires, there is an intense early visualization of creation based on the evidence of the baby's senses. But while the theory of anal babies, on which the relationship of

Dad to the Devil is based, underwrites as science fantasy the assembly lines of technological replication, it is as such not ongoing but leads instead, ultimately, to an underworld of blanks to be filled by the undead. It is the relationship to the dead that, even or especially as repressed, keeps the momentum of visualization up and running.

In his 1936 essay "The Storyteller" Benjamin identified the ending of experience, history-telling, and counsel, which, though dating back in theory to the development of the novel and the advent of information, reached its conclusive crisis point in World War I. Behind the lines of Benjamin's essay, but in line with references to Freud that appear in his other media essays, the shocks that shook experience at its foundation were first internalized as the shell shock epidemic that led Freud to remap the topography of his theory. Before "The Uncanny" and *Beyond the Pleasure Principle*, which then followed, Freud committed to theorization, in his "Introduction to *Psychoanalysis and the War Neuroses*," a splitting of the ego into "Doppelgänger": in one corner the peace ego, in the other its "parasitical" double, the war ego (1955, 209). The divisions of doubles that emerged from the experience-mutating changes brought about by the first total techno war projected a new standard of survival, that of the fit with technologization, a psychic fit best secured through the unbalancing acts of dissociation. What Freud theorized in "Fetishism" as the simulcast of seeing and not-seeing attends the psychoanalytic sensorium as it expands from the limits of visualization of repression and the unconscious to the borderline between neurosis and psychosis (inside psychosis).

By aligning its ending with the end of the protagonist's life and encompassing thereby the sense or direction of a life, the novel administered inoculations against and with death and the dead. Benjamin corrects critic Moritz Heimann's assignment to an individual's early death the role of organizing the meaning of that individual life as it unfolds: "Nothing is more dubious than this sentence – but for the sole reason that the tense is wrong. A man – so says the truth that was meant here – who died at thirty-five will appear to remembrance at every point in his life as a man who dies at the age of thirty-five" (Benjamin 2002, 156). To push further and further out the contact with the dead also means to internalize more and more the point of separation as after-the-fact inoculation administered by, for, and as remembrance. As Karl Kraus (1954) before him and Roland Barthes (1957) and Derrida since then, Benjamin recognized that any system of inoculation builds up to a crisis point of surfeit and backfire: the effect of immunization turns against itself and releases at the border to psychosis new and improved bogies of uncontainment.

The changes that Benjamin (in "The Storyteller") identified but also, on the eve of total war's Second Coming, projected, he located not only in the withdrawal of experience but even and especially inside our relations with the dead. "In the course of modern times, dying has been pushed further and further out of the perceptual world of the living. It used to be that there was not a single house, hardly a single room, in which someone had not once died. . . . Today people live in rooms that have never been touched by death – dry dwellers of eternity; and when their end approaches, they are stowed away in sanatoria or hospitals by their heirs" (Benjamin 2002, 150).

It's not that these dwellers withdraw into high and dry regions. Often overlooked here is the role of "dry dwellers" or *Trockenwohner* in the rapid-fire expansion of Berlin after unification, in particular the westward trek of Berlin's wealthy into new and improved neighborhoods, which the Benjamin family followed out, too, from the Tiergarten and Charlottenburg to Grunewald. The neo-buildings for the rich were erected too rapidly to allow time for the elaborate interiors to dry out. As we might find chronicled by Theodor Fontane or illustrated by Heinrich Zille, *Trockenwohner* were poor families hired to move into the fresh units ahead of the proper tenants to dry out with their mortal bodies the unhealthy moisture at the core of the decor. In the span of Benjamin's image, living or dying by proxy or antibody split off from the dead has made over bodily existence and finitude's afterlife – remembrance or haunting – to dry or die out a secularized eternity's interminable decay. Following Friedrich Schiller, for example, and in sync with Freud, whose notion of the transference neurosis as it unfolds in session is a particularly elaborate or calibrated presentation of the inoculative process, Benjamin identifies in his endopsychic allegory of mass culture the place or span of inoculation as the overriding frame of the mass media Sensurround.

TV Führer

Adorno could offer his essays in the study of television as brief updates because he recognized the impact of this medium only as part of the whole influence that the culture industry administered. And yet television, as that which completes the culture industry as system of delusion, is a part exceeding the whole. This excess is the adaptation the TV situation promotes to the evacuation-packing of sublimation as the new norm. In "Prologue to Television" ("Prolog zum Fernsehen") Adorno enters the genealogical frame Benjamin suspended in "The Storyteller" for viewing the regression in innovation. What television concludes as live transmission is the "schema of mass culture" in preparation as our second nature since the late seventeenth-century origin of the novel (Adorno 2003a, 514). As in Benjamin's reading of the inoculative sense or direction of an ending that injects modernity as its original novelty and dooms it to run on empty, the culture industry summons that which has been entombed only to place it at the disposal of its momentum or motility. "While the images recall those that lie buried in the viewer, and which resemble them, the images of television and film, which flash before us and pass away, approximate writing" (2003a, 514). By the two tracks of the hieroglyphic language, now as image, now as writing, the consumer is encompassed or corralled. The image version supplies regression as the shtick in this maneuver while the written variant draws us onward by its archaic representation of modernity. What is thus doubly secured as status quo was best formulated in Adorno's August 4, 1935, letter to Benjamin as the ongoing repression that befalls the recent past, which can come back only as the catastrophic return of prehistory. The present going on recent past, therefore, is the vanishing point where the dead are, the point of injection whose tracks Benjamin followed back to the origin of the novel.

The novel distribution of the dead as their own doubles and antibodies, which paralyzes the motility of experience or *Erfahrung*, is derived from what was new in the press of communication: information. Storytelling, in Benjamin's essay, offers a safe haven for novelty's displacements, from aura to the maternal relation of righteousness that upholds the creaturely world. What drives displacement in the series is that the news gives the event or advent of the other its inoculating shot: "nowadays no event comes to us without already being shot through with explanations" (2002, 147). Understandable in itself, information by its plausibility exhausts the approach and the encounter in understanding, which comes from afar: "information . . . supplies a handle for what is nearest" (2002, 147).

Inasmuch as the image language of the culture industry "awakens" that which "slumbers pre-conceptually" in the audience the TV viewer, according to Adorno, receives owner's manual instruction in how to adapt to an imposed adaptation (2003a, 514). We are manipulated to adapt to the status quo by startled stops and starts (*zurechtstutzen*). The precedent for assuming this controlling interest as the spirit of our times are those moments from the consumer's conscious and unconscious life (the already interred images at the disposal of the culture industry) which can be held responsible (2003a, 514). As seen on TV, the mind warp that concludes the culture industry's promotion of acceptance of our manipulation as psychic reality is that "not the murderer, but rather the murder victim, is guilty" (2003a, 514–15). In his follow-up reflections in "Television as Ideology" ("Fernsehen als Ideologie") Adorno identifies the normalization of criminality as the moral of the TV show. Television completes the culture industry as techno-doubling of our perceptual and libidinal world without any apparent gap, like the hierarchical difference between high and low culture, in which one double is prised loose from the other. The kernel of reality in the TV broadcast is this kernel of perfect doubling. "The initiated viewers may not transfer the scenarios of the TV crime drama to everyday life, but they are encouraged to arrange their experiences in a similarly frozen and mechanical manner" (2003b, 522). On television the trivial romanticism of ill deeds is conjoined with the realism of gadget-loving attention to the properties of techno-external life. "If the procedure for dialing a phone number did not conform to reality in a TV show, the station would not hear the end of it from an indignant audience, which otherwise is willing to accept with pleasure the fiction that a murderer lurks at every corner" (2003b, 522).

In "Prologue to Television" Adorno argues that the culture industry causes sublimation to decay. In Freud's thought, as Adorno knew, sublimation rests on the uneasy settlement of incorporated or interred melancholic identifications. In the culture industry between film and television Adorno projects the effect and degree of sublimation as the ability to treat actual size and proportion aesthetically. While what was projected large in film could at least be interpreted as life-size, Adorno identifies in the receiving area of television an inability to reformat the miniaturist representations. In this sense television is the station of withdrawal of sublimation within the culture industry (2003a, 509). As Freud advised in his reading of Schreber's *Memoirs of My Nervous Illness*, even after the paranoid schizophrenic was able by projection of his delusional system to enter recovery of a new world order in lieu of the former world that had succumbed to repression and psychotic breakdown, it was a "wealth of sublimations" that remained irretrievably lost (Freud 1958a, 73). In other words, sublimation is what is first destroyed at or as the breaking point of psychosis.

At the same time as Adorno picked up the withdrawal of sublimation as a stage in the development of normative TV viewing, D.W. Winnicott was revising the notion of sublimation, conceived, at the bottom line, as the internal provision of respite from the ongoing struggle to relate inner and outer worlds, as the syndication on the inside of a period of transition enacted and secured between mother and infant. Basic dealings with absence, like mourning and remembrance, rely, according to Winnicott, on the impossibility of separation as another form of its possibility, and thus on the successful derivation of potential space from play as well as, ultimately, from the transitional object itself. And yet Winnicott keeps the watershed of transition close to the potential for traumatization. He writes into the fine print of the transitional contract, which his repeated presentation of the transitional object spells out, always in italics: "*Of the transitional object it can be said that it is a matter of agreement between us and the baby that we will never ask the question 'Did you conceive of this or was it presented to you from without?' The important point is that no decision on this point is expected. The question is not to be formulated*" (Winnicott 1992b, 239–40). The transitional object, therefore, which is designed to lead us through good enough mothering to an integrated sense of presence in absence, is the ready occasion for trauma waiting to happen. At first "good enough" sounds like we're cutting reality some slack and making room for hit and miss in healthy development. The truth is, parental guidance is never good enough. The transitional object as defective cornerstone in development attends Winnicott's shift from what he termed "neurotic analysis" to his reclamation for analytic understanding of the institutional containment of psychopathy. The rest area of the in-between, which by the regular mismanagement of the transitional object gives rise to psychic aberrations as normalcy's alternate realities, is addressed by Winnicott on more than one occasion as "no-man's land." For example, in the chapter in *Human Nature* titled "Establishment of Relationship with External Reality": "There is a no-man's land between the subjective and what is objectively perceived that is natural to infancy" (Winnicott 1988, 114). In "The Deprived Child and How He Can Be Compensated for Loss of Family Life," Winnicott delineates the deprivation in the background of the antisocial tendency as the destruction of transitional bridges in this land: "If we deprive a child of the transitional objects and disturb the established transitional phenomena, then the child has only one way out, which is a split in the personality with one half related to a subjective world and the other reacting on a compliance basis to the world which impinges" (1989, 144). The antisocial tendency is trapped inside another "in between" position at the starting block of normal adaptation: too early for mourning, too late for the open break of regression. We come to stand, like peace ego to war ego in Freud's World War I reading of shell shock, in a near-miss relation to psychopathy as our doubling. In the language of the object relations school: there but for the grace of the good object go I.

In the outlines of Adorno's stricken TV world we can make out the postwar changes going into the new Teen Age. In "Prologue to Television" Adorno recognizes the new wrap-around in-group psychology modeled on TV viewing which arose in the United States by the end of World War II (to some degree consciously already toward the end of the war among the first practitioners of what would be identified as family systems therapy) as an advance on earlier models of mass psychology whereby totalitarianism forfeited the future. But he dismisses it, too, as a diversion from the growing alienation of individuals. For "dumbing down" cannot be tied to TV content but to this overall "situation" ("die Situation verdummt") (2003a, 512). "The fateful proximity of television, the cause as well of the allegedly community-building effect of the apparatuses, around which family members and friends, who otherwise have nothing to say to one another, mindlessly gather, not only satisfies a desire, of which no intellectual or spiritual aspect is allowed to develop or remain, unless it can place itself as product and property, but even beclouds in addition the real alienation between people and between people and things" (2003a, 511–12). A clue to Adorno's refusal to consider the Teen Age outside its condemned site (all the while circumscribing the structures transmitting the shock of what's new) can be found in another essay from this TV period, "What Is Meant by Working-through the Past?" ("Was bedeutet: Aufarbeitung der Vergangenheit?"), in which he considers the prospect for integration of former practitioners of or heirs to the psychopathic violence in the recent past. That postwar Germans like to inform one another that they are not mature enough yet for democracy reminds Adorno of juvenile delinquents who, when caught in the antisocial act, talk themselves out of it by saying they're just teenagers (2003c, 559–60). This passing reference to the violent delinquent's self understanding in terms of "affiliation to the group of teenagers" (2003c, 560) belongs to a psychoanalytic perspective in critical theory that would inhabit history as contemporary, which Adorno had to forgo. He could only reject in this essay the postwar German policy of restitution or reparation as retraumatization of the victim-recipients. But the policy set a new precedent for staggering the scheduling of mourning in the aftermath of psychopathic violence. To this end it applied to the work of repair energy or industry independent of both ethical cleansing and murderous excess. In psychopathy as new limit concept we find over and against its threat of annihilation the saving second chance of reparation that its industry makes possible prior to the onset of the capacity for mourning.

Construction, reparation, restitution

Hannah Arendt opens *On Violence* with a consideration of the "technical development of the implements of violence" that by the end of World War II guaranteed that warfare had lost its effectiveness as well as its political significance. The technological revolution that was aided by warfare as its lab space outran and neutralized it (1970, 3–4). For Winnicott, as spelled out in his 1963 article "Struggling through the Doldrums," World War II led to the introduction of deregulated adolescent energy. The teen was sent to this corner by the atom bomb that was dropped on war as we knew it. Together with the withdrawal of the rationalization for discipline as preparation for war, the introduction of effective contraception meant that the postwar teen began containing himself as the site or medium of sex and violence in society. "Adolescence now has to contain itself, to contain itself in a way it has never had to do before" (2000c, 151). Psychopathy is the parallel universal attending this inside view of adolescence as container of turbulence.

In a conference paper from April 1964, Winnicott shares his "Deductions Drawn from a Psychotherapeutic Interview with an Adolescent." First things first: "there is nothing more difficult than to decide whether one is seeing a healthy boy or girl who is in the throes of adolescence or a person who happens to be ill, psychiatrically speaking, in the puberty age. Is one seeing adolescence, or a hold-up or distortion of adolescence due to illness?" (1989 [1964], 326). Or is one facing a hold-up of adolescence due to the establishment of a new norm of proximity to psychopathy? The patient, Jane is the name, seems to be sleeping around but her only problem, as she sees it, is that she's lying around. But already at age 7 she was stealing any change lying about and then lied about it. Jane can't say why she stole change or that she ever knew the reason. Winnicott translates: she was under a compulsion. She quickly confirms: "'It's just like that with lying.'" "There was trouble in the intermediate area of transitional phenomena, the place where sparks fly in moments of intimacy between persons" (1989 [1964], 332).

Winnicott began making the new boundary concept transitionally legible in case studies of children he nipped as budding psychopaths at the onset of their "antisocial tendencies." His signature intervention, as underscored, for example, in "The Antisocial Tendency" (1992c), was to characterize the initial "nuisance behaviour" as expression of "hope" that illuminates the "importance of the environment." The etymology of "hope" includes in the word's Germanic prehistory (preserved to this day as *verhoffen* in the German "language of hunters") some of the senses Winnicott pursued with his clients at great length. In a word, hope begins as the startle response to a sudden change in our environment, whereby we (humans and animals alike) take the moment of hesitation to try out in our minds a new next move. For Freud this ability to reconsider a plan of action as trial offer was the crux of what he called reality testing, which he assigned with great emphasis to the work of mourning. As with original hoping, we test in and beyond the interruption of loss a new frontier between life and death. Between hope and mourning, however, lies the span of interruption and deprivation which the delinquent, identified by Winnicott as mascot of our group or adolescent psychology, struggles to catch up with or reclaim, but for the time being in all the wrong places.

Because teens try to start over anew, independent of tradition or parental guidance, they form groups based on cursory identifications among peers. An adolescent peer group coheres best under duress. But in the absence of external stimulation, Winnicott emphasizes the significance of group economizing with symptoms on a sliding scale of psychopathology. Teen traits range from psychotic symptoms to normal deceptiveness and self-deception. "From this it follows that in a group of adolescents the various extreme tendencies tend to be represented by the more ill members of the group" (2000c, 153). The teen group members rely on the identified patient or scapegoat, whose acting out, which exceeds what individual group members may be willing or able to do, receives the support of those who, thus, feel real and coherent. Over time – in its passage lies the cure for normal adolescence – the teen admits compromise as allowable and thus begins to discover ways in which "the relentlessness of essential truth can be softened" (2000c, 151). Identification with the parents is Winnicott's chief example of a compromise (or truth softener) that can be admitted only in time, after passage through the turbulence of feeling now futile, now real.

In a 1967 talk titled "Delinquency as a Sign of Hope," Winnicott summarizes his work with children whose antisocial tendency is linked inherently with deprivation: "For the child that we are studying, it can be said that *things went well enough and then they did not go well enough.* A change occurred which altered the whole life of the child and this change in the environment happened when the child was old enough to know about things" (1990, 91). After the change, which introduced uncontainable anxiety, the child manages to attain a neutral state of compliance. "Then, for some reason or other, hope begins to appear, and this means that the child, without being conscious of what is going on, begins to have the urge to get back behind the moment of deprivation and so to undo the fear of the *unthinkable anxiety or confusion that resulted before the neutral state became organized*" (1990, 92). The compliant child becomes difficult whenever conditions give a degree of new hope. It is the antisocial child who retrieves a memory of the time before the deprivation. "In this way the child has reached back either to the lost capacity to find objects or to the lost security of the framework. The child has reached back to a creative relationship to external reality or to the period in which spontaneity was safe, even if it involved aggressive impulses" (1990, 98).

In "Some Psychological Aspects of Juvenile Delinquency," Winnicott describes how the state of the child pursuant to the loss of the nearly achieved norm turns on the realization of violence: "Unless he gets into trouble, the delinquent can only become progressively more and more inhibited in love, and consequently more and more depressed and depersonalised, and eventually unable to feel the reality of things at all, except the reality of violence" (2000a, 116). The emergency brake or break is the emergence of hope coinciding with the passage to the act. According to "The Antisocial Tendency," therefore, the actively antisocial child is looking for something; failing to find it, he seeks it elsewhere, which is the return of hopefulness. From the mother's arms and body to the local police station, the delinquent seeks environmental stability that will withstand impulsive behavior (1992c, 311), while by the very motility of his acting out in the relay of environments he retains a relationship to what Winnicott called the spontaneous self.

In "Contemporary Concepts of Adolescent Development and their Implications for Higher Education," Winnicott addresses the shifting significance of the fantasy content of death from childhood to adolescence. In childhood, "in the fantasy of early growth, there is contained *death*" (1996, 144). In adolescence this bottom deadline is exchanged for one of near-murder. "If the child is to become adult, then this move is achieved over the dead body of an adult" (1996, 145). Even when the period of puberty is uninterrupted by losses, acute problems of management can arise "because growing up means taking the parent's place" (1996, 144). "In the unconscious fantasy, growing up is inherently an aggressive act.

And the child is now no longer child-size" (1996, 144). Because a switch begins to be made from "death" to "murder" the need to be able to mourn rises in proportion to this realization of the capacity for psychopathic violence.

Winnicott advises parents not to relinquish responsibility but to confront their teens, though in a way that promotes "containment that is non-retaliatory" (1996, 150). It's cheating at the "life-game" to "abdicate just as they come to killing you" (1996, 146). "Lost is all the imaginative activity and striving of immaturity. Rebellion no longer makes sense, and the adolescent who wins too early is caught in his own trap, must turn dictator, and must stand up waiting to be killed – to be killed not by a new generation of his own children, but by siblings. Naturally, he seeks to control them" (1996, 146). As Winnicott argues in his 1964 article "Youth Will Not Sleep," the danger that "the group-loyal teenager" will activate his "potential violence" when the "compulsive activities of a few truly deprived boys and girls" start up violence in a gang (2000d, 157) can only be met with holding and containing while we wait it out. The short-term solution to teen turbulence is to raise the cursory connections of teen group bonding to the level of society-wide membership. A greater danger lies in this false solution, "the worst result of today's adolescent tendency to group violence," which would be the one the Nazis found: "Hitler solved the adolescent problem overnight by offering youth the role of superego to the community" (2000d, 156). The Third Reich thus jumped the gun and catapulted the phases of teen group therapy, power through joy, into society as its very momentum. Without the future mourning in murder what's left for metabolization of the death that indwells adolescence is the Big Brother relationship projected society-wide.

Winnicott opens "Aggression in Relation to Emotional Development" with the figment that society is in danger. What's dangerous is the repression of personal aggressiveness in individuals. He thus lays down the law binding us to our psychopathic outcasts, which he admits is painful since it draws attention to "dissociations that are hidden in current social acceptance" (1992a, 204). "In a total psychology, being-stolen-from is the same as stealing and is equally aggressive. Being weak is as aggressive as the attack of the strong on the weak. Murder and suicide are fundamentally the same thing. . . . Possession is as aggressive as is greedy acquisition" (1992a, 204). Winnicott is addressing another part of the problem of adolescent proximity to psychopathy, that of midlife crisis or criticism.

Resignation before or perpetuation of adolescence via midlife criticism of adolescence must be shifted away from the destructive fixity of envy,

"envy of the teenager in this teenage age" (2000d, 157). Only thus can antisocial behavior be reclaimed as sign for the times of hope.

> The fact that there is a positive element in antisocial acting out can really help in the consideration of the antisocial element that is actual in some, and potential in nearly all, teenagers. This positive element belongs to the antisocial individual's total personal history; and where the acting out is strongly compulsive, it relates to an environmental letdown in the particular individual's experience. Just as in stealing there is (if one allows for the unconscious) a moment of hope of reaching back over a gap to a legitimate claim on a parent, so in violence there is an attempt to reactivate a firm holding, which in the history of the individual was lost at a stage of childhood dependence. Without such a firm holding a child is unable to discover impulse, and only impulse that is found and assimilated is available for self-control and socialization.
>
> (2000d, 157)

In adolescence looking for a job is as time-consuming and important as going out on dates. But the industry of the teen job search does not yet carry forward from childhood a certain quality of dependability nor impart itself to the social meaning of employment, which would be congruent with reparation in mourning. In "Contemporary Concepts of Adolescent Development" Winnicott writes that it isn't possible yet "for the adolescent to know how much the job, because of its social contribution, lessens the personal sense of guilt (that belongs to unconscious aggressive drives, closely linked with object-relating and with love) and so helps to lessen the fear within, and the degree of suicidal impulse or accident proneness" (1996, 149). Winnicott addressed the problem of psychopathy by intervening in disturbances in development prior to the advent of the capacity for mourning, toward which he, in theory, was ushering his clients. "Mourning itself," Winnicott advises and admits in his 1958 address to social workers, "The Psychology of Separation," "indicates maturity in the . . . ego of the individual" (2000b, 132). The adolescent returns in fundamental ways to the starting block of early childhood. What has changed is the teen's physical ability to act on the wish to kill parents, who in the meantime bear the date mark of expiration. The teen must find room in psychic reality for this death. But first teenagers find themselves, as Winnicott describes it in "Struggling through the Doldrums," "struggling to start again as if they had nothing they could take over from anyone" (2000c, 152). The countdown to mourning commences in childhood and starts up again in adolescence. And yet the split between industry or energy and the developmental processes that support the work of mourning can reopen at any time, for example during midlife. What we call reparation works on re-pairing this divergence, reclaiming it as on a schedule with the development and re-development of object relations.

The antisocial tendencies in children and teens, which can, once consolidated and rationalized for secondary gain, spawn the psychopath, symptomatize deprivations in and of the holding environment prior to the egoic maturity set for mourning, but also at an age old enough to be beyond fateful internalization of this environmental fault line (2000b, 132–33). In Winnicott's estimation there are certain advantages to the industry of the psychopath over the psychotic's playing dead or the neurotic's endless involution of dependency. There is, then, a division of psychic labor whereby the industry that will contribute to reparation and which inhabits a certain proximity to psychopathy precedes the onset of the ability to engage in the work of mourning, which, given time, it in a sense makes possible. The significance of hope thus adds to the re-scratching out of the groove of loss, of being at a loss, a relationship to the future prospect of catching up with the need to be able to mourn.

References

Adorno, Theodor. 2003a. "Prologue to Television." "Prolog zum Fernsehen." In *Gesammelte Schriften*, ed. Rolf Tiedemann, vol. 10/2, 507–17. Frankfurt am Main: Suhrkamp Verlag.

Adorno, Theodor. 2003b "Television as Ideology." "Fernsehen als Ideologie." In *Gesammelte Schriften*, ed. Rolf Tiedemann, vol. 10/2, 518–32. Frankfurt am Main: Suhrkamp Verlag.

Adorno, Theodor. 2003c. "What Is Meant by Working-through the Past?" "Was bedeutet: Aufarbeitung der Vergangenheit?" In *Gesammelte Schriften*, ed. Rolf Tiedemann, vol. 10/2, 555–72. Frankfurt am Main: Suhrkamp Verlag.

Arendt, Hannah. 1970. *On Violence*. Orlando, FL: Harcourt.

Benjamin, Walter. 2002. "The Storyteller. Observations on the Works of Nicolai Leskov," trans. Harry Zohn. In *Selected Writings*, ed. Michael W. Jennings, vol. 3, 143–66. Cambridge, MA: Harvard University Press.

Derrida, Jacques. 2002. *Fichus: Discours de Francfort*. Paris: Éditions Galilée.

Freud, Sigmund. 1955. "Introduction to *Psychoanalysis and the War Neuroses*." In *The Standard Edition of the Complete Psychological Works*, ed. and trans. James Strachey, vol. 17, 207–10. London: Hogarth Press.

Freud, Sigmund. 1957. *Five Lectures on Psychoanalysis. The Standard Edition of the Complete Psychological Works*, ed. and trans. James Strachey, vol. 11. London: Hogarth Press.

Freud, Sigmund. 1958a. "Psychoanalytic Notes on an Autobiographical Account of a Case of Paranoia (Dementia Paranoides)." In *The Standard Edition of the Complete Psychological Works*, ed. and trans. James Strachey, vol. 12, 9–82. London: Hogarth Press.

Freud, Sigmund. 1961a. *Civilization and Its Discontents*. In *The Standard Edition of the Complete Psychological Works*, ed. and trans. James Strachey, vol. 21. London: Hogarth Press.

Kraus, Karl. 1954. *Die Sprache*. Munich: Kösel Verlag.

Winnicott, D.W. 1988. "Establishment of Relationship with External Reality." In *Human Nature*, ed. Christopher Bollas, Madeleine Davis, and Ray Shepherd, 100–15. London: Free Association Books.

Winnicott, D.W. 1989 [1964]. "Deductions Drawn from a Psychotherapeutic Interview with an Adolescent." In *Psychoanalytic Explanations*, ed. C. Winnicott, R. Shepherd, and M. Davis, 325–40. London: Karnac.

Winnicott, D.W. 1989 "The Deprived Child and How He Can Be Compensated for Loss of Family Life." In *The Family and Individual Development*, 132–45. London and New York: Routledge.

Winnicott, D.W. 1990. "Delinquency as a Sign of Hope." In *Home Is Where We Start From*, 90–100. New York and London: W.W. Norton.

Winnicott, D.W. 1992a. "Aggression in Relation to Emotional Development." In *Through Paediatrics to Psycho-Analysis. Collected Papers*, 204–18. New York and London: Brunner-Routledge.

Winnicott, D.W. 1992b. "Transitional Objects and Transitional Phenomena." In *Through Paediatrics to Psycho-Analysis. Collected Papers*, 229–42. New York and London: Brunner-Routledge.

Winnicott, D.W. 1992c. "The Antisocial Tendency." In *Through Paediatrics to Psycho-Analysis. Collected Papers*, 306–15. New York and London: Brunner-Routledge.

Winnicott, D.W. 1996. "Contemporary Concepts of Adolescent Development and Their Implications for Higher Education." In *Playing and Reality*, 138–50. London and New York: Routledge.

Winnicott, D.W. 2000a. "Some Psychological Aspects of Juvenile Delinquency." In *Deprivation and Delinquency*, ed. Clare Winnicott, Ray Shepherd, and Madeleine Davis, 113–19. London and New York: Routledge.

Winnicott, D.W. 2000b. "The Psychology of Separation." In *Deprivation and Delinquency*, ed. Clare Winnicott, Ray Shepherd, and Madeleine Davis, 132–35. London and New York: Routledge.

Winnicott, D.W. 2000c. "Struggling through the Doldrums." In *Deprivation and Delinquency*, ed. Clare Winnicott, Ray Shepherd, and Madeleine Davis, 145–55. London and New York: Routledge.

Winnicott, D.W. 2000d. "Youth Will Not Sleep." In *Deprivation and Delinquency*, ed. Clare Winnicott, Ray Shepherd, and Madeleine Davis, 156–58. London and New York: Routledge.

Chapter 5

The Exception of Psychoanalysis: Adorno and Cavell as Readers of Freud

Daniel Steuer

Psychoanalysis as a threshold science

Psychoanalysis has too often been seen in terms of dichotomous paradigms, as for instance in Peter Gay's question about whether Freud was a "scientific positivist" or was "principally indebted to the cloudy speculations of the romantics or to Jewish mysticism" (1995, xvi). Such dichotomies obscure rather than explain the specificity of psychoanalysis. I shall suggest that Freud's crucial achievement was a new attitude towards the mind-body problem, avoiding both reductionism and psycho-physical parallelism. Instead, the transition between the somatic and the instinctual representatives (in an unknown "substratum" [1933, 98]), the transformational qualities of the drives ("superb in their indefiniteness," and never certain to be seen "clearly" [1933, 124]), and the transitions between the unconscious and consciousness, emerge as threshold spaces.

Freud called the idea of the unconscious psyche "the first Shibboleth of psychoanalysis" (1991, 351). However, the idea itself vacillates between an understanding of consciousness as a "psychic quality" – one amongst others – that may be present or absent (1991, 351), and that of the unconscious as something to be inferred from the incomplete

A Concise Companion to Psychoanalysis, Literature, and Culture, First Edition.
Edited by Laura Marcus and Ankhi Mukherjee.

data of consciousness (1991, 168). The first perspective assigns logical and temporal priority to the unconscious, the second to conscious material. Freud's acknowledgment that all investigation must, of course, set out from "the perceiving surface" of the psychic apparatus, and that all knowledge is "bound up with consciousness" (1991, 357), does not change this fundamental, productive ambiguity at the heart of the Freudian method: the question of priority must remain unresolved so that psychoanalysis can operate within the dimension thus opened up. This hovering over the threshold between two perspectives, then, may be the actual shibboleth.

As a threshold practice, psychoanalysis shares important aspects with the much-discussed state of exception, which is according to Giorgio Agamben "a threshold, or a zone of indifference, where inside and outside do not exclude each other but rather blur with each other" (2005, 23), where the norm (the inside) is suspended, but *not* abolished. Rather, the topological opposition between norm and exception is turned into a topological relation. Carl Schmitt's decisionism constructs this relation by defining the sovereign as the one who decides on (and under) the state of exception, and by hierarchically reading this "sovereign moment" back into the normal case: "The normal case [*das Normale*] proves nothing, the exception proves everything" (Schmitt 2004 [1922], 21).[1] Thus, the exception becomes hegemonic. Agamben modifies this view in two fundamental respects. Firstly, he extends the notion of the state of exception from the legal sphere to that of language: "Just as between language and world, so between the norm and its application there is no internal nexus that allows one to be derived from the other" (Agamben 2005, 40). And secondly, following Benjamin, he does not attempt to establish the missing nexus, hence, in effect, he removes the sovereign.[2]

Discussing grammatical examples and exceptions as analogues of the juridico-political opposition between norm and anomie, Agamben defines the exception as an inclusive exclusion (making the un-grammatical part of grammar), while the grammatical example "*shows* its own signifying and, in this way, suspends its own meaning" (1998, 22), thus functioning "as an *exclusive inclusion*" (1998, 21).[3] The psychoanalytic setting combines both aspects; it includes what is excluded by the norm, i.e. the symptom; and it excludes what takes place in the consulting room by suspending its normal meaning, i.e. the consequences it would have in ordinary life. Thus the psychoanalytic setting can be seen as a space of exception without a sovereign.

On the metapsychological level, the structure of the exception applies equally to censorship: a repressed impulse is included by being excluded from consciousness, it is excluded by being included in the work of counter-cathexis. Symptoms, symptom- and compromise-formation, the mechanisms by, and results in which, the inexpressible finds expression, all belong to this threshold space of exception.

Receiving psychoanalysis: Adorno and Cavell

The space of exception means that psychoanalysis can tell us something about the nature of the political as such. Without a sovereign operating in the psychoanalytic setting, the politics of the interactions that take place within it are not only post-conventional, they are also post-normative. Freud's theoretical framework, intentionally or not, reflects this in its malleability, as do his writings, individually and collectively, as work in progress. The negotiations of psychoanalysis are, in the last instance, interminable. Beyond the desire for fixed foundations, this allows reflection on the conditions that make the emergence of fixed positions and norms possible in the first place.

"In a radical sense," the psychoanalyst Reimut Reiche claims, "psychoanalysis, in the shape of psychoanalytic interpretations, has no business in the other sciences." Psychoanalytic interpretations "must apply themselves to their objects ... in such a way that they transform themselves, through the object, into the object" (2004, 235). This warning not to apply psychoanalysis in an external fashion, but rather to allow one's own thought to be transformed by it, has been heeded by both Adorno and Cavell. In particular, they have made the irreducible openness of psychoanalysis as a threshold practice part of their attitudes towards language and reading. In both, the missing metaphysical nexus between language and world and the absent sovereign – not as something lacking, but as defining the human as a social being – are almost omnipresent, if with different emphases. While Adorno questions the right of using the first person singular, Cavell asks for the conditions for, and effects of, using the first person plural. If Adorno claims that "In many people it is already an impertinence to say 'I'" (2005, 50), following Cavell, we might be tempted to say: "In most places today, it is in most instances impossible to say 'we'." But their focus is equally on the conditions of the (im)possibility of "voice," be it of a text, an individual, or a social entity.

Reading Freud in and through Adorno and Cavell, psychoanalysis becomes an investigation of the *conditions* of the possibility of shared human language, as these conditions form and transform the threshold of what we can express and articulate, for ourselves and for others, about our inner and outer experience, thus forming and re-forming conceptions of our inner and outer nature. If language, in turn, is the condition of the political, then only one side of this threshold – the inner and outer nature as captured by approved speech – can be brought under norms, while neither the other side (the pre-linguistic inner and outer nature), nor the moment of mediation itself (the threshold) can be brought under norms (except through the prejudice of willful sovereign decision). Psychoanalysis, as a threshold practice, establishes the need for a post-normative conception of the political. This will become apparent when we look at some recent arguments in political theory that attempt to account for the openness of the threshold space while, paradoxically, shutting it down. In the fact that Freud, Adorno, and Cavell keep it open lies their interest for literary criticism.

Adorno and Freud: a plea for radical psychoanalysis

> ... each successful expression of the subject, one might say, is a small victory over the play of forces in its own psychology
>
> Adorno, *Minima Moralia*

In his lecture on "The Idea of Natural History," Adorno maintains that understanding the relationship between nature and history would require comprehending "historical being in its most extreme historical determinacy, where it is most historical, as natural being," and, in reverse, comprehending "nature as an historical being where it seems to rest most deeply in itself as nature" (1984 [1932], 117). This double perspective remains operative in his later work, creating a threshold of indeterminacy between nature and history, and – by analogy – between object of thought and concept, and also between body and mind. This is the space in which the non-identical may appear, where the heart of the *res cogitans* beats (Adorno 1997, 6:229),[4] a space Adorno owed to psychoanalysis.

There are both historical and theoretical reasons why Adorno became increasingly critical of the psychoanalytic tradition. But he always remained loyal to what he termed, in his 1946 attack on the revisionists, "radical" psychoanalysis:

> Radical psychoanalysis, by its orientation towards the libido as something pre-social[,] reaches those points, both phylogenetically and ontogenetically, where the social principle of domination coincides with the psychological principle of suppression of the drives.
>
> (Adorno 1997, 8:27)

Adorno agrees with Freud, the incorruptible naturalist and unprejudiced observer, who "at every theoretical step remained aware that it is violence that is internalised by the individual" (1997, 8:24). He disagrees with Freud when the latter affirms an unquestioned reality principle, and turns social conflict into some (inherited) anthropological constant, thus betraying his own sensitivity and insight.

In the 1950s, Adorno saw the "home domain" of psychoanalysis – "the relatively independent, monadological individual as the scene of the unconscious conflict between the instinctual impulse and the ban" (1997, 8:83) – as fast disappearing. Increasingly, an adaptive ego short-circuited heteronomous social demands with an undifferentiated unconscious, and a fetishized economic system could dictate individual behavior, circumventing the mediation between unconscious desire and conscious life. The ban, thus, is the short-circuiting of unconscious reflexes with exterior economic conditions.[5] And this structure, in which the indeterminacy between nature and the social in the individual is eradicated, constitutes the pathological moment.

The individual is situated at the crossroads of a double dialectic between the inner object (the id, ultimately the body) and the ego, and between the ego and the outer object (society, economy). That second dialectic is stalled by fetishism: social and economic activity returns as given natural law and reduces the ego to a rational functioning in the interest of self-preservation. This, in turn, increasingly shuts down the first dialectic. The impoverished unconscious functions on a regressive reflex level only, which allows the short-circuiting with the internalized social system. This is the metapsychological background to the truthful exaggeration that "in many people it is already an impertinence to say 'I'."

To "un-stall" the dialectic within the individual without "un-stalling" the one between the individual and social totality is impossible. This is why successful psychotherapy becomes untrue and carries "the stigma of the damaged, of futile and pathetically exaggerated adaptation"

(1997, 8:57). There is no health to be had in what is ill, no sane life in the insane. Either all heals, or nothing will. These are the psychoanalytic roots of Adorno's "damaged life."[6]

Adorno's reading of Kant's practical philosophy: metacritique as radical psychoanalysis

The first model of *Negative Dialectics*, the "metacritique of practical reason," provides a counter-model to this condition of stalled dialectics by setting out the conditions of the possibility of freedom. It employs three interrelated terms, each of which indicates the influence of the unconscious, and hence the empirical self from which Kant's moral philosophy abstracts: the pre-egoized, archaic impulse; spontaneity; and the supplementary [*Hinzutretende*]. Each of them can be aligned, roughly, with the three dimensions of Freud's metapsychology:

1 The dynamic aspect (the becoming of freedom): the dawning awareness of, and striving for, freedom feeds off the archaic impulse, which is also a required ingredient in any genuinely moral reaction (Adorno 1997, 6:281)
2 The economic aspect (freedom as resulting from the relative strengths of id and ego): the supplementary indicates the repressed part of the play of forces between id and ego in the context of decision formation, the contribution of the unconscious to the becoming practical of reason
3 The topographical aspect (the place of freedom within the status quo): within the historical constellation, "spontaneity" reminds philosophy of what has been excluded; it exceeds the formal, intelligible self, yet expresses its independence from causality, and thus marks the moment of freedom within the conceptual schema of idealism.

Thus, the three terms signify, from three different perspectives, that aspect of the psyche that breaks with the Kantian block, in effect transposing Kant's distinction between the intelligible and the empirical character onto the relationship between the unconscious and consciousness.[7]

Within this framework, Adorno outlines a natural history of reason which, potentially, moves towards a utopian reconciliation of nature and spirit – but, crucially, not a return to a pre-existing state of unity. Utopian reconciliation only marks the possibility of ongoing, un-coerced mediation. The model actually puts far more stress on the emancipatory aspect of the history of subjectivity than the account given in the *Dialectic of Enlightenment*. Freedom emerges, on the biological basis of the unity of the organism, as increasing distance of the self from pure reflexes (1997, 6:217). Psychoanalytic theory registers the resulting dialectic of identity under the name of "repression," which makes the ego *at the same time* the organon of freedom and of compulsion.[8] What breaks through repression is the "impulse, intramental and somatic in one," which "drives beyond the sphere of consciousness, which it nevertheless belongs to" (1997, 6:228). Identity and self-alienation may "accompany each other from the very beginning," making the concept of self-alienation "badly romantic" (1997, 6:216), but their affinity retains the emancipatory potential.

As a component of the will, the impulse becomes the supplementary: "a bolt of lightning between the poles of something long past, which has become almost unrecognizable, and that which one day could be" (Adorno 1997, 6:228). That is, the supplementary, by linking a promise of the past with a possible future,[9] makes the will more than a kind of rational choice agent acting on behalf of self-preservation. Crucially, acknowledgment of this supplementary also requires "full theoretical consciousness" if it is not to fall prey to a "decisionism which cancels out reason in the transition to the action." Only after this warning against "unreflected freedom," does Adorno insist that "praxis also requires something other, something not exhausted in consciousness, something corporeal, mediated into reason and qualitatively divergent from it" (1997, 6:228). Both aspects cross over in Kant's notion of spontaneity, which "is on the one hand an achievement of the consciousness: thinking; on the other hand, unconscious and involuntary, the heartbeat of the *res cogitans* beyond this latter" (1997, 6:229).

For Adorno, the superego is a main obstacle to successful sublimation in the indeterminate zone between id and ego. Thus, psychoanalysis "in its heroic period" engaged in a "ruthless critique" of it as "something truly heteronomous" (1997, 6:269; translation modified), and with the goal, according to Ferenczi, not of replacing one superego with another, but of getting rid of transference altogether. To retain, nevertheless, the notion of a "normal," socially useful superego (as Ferenczi eventually does) means to affirm the reification by which the superego becomes the short-circuiting agent between the unconscious and a fetishized socio-economic system. It is precisely where psychoanalysis passes over in silence the need to reflect the distinction between "normal" and "pathological" superego that it loses its radicality: "The critique of the superego ought to become the critique of the society, which produced it; if it falls silent before this, then it becomes subservient to the prevailing social norm" (1997, 6:270; translation modified). At this point, psychoanalysis becomes aborted enlightenment; a radical psychoanalysis would need to operate beyond such norms.

"No model of freedom is available, except as consciousness intervening in the social total constitution, and through this in the constitution of the individual." Such intervention is possible because consciousness is also "branched-off drive-energy, also impulse" (1997, 6:262). Thus, there is an affinity between identity and the non-identical – frantically denied by Kant – which provides the counter-model to the unresolved opposition between freedom and determinism,[10] while the latter two positions actually "coincide in their innermost core. Both proclaim identity" (1997, 6:261). They are locked in a stalemate similar to the one between Cavell's skeptic and anti-skeptic who do not recognize that they share the (erroneous) assumption that what is at stake in the debate about other minds is knowledge rather than acknowledgment.[11]

The acknowledgment of uncertainty: Cavell's Freud

> As I read Wittgenstein, as well as Freud, what happens [when creatures of a certain species fall into the possession of language and become humans] is that they become victims of expression – readable – their every word and gesture ready to betray their meaning.
>
> Cavell, "Something Out of the Ordinary"

> In assuming the burden of finality in the absence of certainty, an authority stakes the virtue of its community: if its judgments are not accepted as scrupulously fair, in its criteria and in its application of criteria, the community is shown to that extent not to provide a secure human habitation for its members; it fails to take up the slack between the uncertainty of judgment and the finality of decision.
>
> Cavell, *The Claim of Reason*

In Cavell's work, both psychoanalysis and the political are woven into the ordinary which, in his reading of Wittgenstein, is never a given, but continuously lost and regained.[12] This openness of the ordinary is, ultimately, of a piece with the quest for justice: "philosophy participates in two conversations essential to the formation of a reforming polity, namely the argument of the ordinary, which I say must never be won (since in retrieving words from their exile – of fixity, encrustation, capture, illusory or empty purity – no one has a privileged authority), as well as the conversation of justice, which I say must never be lost (specifically by being closed in citing the rules of a current institution" (Cavell 2006b, 290).

The moment of psychoanalysis: Freud and philosophy

Psychoanalysis, Cavell suggests, marks perhaps the last moment "in which the human psyche as such, the idea that there is a life of the mind, hence a death" receives its proof in the only possible form remaining, a negative one, "namely as essentially unknown to itself, say unconscious" (1987, 390). Without the mind's psychoanalytic intuition of itself as unconscious (1987, 391), radical skepticism would finally have succeeded, and, by succeeding, disappear. For, "to lose knowledge of the human possibility of scepticism means to lose knowledge of the human" (1987, 390). If this can be called Cavell's fundamental intuition, then it is at once philosophical, psychoanalytical, and political: the disappearance of skepticism would mark the disappearance of the human and, with it, the political.

For Cavell, Freud's inheritance of Kant renders idealist practice concrete, making psychoanalysis both personal and transcendental. The analyst helps the analysand establish "the conditions which condition that utterly specific life" (1987, 393). Psychoanalysis' main difficulty and limit in this task, as Cavell sees it, is that it shies away from coming to terms with the relationship between reality and fantasy; shies away, that is, from the "intuition that fantasy" – in the absence of a metaphysical nexus between language and world, and in the presence of wishing minds – "shadows anything we can understand reality to be. As Wittgenstein more or less puts an analogous matter: the issue is not to explain how grammar and criteria allow us to relate language to the world but to determine what language relates the world to be" (1987, 393). And this means, as we shall see, "what *our* language relates *our* world to be *for us*"; to determine the extent to which it *is* our shared language and world. The play between revealing and concealing (between the unconscious and the conscious) is thus shifted by Cavell into the play of language, rendering philosophy psychological and confronting psychoanalysis with its philosophical responsibilities.

Reading against (self-)delusion: transference

Towards the end of "The Politics of Interpretation," Cavell suggests a psychoanalytic model of reading in the context of justifying Emerson's, Thoreau's, Austin's, and Wittgenstein's "politics of philosophical interpretation as a withdrawal or rejection of politics, even of society as such" (1984, 49–50). If the "reign of repressive philosophical systematizing ... has depended upon the suppression of the human voice" (1984, 48), then ordinary language philosophy must, in turn, recover this voice "as from an illness." For the reader to come closer to her voice, a text is required which has the "power to overcome the person of its author" (1984, 53), a text which teaches beyond authorial intention.

In Cavell's model, the text takes the position of the analyst – the reader is "in the gaze or hearing of the text" (1984, 52). The "practice" to follow from this is "guided by three principal ideas": (1) access to the text is not through projection but transference; (2) the pleasures of appreciation are succeeded by the risks of seduction; (3) the goal of the encounter is not consummation but freedom, i.e. freedom from the authority of the author, the undoing of transference (1984, 52–53). We are in need of such reading because we are always already seduced; that is, we practice idolatry by confusing what we take to be the authority of text and author with the value of its truth. Our convictions and beliefs are distorted by an attachment to the former, rather than the latter. A redemptive text makes its reader a better reader, one who has learned to read better by herself. To hazard a formulation: redemptive reading is the exit of the reader from the always already incurred dependence on authorial instruction. We free ourselves of the alleged voice of the author, and thus get nearer to our own voices: an individuation exercise which could also be described as learning to let go, to sever oneself from old attachments. Reading, like philosophy, ultimately, is learning to leave. And learning to leave requires being able to distinguish between fantasy (old attachments) and reality (truth), and to let go of the former.[13]

It is a redemptive text's central silence, "the stillness of the text," that defeats skepticism, "as if the withholding of assertion, the containing of the voice, amounts to the foregoing of domination" (1984, 51). Such silence, if not manipulative, will therefore be politically (psychologically) liberating; it suspends judgment and offers the possibility for the reader to break interpretive habits. This model of reading includes the possibility of being one's own reader.

The linguistic social contract: who is talking for/to whom?

Cavell's vision of the founding of a political community (a "we") by declaring separation from others and from nature (2006b, 273), and his vision of the continuous renegotiation of the "linguistic" social contract thereafter, both contain a moment of exception. And neither community nor individuality is possible if renegotiation is replaced with fixed norms. Rousseau's discovery of a new mode of knowledge – "the self as access to the self's society" – and hence of "a new mode of ignorance," or what Marx and Freud see as unconsciousness "of our social present" and "of our private pasts" respectively (Cavell 1999 [1979], 26), opens a space in which to find out how far our "philosophical appeal to what we say" (1999 [1979], 20), and the criteria underlying what we say, are shared, and to what extent the claim to community, implicit in our linguistic utterances, is justified. To speak for oneself politically thus always "means risking the rebuff" (1999 [1979], 27) – theirs of you, yours of them, yours of yourself. In Emersonian terms: you may be as surprised as others by your sudden aversion to conformity; you have committed to language what you didn't know yourself.

The outcome of such aversive moments remains uncertain, and the moments themselves unavoidable: "we wander through the world as strangers to it and to ourselves," our ordinary lives "filled with illusion, trance, confusion, caprice, self-defeat, and intellectual and spiritual violence. ... In such a state of estrangement it must seem a miracle that we can speak for ourselves, let alone speak for others. But so long as this is mysterious, how can we trust any solution to the debate between, for example, libertarians and communitarians, who take sides on the prior and darker question of whom we speak for, and with what right?" (Cavell 2006b, 265). Indeed, if we speak for ourselves or others, we usually do not do so in full realization of the complexity of ourselves and others that a psychoanalytic perspective would reveal. We speak for political or legal beings, maybe for our social masks or for the fantasies we have of ourselves and of others, by, for example, hallucinating our equality as "free fellow-citizens" (Cavell 1999 [1979], 26). One way of understanding Cavell's work as a continuous political and psychoanalytic intervention is to say that he probes the consequences of speaking for ourselves and others without our words actually being "ours" in the full sense, and by trying, thus, to make them more ours by not ignoring the "prior and darker question." Within the dialectic between speaking (including presenting a reading) and the existence of a self, the possibilities of having an autonomous voice, as a condition of the political, are played out.

Discussions of the "right to speak (for)" take for granted what would first need to be established, as if an analyst were to ask the unanalyzed patient what he wanted to do with his life. Politically, we may put this by saying "the genuine social contract is not in effect." We are "exercising our will not to the general but to the particular, to the partial, to the unequal, to private benefit, to privacy. We obey the logic of conspiracy, though we believe this to be true only of *others*. (You could call this Rousseau's self-diagnosis)" (Cavell 1999 [1979], 26). The conspiracy consists in using the private voice *as if* it were the public – to the point of actually believing that it is. The diagnostician, therefore, is not exempt from the diagnosed condition: she is doctor and patient, social critic and conspirator; and Adorno and Cavell are, thus, no less than others implicated in social pathology, in society's hallucinations of justice and community in the face of actual injustice and particularity.

Thus, the crisis of the political, the "tired political debate," might be seen as a version of the skeptical stalemate: the "opposite sides are unable to free themselves of each other because they share a common unarticulated supposition ... the supposition that speaking for oneself and speaking for others are philosophically transparent and separate matters" (Cavell 2006b, 267). Thus, they do not see that they are not yet in a position to speak of a "we," and without such common ground the arguments talk past each other. Whether the stalemate of such arguments can be broken or not depends on whether ordinary lives of inexpressiveness, the chronic suppression of (one's own) voice, can be overcome – a question that must remain open (2006b, 266). The skeptical moments in Cavell are thus at least threefold: to the "classical" doubts about the external world and other minds we must add the doubt about whether our language is still capable of revealing the world, revealing us to each other and ourselves to ourselves. If not, what remains would be dumbness (possibly well-spoken dumbness), infancy (speechless primordial fear), and voicelessness (the absence of the social).

The faculty of judgment and zones of indeterminacy

Cavell repeatedly refers to Freud's explanation of the intellectual function of negation as derived from the process of repression and, ultimately, the primitive organic oral drives of incorporation and rejection. If we accept this lineage, then "the oral, primitive basis of judgment amounts to the judgment of the world, its affirmation or negation in each utterance or outcry." Cavell's generalization is made possible by aligning the oral drives with Wittgenstein's notion of "criteria," and its "twin" (as he calls it), the ordinary concept of a criterion. The latter is used for evaluation, for counting something as "good" or "bad"; the former are "bases for relating the world in words, or as Kant puts the matter, 'applying concepts in judgments'" (Cavell 1994, 148), i.e. for counting something *as* a certain something. If the primary impulses and linguistic criteria are linked in this way, then all human judgment retains the fundamental features Freud ascribes to it:[14]

1 Negation is derived from repression, and the outcome of the process of repression is, ultimately, unpredictable. "Repression" is an ongoing shifting of forces (the "hidden play" of a "delicate balancing" [Freud 1991, 150]). Hence, the function of judgment retains the moment of unpredictability. The same indeterminacy applies to the therapeutic process. Would Dora have stayed in therapy if he had (play-)acted (with) more affection towards her? Freud's answer is that he simply does not know. Some of the factors active in resistance will "remain unknown in any case," and there are necessary limits to taking psychological influence: "Towards which side the decision will incline to fall in the conflict between the motives, towards the removal or the reinforcement of repression, that can never be *calculated*" (Freud 1977, 175; emphasis added).

2 In its intellectual version, the "judgmental instinct" allows the subject to gain freedom from repression and the automatism of the pleasure principle. The opening of "Negation" introduces the "No"-sign as a "certificate of origin"; the end attaches a liberating power to the "creation of the symbol of negation" (Freud 1991, 441) and its use. In the therapeutic setting, "recognition of the unconscious" is expressed in the negative (1991, 442). Thus, negation allows acknowledgment of the unacknowledged.

To the extent that Cavell's work can be read as a micrological investigation into human judgments (the calls and claims, both personal and social, which constitute our lives), and to the extent that such judgment depends on the function of negation as spelled out by Freud, Cavell's philosophy is a form of Freudianism which acknowledges a moment of indeterminacy. And the same holds for Adorno's negative dialectics to the extent that it can be read as a systematic uncovering of the falsehood of positive claims, of the repression intrinsic to all judgment. If Adorno "negates" the idealist concept of "freedom" as absolute spontaneity (the freedom of Buridan's ass, so to speak), then he uncovers the negation (repression) intrinsic to the "positive" definition, i.e. that it ignores that freedom is always a "freedom from" or a "freedom with regard to."

Post-foundationalism, philosophical romanticism, and post-normative politics

The phenomenon of threshold zones of indeterminacy (states of exception without a sovereign) also appears in recent political philosophy in the form of the theoretical distinction between politics and the political, i.e. as "political difference," and in what has been called a philosophical romanticism of the "new." In both cases, however, it is turned from a moment in the process of investigation into a spectral entity. According to Oliver Marchart, post-foundational political theory accepts the impossibility of providing an explicit foundation for the political (or, for that matter, the social). Instead, the difference, *as* difference, between politics and the political is said to constitute an unbridgeable abyss and to turn contingency and undecidability into quasi-transcendental conditions, expressed in various terms, such as "event, antagonism, truth, the real, or freedom" (Marchart 2007, 8). Thus, political post-foundationalism takes on the burden of an ultra-ontology, in so far as it assumes a "political ground of all things social," and describes every ontological and "*also* every political position" as "politically overdetermined. One can only take such a position by, precisely, *taking position* – and this is what we do" (2007, 168).[15] Everything here depends on what it means to be able to "take a position," and on what its conditions are. And, at this point, any answer which implies a foundational or normative dimension will lead to a form of decisionism or dogmatism. Such consequences can only be avoided at the cost of paradox: the political "is a *ground* that can never be reached and still has the status of a foundation, a *cause* that does not determine anything and still produces effects of its absence, and a transcendental *condition* whose emergence is historically conditioned and still assumes supra-historical validity" (2007, 176).

A similar impasse is reached in Nikolas Kompridis' attempt at defining "philosophical romanticism" as a mode of thought that "engages in a normative critique of culture that is continuous with a normative critique of philosophy" (2006a, 4). The "complex and ambiguous normativity of the new" is such that it "cannot be converted into rule-governed or law-like form." Kant's notion of spontaneity, Kompridis suggests, recognized such normativity, but he shied away from "the idea of freedom as a self-determining new beginning" (2006b, 48). Kompridis reads Adorno's arguments against the capitalist new as an argument for the *real* new as "a normative challenge and normative resource" (2006b, 46). However, a critique of normativity as such cannot itself be normative, nor can a norm critique itself. Thus, the argument confuses the new as a challenge to existing norms with the new as a normative resource for such challenges and how they might be met.

Marchart's and Kompridis' arguments follow an intellectual temptation, maybe typical of our times, to turn an absence into a presence, a void into something substantial. Political difference *as* difference, and the new *as* new, take on a pragmatic, normative, and political burden they cannot carry. Both arguments are therefore in danger of losing sight of "agency" (subjectivity), including political agency, as situated between a historical development which is carried forward by supra-individual institutional dynamics and a residual individual psychology which is potentially outside that dynamic. It is this point of a subject's agency, I want to suggest, which Freud, Adorno, and Cavell want to strengthen – and this is only possible by retaining the articulation between nature, history, and the individual.

Fighting aphasia

In his own contribution to Kompridis' volume, Cavell calls it the peculiar task of philosophy today "to prepare us, one by one, for the business of justice" and to confront "the modern obstacle, to that business: I mean a sense of the exhaustion of human possibility, following the exhaustion of divine possibility." This secular task must confront "a general human withdrawal of interest in the world":

> Secret melancholy, Emerson says. Naming a historical phenomenon, this names not an isolated matter of an individual sense of pointlessness in saying anything, but a more general sense of lacking or failing, the language in which to express what has to be said, as if calling philosophical as well as political attention to a shared aphasia.
>
> (2006a, 27)

Might we, Cavell speculates, following Lacan, cast "all psychoanalytic experience of discrepance as of forms of what might be grasped as (a transfiguration of) aphasia"? This, he says, "reconstitutes, or re-enacts, Freud's early ('pre-psychoanalytic') interest in the phenomenon of aphasia; one might call it the phenomenon of disexpressiveness" (2006a, 27).[16] Possibility and the new, the non-identical and the moments restoring to the world its color (see Adorno 1997, 6:66, 370), are the result of the removal of such "disexpressiveness" caused by time's being out of joint, things and voices not attuned to each other and themselves. What is required for this is to follow what Cavell calls Heidegger's and Wittgenstein's invitation "to take steps, but without a path. And that is itself to acknowledge a future, the fact of futurity. Shall we say that this opens the future to the human will? It opens the will, like a hand" (2006a, 30). There is no, nor could there be any, recipe for such transformation of fist into hand, no fixed method that would guarantee the path from knowledge to acknowledgment – from silence to expression, from muteness to voice – all of which the psychoanalytic procedure aims to make possible.

The family resemblance between Adorno's and Cavell's appropriation of Freud results from their avoidance of ways in which indeterminacy can be neutralized: by decisionism (substituting power for reasoning), by reification (hypostatizing the liminal moment of indeterminacy into some central tenet, even if only in a "negative" form as abyss, necessary contingency, or ontological undecidability), and by inversion (treating the logic of the exceptional case as extending over the whole field of normal cases). Freud, Adorno, and Cavell avoid these dangers through engaging in the articulation and re-articulation of indeterminacy in the confrontation of their material with their theoretical and personal convictions and assumptions. Freud confronts case histories and other anthropological material with metapsychological constructions; in Adorno, philosophical reflection is endlessly answerable to cultural artifacts, be they philosophy, music, or literature; and in Cavell the reporting on the process of readings is itself the message. All three recognize and acknowledge indeterminacy, while simultaneously demonstrating that there are limits to meaningful convictions, interpretations, reactions, and practices because the world offers resistance to them. Thus, Freud's psychoanalytic writing provides the original exception to the modern proliferation of false endlessness and change (and the tedium and boredom that go with it), on the one hand, and forms of dogmatic closure (and the terror that goes with it) on the other. In the middle ground between these two possibilities lies a specifically psychoanalytic sensitivity which cannot be subsumed under the Enlightenment or Romantic traditions, however defined. In this sensitivity lies its ongoing significance for literary criticism, as well as other studies of the human by humans. The teaching of literature must be done with open hands, and with the aim of opening hands, learning better, along the way, to say "I" and "we."

Notes

1 All translations from German texts are mine.

2 More precisely, he claims that Schmitt's sovereign was invented against Benjamin's "affirmation of a wholly anomic human action": "The sovereign violence in *Political Theology* responds to the pure violence of Benjamin's essay [*The Critique of Violence*] with the figure of a power that neither makes nor preserves law, but suspends it. Similarly, it is in response to Benjamin's idea of an ultimate undecidability of all legal problems that Schmitt affirms sovereignty as the place of the extreme decision" (Agamben 2005, 54).

3 In Judges 12:6, Agamben writes, exception and example become indistinguishable in the word "shibboleth"; the word is "an exemplary exception or an example that functions as an exception" (Agamben 1998, 23). The story of the Ephraimites who try to flee across the Jordan, and are identified by the men of Gilead because they pronounce the first syllable of "shibboleth" differently, does indeed express the (bio-)political as well as linguistic threshold of belonging by not belonging.

4 I have used Dennis Redmond's online translation of *Negative Dialectics* (Adorno 2001b); page references are to the German edition (Adorno 1997).

5 Freud's theorizing, Adorno thought, mimicked this process. Freud draws conclusions straight from the psychological to historical reality (e.g. patricide): "The short-circuiting of the unconscious with reality gives psychoanalysis its apocryphal traits" (1997, 8:61). Theory reproduces the objective social process.

6 Nevertheless, Geuss' claim (2004, 164) that for Adorno no life can be a success does not follow: the trajectory of a life, exactly because of its meandering deviations from its premises (and promises), can "represent an unregimented [i.e. successful] one." Life may fulfill its vocation indirectly, just as thought, "for the sake of its relation to its object," must break the promise "presupposed by the very form of judgment" (Adorno 2005, 81). Adorno's famous dictum that there is no right life in the false, in its context, is directed against anachronistic attempts at having a bourgeois "home," "property," and "privacy." It is such attempts that are doomed to fail (2005, 38–40).

7 On the Kantian block see Adorno (2001a), especially lectures 2 and 16.

8 See Adorno (1997, 6:222). This makes it difficult to understand Whitebook's claim that Adorno saw the integrated self *only* under the aspect of domination, coercion, etc., and that "no alternative is put in its place" (2004, 60). Reconciliation between ego and impulse actually is successful, non-coercive sublimation. Adorno's vision of a "dynamic metapsychology" aims precisely at an ego that stands in a receptive, nuanced, integrative, and reciprocal relation to instinctual impulses.

9 The closeness to the structure of the Freudian wish should be obvious.

10 Such affinity is "the peak of the dialectic of enlightenment" (Adorno 1997, 6:266f.).

11 See Cavell's "Knowing and Acknowledging" (2002, 238–66) for a full exposition of the argument.

12 For the more or less continuous presence of Freud in Cavell's life and work, see the autobiographical *Little Did I Know* (Cavell 2010).

13 The repetitiveness of *Walden*, Cavell says, is required by "the repetition of each fact of one's attachment to an object gone, an effort to undo or release the ties of association strand by strand" which is also "part of the work of realization of loss that Freud and principally after him Melanie Klein recognize as the work of mourning. They call it reality-testing, a subjection to the verdict of reality that one's attachment to an object is to undergo severing" (1984, 54). This reading of reality testing protects it against Adorno's charge of being affirmative.

14 Cavell's reading of Wittgenstein's "twin notion" of criteria corresponds to Freud's description of the function of judgment: "The function of judgment is concerned in the main with two sorts of decision. It affirms or disaffirms the possession by a thing of a particular attribute [evaluative judgment]; and it asserts or disputes that a presentation has an existence in reality [judgment of existence]" (Freud 1991, 439).

15 The "reifying" moment in this formulation becomes apparent if we remind ourselves that the consensual and social aspect enters the "taking of a position" by virtue of the fact that no one can take a position altogether privately, and that it would be meaningless to do so. This taking of positions as something we simply do is, in fact, what Marx called a "Robinsonade."

16 Adorno conceived the very distinction between the unconscious and the conscious as resulting from an "aphasic" development in which those parts of the psyche which do not keep up with progress are deposited in the former: "The asynchronicity between the unconscious and consciousness is itself a stigma of the contradictory social development. Whatever in the subject cannot keep up, and must foot the bill for progress and enlightenment, is sedimented in the unconscious. The residue turns into the 'atemporal'" (1997, 8:61).

References

Adorno, Theodor. 1984 [1932]. "The Idea of Natural History." *Telos*, 60: 111–24.

Adorno, Theodor. 1997. *Gesammelte Schriften*. 20 vols., ed. Rolf Tiedemann. Frankfurt am Main: Suhrkamp.

Adorno, Theodor. 2001a. *Kant's Critique of Pure Reason*, ed. Rolf Tiedemann. Cambridge: Polity.

Adorno, Theodor. 2001b. *Negative Dialectics*, trans. Dennis Redmond. http://www.efn.org/~dredmond/ndtrans.html. Accessed November 26, 2013.

Adorno, Theodor. 2005. *Minima Moralia*. London: Verso.

Agamben, Giorgio. 1998. *Homo Sacer: Sovereign Power and Bare Life*. Stanford: Stanford University Press.

Agamben, Giorgio. 2005. *State of Exception*. Chicago: University of Chicago Press.

Cavell, Stanley. 1984. *Themes Out of School*. San Francisco: North Point Press.

Cavell, Stanley. 1987. "Freud and Philosophy: A Fragment." *Critical Inquiry*, 13, no. 2: 386–93.

Cavell, Stanley. 1994. *A Pitch of Philosophy*. Cambridge, MA: Harvard University Press.

Cavell, Stanley, 1997. "Something Out of the Ordinary." *Proceedings and Addresses of the American Philosophical Association*, 71, no. 2: 23–37.

Cavell, Stanley. 1999 [1979]. *The Claim of Reason*. New York: Oxford University Press.

Cavell, Stanley. 2002. *Must We Mean What We Say?* Cambridge: Cambridge University Press.

Cavell, Stanley. 2005. *Philosophy the Day after Tomorrow*. Cambridge, MA: Belknap Press.

Cavell, Stanley. 2006a. "The Future of Possibility." In *Philosophical Romanticism*, ed. Nikolas Kompridis, 21–31. London: Routledge.

Cavell, Stanley. 2006b. "The Incessance and the Absence of the Political." In *The Claim to Community*, ed. Andrew Norris, 263–317. Stanford: Stanford University Press.

Cavell, Stanley. 2010. *Little Did I Know: Excerpts from Memory*. Stanford: Stanford University Press.

Freud, Sigmund. 1933. *New Introductory Lectures on Psycho-Analysis*. London: Hogarth Press.

Freud, Sigmund. 1977. *Case Histories I*, ed. Angela Richards. Harmondsworth: Pelican Books.

Freud, Sigmund. 1991. *On Metapsychology: The Theory of Psychoanalysis*, ed. Angela Richards. London: Penguin.

Gay, Peter. 1995. *Freud: A Life for Our Time*. London: Macmillan.

Geuss, Raymond. 2004. "Adorno's Gaps." *Arion*, 12, no. 2: 161–80.

Kompridis, Nikolas. 2006a. "Introduction: Re-inheriting Romanticism." In *Philosophical Romanticism*, ed. Nikolas Kompridis, 1–17. London: Routledge.

Kompridis, Nikolas. 2006b. "The Idea of a New Beginning: A Romantic Source of Normativity and Freedom." In *Philosophical Romanticism*, ed. Nikolas Kompridis, 32–59. London: Routledge.

Marchart, Oliver. 2007. *Post-Foundational Political Thought: Political Difference in Nancy, Lefort, Badiou and Laclau*. Edinburgh: Edinburgh University Press.

Reiche, Reimut. 2004. "Adorno und die Psychoanalyse." In *Die Lebendigkeit der kritischen Gesellschaftstheorie* [The Vitality of Critical Social Theory], ed. Andreas Gruschka and Ulrich Oevermann, 235–54. Wetzlar: Büchse der Pandora.

Schmitt, Carl. 2004 [1922]. *Politische Theologie* [Political Theology]. Berlin: Duncker & Humblot.

Whitebook, Joel. 2004. "Weighty Objects: On Adorno's Kant-Freud Interpretation." In *The Cambridge Companion to Adorno*, ed. Tom Huhn, 51–78. Cambridge: Cambridge University Press.

Chapter 6

Freud's Textual Couch, or the Ambassador's Magic Carpet

Jean-Michel Rabaté

> Give me a lover bold and free,
> Not Eunucht with formality;
> Like an Embassador that beds a Queen
> With the nice caution of a sword between.
>
> John Cleveland,
> "The Antiplatonick," 1653

Should one apply psychoanalysis to literature? Can one do this without having it unravel? Conversely, should one apply literature to psychoanalysis? This question, less flippant or fresh than it sounds, may be a "French" question, since it echoes the title of Pierre Bayard's (2004) witty book, *Can One Apply Literature to Psychoanalysis?* Bayard's inversion of the classical paradigm by which one applies psychoanalysis to literature is not that paradoxical. Such a reversal was anticipated by Lacan, Derrida, Cixous, and Kristeva, by all those who have wanted to remain Freudian without following Freud's reductive hermeneutics when it came to literature. But if the inverted phrase appears to refute Freud's belief that psychoanalysis can be applied to everything, including art and the humanities, the insight follows a recurrent Freudian idea, which is that psychoanalysts should learn from writers and artists

A Concise Companion to Psychoanalysis, Literature, and Culture, First Edition.
Edited by Laura Marcus and Ankhi Mukherjee.

when exploring the unconscious. Bayard's inversion is less polemical than it seems. Freud recommended a similar strategy when he listed literature as one of the foundational disciplines that a psychoanalyst should master in the training. He explains this in *The Question of Lay Analysis*, refusing medical training as a prerequisite for psychoanalysts but insisting on the pedagogical function of the humanities. Freud writes: "the analytical curriculum would include subjects which are far removed from medicine and which a doctor would never require in his practice: the history of civilization, mythology, the psychology of religion, and literature. Unless he is well oriented in these fields, the analyst will be unable to bring understanding to bear upon much of his material" (1950, 118). Freud is not simply alluding to a subjective appropriation of poems, novels, and plays. He uses the term *Literaturwissenschaft* (Freud 1982, 337) a word that conflates literary expertise and a science of literature, a science of the text including literary criticism. Mastering this science of literature will be an essential asset in the training of any analyst.

If the word "literature" defines an area of competence, it is also because Freud, whose main official distinction was the Goethe Prize in 1936, was a literary scholar. He peppered his essays with quotes from Goethe, Shakespeare, and Heine, and his well-stocked library (I'll have more to say about the localization of the library) held more books about literature, mythology, and religion than about psychiatric or psychoanalytic issues. A "science of literature," no doubt, includes a theory of interpretation, a whole hermeneutics moving from the literary field to sexuality, contributing an inexhaustible lore of examples, characters, situations, and jokes. These models help refine individual diagnoses, dig more deeply into the complex dramas of neurotic patients' lives, and find in the chronicles of gods, heroes, and kings paradigms of our transgenerational dramas. In Freud's view, literature is not limited to a passing acquaintance with important writers, but entails a serious immersion in the humanities. There is a specific knowledge, with its attendant pedagogy, that can be mastered by a training blending the medical and the humanistic. Literature offers a privileged mode of entrance to "culture," a term which combines personal engagement with formalized modes of fiction (*Bildung*). They offer a compendium of values and define a civilization (*Kultur*). No psychoanalyst can ignore the benefits derived from its acquisition: psychoanalysis is a province of the humanities.

Is this what Bayard had in mind with his provocative title? To be sure, his chiasmic reversal aims at questioning critical methods elaborated in the name of psychoanalysis, so as to limit or prevent its "applications" to literature. This critique of the assumptions of standard psychoanalytic criticism comes from someone who is both a psychoanalyst and a professor of literature. He must be in a good position to give voice to a general dissatisfaction with psychoanalytic literary criticism. The current consensus is that psychoanalytic criticism is obsolete. No American graduate program will accept a candidate with a plan to study Hamlet's inhibitions or examine Dostoevsky's castration complex. Already in the 1950s, Nabokov vociferously attacked Freud. He was then in a minority when he railed against "the Viennese quack" and derided Freud's sexual obsession. Indeed, the Freudianized critical literature of the 1950s is painful to read: every steeple is a penis, every vale a vulva. Nabokov's strictures are now universally shared. What is more, the term "application" sounds like an echo of Bergson's definition of laughter caused by the "application" of the mechanical to the human. The very idea of an "applied" discourse triggers a wan smile, which broadens to a grin when one thinks that this discourse is "plaqué," that is, mechanically welded onto literary singularity.

Looking at books like Sarah Kofman's (1970) survey of Freud's writings on art or Jean Bellemin-Noël's (1979) concept of a textual unconscious, Bayard acknowledges that Freud's theory grants a certain pre-eminence to artists and writers, all credited with having discovered Freudian ideas before he did. Yet what is given with one hand is taken with the other: those creators had no awareness of the process, any knowledge of the laws of creation is denied to them. Writers and artists don't know what they are doing when they are creating. Only psychoanalytic interpretation can make sense of their brilliant but opaque intuitions. Whether these interpretations rely on psychobiography as practiced by Marie Bonaparte or avoid it like Bellemin-Noël, who launched the concept of a "textual unconscious" not reducible to that of the author, Bayard remains skeptical. He does not spare Lacan, who alternated "critical texts in which the author is taken into account" and "texts in which the readings are not founded in any privileged manner on the life of the author, as with *Hamlet*" (Bayard 2004, 37). True, Lacan criticized biographical readings of Poe or Shakespeare, but he remained a structuralist at heart, which led him to deny agency to the writers' subjectivity. Moreover, Lacan disconcertingly returned to psychobiography at the end of his long career when dealing with Joyce (see Rabaté 2001).

If most psychoanalytic schools, whether psychobiographical, structuralist, or textualist, share a belief in the superiority of psychoanalytic discourse over literature, such a belief generates mere variations on the genre of psychobiographical reconstructions. They rely on a hermeneutics of suspicion deemed powerful enough to disentangle the hidden meanings lurking in the works, to be then presented as an extension of the author's psyche. Since these meanings are by definition unconscious, the author can know nothing of the dark forces that operated to make the work happen. The danger is that these readings yield results that conform to the initial theory. They remain teleological interpretations that function more or less like religious readings: what is found in literary texts is less a product of the investigation than of its origins and its presuppositions. Psychoanalytical readings are thus not different from biblical interpretations since, like religious readings, they assume that any text will confirm the Freudian doctrine. They reiterate psychoanalytic theses about the Oedipus complex, archaic fantasies, the primal scene, the role of childhood memories, and so on. This does not mean that the results are false or the methods wrong, but more damagingly, that they are entirely predictable. It is such a predictability that leads to boredom and to theoretical sterility.

Bayard's contention is simple: in order to avoid this entropy, psychoanalysis should start learning from literature – really. For this, one should examine how literary texts reflect psychic phenomena. Applied literature would focus on moments of emergence, describe how a new knowledge is passed on to readers. Admittedly, this strategy is unlikely to convince psychoanalysts, who will feel contested by it, or critics coming from schools that have no patience with psychoanalysis. As if to confirm these misgivings, the examples provided are barely satisfactory. In the plays and novels given as examples, one recognizes the canon explored by Bayard in previous books. Laclos, Proust, Maupassant, Agatha Christie, and Shakespeare are the mainstays of his demonstration, which is to show that literature thinks. Literature thinks by itself, thus staging complex psychological problems. Here is the rub: one does not need psychoanalysis to convince teachers and readers that literature is capable of "thought," able to deal with important psychological issues.[1] A chapter recapitulates predecessors and successors of Freud, all those who didn't read him but "knew" him nevertheless. This section, entitled "How Does Literature Think?," fizzles out when it merely re-states Susan Sontag's *Against Interpretation*. What do we gain, if we are just told that anger was convincingly depicted in Homer's *Iliad*, even if it was written before psychoanalysis was invented? We accept the idea that the invention of psychology has been parallel to the development of literature, just as it seems obvious that Ibsen, Maupassant, Strindberg, and Nietzsche were Freud's predecessors. This confirms that the zeitgeist is at work, which is hardly news. Bayard avoids engaging with a scientific conversation that would start from the neurosciences and cognitive mapping, and would see their insights anticipated by Homer or Proust.

From an Anglo-American position, it would seem more urgent to historicize these parallel efforts and discourses. This might lead us to insist on the links between *Madame Bovary* and the invention of hysteria by medical discourse, which culminated with Charcot's theories. Indeed, literature became a field of predilection for psychoanalysis at the time that it was being invented. Freud, Rank, Ferenczi, Jung, Bion all meant to test their hypotheses by applying them to culture, and above all to literature. When this discourse was systematized, it lost its power of invention. If one agrees that there has been an exhaustion of unconscious hermeneutics after Freud and that the solution should come from literature, is it sufficient to argue that we need to deduce theoretical schemes from literary models? This remains programmatic: Bayard gestures in the direction of a new conception of subjectivity found in literary texts, which might avoid the closure of applied psychoanalysis. Given its riches, its diversity, and its subversive potentialities, literature would signal the disappearance of psychoanalysis as an interpretive paradigm (Bayard 2004, 164). The main chance of success of "applied literature" would be to limit the grandiosity implied by the wish to elaborate a system capable of replacing previous hermeneutics. There is no universal method of interpretation available, hence a psychoanalyst reading literature will never say "we" but speak in the first person. Is this subjectivist conclusion inevitable? Have we not abandoned Freud's notion of a *Literaturwissenschaft,* and thrown out the baby of culture with the dirty water of tainted hermeneutics?

Bayard's program seems to miss the key issue of what constitutes a text's textuality, its writing as such. His spin on the debate about psychoanalysis and literature paints him into a subjectivist corner; the psychoanalyst turned literary critic becomes a hedonistic reader who enjoys the peace of a vast, walled-in library. Yet I would contend that if books have something to teach, it will be more than a subtle psychology of human emotions. Once we have begun splicing literature and psychoanalysis, we cannot remain in contemplative peace, meditating on how to use famous novels to make sense of affects. Promoting a new restlessness linking literary theory and practice, I will want to revisit Freud's program, beginning by admitting that if his interpretive practice cannot be reduced to applied psychoanalysis, it is because it gives us more productive metaphors. Starting from the materiality of Freud's clinic, I will find in the "ambassador" an image of the unconscious as it returns to us mediated by texts. Hopefully, this should answer my initial question: how to put literature on the couch without having it unravel?

The issue lies perhaps not in *what* but in *how* we learn from literature. I will argue that literature teaches us something by having us play the role of an "ambassador." From which court? In order to answer this last question, I will have to connect three images: Freud's study and his couch, a famous historical painting, and a celebrated novel by Henry James. This link is based upon a visual superposition: as soon as one looks at Freud's couch and at Holbein's *The Ambassadors* side by side, the resemblance is striking. The carpet on Freud's couch is almost identical with the carpet painted on a shelf covered with scientific instruments in *The Ambassadors*. Freud may have seen Holbein's painting in the National Gallery when he visited London as a young man. Henry James saw it when he drafted his novel. In the same way, many of the allegorical objects visible between the two French ambassadors look strangely like the curios displayed in Freud's study, now accessible to the public in what is the London Freud Museum. If this visual link, perhaps due to objective chance, teaches us something, it will say something about the practice of psychoanalysis itself. A consideration of Freud's things, the objects of his material world, will lead us to examine several versions of *The Ambassadors*, from Holbein to Henry James.

Freud's decision to combine a lush Persian carpet on a couch facing a desk that held rows of antique statues obeyed hidden rules, evoking either a private game to be played daily or a pedagogical interaction with his analysands. Let us meditate on the setting chosen by Freud: on his writing desk there were always two or three rows of antique statues that he had collected patiently; these were also found above and around the couch. The couch was decorated with this rich, thick, oriental wool carpet. Immediately, two types of metaphor come to mind. On the one hand, the statues evoke the archeological metaphor systematically used by Freud to characterize the discovery of the unconscious. His carefully chosen antiques embody antiquity, they point to the existence of an ancient and partly forgotten past, whose symbols can be understood thanks to some intellectual exploration. Freud told his patient the Wolf Man: "The psychoanalyst, like the archeologist in his excavations, must uncover layer after layer of the patient's psyche, before coming to the deepest, most valuable treasures" (Wolf Man 1971, 139, quoted in Gay 1989, 16; see also Kuspit 1989). In this case, indeed, it is the psychoanalyst who does all the work; the patient will be "excavated" so as to bring back to light the treasures that were hidden through the layers of a given psyche.

Yet a different notion is conveyed by the rug's oriental wool, the Qashqai Shekalu carpet. The exotic rug signals a more feminine process since it reminds us of the fact that in the Freud household, the women were adept at needlework, crocheting, knitting, and weaving. Throughout her life, Anna Freud used to make her clothes by hand. Her huge wooden loom remains in the Freud Museum today. Anna Freud, like her father no doubt, thought that weaving was both useful and therapeutic. Her father commented on her "passion" in those terms: "If the day comes when there is no more psychoanalysis, you can be a seamstress in Tel Aviv" (Behling 2005, 116). Liliane Weissberg (2010) has studied the images of weaving and unweaving in Freud's works, arguing that they had something to do with the textile professions in which so many family members distinguished themselves. This was especially the case for his half-brother Emanuel Freud and his brother Philip, who founded a cloth-making factory in Manchester. Freud's anglophile leanings (his preference for Shakespeare over Goethe is obvious) have something to do with the success story of that branch of his family. When, in 1875, the 19-year-old Sigmund visited Manchester as a student, he was impressed by the possibility of such a career. He went back to Manchester in 1908 to visit Emanuel and Philip, and it was during this second trip that he visited the National Portrait Gallery. Did he also go London's National Gallery? This is most likely, although undocumented.

What is important at this juncture is to note that the image of weaving suggests something different from that of excavating. In the weaving of a metaphorical piece of cloth on the couch, it is as if the patient was doing most of the work; the psychoanalyst more often than not unweaves by being silent or dropping timely comments. This brings us closer to the constructivist view of interpretation put forward in Freud's later essays, such as "Constructions in Psychoanalysis" from 1937. There, Freud begins by quoting in English the motto, "Heads I win, tails you lose," only to dismiss the accusation that psychoanalytic interpretations can never be refuted. Even when people agree with one interpretation, a psychoanalyst will not accept this as a positive confirmation, but if a patient says: "I had never thought of that," something is revealed. Freud's imagined collaboration with an analysand puts him in the place of a Penelope who, inverting the Homeric paradigm, unweaves during the day what has been woven at night.

Let us pause at the threshold or at the loom, so as to stress links between the collection of antiques, clearly meant to embody a mythical audience, and the gaudy carpet on the couch. Freud would rearrange the rows of figures every day, recreating another gaze bearing on the analysand and on him. In a letter of July 17, 1899, he described to Fliess a statuette of Janus he had just bought in those terms: "The ancient gods still exist, because I obtained a few recently, among them a stone Janus who looks at me with his two faces in a very superior manner" (Freud 1985, 361).[2] The divine, human, and animal representations that he arranged thus were to incarnate an Other audience. Through their juxtapositions, he would sketch new constellations. The whole apparatus combines three features: the embodiment of a vertical past, the present agency of a collaborative work of weaving, and a gaze coming from elsewhere to see people and things in a different light. Freud's office implied a triangulation between culture (all his books), the statues, and the rug on the couch. If archeology betrayed Freud's belief in a truth found in psychic depths, the process of weaving suggests a continuous weaving linking patient and analyst. This weaving calls up the etymology of *text*, deriving, as Roland Barthes would repeat endlessly, from Latin *textum, texere*, hence, to weave.

The orientalism of the Qashqai Shekalu wool rug might be situated in the context of a fascination with the Orient that was dominant in Europe before World War I. The craving for the oriental in all shapes, whether it came via Venice, St Petersburg, or Tokyo, enhanced the pleasure of the imagination. Thus Proust could transform a Breton port like Balbec into a Persian temple via the magic of its name. Similarly Walter Benjamin points out that the invention of psychoanalysis was inseparable from a material arrangement of rooms, plush sofas, thick curtains, and deep armchairs, in short from a whole bourgeois "philosophy of furniture" elaborated at the end of the nineteenth century:

> It is one of the tacit suppositions of psychoanalysis that the clear-cut antithesis of sleeping and waking has no value for determining the empirical form of consciousness of the human being, but instead yields before an unending variety of concrete states of consciousness conditioned by every conceivable level of wakefulness within all possible centers. The situation of consciousness as patterned and checkered by sleep and waking need only be transferred from the individual to the collective. Of course, much that is external to the former is internal to the latter: architecture, fashion – yes, even the weather – are, in the

> interior of the collective, what the sensoria of organs, the feeling of sickness in health, are inside the individual. And so long as they preserve this unconscious, amorphous dream configuration, they are as much natural processes as digestion, breathing and the like. They stand in the cycle of the eternally selfsame, until the collective seizes upon them in politics and history emerges.
>
> (Benjamin 1999, 389–90)

In this context, Freud's careful arrangement of his couch and of his favorite treasures would play the role of dream-machines, or more precisely, of dream-catching machines. By insisting on the private nature of his own assemblages, Freud brought to the fore his process of selection: "To live in these interiors was to have woven a dense fabric about oneself, to have secluded oneself within a spider's web, in whose toils world events hang loosely suspended like so many insect bodies sucked dry" (Benjamin 1999, 216). Yet Freud let some air in by producing something like a private arcade, a "passage Viennois," one might say. This, according to Benjamin, would be a space in which the inside and the outside always communicate: "Arcades are houses or passages having no outside – like the dream" (1999, 406).

As with the densest and most significant dream of *The Interpretation of Dreams*, the dream of Irma's injection, the stuffy Viennese interior presents a riddle that brings along its own "solution." The riddle and the solution derive from a visual clue, the superposition, nay, the quasi-identity, of Holbein's oriental carpet on the shelf between the French ambassadors and the famous Qashqai Shekalu wool carpet with which Freud covered his couch. Holbein's *Ambassadors* depicts two French courtiers, Jean de Dinteville and Georges de Selves, who met briefly in London in the spring of 1533. At the time, Holbein was already the main court painter in England, when he painted the double portrait. Jean de Dinteville, soon to fall from favor with the French king, brought the painting back home, and hung it in the castle of Polisy, where it remained for several centuries. De Dinteville was portrayed several times: he is the Moses of the wonderfully enigmatic *Moses and Aaron before Pharaoh: Allegory of the Dinteville Family* in the New York Metropolitan Museum of Art (see Foister, Roy, and Wyld 1998, 24).

This celebrated double portrait is familiar to readers of Lacan, who used it to illustrate his theory of the gaze in Seminar XI. I will briefly allude to his commentary. In Seminar XI, Lacan takes as his point of departure an analysis of the strange anamorphic skull that dominates the foreground of the painting. His remarks are inspired by Jurgis Baltrusaitis' book *Anamorphoses*. Lacan states:

> The two figures are frozen, stiffened in their showy adornments. Between them is a series of objects that represent in the painting of the period the symbols of *vanitas*. At the same period, Cornelius Agrippa wrote his *De vanitate scientiarum*, aimed as much at the arts as the sciences, and these objects are all symbolic of the sciences and art as they were grouped at the time in the *trivium* and *quadrivium*. What, then, before this display of the domain of appearance in all its most fascinating forms, is this object, which from some angles appears to be flying through the air, at others to be titled? You cannot know – for you turn away, thus escaping the fascination of the picture.
>
> Begin by walking out of the room in which no doubt it has long held your attention. It is then that, turning round as you leave – as the author of the *Anamorphoses* describes it – you apprehend in this form ... What? A skull.
>
> (Lacan 1981, 88)

Lacan even compares the anamorphic skull with Salvador Dalí's soft watches, before moving from the skull to death and negativity. Holbein would have made visible an emblem of both erection and castration, hence made the phallus appear in such a way that it speaks directly to our gaze. Our gaze is pinned and imprisoned, caught in this "pulsatile, dazzling and spread out function." Lacan generalizes this function to all pictures and concludes: "This picture is simply what any picture is, a trap for the gaze. In any picture, it is precisely in seeking the gaze in each of its points that you will see it disappear" (1981, 89). To reach these insights, Lacan's relay has been Merleau-Ponty's *The Visible and the Invisible*, a book in which the exploration of the visible opens up to an investigation of the "prose of the world." Merleau-Ponty's phenomenology of the eye and the gaze leads Lacan to posit the existence of a materialization of the Gaze of the Other in some detail of the painting – here, a disquieting skull distorted by anamorphic projection. The gaze of the Other comes from the Unconscious via the suggestion of the power of death and castration embodied in the skull. Thus one can say that Holbein's painting projects also a material allegory of the psychoanalytic situation.

Lacan doesn't gloss all the details of the painting. There is one that often escapes the eye of art critics: it is the little brooch that Jean de Dinteville has pinned to his black hat. We may need a magnifying glass to see that the figure it carries is a little skull in gold. Not only is it a smaller skull that is almost invisible, but the slanting orientation of the beret on which it is pinned is rigorously parallel to the plane of the anamorphic skull. Those two "details," both skulls, one in precious metal, the other in bone, but partly hallucinated, suggest that Death traverses the painting on an oblique diagonal. Meanwhile, the two noblemen stare fixedly in front of them as if their eyes were searching for ours. We would be deluded if we tried to outstare them. Let's pay attention to what they do not see. Like any textual critic, we have to focus on apparently insignificant details. Why does the anamorphized skull project its shadow to the left, whereas the objects referring to the sciences, and allegorizing *Vanitas* on the shelves, project their shadows to the right? Holbein implies that the skull's origin is otherworldly: the symbol of death is bathed in the light of a different sun.

Is this other sun Dürer's celebrated "black sun" of melancholy, another variation on the *vanitas* theme? Jean de Dinteville was melancholy, ill at ease, and homesick during his stay in London in 1533: thoughts of death were never far from him. He complained in May 1533: "I am the most melancholy, weary and wearisome ambassador that ever was seen." And again in a letter of June 4: "I am, and have been, very weary and wearisome" (quoted in Hervey 1900, 16). Besides, the time was rife for huge changes – this was the summer when the English king married an already pregnant Ann Boleyn. Henry VIII was divorcing Catherine of Aragon, thus precipitating a schism with the Catholic Church. Peace reigned for once between France and England, but the situation was fraught with tensions. The two French gentlemen were made to witness this shift, and were conscious that disunity was looming. Hence the lute with a broken string, and the curious presence of a Lutheran hymn-book.

In Holbein's painting, the rug is a setting for the most precise mathematical instruments of the day, a celestial globe, a shepherd's dial, two quadrants, a small dial, a polyhedral sundial, and a *torquetum*. The lower wooden shelf, with the lute, a book of mathematics, another globe, and the hymnal, remains bare. Above, the oriental rug frames a dialogue between the left hand of Jean de Dinteville, which curves downward openly, and the right hand of Georges de Selve, who clutches his gloves and holds his coat. The triangulation of the two men's gazes and the gaze of the Other calls up the set-up chosen by Freud for the psychoanalytic session: Freud seated in his deep armchair gazes in front of him, while the analysand, lying on the couch, talks or is silent. All those frames and props are necessary if one wants to materialize the locus of the Other, in other words, prepare one for an unlocking of unconscious knowledge.

A similar triangulation takes place in Henry James's novel. To understand it, we do not have to put Henry James on Freud's couch: true to Freud's own dictum, James had understood the process by himself. The fact that he decided to make a novel of this shows that a painting is already a text, at least in so far as it can generate innumerable texts. James had seen Holbein's double portrait in London while he was thinking of his novel (Poole 2008, xxxi). This took place when Freud had just published his *Interpretation of Dreams* and when Mary F.S. Hervey (1900) had proved definitively that the two characters depicted by Holbein were French ambassadors. We need another novelist, J.M. Coetzee, to verify that James' novel is indeed a sketch of the Freudian unconscious. Coetzee analyzes the text itself, letting its semantic structure speak, in order to show how *The Ambassadors* is a text that works with the Unconscious. He discusses the relationship between form and meaning in passive constructions. Briefly considering the plot of *The Ambassadors*, Coetzee adds this:

> In Henry James's *The Ambassadors*, Lambert Strether, out for a day in the country, spies the guilty lovers Chad Newsome and Madame de Vionnet boating down the river. "It was suddenly as if these figures, or something like them, had been wanted in the picture, had been more or less wanted all day, and had now drifted into sight ..." The passive *wanted*, stressed by repetition, has a double signification: (1) The lovers in the boat reveal that the rural scene, considered as a picture, has in fact been aesthetically incomplete until this moment. (2) The appearance of the lovers solves a mystery, adds the last piece (the piece that was wanting) to a puzzle which Strether, up to this minute, has not wanted to admit he wants solved, since life is so much easier if lies are believed. In the complex play that James performs here, the absence marked by the agentless form is the absence of a drive to find out the truth; and that drive has been suppressed by a hitherto stronger agency, the desire in Strether for the easy, the beautiful, the romantic. What is marked at this instant of the narrative is therefore a moment of self-realization at which ... the moral agent supplants the aesthetic in Strether. And all without Strether's yet being aware of it: the drama takes place in the vacant arena where the agent phrase might have been – as good a syntactic representation of the unconscious one is likely to find.
>
> (Coetzee 1992, 174–75)

Space restrictions prevent me from engaging in a detailed discussion of this famous novel, but one will readily concede that, being contemporary with Freud's exploration of the Unconscious, *The Ambassadors* attempts something similar through fiction. Strether, our "hero," is this clumsy "ambassador" sent by a mother who is also his fiancée to try and bring Chad, the wayward son, back to the fold. He betrays his mission by falling in love twice, without fully realizing it, first with the seductive and playful Miss Gostrey, then with Chad's lover, the beautiful Madame de Vionnet. The fact that Strether is unaware of his own feelings creates an exquisite game of hide-and-seek with the reader, who generally guesses the truth before the hero faces it close to the end, as we have seen.

This game entails the unconscious, which is stressed by the recurrence of the adjective "unconscious" repeated six times in the novel. The truth of Chad's and Madame de Vionnet's sexual relationship is something that has been obvious for some time but that Strether could not face, preferring to lie to himself by believing the couple's deliberate equivocations. An indication of this process of revelation is provided early in the novel by an exchange between Strether and Miss Gostrey. They discuss the consequences that Strether's trip to Paris cannot fail to have on Chad's attitude:

> "You see more in it," he presently returned, "than I."
> "Of course I see *you* in it."
> "Well then you see more in 'me'!"
> "Than you in yourself? Very likely. That's always one's right."
> (James 2008, 69)

This dialogue explains what this novel, like all novels and all paintings, is doing. It presents a knowledge about ourselves that we had without knowing it. This is why knowledge will be the only thing that Strether will gain in the end. The outcome of his melancholy trip is that he loses both the prospect of getting rich by marrying Mrs. Newsome and the prospect of love by staying in Paris with Maria Gostrey, when she has all but offered marriage. Strether decides to return to Woollett, Massachusetts, to a drab bourgeois life devoid of any illusion – he will return to die, in fact. Just as we never learn the name of the famous object mass-produced in Woollett (is it a tooth-pick, as some critics think?), we will never fathom the rationale for his return home. One lesson is that the loss of everything is not too great a price to pay if one can attain knowledge. This disappointing knowledge goes beyond the "truth" about sexuality and love; it has to comprehend life and death. Strether will return to face death, having rejected all hedonistic seductions. The vision of a good life in Paris remains a fantasy, a reminder of a past irrevocably lost. We are just told that he will go back to "a great difference" (2008, 469), which, with a wink in the direction of Derrida, we can interpret as having to do with writing. The "sword between" of my epigraph will turn into the writer's pen. No epithalamium is expected, just the unfolding of text as process.

This melancholic truth brought about by the novel is an issue that Freud faced at the end of his life, having settled in London. His stoicism in the face of death allows us to answer one question I have left dangling: from which court do the ambassadors come? Apparently, Freud gave an answer in a letter written in December 1938 to thank the novelist Rachel Berdach who had sent him *The Emperor, the Sages and Death*, a novel in which death figures prominently. The setting of her novel (1962), calls up the historical situation of Holbein's *Ambassadors*. Freud wrote:

> Your mysterious and beautiful book has pleased me to an extent that makes me unsure of my judgment. I wonder whether it is the transformation of Jewish suffering or surprise that so much psychoanalytical insight should have existed at the court of the brilliant and despotic Staufer which makes me say that I haven't read anything so substantial and poetically accomplished for a long time. ... Who are you? Where did you acquire all the knowledge expressed in your book? Judging by the priority you grant to death, one is led to conclude that you are very young.
>
> (Freud 1992, 1192)

Berdach's novel is situated in the thirteenth century, at a time when the Holy Roman Emperor Frederick II (Friedrich II von Hohenstaufen) and Rabbi Jacob Charif Ben Aron are intimate friends despite everything that separates them. The novel begins and ends with the rabbi's death. His ethical concerns and religious piety clash with the scientific optimism of Frederick, who had tried to bring together all the scientists of the world, Arabs, Greeks, Jews, and Christians, allowing them to exchange their views on medicine, astronomy, and astrology. Three centuries later, all those sciences would be piled up on two shelves by the French ambassadors in London. In Berdach's novel, given the "heretic" complicity between the ruler and the rabbi at the end, the latter's death is represented as a peaceful surrender to the Angel of Death, Azrael. The angel, who takes him on his wings while the whole world appears to him as deprived of any life, might also be figured twice by Holbein's anamorphic skull and Jean de Dinteville's hat brooch with a gold skull.

Freud imagined Rachel Berdach to be a young person because she tended to see death everywhere. His wrong guess baffled Max Schur

(1972, 516). In fact, Berdach was middle-aged at the time she wrote the book, although she had drafted it when she was younger, after the loss of a dear friend. Freud's thesis is exposed in *Beyond the Pleasure Principle*. When we are young, we think that death is a sad but common fate, an *anangke* against which there is nothing to be done. A young person tends to see death as the ultimate truth of life so as to find comfort in advance, to anticipate future losses. An older person has less to lose and everything to gain by betting on knowledge, which, for Freud, meant "science." Like Strether, they will be less afraid of dying, less tempted to take death as a final answer. And perhaps they will appreciate more readily the intimate connection between death and writing. Freud, who owned a beautiful Egyptian statue of Thoth, the god of writing, knew this: the process of textualization that constitutes the unconscious is tributary to the death drive, a drive that acquires more and more importance in his metapsychology.

This insight is shared, it seems, by James Joyce when he has Stephen Dedalus meditate on Thoth during a pause in his speech about Shakespeare. Stephen muses on literary ghosts, on the power of dead writers once their thoughts have been "coffined" in books:

> Coffined thoughts around me, in mummycases, embalmed in spice of words. Thoth, god of libraries, a birdgod, moonycrowned. And I heard the words of that Egyptian highpriest. *In painted chambers loaded with tilebooks.*
>
> They are still. Once quick in the brains of men. Still: but an itch of death is in them, to tell me in my ear a maudlin tale, urge me to wreak their will.
>
> (Joyce 1993, 159)

Significantly, Stephen is quoting Moses here. One should read carefully this entire episode of *Ulysses*: it shows why a psychoanalytic reading of literature needs the fallacy of biographical criticism (even if, as with Shakespeare, we are not sure whether the man we are discussing is the famous writer of the plays and sonnets) in order to go beyond it, before reaching a point when any great writer will appear to be "all in all in all of us" (Joyce 1993, 175).

Thus, the knowledge provided by literature is not a knowledge about facts, nor about feelings, nor is it about the correlation between fact and theory, or between affects and ideation, as Bayard claims. It will not bring a truth about anger or guilt, as when we rail against parents on the couch; it does not consist in an accurate evocation of passions. It is a knowledge from beyond, a knowledge about the limits of life and death, no doubt an obscure knowledge. As such it structures the *form* that the acquisition of any knowledge will take. Like literature, this knowledge is founded on the agency of death and writing, a writing that can model for us the working of our own psychic apparatus. Such knowledge mobilizes the countless dead speakers, myriad dead words that we revive when reading a text. Here is a paradoxical knowledge because it is a knowledge that does not know, or at least does not know all. It does not "apply" to anything nor can it be "applied." It does not apply but it "deploys" and unfolds. By unfolding its images continuously, it transgresses its limits as soon as they appear. If we work psychoanalytically with literature, exploring those darker spaces, we will learn to work with unknowing, that is, we learn to trust our unconscious. Even if we plunge deeper into an abyssal "other" scene, we are told by a voice coming from elsewhere that we will return. And if, having thus returned, we keep on acquiring knowledge and turn the process into a method, then we can call ourselves the ambassadors of the unconscious.

Notes

1 Among many brilliant treatments of this topic, I will select Gourgouris (2003) and Wood (2005).

2 It is in this letter that Freud quotes the epigraph of the *Traumdeutung*: "Flectere si nequeo superos, Acheronta movebo." ("If I cannot deflect the will of Heaven, then I will move Hell.")

References

Bayard, Pierre. 2004. *Peut-on appliquer la littérature à la psychanalyse?* Paris: Minuit.

Behling, Katja. 2005. *Martha Freud: A Biography*, trans. R.D.V. Glasgow. Cambridge: Polity.

Bellemin-Noël, Jean. 1979. *Vers l'inconscient du texte*. Paris: Presses Universitaires de France.

Benjamin, Walter. 1999. *The Arcades Project*, trans. Howard Eiland and Kevin McLaughlin. Cambridge, MA: Harvard University Press.

Berdach, Rachel. 1962. *The Emperor, the Sages and Death*, trans. William Wolf. New York: Thomas Yoseloff.

Coetzee, J.M. 1992. *Doubling the Point: Essays and Interviews*, ed. David Attwell. Cambridge, MA: Harvard University Press.

Foister, Susan, Ashok Roy, and Martin Wyld. 1998. *Making and Meaning: Holbein's Ambassadors*. London: National Gallery Publications.

Freud, Sigmund. 1950. *The Question of Lay Analysis*, trans. Nancy Procter-Gregg. New York: Norton.

Freud, Sigmund. 1982. *Die Frage der Laienanalyse (VII), Studienausgabe, Schriften zur Behandlungstechnik*. Frankfurt: Fischer.

Freud, Sigmund. 1985. *The Complete Letters of Sigmund Freud to Wilhelm Fliess*, ed. Jeffery Moussaieff Masson. Cambridge, MA: Harvard University Press.

Freud, Sigmund. 1992. *The Letters of Sigmund Freud*, selected and ed. Ernst L. Freud. London: Dover.

Gay, Peter. 1989. "Introduction." In *Sigmund Freud and Art: His Personal Collection of Antiquities*, ed. Lynn Gamwell and Richard Wells, 15–19. Binghamton: State University of New York Press; London: Freud Museum.

Gourgouris, Stathis. 2003. *Does Literature Think?* Stanford: Stanford University Press.

Hervey, Mary. 1900. *Holbein's Ambassadors: The Picture and the Men*. London: George Bell & Sons.

James, Henry. 2008. *The Ambassadors*. London: Penguin.

Joyce, James. 1993. *Ulysses*, ed. Hans Walter Gabler. New York: Vintage.

Kofman, Sarah. 1970. *L'Enfance de l'art: Une interprétation de l'esthétique freudienne*. Paris: Payot.

Kuspit, Donald. 1989. "A Mighty Metaphor: The Analogy of Archaeology and Psychoanalysis." In *Sigmund Freud and Art: His Personal Collection of Antiquities*, ed. Lynn Gamwell and Richard Wells, 133–51. Binghamton: State University of New York Press; London: Freud Museum.

Lacan, Jacques. 1981 *The Four Fundamental Concepts of Psychoanalysis*, trans. Alan Sheridan. New York: Norton.

Poole, Adrian. 2008. Introduction to *The Ambassadors*, by Henry James. London: Penguin.

Rabaté, Jean-Michel. 2001. *Jacques Lacan: Psychoanalysis and the Subject of Literature*. Houndmills: Palgrave.

Schur, Max. 1972. *Freud: Living and Dying*. London: Hogarth.

Weissberg, Liliane. 2010. "Ariadne's Thread," *MLN*, vol. 125/3, April, pp. 661–81.

Wolf Man. 1971. *The Wolf-Man by the Wolf-Man*, ed. Muriel Gardiner. London: Hogarth Press.

Wood, Michael. 2005. *Literature and the Taste of Knowledge*. Cambridge: Cambridge University Press.

Part II

Literatures

Chapter 7

Freud's Double

Nicholas Royle

"Freud's Double": the meaning of this phrase is at least double. It evokes, first of all perhaps, the concept or theory of "the double" in the writings of Sigmund Freud (1856–1939). The following pages will accordingly attempt to provide an account of the double as it emerges from Freud's work. Particular attention will be paid to his essay on "The Uncanny" (1953–74, 17:219–56), first published in German ("Das Unheimliche") in 1919. I hope to show how Freud's writing on the double illuminates the question of literature, the relations between literature and psychoanalysis, and the strange interweavings of fiction and real life. The title-phrase can also be understood to refer to "the double of Freud," that is to say, the idea of Freud himself having a double. In addition, then, this essay will be concerned with the, in some ways perhaps rather weird or implausible, hypothesis that Freud had or has a double, a doppelgänger or alter ego. Leaning a little more in that direction, it may be noted that the two-word title-phrase can also be read in English as a complete sentence: Freud's double, I tell you, *Freud is (at least) double.*

By way of reassurance, permit me to stress at the outset that I am not proposing some maverick or mystical interpretation of Freud. Rather, this essay seeks to provide a critical sense of why he remains one of the most fascinating, sharp-sighted, and enlightening thinkers of the past

A Concise Companion to Psychoanalysis, Literature, and Culture, First Edition.
Edited by Laura Marcus and Ankhi Mukherjee.

two hundred years. As I hope may become clear, Freud's thinking on "the double" continues to have profound significance not only for the study of literature, film, and art, but also for more general philosophical, ethical, and political questions about who we think we are and how we construe the world.

The double is uncanny. It is weird, eerie, spooky, strangely disorienting to think about. It is uncanny because it involves a strangeness contaminated with sameness, difference as repetition. It is one thing *and* something else. The double is a matter of life and death. On the one hand, it seems to illustrate or promise immortality: you can be repeated, replicated, duplicated. The life of an individual is no longer precariously confined to a single body. On the other hand, it is the very disordering of identity. The individual is no longer individual. There is a dividing of the one, division within the self. Seeing your double you are obliged to suppose that your own identity is dissolving or has already come to an end. The double thus comes to figure as, in Freud's phrase, "the uncanny harbinger of death" (1953–74, 17:235).

Making particular reference to Otto Rank's work *The Double: A Psychoanalytic Study* (1989), first published in 1914 (as *Der Doppelgänger*), Freud comments that the double has to do with "reflections in mirrors, with shadows, with guardian spirits, with the belief in the soul and with the fear of death." The idea of the double was "originally an insurance against the destruction of the ego." It springs, Freud argues, "from the soil of unbounded self-love, from the primary narcissism which dominates the mind of the child and of primitive man." Even if we do not persist in thinking on this topic like children (which is always, for better or for worse, a possibility) or like the ancient Egyptians (Freud's in some ways unconvincing example of "primitive man"), the idea of the double comes back in "the later stages of the ego's development" in the form of that "special agency" that we call *conscience* (1953–74, 17:235). But these observations, Freud goes on to suggest, do not help us understand "the extraordinarily strong feeling of something uncanny" (1953–74, 17:236) around the idea of the double. He concludes:

> When all is said and done, the quality of uncanniness can only come from the fact of the "double" being a creation dating back to a very early mental stage, long since surmounted – a stage, incidentally, at which it wore a more friendly aspect. The "double" has become a thing of terror, just as, after the collapse of their religion, the gods turned into demons.
> (Freud 1953–74, 17:236)

Freud's reflections on this topic have a richness that extends far beyond their value and pertinence in relation to specific cases of "the double in literature." Nonetheless that theme – the double in literature – provides a powerful source and resource for these reflections. Freud begins his reflections with literature, and more specifically with E.T.A. Hoffmann's *The Devil's Elixir* (1815). Other celebrated literary examples would include James Hogg's *The Confessions of a Justified Sinner* (1824), Edgar Allan Poe's "William Wilson" (1839), Fyodor Dostoevsky's *The Double* (1846), Robert Louis Stevenson's *Strange Case of Dr Jekyll and Mr Hyde* (1886), and Joseph Conrad's "The Secret Sharer" (1910). But what analysis of the double in literature does is to open up a Pandora's box or, in Hamlet's phrase, "to hold, as 'twere, the mirror up to nature" (Shakespeare 1998, 248), generating effects that transform our thinking about everything in the world, and more besides (religion and posthumous life, genetic engineering, parallel universes, and so on). Nothing perhaps brings out the strangely treacherous, at once beautiful and appalling, relation between literature and real life better than the double. In one direction the double leads us, hand in hand, to the great questions of the universe, death, and existence beyond this world – for isn't religion, of whatever kind, essentially predicated on a theory of the double, on the supposition of being able to repeat oneself, duplicate one's being in another dimension, in another world, in a higher sphere or otherwise? And in another direction it leads into the mirror-world of language itself, to "double meaning," ambiguity, and the constitutively double nature of puns, homonymy, and irony. And finally, in a duplicitous fashion, it keeps us coming back to the very strangeness of being in the world – of seeing oneself in a mirror (is that really "me"?), of narcissism and otherness, of self-consciousness and self-identity, and so on.

In order to begin to grasp the subtlety and complexity of Freud's reflections on the uncanniness of the double, then, let us turn to consider more closely the essay in which they appear. Here is the opening paragraph of "The Uncanny," in Strachey's translation:

> It is only rarely that a psychoanalyst feels impelled to investigate the subject of aesthetics, even when aesthetics is understood to mean not merely the theory of beauty but the theory of the qualities of feeling. He works in other strata of mental life and has little to do with the subdued impulses which, inhibited in their aims and dependent on a host of concurrent factors, usually furnish the material for the study of aesthetics.

> But it does occasionally happen that he has to interest himself in some particular province of that subject; and this province usually proves to be a rather remote one, and one which has been neglected in the specialist literature of aesthetics.
>
> (Freud 1953–74, 17:219)

This paragraph seems quite straightforward: Freud is setting us up for an account of the uncanny (as the title of his essay has promised), and he commences by pointing out that this is not a subject that a psychoanalyst usually tackles. A psychoanalyst works in other areas of the mind: he deals with sick people, not with aesthetics. But then sometimes it does prove necessary to deal with some aspect of this discipline and it turns out to be one that the specialists in that field have generally ignored.

The preceding three sentences offer a paraphrase of the opening sentences of Freud's essay. As such they may serve to illustrate Bill Readings' observation that paraphrase is "a philosophical joke" (Readings 1991, xxi) and thus also to suggest how easy it is to make a mess of Freud. To paraphrase is to alter, to use different words and thereby transform the original into something else, no longer itself. It is to change the context, meaning, voice, and tone. To read Freud well, or at least to read him with a minimal degree of critical care, is to realize, first of all, that his work resists paraphrase. It is to see, also, that his writing is a kind of event, a work of strange energies that are not necessarily, and in some respects not at all, within his control or restricted to "what Freud meant." In this way we can start to see the crucial importance of what Sarah Kofman, in her essay "The Double Reading," calls the differences between "what Freud openly says and what he in fact does" (Kofman 2007, 45).

We could devote many pages to commenting on this opening paragraph of Freud's essay. We could spend a great deal of time exploring what he says, as well as what he does *not* say, on the subject of "the uncanny" (a phrase that, notably, does not appear in the paragraph itself). Suffice for the moment to offer just a few observations:

1 The paragraph involves playing with time, with a sense of what is frequent or habitual and what is not. This is especially notable in the phrase "only rarely" in the first sentence and "occasionally" in the third. For Freud's unnamed subject ("the uncanny") a kind of rarity value is implied, a sense of needing to put special time aside for it.

2 Freud's paragraph deploys intriguing spatial and topographical metaphors: the uncanny has to do with "other strata of mental life"; it is a "province," and indeed "a rather remote one." Freud's topic thus implicitly acquires a kind of mysterious, even alluring quality, like a far-off kingdom in a fairytale or a distant realm in the past. The literary thus already beckons.

3 Despite the non-literal language (the metaphor of the remote and neglected province, for example), the tone of the paragraph seems quite matter-of-fact, detached, and scientific. The combination of figurative and matter-of-fact language might seem to gesture towards a lurking and indeed profound question, viz: what *is* the most appropriate language for describing "qualities of feeling" or the real nature of "mental life"? One of Freud's most complex legacies, for our understanding of everyday life as well as of literature, has to do with his upsetting of the literal and metaphorical. You might suppose that his writings would seek to emphasize the true and actual existence, for example of the "sexual instincts," the "ego-instincts," or the "death instincts"; but in fact he is quite explicit about their poetic or "mythological" nature. As he puts it in "Anxiety and Instinctual Life": "The theory of the instincts is so to say our mythology. Instincts are mythical entities, magnificent in their indefiniteness" (Freud 1953–74, 22:95).

4 Freud's paragraph exploits an enigmatic vocabulary of compulsion: the author "feels impelled to investigate"; "he has to interest himself in some particular province." Exploring the subject of the uncanny is not optional: it is strangely necessary. Freud cannot prevent himself. While we might think of Freud as a bit of a know-all, or as someone who seems to think of himself as a bit of a know-all, here he seems to be testifying to a striking ambiguity about agency and volition. This ambiguity is underscored, near the end of the essay, when he rather bizarrely observes: "We have drifted into this field of research half involuntarily" (1953–74, 17:251). Does Freud choose to write on the uncanny or does the uncanny somehow choose him?

5 Finally, a small but nonetheless crucial stylistic or grammatical feature of Freud's opening paragraph: he does not write about himself in the first person but in the third (the writer is "a psychoanalyst," "he"). Freud is not himself, or rather: *he makes himself double*. It is a conventional mode of proceeding, especially in scientific discourse, to write in the third person, but what this particular writer is saying, in these three opening sentences, generates uncertainty about just

> what the conventional might be: the topic ("the uncanny"), as evoked here, is evidently as foreign to the psychoanalyst as it is to the scholar of aesthetics. The consequent enigma about what kind of topic we are being drawn into is compounded by the oddity of the fact that, in this opening paragraph, Freud is clearly talking about himself but he does so *as if he were another*.

Already, then, in the apparently rather anodyne opening paragraph of "The Uncanny," we have an intimation of what will transpire to have been perhaps the most insidious and intractable aspect of the topic that is under investigation: the uncanny is bound up with the notion of the double. The theory of the uncanny and the theory of the double have a strange way of turning into one another. The uncanny is double. Only a page later, in fact, we see this doubling of Freud made even more explicit and dramatic, when he declares apropos people's varying "sensitivity" to uncanny feelings: "The writer of the present contribution, indeed, must himself plead guilty to a special obtuseness in the matter, where extreme delicacy of perception would be more in place. It is long since he has experienced or heard of anything which has given him an uncanny impression, and he must start by translating himself into that state of feeling, by awakening in himself the possibility of experiencing it" (1953–74, 17:220). Despite feeling "compelled" to explore this topic, then, the writer (still writing as if he were his own double) apparently has no recent experience of what it is he is supposed to be discussing.

Of course, we are discussing Freud here in English, on the basis of the so-called English "Standard Edition": an entire book or indeed library could be written about "Freud in English" – about how "Freud in English" is, and is not, a sort of double for "Freud in German", and about how different English translations – Strachey's, for example, or David McLintock's in the so-called "New Penguin Freud" (Freud 2003) – produce a different "Freud." When reading Freud in English it is necessary to be mindful of a sense of the untranslatable – of how, for example, "unheimlich" is not "uncanny," "doppelgänger" is not "double," voice and tone are not the same across different languages, and so on. Translation entails what Jacques Derrida calls a "double bind." His use of this term derives in part from Gregory Bateson (1956) but it is in no small measure inspired also by Freud, and especially by "The Uncanny," an essay that is, for Derrida, interminably caught up in "the play of the double" (Derrida 1981, 268). (In fact, like so many other things, the notion of double bind can be related back to Shakespeare: the guilty

Claudius, in *Hamlet*, cannot focus his mind sufficiently to be able to pray but is "like a man to double business bound" [Shakespeare 1998, 272].) As Derrida puts it: "what remains *untranslatable* is at bottom the only thing to translate, the only thing *translatable*" (Derrida 1992, 257–58). And this is not just a matter of translation between languages, between German and English or French, etc. As we have noted, Freud draws on the figure of translation to describe the very project of writing "The Uncanny": the writer must *translate himself* into "the possibility of experiencing [the uncanny]." As if it were indeed *impossible*, nevertheless "he must start by translating himself into that state of feeling." Evidently continuing with this half-veiled motif of double talk concerning "the uncanny and translation," Freud remarks just a page further on: "we ourselves speak a language that is foreign" (1953–74, 17:221). This statement has a kind of stand-alone, haunting character. It poses as a troubling formula or aphorism. We think we are speaking in our own language but it is not really ours. Our words are borrowed. Language does not belong to us or indeed to anyone, even if we sometimes like to think it does.

Freud's writing may seem clear, orderly and to the point, but there is always more going on than meets the eye or ear. In a discussion of detective fiction, Roger Caillois once remarked that "the story opens on a rigged set" (Caillois 1983, 4). When you start reading a detective story, you know – or a part of you knows, even if you choose to ignore the fact – that in some sense the story is already over: someone ("the narrator" or "the author") already knows what happens, already knows whodunit. The opening of the detective story is necessarily deceptive. It constitutes a sort of *trompe l'oeil* and often contains clues that will transpire to be significant later. Freud has a particular term for this "choosing to ignore": it is called *disavowal*, in other words the kind of scenario in which you say to yourself, *I know this is not really how things are but I am going to carry on as if it were*. Disavowal is indeed arguably one of the most powerful and disturbing ideas in psychoanalysis and, like so many of Freud's ideas, it entails a double logic. It involves a sort of splitting whereby you recognize the truth while also pretending that you don't. In disavowal you are double. Roland Barthes gives a neat instance of this in the context of reading a work of literature such as a novel or short story. Drawn into the world of the text, the reader thinks: "*I know these are only words but all the same* … (I am moved as though these words were uttering a reality)" (Barthes 1990, 47). Freud's case studies (such as "Dora" or "The Wolf Man") have sometimes been compared to works of detective fiction, but the model of the detective story casts helpful light on many other Freud texts. It corresponds, too, with Freud's admiration for Goethe as a writer who is both "a great self-revealer" and "a careful concealer" (1953–74, 21:212). At once revealing and carefully concealing, "The Uncanny" is an essay that opens on a rigged set.

The uncanny is mysterious and strange, ghostly, eerie, weird. It is not simply what is strange but what is *uncomfortably* strange, a disorienting strangeness that has a certain *familiarity* about it. Uncanniness is somehow connected with return or coming back. The uncanny is a *revenant*: this French word has flitted across into English, in the sense of "a ghost" or "someone who returns from the dead." "Revenant" literally means that which *comes back*. The uncanny gets up to all kinds of revenantics. The rigged set of the opening of Freud's essay is in fact already hinted at in the Standard Edition by the fact that Strachey chooses to put the word "uncanny" in quotation marks in the title: it is "The 'Uncanny'." The scare quotes really can have an unsettling quality: it is as if the translator wants to signify from the very beginning that this topic is one that cannot be translated or pinned down. Most critics (including the present writer) tend to drop these "double" quotes, considering them overly fussy: once you start putting words in quotes, where would you end?

The theory of the uncanny is, among other things, a theory of words themselves being double, at odds with themselves, beside themselves. In this respect it is crucial to note that the force and meaning of "Freud's double" (of how doubling figures in his work) necessarily includes everything he has to say, for example in *The Interpretation of Dreams* (Standard Edition, volume 4), *The Psychopathology of Everyday Life* (Standard Edition, volume 6) and *Jokes and their Relation to the Unconscious* (Standard Edition, volume 8), about double meaning, double entendre, ambiguity, antithetical meaning, substitutability, and so on. One of the first things he does in "The Uncanny," after his opening paragraph or so, is to turn to dictionaries and start exploring the German word *heimlich* (familiar, tame, intimate, friendly, etc.) – that is to say, the opposite of the *unheimlich* (fearful, weird, ghostly, etc.) – only to discover (though the "discovery" is rigged: obviously he knew all about this in advance) that the *heimlich* has a disturbing propensity to shade off and become "identical with its opposite" (1953–74, 17:224), the *unheimlich*. The adjective *heimlich* (originally linked to the German *Heim*, meaning "home") is a rough equivalent of the English word *canny*, and indeed one of the curious things about Freud's discussion of *heimlich/unheimlich* is the sort of eerie doubling or shadowing that can be seen to occur in their English counterparts, *canny/uncanny*. For the word *canny* (which originally seems to have been linked to the Old English verb *can*, meaning "to know") has an oddly similar propensity to drift in meaning from "knowing," "skillful," or "shrewd" (in a positive, respectful, or admiring sense) to *unnaturally* "knowing," "skillful," or "shrewd" (in a disquieting, mysterious, or enigmatic sense). In other words, *canny* can connote something unnatural, beyond the normal, even magical or supernatural. *Canny*, like the German *heimlich*, has a peculiar capacity to become (in Freud's phrase) "identical with its opposite": *uncanny*.

Freud's writing is canny. It has a remarkable kind of knowingness, skill, and shrewdness. It is canny in the sense of "agreeable," "nice," "tidy," "gentle," "cautious," but also in the sense of "sly." As Patrick J. Mahony has shown in his admirable examination of the form and style of "The Uncanny," Freud can be eerily deceptive: "his wonderful ease of expression and his masterfully articulated syntax make his writing appear, at first blush, clear and less ambiguous than it is" (Mahony 1987, 77). No sentence in "The Uncanny" is quite what it seems, even or especially when it appears inconsistent or incoherent. Numerous critics have pointed out problems, inconsistencies, and contradictions in Freud's essay, in particular as regards (1) his evident assumption that "the uncanny" can be exhaustively described, categorized, and classified (an assumption undermined in advance by what Cixous calls "The author's double: Hesitation" [2011, 15]); and (2) his preoccupation with "castration anxiety" and his corresponding inattentiveness to a female perspective. Some critical readings of Freud, such as those offered by Derrida (1987), Weber (2000), and Cixous (2011), are a good deal more careful and intellectually stimulating than others. But Freud-bashing is likely to remain a widespread phenomenon. As Freud himself clearly understood, his writings seem to make people feel like "neurotics under treatment" (1953–74, 19:221). Resistance to psychoanalysis is what makes psychoanalysis psychoanalysis.

Freud's texts are also canny, however, in ways that go beyond the author's stated intentions or meanings. Here it may be helpful to recall a comment made by Stephen Dedalus in James Joyce's *Ulysses*: "A man of genius makes no mistakes. His errors are volitional and are the portals of discovery" (Joyce 1969, 190). It is clear that Freud gets things wrong, he contradicts himself, his supposedly rationalistic theories and systems are inflected with forms of superstitious or magical thinking, and so on.[1] But the canniness of Freud's writing has to do with the fact that when we think we have spotted the limits or found a flaw in what he is saying, this is where his work lets us start seeing new things, thinking new possibilities: his sentences, his metaphors, even his elisions or silences, are "portals of discovery," in Joyce's phrase.

It is in this context that we might understand Michel Foucault's contention that Freud was not an author so much as a "founder of discursivity" (Foucault 1979, 154). Or to put it slightly differently, we are still in the process of discovering what kind of author Freud is. It is here, too, that we might think differently about "genius." It may be tempting to follow the Joycean and more broadly Romantic conception of the artist as "genius," but Freud's genius can perhaps more productively be thought about in terms of something he releases rather than possesses – something that his essay on "The Uncanny" gives or opens up, above and beyond any controlling idea of conscious intention or calculated effect. Of course, we respond to the sense that Freud is extraordinarily clever, immensely well read, and among the most remarkable modern essayists. Moreover his writing encourages this response, in part through its use of a language of mastery – from its often magisterial tone and its "masterfully articulated syntax" (in Mahony's phrase) to its sophisticated allusions to classical, German, and English literature, for example. His texts depend on – and indeed do new and strange things with – the rhetoric of authority. Freud's writing is supremely canny in its shifts and turns of phrase, its way with words, its know-how when it comes to letting the reader know that *this* writer knows an enormous amount. Mastery and authoritativeness are consistently undercut, however, by a feeling of loss of control, a failure to pin down, Freudian slips of the first order.

Mastery in the context of the uncanny, then, is a slippery thing. At one point in the essay Freud speaks of E.T.A. Hoffmann as "the unrivalled master of the uncanny in literature" (1953–74, 17:233), but this seems to be a tribute, once again, of a quite conventional, Romantic type (like speaking of Leonardo da Vinci as "a universal genius" [1953–74, 11:63]). The uncanny has no master. This is the case not only apropos the numerous ways in which Freud's account of Hoffmann's story "The Sandman," for example, can be seen as misguided or erroneous – in its skewed reckoning with the figure of woman, in its failure to consider the epistolary form of the text, in its inattentiveness to the comical or satirical elements of the story, in its suppression of the question of the death drive or what Hoffmann's story itself calls "the presentiment of a dark power which strives to ruin us within our own selves" (Hoffmann 1982, 96), and so on. (For extended commentary and analysis in these contexts, see, inter alia, Cixous 2011, Kofman 1991, Royle 2003, and

Weber 2000.) Whenever one supposes that one has mastered the uncanny, it has already gone – only, perhaps, to show up again (like the Ghost as "old mole" in *Hamlet*) unpredictably elsewhere.

We might clarify this elusiveness through the example of the figure of the double itself: there is a simple conception of the double (a character called Dr. Jekyll, for example, who turns into another, called Mr. Hyde) and a more complex conception, in which it is no longer possible to know which comes first or indeed whether there is a "first." It is in this context that Jacques Derrida speaks of the double as entailing a logic of "duplicity without original" (1987, 342). The uncanny is not an object but a feeling, usually fleeting, a feeling that makes us "strangers to ourselves," in Julia Kristeva's phrase (1991). It is a foreign body. It is a matter of what Jacques Lacan called "extimacy" (1992, 139), the experience of something insidious but external, something intimate but alien in the self. Extimacy, we could say, is a duplicitous figure, doubling within. Critical reflection on the uncanny, then, leads us away from the reductive idea, noted by Adam Phillips, that "intimacy is by definition personal intimacy" (Bersani and Phillips 2008, vii). It leads us (back) towards the strangeness of literature.

Let us conclude by considering briefly the example of Dostoevsky's *The Double*. This is how the novel begins:

> It was a little before eight o'clock in the morning when Titular Councillor Yakov Petrovich Golyadkin woke from a long sleep, yawned, stretched, and finally opened his eyes completely. He lay motionless in bed, however, for a couple of minutes more, like a man who is not yet quite sure whether he is awake or still asleep, and whether what is happening around him is real and actual or only the continuation of his disordered dreams. Soon, however, Mr. Golyadkin's senses began to receive more clearly and distinctly their usual ordinary impressions. The dingy-green, smoke-begrimed, dusty walls of his little room, his mahogany chest-of-drawers, the imitation mahogany chairs, the red-painted table, the Turkish divan covered in reddish oil-cloth with a pattern of little green flowers, and finally the clothes hastily removed the night before and flung down in a heap on the sofa, all looked familiarly back at him. Finally, the dull, dirty, grey autumn day peered into the room at him through the cloudy window-panes with a grimace so sour and bad-tempered that Mr. Golyadkin could no longer have the slightest doubt: he was not in some far-distant realm but in the capital, in the town of St Petersburg, in his own flat on the fourth floor of a large and imposing building in Shestilavochny Street.
>
> (Dostoevsky 1972, 127)

Like so many other literary works that we might describe as uncanny, Dostoevsky's begins at home – literally, in the protagonist's flat in St Petersburg. It starts out from the everyday and ordinary, indeed from the tiresomely or distastefully familiar, before moving into the radically unfamiliar. As Freud shows, better even than he realizes, uncanniness has to do with a peculiar jumbling of the familiar and unfamiliar. The novel is called *The Double*, and so from the very opening words the reader is curious to know how this figure or concept is to play its part. In fact, as so often in his writing, Dostoevsky teases his readers with various sorts of narrative prevarication – protraction, dilatoriness, suspense, and digression – and it is a good while before we actually come to discover that Mr. Golyadkin indeed appears to have a double and that this encounter (or entrapping web of encounters) with the double is the focus of the novel.

While these initial sentences evoke a strong sense of the ordinary, actual, daily life of a man waking up in his flat, however, there are also a number of odd things going on. What might appear familiar is already tinged with the unfamiliar. In the first place, Dostoevsky's description unsettles any simple or reassuring conviction about the distinction between being awake and being asleep. This corresponds with Freud's suggestion that "an uncanny effect is often and easily produced when the distinction between imagination and reality is effaced" (1953–74, 17:244). An uncertainty about whether the scene is real or not, a scene from waking life or from the world of dreams, constitutes the very subject of Dostoevsky's writing. This sort of narrative delirium is so peculiar to him it might be called Dostoevsky's signature. Already, in fact, we have a sort of logic of the double at work: the scene with which we are presented is uncertainly real and imaginary, wakeful and a "continuation of ... disordered dreams." And the duplicity is highlighted in at least two further respects. First, there is the oddness of a scene that *looks back*. Mr. Golyadkin looks around his little room and "all looked familiarly back at him." Likewise the day itself "peered into the room at him ... with a grimace." It is a peculiar "double" scene, doubly seen, like a two-way mirror. Second, and more fundamentally, what makes these opening sentences markedly "literary" in the first instance, above and beyond anything else, is that they are written in the third person, about a man called Mr. Golyadkin, as if from an external perspective, while at the same time informing the reader about what is going on inside Mr. Golyadkin's mind and body – above all his experience of uncertainty as to "whether he is awake or still asleep."

Dostoevsky's novel will go on to relate a proliferation of strange and disturbing experiences, all devolving from the trope (if it can with any real conviction be called that) of Mr. Golyadkin's having a double, a double whose reality (like that of the ghosts in Henry James' *The Turn of the Screw*) remains undecidable. But in a sense nothing is more bizarre than what we might call the original or primal literary scene, in which a speaker or writer (Dostoevsky or his "narrator") tells us what someone else (here Mr. Golyadkin) is thinking and feeling. In this space the identities of author, narrator, and character substitute, overlap, double up. It is the space of what might be called *literary extimacy*. Literary fiction, in this respect, is double writing par excellence.

Freud's "The Uncanny" makes use of literature in similar fashion. As we have seen, its very opening paragraph figures Freud in the third person. Elsewhere, in a haunting and deceptive footnote, Freud tells a story about his own double:

> I was sitting alone in my *wagon-lit* compartment when a more than usually violent jolt of the train swung back the door of the adjoining washing-cabinet, and an elderly gentleman in a dressing-gown and a travelling cap came in. I assumed that in leaving the washing-cabinet, which lay between the two compartments, he had taken the wrong direction and come into my compartment by mistake. Jumping up with the intention of putting him right, I at once realized to my dismay that the intruder was nothing by my own reflection in the looking-glass on the open door.
>
> (1953–74, 17:248n1)

What makes this embedded story within Freud's essay *literary* is in part the duplicitous way in which it operates: is the narrator/intruder "sitting" or "standing," motionless or coming in? Where does Freud's "I" stop and the mirror begin? Near the end of his essay Freud writes of the "*peculiarly* directive power" that a storyteller has over us: "by means of the moods he can put us into, he is able to guide the current of our emotions, to dam it up in one direction and make it flow in another, and he often obtains variety of effects from the same material" (1953–74, 17:251). What is perhaps ultimately most haunting about Freud is the "peculiarly directive power" of his own writing – in particular, the way in which it mimics or duplicates such literary effects, while also forging a discourse of its own, a new kind of *writing double*.

Note

1 For a good account of Freud's sympathetic interest in spiritualism, telepathy, and psychical research, see Jones (1957).

References

Barthes, Roland. 1990. *The Pleasure of the Text*, trans. Richard Miller. Oxford: Basil Blackwell.

Bateson, Gregory. 1956. "Towards a Theory of Schizophrenia." *Behavioral Science* 1, no. 4: 251–64.

Bersani, Leo, and Adam Phillips. 2008. *Intimacies*. Chicago: Chicago University Press.

Caillois, Roger. 1983. "The Detective Novel as Game," trans. William W. Stowe. In *The Poetics of Murder: Detective Fiction and Literary Theory*, ed. Glenn W. Most and William W. Stowe, 1–12. New York: Harcourt Brace Jovanovich.

Cixous, Hélène. 2011. "Fiction and Its Phantoms: A Reading of Freud's *Das Unheimliche* (The 'Uncanny')," trans. Robert Denommé, revised Eric Prenowitz. In *Volleys of Humanity: Essays 1972–2009*, ed. Eric Prenowitz, 15–40. Edinburgh: Edinburgh University Press.

Derrida, Jacques. 1981. "The Double Session." In *Dissemination*, 173–285, trans. Barbara Johnson. Chicago: Chicago University Press.

Derrida, Jacques. 1987. "To Speculate – on 'Freud'." In *The Post Card: From Socrates to Freud and Beyond*, 257–409, trans. Alan Bass. Chicago: Chicago University Press.

Dostoevsky, Fyodor. 1972. *The Double*. In *Notes from Underground / The Double*, 127–287, trans. Jessie Coulson. Harmondsworth: Penguin.

Foucault, Michel. 1979. "What Is an Author?," trans. Josué V. Harari. In *Textual Strategies: Perspectives in Post-Structuralist Criticism*, ed. Josué V. Harari, 141–60. London: Methuen.

Freud, Sigmund. 1953–74. *The Standard Edition of the Complete Psychological Works of Sigmund Freud*. 24 vols., ed. James Strachey, with the assistance of Anna Freud, Alix Strachey, and Alan Tyson, trans. James Strachey. London: Hogarth Press.

Freud, Sigmund. 2003. *The Uncanny*, trans. David McClintock. London: Penguin.

Hoffmann, E.T.A. 1982. "The Sandman." In *Tales of Hoffmann*, 85–125, trans. R.J. Hollingdale. Harmondsworth: Penguin.

Jones, Ernest. 1957. "Occultism." In *Sigmund Freud: Life and Works*, 3:402–36. London: Hogarth Press.

Joyce, James. 1969. *Ulysses*. Harmondsworth: Penguin.

Kofman, Sarah. 1991. *Freud and Fiction*, trans. Sarah Wykes. Cambridge: Polity.

Kofman, Sarah. 2007. "The Double Reading," trans. Winifred Woodhull. In *Selected Writings*, ed. Thomas Albrecht, with Georgia Albert and Elizabeth Rottenberg, 37–55. Stanford: Stanford University Press.

Kristeva, Julia. 1991. *Strangers to Ourselves*, trans. Leon C. Roudiez. New York: Columbia University Press.

Lacan, Jacques. 1992. *The Ethics of Psychoanalysis, 1959–60: The Seminar of Jacques Lacan*, ed. Jacques-Alain Miller, trans. Dennis Porter. London: Routledge.

Mahony, Patrick J. 1987. "Proportions of Certainty." In *Freud as a Writer*, 75–96. New Haven: Yale University Press.

Rank, Otto. 1989. *The Double: A Psychoanalytic Study*, trans. Harry Tucker Jr. London: Maresfield Library.

Readings, Bill. 1991. *Introducing Lyotard: Art and Politics*. London: Routledge.

Royle, Nicholas. 2003. *The Uncanny*. Manchester: Manchester University Press.

Shakespeare, William. 1998. *Hamlet*, ed. G.R. Hibbard. Oxford: Oxford University Press.

Weber, Samuel. 2000. "Uncanny Thinking." In *The Legend of Freud*, expanded edn., 1–30. Stanford: Stanford University Press.

Chapter 8

Medieval Dreams

Nicolette Zeeman

At one point Chaucer's red-stockinged Wife of Bath describes how she invented a dream with which to seduce her most recent husband, a much younger clerk:

> I bar hym on honde he hadde enchanted* me — deceived me
> ... I seyde I mette* of hym al nyght, — dreamed
> He wolde han slayne* me as I lay upright,* — would have slain; on my back
> And al my bed was ful of verray blood.

Invoking the medieval dreambooks to the effect that "blood bitokeneth gold," she recounts how she told him that she hoped he would "do her good," and concludes:

> And al was fals; I dremed of it right naught,
> But as I folwed ay* my dames loore.*[1] — always; my mother's teaching

Medieval dream theory variously attributed dreams to supernatural, cosmological, or bodily causes (see p. 141 below); the Wife's dream suggests that in other respects too the material forces of the cosmos may determine the subject – at the very least she alludes to the humoral

A Concise Companion to Psychoanalysis, Literature, and Culture, First Edition.
Edited by Laura Marcus and Ankhi Mukherjee.

theory that associated the "sanguine" temperament, and the color red, with a heightened sexual drive: according to Avicenna's *Canon of Medicine*, the sanguine person dreams of "red objects, large amounts of blood coming out of his body, or that he is swimming in blood, and similar things".[2] But of course the Wife's dream is invented; she is performing the language of material determinism for what she claims are her own, conscious, purposes. She identifies with a tradition of female manipulators of men ("I folwed ay my dames loore"), and, even if this is to invoke a separate set of cultural determinations (the devious ways of dealing with men that medieval culture attributes to women), she insists on the fantasy of personal autonomy and artfulness.

But the Wife's dream also speaks of desire in other ways. Its language of violent wounding, for instance, invokes a longstanding western version of love that is simultaneously sublimatory, masochistic, and visceral (compare the roundel "Your yen [eyes] two wol slee me sodenly" [Chaucer 1987, 659]). Lacan described this tradition of "courtly love" as involving narcissistic and sublimatory illusions of reciprocity, art, and autonomy, but also participation within the "symbolic order that preexists the infantile subject and in accordance with which he will have to structure himself" (Lacan 1980, 234); by claiming to relinquish control willingly, love's rhetoric of frustration and pain masks, but also encodes, the impossibility of the sexual relation. Desire in the Wife's dream is the desire of the other (see also Lacan 1980, 54; 1998, 65–72).[3] This is, after all, the sacrificial moment when the Wife will give up her long-standing practice of marrying old men for their goods in order to pass both her body and her accumulated wealth on to a man who is likely to outlive her (and who will himself prove physically violent). Of course the Wife's bloody dream could be a reference to menstrual blood, in which Freud might have seen the desire for an erotic or pleasant life without pregnancy (see Freud 2006, 139); but the fantasy of menstruation might just be a further gift to the (fortune-seeking?) clerk – no heirs. Like the dream of the analysand, then, the Wife's dream strategy is "a provocation, a masked avowal, or a diversion" from what is really being said (Lacan 1980, 58).

In my reading of medieval dream poems, I'm going to be using Freudian and Lacanian dream theory: Freud's foundational belief that the dream and the literary text provide unparalleled degrees of access to the work of the mind; his connected sense of the multiplicitous, devious, and denying modes by which dreams (and literary texts) signify and censor themselves; and Lacan's view, that in pointing towards the unconscious, the dream and the literary text gesture at desire, but also at that which cannot be symbolized, trauma and the real. Partly as a result of this Lacanian emphasis, though also in line with wider practice in later Freudian psychology, my readings will downplay Freud's emphasis on dreaming as unconscious wish-fulfillment (though even Freud later admitted that repetition in the dreams of patients suffering traumatic neuroses might upset "the function of dreaming," expressing instead the death drive [1953–74, 18:13, 32–33).[4] My readings will reflect the fact that medieval literary dreams respond to a number of different types of psychoanalytic interpretation. The many different ways they do this, however, reflect Freud's rich sense of the diverse modes by which the dream and the literary text signify.

The seminal text of Freud's own self-analysis, *Interpreting Dreams*, contains extensive discussion of universal dream symbols, and was expanded in subsequent editions as Freud and his collaborators inserted further dream materials in the belief they would increase the book's applicability and objectivity; but Freud finally came to disagree with thinkers such as Rank and Jung over universal symbolism (Marinelli and Meyer 2003). Ultimately, he denied that the dream could be read without reference to the patient's personal history: dreams were, he said, "wholly egotistical" and the "I" could appear under many guises within them (Freud 2006, 337–38).[5] These guises and detours were just some of the tools of censorship by which the dream both articulated and disguised the wishes that underlay it (2006, 148–76). They gave rise to Freud's dazzlingly inventive, imaginative, and "literary" dream readings.

He was very much aware that many of the features he identified in dreams are also found in the artwork and the literary text. Put together in a manner "rather like the way a poet works," the Freudian dream is characterized by the *Verdichtung*, "compression" (previously translated as "condensation"), of multiple thoughts into single images, and by the *Verschiebung*, "displacement," of ideas and feelings onto other, and sometimes unconnected, phenomena (Freud 2006, 354–55, 295–325).[6] It can signify literally or figurally, and its form (observed clarity, for example) can be part of its "content" (2006, 344–46). Not only does the dream reveal a constant "preference" for expressing dream thought in pictorial and visual form, replacing abstract formulations with "concrete" ones, but, as Freud interprets it, it is also regularly structured round language, in particular its sound, and full of "puns, quotations, songs and proverbs" (2006, 360; for further elaboration of this idea, see 61–62, 355–64, 422–41). Freud himself noted that the telling of a dream is already an interpretation, as well as a potential rationalization, and a form of censorship or falsification (2006, 58–59); if this means that it is almost impossible in *Interpreting Dreams* to draw a boundary line between the telling and interpretation of a dream, it also implicitly reveals that the activity of dream interpretation is remarkably similar to dream work itself.

Dreams have played a less central role in later Anglo-American psychoanalytic practice, due to its emphasis on ego psychology and on cognitive behavioral therapy, both of which involve more focus on the conscious subject. Whereas for Freud dreams are the road to the unconscious, many Anglo-American practitioners, when they use dreams, pay more attention to the overt content of the dream and its role in the psychoanalytic exchange as a whole (Lane and Harris 2002).

Lacan has quite a bit to say about dreams. Like Freud, he is clear that characteristic operations of dreamwork, such as compression/condensation, are "connatural with poetry to the point that it envelops the traditional function proper to poetry" (1980, 160). Lacan's claim that "dreamwork follows the laws of the signifier," of course, means much more than this, by identifying in the dream "a signifying flow, the mystery of which lies in the fact that the subject does not even know where to pretend to be its organiser," as a "derivation" of which "the channel of desire flows" (1980, 161, 259; see also 57–58). This is not about being recognized as the subject of either desire or sight: "our position in the dream is profoundly that of someone who does not see" (Lacan 1979, 75); the dream is "the world, the world of being, full of knowledge ... the body insofar as it speaks" (1979, 55). What is more, if dream thought exists in slippages and "missed encounters," it reveals an "it *shows*," a "character of emergence, of contrast, of stain" (Lacan 1998, 126).

Lacan is in some ways a more literal dream reader than Freud, as we see in his discussions of the "dream of the burning child": a father sleeps in a room adjacent to the one where his dead child is lying, while the old man, who should be watching the child, has also fallen asleep, allowing the corpse to be burnt by a fallen candle; the father dreams that the child comes to him, touching his arm and saying, "Father, can't you see I'm burning?" (Freud 2006, 526–27). Lacan returns slightly obsessively to this dream, describing it as one "in a category of its own – a dream suspended around the most anguishing mystery" (Lacan 1979, 34). This is certainly not dream as "a phantasy fulfilling a wish" but an articulation of desire manifested "by the loss expressed in an image at the most cruel point of the object." For Lacan the real of this dream is accessed in its repetitions, its obscured seeing (he says it can scarcely even be remembered), and its displacement of the subject: "it is only in the dream that this truly unique encounter can occur. Only a rite, an endlessly repeated act, can commemorate this not very memorable encounter – for no-one can say what the death of a child is, except the father *qua* father, that is to say, no conscious being." Lacan's remarks here are intense and in many ways poetic, as he repeats the child's haunting words, "Father, can't you see I'm burning?": "This sentence is itself a firebrand – of itself it brings fire where it falls – and one cannot see what is burning, for the flames blind us to the fact that the fire bears on the *Unterlegt*, on the *Untertragen*, on the real" (1979, 59). It is this, and not any noise or light from the adjoining room, Lacan insists, that is the "reality" (*réalité*) that wakes the father (1979, 60).[7]

These writings have been hugely influential in psychoanalytic literary studies. Intriguingly, there are also parallels between the ways that medieval writers theorize dreams and imaginative texts – including imaginative "dream" texts. Medieval writers, for instance, characterize them both in terms of an image-using, visual dimension, often counterpointing this with representations (sometimes embodied or personified) of the spoken or written word. Just as dreams pose problems of interpretation (see Kruger 1992, 7–16), so medieval literature is also acutely alert to the complex hermeneutics involved in commentary, literary "retelling," and even notionally fresh composition. Medieval theorists also consider that dreams and imaginative texts pose very similar questions about their own origins and ontology. Dream theory (often associated with the sixth-century Macrobius, but in fact explored by both medieval religious thinkers and natural philosophers) divides dreams into a spectrum of categories ranging from supposedly authoritative, philosophical, and revelatory visions to those derived from contingent situations, particular persons, and local and bodily effects. Medieval imaginative writing, especially in the vernacular, also locates itself at the interface of the authoritative textual archive and the "new" and non-authoritative interventions of the imaginative writer, often characterized in terms of material particularity, bodiliness, partiality, and desire (see Kruger 1992; Minnis and Scott 1988; Wogan-Browne, Watson, Taylor, and Evans 1999). By no means all medieval imaginative texts are dream poems. Nevertheless, when medieval imaginative writers use the figure of the dream to signal the imaginative text they are alluding to many of its dream-like features – its figurality, its verbalism, its complex modes of reference, the hermeneutic activity that it implies and demands – and its ambiguous origins in the culturally and linguistically imbricated subject.[8]

Guillaume de Lorris' unfinished but widely read thirteenth-century French *Roman de la rose* is highly alert to the divided languages of desiring and dreaming. The narrator/lover walks out into a landscape, where he finds a walled garden, within which he finds the "rose" that will function as the object of his desire:

> Within my twenty yer of age,
> Whan that Love taketh his cariage* [feudal tax]
> Of yonge folk, I wente soone
> To bedde, as I was wont to done,
> And faste* I slepte; and in slepyng [soon]
> Me mette such a swevenyng* [I dreamed such a dream]
> That lyked me wonders wel.
> But in that sweven is never a del* [no part]
> That it nys afterward befalle,* [that it did not happen after]
> Ryght as this drem wol tel us alle.
> Now this drem wol I ryme aright
> To make your hertes gaye and lyght,
> For Love it prayeth, and also
> Commaundeth me that it be so.[9]

The poem interleaves the claims of amorous and literary intentionalism ("I wente soone / To bedde," "this drem wol I ryme aright") with the determinations of love and dreams ("Whan that Love taketh his cariage / Of yonge folk," "Love it prayeth, and also / Commaundeth me," "Me mette such a swevenyng" – *mette* is here a reflexive verb). The poem's landscape and its inhabitants (Ydelnesse, Curtesie, Richesse, the God of Love and Daunger [Disdain]), link the psychic and the cultural/linguistic; and, although the narrator describes himself as actively choosing to enter the landscape, it is clear that he is in fact subject to its "lures," its leading paths, walls, apertures, new terrains, and its inviting figures. When he passes from sunlit spaces into a dark wood, his subjection is rearticulated as coercion, and the God of Love, who figures "love" both as affect and as the social requirement to love, begins to stalk him with his bow and arrows. This is desire as the desire of the Other, and its object-cause is both substitutive and secondary, as we note when the narrator sees the rose: he looks into a well in which marvelous crystals enable him to observe a rosebed filled with what appear to be many beautiful roses and rosebuds, and then immediately chooses one as "more unto my pay [pleasure] / Than ony other that I say [saw]" (ll. 1721–22). The poem thus circles round its inaccessible "petit object a" in a series of repeating structures that reiterate "falling in love" (following paths into the garden, being shot by the God of Love, looking in the pool, seeing the rose), but also then re-enact the bars to love (feminine *daunger* and *shame*, and powerful but unspecified forms of masculine possessiveness such as *wikkid-tunge* and *jelousie*: ll. 3788, 3799, 3828). Hult (1986) has argued that the poem's unfinished nature is a structurally inevitable consequence of its formulation of desire. "Courtly love," for Lacan the skill of "elegantly pulling off" the impossibility of the sexual relation, is not just about the arts and pleasures of self-denial; it is also an acknowledgment that desire has no end (Lacan 1998, 69; on self-denial, see Fradenburg 2002).

The lover sees the rose mysteriously reflected in a well marked "Here starf [died] the fayre Narcisus" (l. 1468). There has been much debate over whether this reference to Narcissus emblematizes love's vanity, cruelty, solipsism, or impossibility (Hult 1986, 263–83). What we can surely say is that Narcissus is doubled and uncanny. Dying for love of his own image and memorialized in the fountain, in the poem both absent and present, both dead and alive, he appears at the center of its fantasized love relation like the return of something already known, but repressed, about desire (Freud 1953–74, 17:217–52). Only partially seen (he is a mere reference, after all), he is also a reminder of the imbrication of desire and the death drive, of the "it speaks" that Lacan finds "where there is pain." In fact, Lacan uses, not Narcissus, but Actaeon, a very similar mythical figure, to make the same point: Actaeon is "perpetually slipped by dogs that have been tracked down from the beginning, and which he strives to draw back into pursuit, without being able to slacken the chase"; he seeks "the chthonian Diana in the damp shade," whose offering comes with "the smooth surface of death" (Lacan 1980, 124–25; see also 145). Jean de Meun takes up this mortificatory dimension of Guillaume de Lorris' vision of love in the later part of his learned, satirical, reifying, and pornographic continuation of the poem. Here, the object-cause of desire is imagined first through a bizarre and comic version of Pygmalion's statue and then finally as a grotesquely concretized genital "shrine," a small "opening" in a tower between "two pillars," in which there was a "sanctuary, more fragrant than a pomander" into which the "pilgrim" lover proceeds to insert his pilgrim's "staff" and rummage around.[10] In these last lines of the poem, the fantasy love object of Guillaume's exquisite and euphemistic love narrative is unveiled as a grotesque and fetishistic substitute, while the "lover" himself is reduced to the tools of his sexual work (on buildings and luggage as genitalia, see Freud, 2006, 361, 371).

In Langland's *Piers Plowman* (written and revised c.1360–90), the interplay of desire and its objects is formulated in religious terms. Unusually among medieval dream poems, this text is made up of multiple dreams. With one exception (the vision of Christ's crucifixion and harrowing of hell), these all end with some kind of crisis and upset, or with a disappearance or loss, or with both, leaving the dreamer in a state of increasing disturbance and disfunctionality, "witlees nerhande ... as a freke that fey were" ("almost out of my mind ... like a doomed person," Langland 1995, 13.1–2). Although both Freud and Lacan agree that one function of dreams is to support the wish for sleep by "naturalizing" any phenomenon from the waking world that might disrupt it, Lacan also insists on the power of dream experience to wake the dreamer. It is this that we see in the disturbing dreams of *Piers Plowman*.

Repeatedly they describe an attempt to reform society or teach people to "do well," and repeatedly the mechanisms of change turn out to be, if not downright corrupt, then inadequate, and open to misunderstanding, abuse, and complacency. I have argued elsewhere that the psychological corollary of this endemic cycle of decline is another pattern that also repeats across the poem, in which a spiritual seeker (often the dreamer himself) gets diverted by objects that appear to satisfy his quest; he is then rebuked and frustrated by a teacher or authority figure who finally him- or herself disappears. The result is a kind of pause or void in the narrative, which produces the effect of newly intense desire, not only in the disappointed seeker, but also in the reader (Zeeman 2006). In one of the most famously confusing moments of the poem, for instance, Piers Plowman offers the community a "pardon," which looks like a covenantal agreement from God to save those who do what they can; a priest proposes to explicate it to Piers, only to announce that, according to his understanding of medieval ecclesiastical indulgences, this is not a pardon at all. In "pure tene [anger]" Piers then tears the pardon up and appears to blame himself, saying that he will give up trying to serve the community and devote himself to penance. Everyone vanishes and the dreamer awakes, looking about, "meteless and moneilees [without food or money] on Malverne hulles' (7.115, 140–43). Despite its mysteriousness, the incident is entirely characteristic of the poem in the way that it uses a cycle of guilt, repression, frustration, and disappointment to produce a startlingly open and non-prescriptive sense of desire. No doubt this is part of the poem's attempt to inculcate the desire for immaterial and spiritual things, but what it repeatedly lays bare are the repressions and detours of desire itself.

Another way of describing this would be to say that desire in the poem always "goes wrong" by getting diverted onto an object that looks as if it will satisfy it. As seen in the pardon incident, these objects tend to be ecclesiastical and educative institutions, practices, formulations, words, and concepts – objects that are not bad in themselves, but that might be abused, or, equally dangerously, be used in a spirit of complacency and indifference. The real problem with these objects, in other words, is that they might be thought to be the solution: they masquerade as the ends of desire. The poem's devastating revelation (which of course it claims is a spiritual one) is that anything that claims to be desire's end can only be a substitute, a fetish, an "objet petit a." This, I suggest, and not local ecclesiastical corruption, is the real reason that, at the apocalyptic conclusion of the poem, the personification Conscience leaves even the established Church, calling out for grace and Piers Plowman (who is in fact one of the most absent of the poem's absent objects of desire); it is a desperate moment, and the dreamer wakes, "And sitthe he gradde [cried out] after Grace, til I gan awake" (20.387). With that, the poem ends, and one more void opens up for desire.

My last example comes from Chaucer, all of whose dream poems address questions of desire and loss, but often in strangely comedic forms (Fradenburg 1990). Several of Chaucer's narrators are the butt of other protagonists' jokes, and, although they hold themselves aloof, insinuating that the joke is on the others, this insinuation is never entirely successful. This is certainly true of Geffrey in *The House of Fame* (c.1379–80), for whom I propose that the discomforting effect of being seen, rebuked, and laughed at, from a position that he cannot properly grasp or understand, involves something akin to noticing oneself within the gaze. Lacan's story about the gaze in the sardine can, after all, also has a comedic dimension. When the fisherman Petit-Jean points out the can floating in the sea, exclaiming, "You see that can? Do you see it? Well, it doesn't see you!" Lacan comments that "it was looking at me at the level of the point of light, the point at which everything that looks at me is situated." And part of Lacan's sense of himself as the focus of the gaze here must be due to his being the irritable recipient both of the fishermen's look and their humor:

> it is because I, at that moment – as I appeared to those fellows who were earning their livings with great difficulty ... looked like nothing on earth. In short, I was rather out of place in the picture. And it was because I felt this that I was not terribly amused at hearing myself addressed in this humorous, ironical way.
>
> (1979, 95–96)

The House of Fame is an extended riff on the challenges of being enmeshed in the textual and cultural tradition, both for the writer and for those he writes about. Like most of Chaucer's dream poems, it is divided into narrative sections, a vivid example of dream displacement. It begins with the poet dreaming he is in a glass temple dedicated to Venus, in which the story of the *Aeneid*, up to the death of Dido, is engraved, apparently on a brass "table." As Chaucer narrates the tale, however, reiterating "ther saugh I," it becomes increasingly unclear whether he is describing graven texts or images. The story culminates with Dido's lament about the unfairness of her literary "fame" through Aeneas' shameful behavior: "That I have don rekever [recover] I never, / That I ne shal be seyde, allas, / Yshamed be thourgh Eneas" (Chaucer 1987, 347–73 [ll. 354–56]). This is followed by her suicide and Chaucer's comment that if we want to know more we should read "Virgile in Eneydos / Or the Epistle of Ovyde" (ll. 378–79), two notoriously contradictory versions of the tale. What initially seems to be a love narrative turns out to be one more tale of unhappy desire and death; textual and imagistic forms of cultural transmission turn out to be opaque, conflictual, and unreliable; and for Dido the experience of being the object of such texts and images is the disempowering and mortificatory one of finding yourself within the gaze – of never being looked at "there at the place from which I see you" (Lacan 1979, 103; translation modified).

In the next section, the narrator goes outside the temple into a vast field of sand, where a Dante-esque golden eagle swoops down to pick him up (see *Purgatorio* 9.19–20, 2.17–24; *Paradiso* 18–20). The eagle announces that he has been sent by Jove to reward Geffrey with *tydynges* of "Loves folk" (l. 675), and carries the poet up into the sky, showing him the stars, the castle of Fame, and a spinning twig-house; it is to this place that all the true and false words ever spoken or written apparently ascend, like the air they are, finding their natural position in the heavens. All this looks rather like wish-fulfillment. Chaucer, seeking poetic material with which to develop his literary career, fantasizes that it has been provided by a divinely appreciative audience and patron, who have been concerned about his welfare; at the end of a day's work, the eagle explains to him, "Thou goost hom to thy hous anoon, / And, also domb as any stoon, / Thou sittest at another book / Tyl fully daswed [dazed] ys thy look" (ll. 655–58). The poem not only provides the poet with visionary poetic "matter" but also, it seems, his own iconic "pillar" in Fame's house. Here, among all the other authors, Homer, Guido delle Colonne, and "Englyssh Gaufride" (the future author of *Troilus and Criseyde*?) stand on their own pillars, upholding the story of Troy (ll. 1466–72; Cooper 1999, 58–59). Even the poet's denial that he has come in pursuit of fame looks like the most ordinary form of dream censorship (ll. 1874–77).

But there is more to it than this. For a start, the eagle is a dream compression, a doubled figure who speaks uncannily, "Ryght in the same vois and stevene / That useth oon I koude nevene [name]" (ll. 561–62). He may look like a hot literary allusion to an important Italian text, but he turns out to be an irrepressible and familiar pedagogue, who bombards the reluctant Geffrey with elaborate explanations of poetical cosmology and physics, repeatedly interpellating him from his (grammar school?) past:[11]

> "Wilt thou lere* of sterres aught?" — learn
> "Nay, certeynly," quod y, "ryght naught."
> "And why?" "For y am now to old."
> "Elles I wolde the have told,"
> Quod he, "the sterres names, lo,
> And al the hevenes sygnes therto,
> And which they ben." "No fors,"* quod y. — I don't care
> (ll. 993–99)

In fact no love tidings ever appear in the poem. In the closing lines, Geffrey catches sight of someone who seems to be "A man of gret auctorite" (is this a wish for the fantasy oeuvres of the future or another mortificatory allusion to the works of the past?), but with that, the poem concludes, in the middle of a sentence. There is no end to desire – or the poem.

At its center is the "house" of Fame itself, a fantastical, sculpted artwork, but built on melting ice and in partial decay. The sound that emanates from it is empty and wordless, "lyk betynge of the see ... ayen [against] the roches holowe" (ll. 1034–35); once the poet is inside, he finds that it contains embodied voices, but they are words that have become not living persons, but mere images (or dead idols: Zeeman 2002, 48–49). The goddess Fame, who randomly passes out fame or obscurity to her suitors, is a spectral figure, oscillating in size, and covered with eyes, ears, and tongues:

> as feele* eyen hadde she — many
> As fetheres upon foules be ...
> And, soth to tellen, also she
> Had also fele upstondyng eres
> And tonges, as on bestes heres.* — hairs
> (ll.1381–82, 1388–90)

Here, in bizarre and comedic form, is the inhuman gaze obscurely to be seen in the literary tradition and the artwork; its work is surely "to catch in its trap" the poet who has earlier been described as dumb and dazed before his books (see Lacan 1979, 92, 100). We should not be surprised to discover that Dido's predicament, transfixed by the gaze of the other in textual form, is a version of that of the startled author and dreamer of the poem.

Notes

1 *Canterbury Tales*, III.575–83 (Chaucer 1987, 1–328).
2 Avicenna 1556, Lib.1, fen. 2, doct. 3, cap. 7; Morris 1886, 157; Kosmer 1975, 6–8. For the Wife's red clothing, see Chaucer 1987: *Canterbury Tales*, General Prologue, 456; III.559.
3 For recent psychoanalytic readings of "courtly love," see Fradenburg (2002), Gaunt (2006), Kay (1999).
4 Lacan relates dreams and neurosis rather differently: "neurosis consists in dreaming, not perverse acts. Neurotics ... dream of being perverts" (1998, 87).
5 On dream symbolism, see Freud 2006, 257–92, 361–84, 408–13.
6 On the disjuncture of affect in dreams, see Freud 2006, 86, 154, 171, 396.
7 See also all of Lacan (1979, 53–64), and Bowie (1991, 105–6). On the "screen" or "trompe l'oeil" that indicates something behind, see Lacan 1979, 60, 103.
8 For other psychoanalytic readings of medieval dream poems, see Fradenburg (1990); Gilbert (2011, 151–214); Hasler (2011, 43–62).
9 Cited in the translation attributed to Chaucer (1987, 685–767 [ll. 21–34]).
10 There is no Middle English translation here: *Roman de la rose*, ll. 20791–814, 21587–676.
11 Christopher Cannon has proposed in a personal communication that Chaucer alludes to his teacher of "poetry," his grammar school master; see also Spearing (1976, 88).

References

Avicenna. 1556. *Medicorum Arabum principis liber canonis*. Basle.
Bowie, Malcolm. 1991. *Lacan*. London: Fontana.
Chaucer. 1987. *The Riverside Chaucer*, 3rd edn., ed. Larry D. Benson. Oxford: Oxford University Press.
Cooper, Helen. 1999. "The Four Last Things in Dante and Chaucer: Ugolino in the House of Rumour." *New Medieval Literatures*, 3: 39–66.

Dante Alighieri. 2006–7. *The Divine Comedy,* 3 vols., trans. and ed. Robin Kirkpatrick. London: Penguin

Fradenburg, Aranye L.O. 2002. *Sacrifice your Love: Psychoanalysis, Historicism, Chaucer*. Minneapolis: University of Minnesota Press.

Fradenburg, Louise O. 1990. "'Voice Memorial': Loss and Reparation in Chaucer's Poetry." *Exemplaria,* 2: 169–202.

Freud, Sigmund. 1953–74. *The Standard Edition of the Complete Psychological Works of Sigmund Freud,* 24 vols., ed. James Strachey, with the assistance of Anna Freud, Alix Strachey, and Alan Tyson, trans. James Strachey. London: Hogarth Press.

Freud, Sigmund. 2006. *Interpreting Dreams,* trans. J.A. Underwood. London: Penguin.

Gaunt, Simon. 2006. *Love and Death in Medieval French and Occitan Courtly Literature*. Oxford: Oxford University Press.

Gilbert, Jane. 2011. *Living Death in Medieval French and English Literature.* Cambridge: Cambridge University Press.

Guillaume de Lorris and Jean de Meun. 1993. *Le Roman de la rose,* ed. Armand Strubel. Paris: Livre de Poche.

Hasler, Antony J. 2011. *Court Poetry in Late Medieval England and Scotland.* Cambridge: Cambridge University Press.

Hult, David F. 1986. *Self-Fulfilling Prophecies: Readership and Authority in the First* Roman de la rose. Cambridge: Cambridge University Press.

Kay, Sarah. 1999. "Desire and Subjectivity." In *The Troubadours: An Introduction,* ed. Simon Gaunt and Sarah Kay, 212–27. Cambridge: Cambridge University Press.

Kosmer, Ellen. 1975. "The 'noyous humoure of lecherie'." *The Art Bulletin,* 57: 1–8.

Kruger, Steven F. 1992. *Dreaming in the Middle Ages*. Cambridge: Cambridge University Press.

Lacan, Jacques. 1979. *The Four Fundamental Concepts of Psycho-analysis,* ed. Jacques-Alain Miller, trans. Alan Sheridan. Harmondsworth: Penguin.

Lacan, Jacques. 1980. *Écrits: A Selection,* trans. Alan Sheridan. London: Tavistock.

Lacan, Jacques. 1998. *The Seminar of Jacques Lacan,* Book XX: *On Feminine Sexuality, the Limits of Love and Knowledge, Encore 1972–1973,* ed. Jacques-Alain Miller, trans. Bruce Fink. New York : Norton.

Lane, Robert C., and Max Harris. 2002. "The Changing Place of the Dream in Psychoanalytic History, Part I: Freud, Ego Psychology, and the Interpersonal School." *Psychoanalytic Review,* 89: 829–59.

Langland, William. 1995. *The Vision of Piers Plowman: A Critical Edition of the B Text,* 2nd edn., ed. A.V.C. Schmidt. London: Everyman.

Marinelli, Lydia, and Andreas Meyer. 2003. *Dreaming by the Book: Freud's* The Interpretation of Dreams *and the History of the Psychoanalytic Movement,* trans. Susan Fairfield. New York: Other Press.

Minnis, Alastair J., and A.B. Scott, eds., with the assistance of David Wallace, 1988. *Medieval Literary Theory and Criticism c.1100–c.1375: The Commentary Tradition*. Oxford: Oxford University Press.

Morris, Richard, ed. 1866. *Dan Michel's Ayenbite of Inwit, or Remorse of Conscience*. Early English Text Society 23. London: Trübner.

Spearing, A.C. 1976. *Medieval Dream Poetry*. Cambridge: Cambridge University Press.

Wogan-Browne, Jocelyn, Nicholas Watson, Andrew Taylor, and Ruth Evans, eds. 1999. *The Idea of the Vernacular: An Anthology of Middle English Literary Theory 1280–1520*. Exeter: University of Exeter Press.

Zeeman, Nicolette. 2002. "The Idol of the Text." In *Images, Idolatry, and Iconoclasm in Late Medieval England: Textuality and the Visual Image*, ed. Jeremy Dimmick, James Simpson, and Nicolette Zeeman, 43–62. Oxford: Oxford University Press.

Zeeman, Nicolette. 2006. *Piers Plowman and the Medieval Discourse of Desire*. Cambridge: Cambridge University Press.

Chapter 9

Queer Desire, Psychoanalytic Hermeneutics, and Love Lyric

Tim Dean

When, in an encounter between psychoanalysis and literary criticism, queer theory is added to the mix, the resulting *ménage à trois* risks becoming one of those situations in which the participants remain disturbingly aware that desire and attention are not distributed equally. Someone ends up feeling left out, even while ostensibly being included (group sex fails when a couple emerges). In order not to make literature serve an exclusively subordinate role, as exemplar or illustration, in the conceptual encounter between psychoanalysis and queer theory, I want to begin by considering some lines from a poem. The lyric is spoken in the voice of serial killer Jeffrey Dahmer:

> Oh do not leave me now.
> All that I ever wanted is compressed
> In your sole body. As you turn to go
> I know that I must keep you, and know how,
> For I must hold the ribbed arch of your chest
> And taste your boyish glow.
>
> (Gunn 2000, 85)

This is the opening stanza of Thom Gunn's "Hitch-hiker," the first in a sequence of five poems titled "Troubadour," which bears the dedication,

A Concise Companion to Psychoanalysis, Literature, and Culture, First Edition.
Edited by Laura Marcus and Ankhi Mukherjee.

"songs for Jeffrey Dahmer." Here the conventional sentiments of love poetry – the desire to possess, even "taste," the beloved – are darkened irremediably by our knowledge that the serial killer ate several of his victims. Shortly after his arrest, in July 1991, Dahmer confessed to killing seventeen young men and boys, most of whom he had sex with (pre- and post-mortem), all of whom he dismembered, and several of whose body parts he consumed. His first victim was a hitch-hiker named Stephen Hicks, whom Dahmer killed, in 1978, when he was just 18 years old.

Doubtless the desire to incorporate the beloved through cannibalism invites a psychoanalytic interpretation. Yet what is striking about "Hitch-hiker" is how the poet couches Dahmer's desire in the language of longing and adoration ("All that I ever wanted is compressed / In your sole body"), rather than in terms of sickness or dysfunction. If it is not only Dahmer's heinous acts but his *desire* that should be understood as pathological, then by framing that desire in the language of Elizabethan love poetry Gunn suggests that our culturally valorized notion of romantic love may be fundamentally flawed. And by speaking this love lyric in a serial killer's voice, he asks us to see how it is not just Dahmer but amatory desire itself that, in its impulse to possess the beloved, is prone to pathology.

In this way, "Troubadour" enters the hermeneutic contest over Dahmer's psychology and his motives for killing – a contest in which forms of psychoanalytic interpretation and queer sexuality have been central. Since, as Martha Schmidt (1994, 82) observes, "in the mainstream press, his crimes were immediately defined as specifically gay crimes," the public attempt to comprehend Dahmer influenced how gay male sexuality was understood during the decade in which queer theory and politics emerged. The early 1990s was the time when queer theory exploded onto the academic scene, coming out of deconstruction, AIDS activism, and women-of-color feminism; it was also the moment when figures such as Dahmer were being invoked in debates about the social status of homosexuality. Looking back on the controversies surrounding Dahmer and queerness two decades later, I would like to use Gunn's "Troubadour" to help think through the stakes of articulating psychoanalysis with queer theory for the purpose of interpreting erotic desire. I want to follow Gunn in characterizing Dahmer's desire as not aberrant but typical or conventional. The excessiveness of erotic desire pictured in "Troubadour" – "my desire to own the elusive one / I have not even possessed" (Gunn 2000, 85) – is both irrational and yet a recurrent feature of human wanting. We might say that, from a psychoanalytic perspective, what is normative for erotic desire (whether gay, straight, or queer) is for it to appear as non-normative or constitutively excessive. It is normal for sexual desire to seem crazy.

This apparently paradoxical formulation provides an opportunity to clarify a distinction that is central to queer theory. What Michael Warner (1999) calls "the trouble with normal" refers to the two different senses – statistical and evaluative – in which "normal" has functioned since the nineteenth century. The Victorian passion for classification, tabulation, and statistics led to a widespread preoccupation with mathematical norms or statistical averages derived from large populations. The trouble comes when these statistical norms are confused with evaluative or moral norms, that is, when being statistically normal becomes a positive ideal. There is no necessary reason that the statistically average should be regarded as morally desirable, yet this is the direction in which social normalization has been pushing western societies for more than a century. Georges Canguilhem (1991), the French historian of medicine who influenced Foucault, demonstrated as early as the 1940s that variation from the norms of human biology need not imply pathology. Owing to the medical conflation of statistical with evaluative norms, however, "normal" has become something that it is considered imperative to be – especially in the realm of sexuality.

Queer theory follows Canguilhem in its claim that falling outside the pale of the normal need not render one thereby pathological. You may not be normal, in the sense of typical or statistically average, but that does not make you necessarily deviant or sick. There are options beyond the normal–pathological binary; indeed, *queer* emerges as a strategic alternative to this medicalizing perspective on sexuality. A queer approach to sex reminds us that, if anything, *variation is the norm* – variation in the gender and number of partners, variation in the kind of acts preferred, variation in the context in which any erotic act may be performed, variation in its frequency. These variations occur not only among different people and cultures but also over the lifespan of an individual. And yet in spite of our knowledge about the variety of sex, we tend to believe that there remains an ideal template, a desirable norm, for consensual erotic activity. The strength of our individual preferences inculcates a conviction that we know what sex is and should be, when in fact there is no best way of having sex, no ideal form it should take (see Rubin 1984). Nevertheless, the further someone's activities or fantasies depart from erotic ideals, the more she worries about sexual pathology. We subject our own desires to interpretation in the name of normalization. What does it mean that I think about doing *that*? Is my desire normal?

The fascination elicited by Dahmer's case has a similar source. What does it mean that he wished to sexually possess his male partners, even to the point of killing, dismembering, and consuming them? How should we interpret his desire in light of his acts – and, more important, how can we differentiate his erotic desire from our own? Are queer theorists claiming that Dahmer is somehow normal or his behavior acceptable? This last question is easily answered in the negative. Yet a queer perspective, such as Gunn gives us in "Troubadour," complicates that easy answer by disentangling Dahmer's desire from his acts, rather than simply seeing the latter as an inevitable expression of the former. What Gunn's poems in the serial killer's voice suggest is that, although his acts were beyond-the-pale abhorrent, his desires may be recognizably familiar when read in light of the western lyric tradition. To disarticulate his desire from his acts makes Dahmer less reassuringly alien – but perhaps more interesting.

I will return to this feature of the Dahmer poems, but first I want to elaborate the significance of the distinction between desire and sexual acts. Queer theory draws inspiration from Michel Foucault's challenge to the commonsense view that regards action as expressing psychological identity by way of the mediation of desire. Foucault (1978) showed how normalization works by interpreting discrete acts as the signs of desire that betray identity. You do certain things because of the *kind* of person you are. Taking homosexuality as his example, Foucault characterized the transformation of acts into identity thus:

> As defined by the ancient civil or canonical codes, sodomy was a category of forbidden acts; their perpetrator was nothing more than the juridical subject of them. The nineteenth-century homosexual became a personage, a past, a case history, and a childhood, in addition to being a type of life, a life form, and a morphology. ... Nothing that went into his total composition was unaffected by his sexuality. It was everywhere present in him: at the root of all his actions because it was their insidious and indefinitely active principle. ... It was consubstantial with him, less as a habitual sin than as a singular nature. We must not forget that the psychological, psychiatric, medical category of homosexuality was constituted from the moment it was characterized. ... The sodomite had been a temporary aberration; the homosexual was now a species.
>
> (Foucault 1978, 43)

Previously regarded as "a temporary aberration" in which anyone might indulge, same-sex erotic acts became, in the nineteenth century, signs of a new kind of person, the homosexual. Foucault claims that the idea of sexual identity is not just relatively recent but also, more significantly, that it comes into existence as part of a broader project of normalization. Interpreting homosexuals as "a species" makes them easier to locate, tabulate, and control. The crucial point here – one that has been made also by psychoanalysis – is that sexual identity is a normalizing concept.

On the question of sexual identity, psychoanalysis and queer theory have more in common than typically is supposed. Anglo-American interpreters of Foucault tend to conflate his critical remarks about the normalizing effects of psychology and psychiatry (apparent in the passage above) with a general indictment of psychoanalysis – although Foucault was always careful to differentiate the latter from the disciplinary practices of both psychiatry and psychology. By medicalizing sexuality, psychiatry treats it from the vantage point of expertise, whereas Freud insisted that the unconscious turns the expert into a layperson (Freud 1957 [1910], 12). The expert is the one who approaches sexuality diagnostically, classifying it as normal or pathological; the unconscious casts doubt on the very notion of the normal. And whereas psychology takes for granted the reality of individual sexual identities, psychoanalysis emphasizes all the ways in which unconscious mental life undoes identity. Paying attention to unconscious desire enables one to appreciate social and subjective identities as so many chimera of consciousness.

From a psychoanalytic perspective, identity represents a ruse of the imaginary, an illusion of the ego. Identity has little to do with sexual preference and everything to do with ego preference, that is, how I like to imagine myself. Psychoanalytically, the very notion of "sexual identity" is a contradiction in terms – albeit one we seem reluctant to dispel. I'm describing identities as illusory, not merely constructed, because the human ego is formed through a process of misrecognition that creates something bounded and whole from what actually is fragmentary and uncoordinated (Lacan 1988). We love our identities because we love the illusion of mastery they confer over the chaos of experience. My ego reassures me that *I'm not like that*; it erects a wall of difference and thereby severs connections with what surrounds me. Rather than initiating connections, group identity simply reinforces the perception of difference by extending imaginary identification to others who may be misrecognized as sufficiently like me. This kind of imaginary identification, part and parcel of basic ego formation, unleashes murderous aggressivity whenever the artificial boundaries of identity are challenged. We cannot rely on the ego as a basis for either ethics or emancipatory politics.

Queer theory, even when not psychoanalytically informed, shares this skepticism about identity. The skepticism has multiple sources, both conceptual and political. As I've suggested, Foucault regards sexual identities as crucial components of the apparatus of normalization, even when those identities are taken up as points of resistance. Queer politics is less about diversifying sexual identities than about resisting normalization, of which proliferating identities are a symptom. At its debut, circa 1990, queer theory combined a Foucauldian critique of normalization with a deconstructive critique of identity by way of the Derridean principle of repetition-with-a-difference. Sexual and gender identities would be destabilized by revealing their dependence on citation, repetition, and performativity (Butler 1990).

At the same time as critics such as Judith Butler were staging these theoretical maneuvers, debates within feminism increasingly revealed the disunity and fractured nature of the category of woman. Feminist identity politics were challenged by women of color, particularly by the intersectional argument put forth by legal scholar Kimberlé Crenshaw (1991), who argued that racial discrimination is inseparable from sexual discrimination – and therefore that they need to be thought about together rather than separately. The intersectionality approach, hugely influential in the development of "queer of color" critique in the twenty-first century, would likely direct attention to the fact that many (though not all) of Dahmer's victims were non-white and were selected because, as socially undervalued, they were less likely to be missed. There may be a racial as well as a sexual component to Dahmer's desire. The drawback to "queer of color" critique, however, lies in how it often seems intent on reinstating racialized identities and hierarchies, even as intersectionality constitutes an ostensible critique of identity. For some of its practitioners in the United States, you must be recognizable as non-white to qualify as authentically queer and properly political.

The trouble with queer politics is that it perpetually risks degenerating into another version of the identity politics that it was invented to outwit. It is for this reason that the pernicious notion of "queer identities" must be strenuously resisted; pluralizing identity does nothing to alter how identities are structured or the defensive aggressivity with which they operate. The critical force of queerness dissipates as soon as it resolves itself into identity formations, including group identities. There are no queer egos, only queer desires and practices. This claim is Foucauldian, insofar as it emphasizes how practices offer the potential for disentangling action from identity. However, the claim is also psychoanalytic, insofar as it suggests that erotic desire is less an expression of identity than a departure from it. Since the question of desire, so central to this chapter, remains a point of contention between Foucault and psychoanalysis, it is worth examining more closely what different thinkers mean by this apparently self-evident term.

In her first book, *Subjects of Desire*, Butler elaborates a theory of desire out of Hegelian dialectics. Here desire is above all the desire for recognition: master and slave are joined in their struggle for recognition by the other; without the other neither can exist (Butler 1987). Although Butler and, following her, a large swathe of sex/gender theory understands desire in these terms, as constituted through an other, we might note that the dialectic thus pictured should be characterized as imaginary. What Hegel's master–slave dialectic offers is a philosophical account of the formation of the ego; identities constituted through an imaginary other are no different from any identity. Demonstrating that an identity category depends on what it excludes does not get criticism or politics beyond the vectors of the imaginary domain (Dean 2000, 174–214).

By contrast, what Lacan offers the present discussion is an account of desire as unconscious. According to this alternative account, human desire is constituted through the displacements of language and the real (*real* as a term for the blockages in language), not through imaginary recognition. Whether or not one concedes that Butler has misunderstood psychoanalysis at a fundamental level, nevertheless we need to register that the Lacanian account of desire contradicts hers. The advantage of the psychoanalytic description of desire, conceptually and politically speaking, is that it renders desire as definitively unmasterable. Forever in excess of the ego, desire runs counter to identity. That is what I meant by characterizing the notion of sexual identity as a contradiction in terms.

Since it is crucial for sexual politics to move beyond the futile project of acknowledging every identity in its particularity, I want to clarify further what the alternative understanding of desire entails. For Lacan, desire is defined not by its content but by the way it detours a human body's needs through the alien register of signs and symbols. "Desire is neither the appetite for satisfaction, nor the demand for love, but the difference that results from the subtraction of the first from the second, the phenomenon of their splitting," he claims (Lacan 1977, 287). Desire remains an eternal problem because, as the surplus of articulated demand over bodily need, it comes into existence as excess. Since by definition nothing can satisfy it, desire cannot be said to have a "proper" object. Human sexuality, divorced from nature by linguistic mediation, does not have heterosexual reproduction as its model. Indeed, if erotic desire is constitutively excessive, then it makes little sense to divide its manifestations into normal and pathological (this is another way in which psychoanalysis departs from psychiatry). We might even say that, by contrast with animal instinct, human desire is born queer.

Yet this psychoanalytic account remains at odds with Foucault's understanding of desire. The simplest way of characterizing the difference would be to say that whereas for Lacan desire is de-individuating, for Foucault it represents precisely a principle of individuation. Viewing desire as unconscious, incompletely comprehended by the ego, Lacan treats desire as an unconquerable excess that decenters selfhood. By contrast, Foucault argues that the interpretation of desire has been constituted historically as the key to selfhood and identity. As he once ventriloquized it in an interview, "Tell me what your desire is, and I'll tell you who you are" (Foucault 2011, 389). The problem is that desire has become an index of subjective truth; and psychoanalysis, no matter its skepticism about normalization and identity, has played a significant role in the long historical process whereby desire and truth have been knotted together. Once desire becomes indexical, the business of hermeneutics starts booming. We are all in need of codes for deciphering desire's secret meanings, because now we not only desire specific objects but also *desire to interpret desire*.

Foucault's skepticism vis-à-vis the category of desire thus stems from his tracing techniques of normalization back to what he calls the hermeneutics of the self. The connection between normalization and hermeneutics is essentially what the three volumes of his *History of Sexuality* endeavor to chart and explain. In the final decade of his life, Foucault became preoccupied by how normalizing diagnoses that interpret the truth of our desires are not simply external impositions, something that institutions do to us; such diagnoses are also something that we do to ourselves. I subject my own desires to interpretation in order to ascertain who I am and whether or not I'm normal.

The significance of Foucault's critique for our purposes here concerns how psychoanalysis and literary criticism are both hermeneutic practices, systems of interpretation. Although the former interprets subjectivity while the latter interprets literary texts, nevertheless both psychoanalysis and literary criticism decipher meaning through images, symbols, and metaphors; both depend fundamentally on language and its ruses. This, after all, is why psychoanalysis has such a rich history of employment in literary criticism, a history that reaches back to Freud's own discussions of literary works and aesthetic artifacts.[1] If we were not creatures of language, enmeshed in semiotic networks, we would have no need for hermeneutic systems. What Foucault makes clear, by focusing on the power relations within which interpretation assumes its historical importance, are the politics and ethics of the hermeneutics of the self. And what queer theory takes from this is the critical insight that modern hermeneutics, far from operating neutrally, tends to function in the service of normalization by construing heterosexuality as the paradigm through which everything makes sense. *Heteronormativity* is the name for this broad interpretive framework.

A good example of heteronormativity in action would be the tendency to assume, when discussing Shakespeare's Sonnet 18, for instance, that the love lyric is addressed from a man to a woman: "Shall I compare thee to a summer's day? / Thou art more lovely and more temperate," and so on (Shakespeare 2002, 417). Although Shakespeare scholars agree that this sonnet is one of many addressed to the "fair youth" or young man, most non-experts who encounter this poem in isolation, outside the context of Shakespeare's sonnet sequence, invariably take it to exemplify heterosexual love. Since there are no gendered pronouns in the poem, that assumption is heteronormative: it assumes that love lyric, especially when undertaken by canonical poets, is paradigmatically heterosexual. The force of that assumption is illustrated by how tough it can be to get undergraduates to use the masculine pronoun "he" when referring to the poem's addressee, even after they've learned about the role of the "fair youth" in the sonnet sequence.

The flip side of the heteronormative hermeneutic consists in a tendency to assume that if this poem's addressee is male, then Shakespeare must be gay. Although the proposition sounds somewhat sacrilegious ("Shakespeare was *what*?"), it is also reassuring because it keeps sexuality confined within familiar categories of intelligibility. Desire stays safe as long as we can interpret it in terms of identity. Yet, rather than attempting to diagnose the historically distant figure of Shakespeare through modern sexual categories, we might instead register how there is something queerly indecipherable about his famous sonnet sequence.

Critic Joel Fineman (1986) argues, in what after a quarter-century remains the best psychoanalytic reading of the sonnets, that through these poems Shakespeare invented a fractured poetic speaker whose ambiguous doubleness subsequently became the paradigm of literary subjectivity. Although Fineman was writing before queer theory existed as such, his thesis underscores how, at this crucial moment in the history of English love lyric, amatory desire is being formulated in something other than straightforwardly heterosexual terms (see also Sedgwick 1985, 28–48).

This context helps to illuminate what Gunn is doing in "Troubadour" by vocalizing Dahmer's desire through Elizabethan poetic conventions.[2] It is less that Gunn is "queering" the conventions of love lyric than that he's bringing out what is already queer in them. Dahmer is perfect for this endeavor not because he was gay but because his desire was so extreme, his relation to the beloved so vividly excessive. And "Troubadour" is perfect for my purposes because the sequence takes as its subject a figure whom no right-thinking homosexual would want to claim as his own. It is easy enough to discuss queer theory and literary criticism by focusing on Shakespeare, with his enormous cultural prestige, but much more challenging to take an example such as Dahmer, with whom nobody wishes to identify. Queer criticism is at its most powerful not when discussing the good gay poets or showing how hip and transgressive the bad ones really are, but instead when its interpretive politics no longer rely on our sympathy or the possibility of identification. It is because there are no viable terms, whether political or literary, through which Dahmer can be redeemed that Gunn's poetic sequence is so remarkable.

Various critics have discussed how Dahmer was figured as a monster (Tithecott 1997; Schmid 2005, 220–29). The nature of his crimes – their combining butchery with same-sex necrophilia and cannibalism – made him appear inhuman. His sexual activity, violating human law and natural law alike, rendered him monstrous; uncivilized, he was not even a savage. As Arnold I. Davidson (2002, 97) points out in his study of the role of monstrosity in the history of sexuality, monsters solicit interpretation because it is believed that their existence has a rationality that can be decoded and explained. The hermeneutic principle employed to explain Dahmer was his sexuality. Since he appeared sufficiently presentable to seduce his victims in gay bars, his actions contaminated the gay community's image in Milwaukee, Wisconsin, after his arrest there (Schmidt 1994). His monstrosity rubbed off. During the 1990s, gay men – and particularly their pursuit of casual, anonymous sex – increasingly were regarded as fundamentally deviant, if not outright monstrous, by association with Dahmer. It was as if he'd butchered not only a series of male lovers but the gay rights movement itself. Unsurprisingly, gays (and many lesbians) reacted to the media construction of the serial killer as gay by defining themselves in opposition less to heterosexuals than to Dahmer. He offered a ubiquitous image against which to shore up one's ego ("I may be queer but at least I'm not like that").

If Dahmer was toxic to gay identity, this was all the more so because his monstrosity was not easily detectable. Sociologist Martha Schmidt quotes a gay social worker she interviewed in Milwaukee after Dahmer's arrest:

> People try to place all this as out of the ordinary. How could this monster be roaming the streets? I mean he wasn't some hunchback of Notre Dame, snatching people away. He was just a regular normal looking guy who blended into the community. That's what makes it so terrifying.
>
> (quoted in Schmidt 1994, 93)

Dahmer passed as virtually normal; as undetectable, he appeared even more disturbing. Since we prefer our serial killers, like our homosexuals, to be readily identifiable, our fear of them is often greater when they resist the culture's standard hermeneutic schemes. As "a regular normal looking guy who blended into the community," Dahmer was terrifying less because he could get me than because he could, in fact, *be* me (who doesn't know what it feels like to want to "taste [a] boyish glow"?). If Dahmer's sexuality made him seem monstrous, then his normal appearance threatened to make that monstrosity contagious.

It is not difficult to grasp how Dahmer, dramatizing the fatality of gay sex, would intensify public terror surrounding "that other serial killer, AIDS" (Hirsch 1996, 453). Indeed, he quickly came to symbolize the phobic idea that sex between men is deadly. Given Dahmer's symbolic association with the epidemic, it is perhaps unsurprising that Thom Gunn, widely considered a pre-eminent poet of AIDS after his book *The Man with Night Sweats* (1992), would take the serial killer as a poetic subject. In this context, we might recall also that the politics of AIDS was central to the emergence of queer theory, insofar as the epidemic demonstrated the necessity of forging alliances across identity lines. AIDS activists, countering its misrecognition as a gay disease, emphasized that HIV does not discriminate on the basis of identity categories. Further, they developed a coalitional politics among the groups most affected by the disease – a politics that brought gay men into closer cooperation with other stigmatized constituencies than previously had been the case. By thus helping to render obsolescent the identity-based activism of earlier decades, AIDS was instrumental in producing a specifically queer consciousness.

This historical synopsis, in addition to elaborating the conditions under which queer theory appeared on the academic scene in the 1990s, deepens our appreciation of the Dahmer poems. If, in *The Man with Night Sweats*, Gunn memorialized a generation of men dead from AIDS, in "Troubadour" he goes a step further by bringing Dahmer back into the fold of the human. He shows how the deeply stigmatized and socially dead may be given symbolic life via the preservative power of poetry – a power that depends less on the prowess of the individual poet than on the longevity of literary forms and conventions. Rather than "othering" Dahmer as monstrous, which keeps him at a safe distance, Gunn brings Dahmer closer by allowing him to inhabit the lyric "I" and then couching his voice in the idioms of a distinguished poetic tradition.

This vocal strategy has a double effect: on the one hand, it brings Dahmer closer by stressing his common humanity, while on the other, it lends his voice the impersonal distance of a tradition that is centuries old. That distance is one of historical time but also of thwarted intimacy; as Gunn remarks elsewhere, "Love poetry started as the fantasies of troubadours, who by definition had to love at a distance" (Gunn 1985, 166). Medieval lyricists who sang in Provençal, troubadours were itinerant poets – hitch-hikers of a sort – whose poems of courtly love praised the inaccessible, impossibly idealized lady of chivalric fantasy. (The conventions of courtly love are central to the ambiguous praise that characterizes Shakespeare's sonnets, too.) Gunn's "Troubadour," in turn, pictures Dahmer endeavoring to overcome the distance between him and his idealized love objects through the extreme measure of cannibalistic incorporation.

The sequence's recurring metaphors of hunger and consumption make clear that Gunn is not glossing over the horror of Dahmer's crimes. Yet, by situating him in the love lyric tradition, he's suggesting that Dahmer's desire, far from being monstrous, may be familiar. It is precisely the excessiveness of his desire that makes him human; or, to put it another way, the inhuman dimension of Dahmer's desire is not his alone. My claim is that Gunn is doing something that is at once psychoanalytic and profoundly ethical, in the sense that psychoanalysis brings queerness into the realm of the human by redefining, through its concept of the unconscious, what the human is. Gunn's ethics lies in his making it that much harder – in the terms of one queer meditation on Dahmer – "to disavow kinship with monstrosity" (Hirsch 1996, 463). Through poetic means he counters the repudiation of Dahmer without rendering him as a figure of emulation or sympathy. The poet brings us into intimate relation with the serial killer, depathologizing his desire while yet refusing to normalize him through identification.

The distinction I'm trying to make here, by articulating queer theory with psychoanalysis, hinges upon the difference between an imaginary politics of identification and an impersonal ethics of formal similitude. I want to be clear that, even as Gunn gives Dahmer the lyric "I" for an entire poetic sequence, "Troubadour" is not proposing the serial killer as a queer role model. There is no politics derivable from Dahmer's transgressions. There is, however, an ethics to be found in acknowledging how his monstrosity remains cognate with our own. "A Borrowed Man," the fourth poem in Gunn's sequence, dramatizes the formal similitudes underlying that kinship. The dark irony of this poem's title – Dahmer did not "borrow" men, he took them for keeps – points to the role of dismemberment in both the serial killer's desire and the courtly love tradition, where the poetic device of the blazon composes an ideal beloved by listing her or his various parts. Here the speaker conjures his beloved, his "borrowed man," piece by piece:

> I beg from memory each limb,
> Each body-part that spoiled with time:
> The sidelong hungry look of him,
> From him a stammer, from another
> A single blue bicep with Mother,
> From one a scalp, with hair's regalia,
> From one large hands and lazy grin,
> From someone reddened genitalia,
> And last the image of the chest
> From my original conquest.
>
> (Gunn 2000, 89)

Mutability remains a deep theme of lyric because time's passing destroys beauty and hence the source of love. Here, however, time ruins the beloved in the more literal form of putrefying flesh ("Each body-part that spoiled with time"). That macabre literalization of a well-worn poetic theme is counterbalanced by Gunn's cataloging the less tangible components of Dahmer's men – "the sidelong hungry look," "a stammer," a "lazy grin." It is hard to know how one might cannibalize a stammer.

As in any poetic blazon, many of the desirable components are utterly conventional (the tattooed bicep, the large hands, the well-worked genitalia), not least because the conventionality of the device itself is what poets since Shakespeare have been foregrounding, all the better to ironize it. If the blazon device had become a cliché as early as the sixteenth century, then Gunn vivifies it by emphasizing its reliance on not only dismemberment but also seriality. We have here a series of body parts collated from a series of lovers, all of whom became victims of a serial killer who now is the subject of a series of poems. The blazon of "A Borrowed Man" thus suggests formal resemblances, based on seriality, between cannibal killer and love poet. Indeed, insofar as he or she cuts and consumes fragments from other textual bodies, every poet participates in cannibalism to some degree. Putting the matter in this way helps to clarify how the resemblances are formal rather than psychological: here similitude depends not on imaginary identification but on the formal kinship of seriality.

Seriality challenges the closure of identity by holding open the prospect of additional parts. If there is always the possibility of more, then excess has become the condition of desire. By virtue of its tendency toward fragmentation and excess, erotic desire represents less the fulfillment of imaginary wholeness than its undoing. What Gunn provides in "Troubadour" is an extreme example of how human desire works. To the extent that Dahmer is exemplary rather than aberrant, his is not an example we are meant to follow. If desire threatens the ego's illusion of imaginary integrity (along with its ideological correlates), then Gunn's poetic sequence challenges also our illusions about desire itself.

Acknowledgments

Thanks to Joe Aldinger, Carrie Bramen, Victoria Brockmeier, Sarah Maguire, Steven Ruszczycky, David Schmid, and Ramón Soto-Crespo for help of various kinds with this essay.

Notes

1 Restrictions on space prevent me from pursuing the significant ways in which psychoanalysis, thanks to its method of free association, also resists hermeneutic schemes (see Laplanche 1996). I have discussed elsewhere (Dean 2002) the anti-hermeneutic ethic of French psychoanalysis.

2 Although various sonnets play on the multiple meanings of "strain," the Shakespearean text that Gunn alludes to most directly in "Hitch-hiker" is *Twelfth Night*, since the closing lines of his poem –

> The strain of feeling loss, but after these
> Strain of the full possession once again
> That has a dying fall.
> (Gunn 2000, 86)

– conjure the opening lines of Shakespeare's play:

> If music be the food of love, play on;
> Give me excess of it, that, surfeiting,
> The appetite may sicken, and so die.
> That strain again! it had a dying fall.
> (Act I, scene i, lines 1–4)

Layering allusions, Gunn situates his lyric speaker in a Shakespearean tradition rather than a deviant one.

References

Butler, Judith. 1987. *Subjects of Desire: Hegelian Reflections in Twentieth-Century France*. New York: Columbia University Press.

Butler, Judith. 1990. *Gender Trouble: Feminism and the Subversion of Identity*. New York: Routledge.

Canguilhem, Georges. 1991. *The Normal and the Pathological*, trans. Carolyn R. Fawcett. New York: Zone Books.

Crenshaw, Kimberlé. 1991. "Mapping the Margins: Intersectionality, Identity Politics, and Violence against Women of Color." *Stanford Law Review*, 43: 1241–99.

Davidson, Arnold I. 2002. "The Horror of Monsters." In *The Emergence of Sexuality: Historical Epistemology and the Formation of Concepts*, 93–124. Cambridge, MA: Harvard University Press.

Dean, Tim. 2000. *Beyond Sexuality*. Chicago: University of Chicago Press.

Dean, Tim. 2002. "Art as Symptom: Žižek and the Ethics of Psychoanalytic Criticism." *Diacritics*, 32: 21–41.

Fineman, Joel. 1986. *Shakespeare's Perjur'd Eye: The Invention of Poetic Subjectivity in the Sonnets*. Berkeley: University of California Press.

Foucault, Michel. 1978. *The History of Sexuality*, vol. 1: *An Introduction*, trans. Robert Hurley. New York: Random House.

Foucault, Michel. 2011. "The Gay Science," trans. Nicolae Morar and Daniel W. Smith. *Critical Inquiry*, 37: 385–403.

Freud, Sigmund. 1957 [1910]. "Five Lectures on Psycho-Analysis." In *The Standard Edition of the Complete Psychological Works of Sigmund Freud*, 24 vols., ed. James Strachey, with the assistance of Anna Freud,

Alix Strachey, and Alan Tyson, trans. James Strachey, vol. 11, 1–55. London: Hogarth Press.

Gunn, Thom. 1985. *The Occasions of Poetry: Essays in Criticism and Autobiography*. San Francisco: North Point Press.

Gunn, Thom. 1992. *The Man with Night Sweats*. New York: Farrar, Straus & Giroux.

Gunn, Thom. 2000. *Boss Cupid*. New York: Farrar, Straus & Giroux.

Hirsch, David A.H. 1996. "Dahmer's Effects: Gay Serial Killer Goes to Market." In *Disciplinarity and Dissent in Cultural Studies*, ed. Cary Nelson and Dilip Parameshwar Gaonkar, 441–72. New York: Routledge.

Lacan, Jacques. 1977. "The Signification of the Phallus." In *Écrits: A Selection*, trans. Alan Sheridan, 281–91. New York: Norton.

Lacan, Jacques. 1988. *The Seminar of Jacques Lacan*, Book II: *The Ego in Freud's Theory and in the Technique of Psychoanalysis, 1954–1955*, ed. Jacques-Alain Miller, trans. Sylvana Tomaselli. Cambridge: Cambridge University Press.

Laplanche, Jean. 1996. "Psychoanalysis as Anti-Hermeneutics." *Radical Philosophy*, 79: 7–12.

Rubin, Gayle. 1984. "Thinking Sex: Notes for a Radical Theory of the Politics of Sexuality." In *Pleasure and Danger: Exploring Female Sexuality*, ed. Carole S. Vance, 267–319. London: Routledge.

Schmid, David. 2005. *Natural Born Celebrities: Serial Killers in American Culture*. Chicago: University of Chicago Press.

Schmidt, Martha A. 1994. "Dahmer Discourse and Gay Identity: The Paradox of Queer Politics." *Critical Sociology*, 20: 81–105.

Sedgwick, Eve Kosofsky. 1985. *Between Men: English Literature and Male Homosocial Desire*. New York: Columbia University Press.

Shakespeare, William. 1994. *Twelfth Night, or What You Will*, ed. Robert Warren and Stanley Wells. Oxford: Oxford University Press.

Shakespeare, William. 2002. *Complete Sonnets and Poems*, ed. Colin Burrow. Oxford: Oxford University Press.

Tithecott, Richard. 1997. *Of Men and Monsters: Jeffrey Dahmer and the Construction of the Serial Killer*. Madison: University of Wisconsin Press.

Warner, Michael. 1999. *The Trouble with Normal: Sex, Politics, and the Ethics of Queer Life*. New York: Free Press.

Chapter 10

Psychoanalysis, Literature, and the "Case" of Adolescence

Pamela Thurschwell

> The school must never forget that it has to deal with immature individuals who cannot be denied a right to linger at certain stages of development and even at certain disagreeable ones. The school must not take on itself the inexorable character of life: it must not seek to be more than a *game* of life.
>
> Freud, "Contributions to a Discussion on Suicide"

Any parent will tell you that adolescence is a difficult time but it is also a difficult *time*. Adolescent temporality is oddly constructed. Our modern view of the adolescent has been created by holding together two opposing understandings of temporality: on the one hand, adolescence is usually seen as a passing phase, a few brief moments in time on the trajectory from childhood to adulthood. On the other hand, at the end of the nineteenth century and the beginning of the twentieth the adolescent is also being redefined as a "case" and as an identity, as a specific locus for concerns about the potential criminality, waywardness, or deviance that accompany the insecure and inviting lagtime between childhood and adulthood (before taking that apparently logical next step into economic productivity and sexual reproduction) (Chinn 2009; DeLuzio 2007; Gilbert 2004).

A Concise Companion to Psychoanalysis, Literature, and Culture, First Edition.
Edited by Laura Marcus and Ankhi Mukherjee.

At the beginning of the twentieth century adolescence as an identity is more often assigned and defined by others (in a Foucauldian disciplinary fashion).[1] But by the middle and end of the century, because of the increasing economic autonomy and cultural significance of adolescents, adolescence comes to be a chosen, often idealized time of life. As the twentieth century progresses that "phase" will be filled by definite markers of shared identity: subcultural styles, music, clothing, etc. – all contributing to the birth of the marketing phenomenon and identity, the teenager (Savage 2008). But the tension between adolescence as phase and adolescence as identity (whether that identity is seen as full of social promise, or social menace, or both) remains. In this essay I want to ask what happens when we try to conceive of adolescence as a "case," especially when that word "case" proliferates its meanings, to encompass both a case of measles and a case history.[2] Is adolescence something you catch, or something you are? If the symptoms of adolescence are a part of a case history, will the cure inevitably involve the injunction to grow out of it, and leave those symptoms behind?

My evoking of adolescence as a "case" here owes a debt to Foucault's oft-cited formulation about the consolidation of homosexual identity at the end of the nineteenth century. In his words, "The nineteenth-century homosexual became a personage, a past, a case history and a childhood" (Foucault 1990, 43). Might the adolescent too fit aspects of Foucault's description? There have been abundant medical, historical, and theoretical connections made between adolescence and homosexuality, most of which uncomfortably posit a youthful homosexuality as a "stage along the way" to adult heterosexuality, either for the individual or the species.[3] Early sexologists used the terminology of nineteenth-century racial science to posit "inverts" as evolutionary throwbacks (Somerville 2000), while homosexuality has also often been figured as an "adolescent" sexuality, the realm of schoolboy and schoolgirl crushes and furtive first sexual experiences with classmates. Homosexual desire has been consistently portrayed as a stage that one grows out of eventually on the "correct" trajectory towards adult procreative heterosexuality. For psychoanalysis, for instance, if one does not abandon one's early homosexuality, one has not negotiated the Oedipus crisis successfully and remains mired in an infantile narcissism. Queer theorists and feminist critics have analyzed this version of the straitjacket, straight Freud who posits homosexuality as a learner's sexuality (Warner 1990). Other critics have emphasized the ways in which this Freud is always in tension with another Freud, the shadow

Freud of *The Three Essays on Sexuality* who dwells primarily in the footnotes, recognizing the waywardness of desire and the near-impossibility of achieving the normal, the Freud who recognizes that heterosexuality needs just as much of an explanation as homosexuality (Davidson 1987). But this attractive "modern" Freud usually has been seen to give way to the more normalizing and narrativizing one, the familiar, teleological Freud who sends us toward the procreative sexual act, the sexual climax, and adulthood (Thurschwell 2009, 47–58).

Seen through this lens, adolescence, like homosexuality, turns on a problem of time and narrative. What kinds of narrative might allow us to dwell with the adolescent without too quickly hurrying him or her along to the next stage? My project in this essay both converges with, and differs from, the spate of recent work on queer temporality which has argued for specific queer resistances to the ways in which heteronormative teleologies or reproductive futurism are inescapably mapped on to time and history in the abstract.[4] In his polemical book, *No Future: Queer Theory and the Death Drive*, Lee Edelman argues that the figure of the child has taken on the weight of representing *the* future for western culture, and not just any future, but a future that cannot be argued with – a hopeful future, better than the present. He parodies this non-choice in the form of a question: "'We're fighting for the children. Whose side are you on?'" It appears as if there could be only one answer to this question but Edelman chooses the other. As he writes: "at the heart of my polemical engagement with the cultural text of politics and the politics of cultural texts lies a simple provocation: that queerness names the side of those not 'fighting for the children,' the side outside the consensus by which all politics confirms the absolute of reproductive futurism" (Edelman 2004, 3). Edelman argues that an unquestioning political goal such as the "good of the child" masquerades as a non-politics; that the shared cultural project of protecting the innocent and guaranteeing some sort of better future (a goal that reverberates for both the far right and the far left of liberal political discourse) relies on an assumed and unmarked heterosexual procreative futurity that erases queer alternatives. With such presuppositions, when we project the child into a heteronormative future, "we accept the teleology of the child (and, in a sense, narrative itself) as heterosexually determined" (2004, 3). Edelman instead embraces what has been a historically dangerous identification of homosexuality with the death drive: "queer theory, as I construe it, marks the 'other' side of politics; the 'side' where narrative realization and derealization overlap, where the energies of vitalization ceaselessly turn against themselves; the 'side' outside all political sides, committed as they are, on every side, to futurism's unquestioned good" (2004, 7).

I want to argue here, perhaps paradoxically, that adolescence as a stage of life (apparently always pointed toward the future), might also be capable of staging some of the same refusals that Edelman calls for; in other words, adolescence might be the developmental stage that just says no to development.[5] The very title of Edelman's book suggests to me that there is a significant term missing in his argument. For me, "No Future" rather than conjuring up children or queers, evokes a group of 19- and 20-year-old social outcasts who formed a band called the Sex Pistols that combined an all-encompassing political disaffection with adolescent rage.[6] They wrote a song called "God Save the Queen" with a chorus of "No Future" which they sang in such a way that it wasn't clear whether "No Future" was a threat or a promise, a hand they'd been unfairly dealt or a position they wanted to embrace, their own version of the death drive, in fact, but a death drive very clearly embedded in their historical and political moment.[7] Despite his title Edelman doesn't mention punk; his argument is about the uses of the child as figuring innocence and needing protection, the apparently universal, but really heteronormative requirement that we (adults) secure them (children) a future. But this neglect of that middle term, adolescence – especially the adolescent with his or her own politics, culture, and historical moment – seems like a strange aporia in Edelman's argument. Placed between the adult and the child, the adolescent too might harbor an ambivalent and potentially non-teleological relation to a time that he or she hasn't chosen, and to a future he or she might want to avoid (Bruhm and Hurley 2004). This is the case I want to make for adolescence in relation to psychoanalysis and literature, in what follows.

So what might it mean to be (or have) a "case" of adolescence? Foucault argues that it is the clinical sciences which make possible our modern notion of the case study:

> The examination, surrounded by all its documentary techniques, makes each individual a "case": a case which at one and the same time constitutes an object for a branch of knowledge and a hold for a branch of power. The case is no longer, as in casuistry or jurisprudence, a set of circumstances defining an act and capable of modifying the application of a rule; it is the individual as he may be described, judged, measured,

> compared with others, in his very individuality; and it is also the individual who has to be trained or corrected, classified, normalized, excluded, etc.
>
> (Foucault 1977, 191)

For the idea of "the case study" to have any force one must assume that the individual story can be exemplary while maintaining its uniqueness – the case study, as Foucault describes it, is in the service of the possibility of correction and normalization (if not for that particular "case" then for others who might look at it and know what not to do). The case study combines respect for the single instance, the unique individual who stands out from the herd as a "case," with an ideal of the knowledge of the generality that the case can provide. The problem with the adolescent as "case," as I've been indicating, is in part in how we might imagine the procedures for normalization or classification if the adolescent is not a set identity but a moving target: a chronology, a sexuality, a body, a set of desires and habits, in flux, moving through time responding to different narrative and cultural injunctions; on the one hand towards an imagined endpoint of adulthood, on another, perhaps away from it, towards maintaining an identity that is bound up in youth and ephemerality. With that in mind I want to look at two instances of normalization resisted – individuals who will not be trained or corrected, and whose very resistance serves to make them worthy of study as "cases."

I'll now turn to Freud's 1920 "The Psychogenesis of a Case of Homosexuality in a Woman" and Willa Cather's 1905 short story, "Paul's Case: A Study in Temperament." Neither of these works is usually thought of as being about adolescence per se, although both have been seen as significant interventions into early twentieth-century discourses on homosexuality. There are multiple structural similarities between the two works. The titles suggest that both protagonists should be viewed as medicalized "cases." (In the title of the Freud it is initially "homosexuality" that is the case, parallel to a case of measles, rather than the woman herself. But as this is one of Freud's case histories, about a case of homosexuality, "case" is used in both senses.) However, as we read through the text of each "case" we discover it's not precisely clear what the locus of the problem is; both works raise the question "What is this case a case of?"[8] To continue with my list of connections between the texts: in both narratives professional observers encounter a core of refusal and resistance emanating from the adolescents they attempt to define and discipline, and in both works there is a certain kind of narrative revulsion towards, or at least distrust of, the adolescent. In Cather's story, the narrative moves from a position of suspicion, disgust, and judgment to a position of guarded sympathy, whereas in Freud, if anything the movement is from sympathy to distrust and exasperation. This distrust of the adolescent goes along with, and is perhaps inspired by, a sneaking suspicion that the professional observers are being made to look foolish, are in fact less knowledgeable than the adolescent who is the subject of their scrutiny. Finally both works suggest a significant relationship between homosexuality and suicide only to refuse to speculate any further on the nature of that relationship.

I'd like to propose adolescence as a category, alongside the other categories such as homosexuality, gender, decadence, and modernism, that have been deployed to analyze these two texts. In what follows what I'll show to be specific to adolescence is a resistance to "adult" narrative teleologies, and a version of atemporality, a desire to live in a different relation to time from that which has been imposed.

Before I turn to readings of the two works I will briefly consider what kind of "case" adolescence has been for psychoanalysis. Queer and feminist psychoanalytic criticism has repeatedly discussed Freud's trouble with women and his trouble with homosexuality, the ways in which his historically blinkered perspective on to these two categories disturbs and up-ends his most generalizing formulations, such as the Oedipus complex, that are meant to explain the universal psychosexual development of a subject who, it turns out, is inevitably male and heterosexual. But what if Freud also has a separate and equally troubled relation to adolescence?

Childhood and infancy have always had a doubly privileged place in the history of the psychoanalytic movement. On the one hand, the child has been important as the potential subject of analysis (the problem of child analysis was brought to the fore in the heated debates between the followers of Anna Freud and Melanie Klein over the question of whether it was possible to analyze a child as one would an adult). On the other hand, less contentiously, the child has been important as the object of psychoanalysis (the crucial place of infancy and childhood as an originary point, as an object to be retrieved or constructed). So the child in analysis has been massively deliberated and debated, from "Little Hans" to the controversial discussions and beyond (Riley 1983; Rose 1993; Thurschwell 2012). The adolescent, by contrast, has been left relatively alone – although not totally alone, perhaps not as alone as it initially appears. In fact if we begin to look at the ages of some of Freud's crucial early patients who became his most important case histories, we can see we are in the world of late adolescence: "Dora" and "A Case of Female Homosexuality" deal with 18-year-olds; Katharina in *Studies on Hysteria* is around 18; and Breuer's patient Anna O. was 21 when her illness began. However, adolescence is not a category in which Freud is particularly interested in his discussions of these cases. While in practice he often treats adolescent patients, theoretically for Freud adolescence becomes a kind of excluded middle.[9]

Freud (1977) does, of course, discuss adolescence in the third section of his *Three Essays on Sexuality*, "Transformations of Puberty."[10] However despite the existence of this third essay, Freud seems not greatly interested in puberty. It's the shortest of the three essays and, I think most readers would agree, the least memorable, with subtitles, such as "After-Effects of Infantile Object Choice," that seem to give the game away, that Freud's real interest lies elsewhere. In fact the transformations of puberty are mostly just what the subtitle indicates, after-effects; re-enactings of infantile scenes and choices, a sort of half-hearted re-run of the original Oedipus crisis.

For Freud in this essay, adolescence is perhaps most significant as the moment when libido begins to diverge in relation to sexual difference. It is at that time "that the sharp distinction is established between masculine and feminine characters. From that time on, this contrast has a more decisive influence than any other upon the shaping of human life" (Freud 1977, 141). The major accomplishment of adolescence as Freud defines it, is the boy's; it is his finally detaching himself from the overwhelming Oedipal relation to his parents which allows him to enter into a wider culture:

> At the same time as these plain incestuous phantasies are overcome and repudiated, one of the most significant, but also one of the most painful, psychical achievements of the pubertal period is completed: detachment from parental authority, a process that alone makes possible the opposition, which is so important for the progress of civilization, between the new generation and the old.
>
> (Freud 1977, 150)

That "opposition" between new and old – which registers so starkly in the realm of literature and art, via the modernist rejection of antecedents – is pictured here as an adolescent achievement. Here for Freud, what is specific to adolescence is, for boys, a cultural achievement: the detachment from parental authority, the rebellion against the past which makes the new and forward-looking possible. For girls, the changes of adolescence are portrayed as primarily biological.[11]

Appropriately, given the opposition between old and young generations, when Sigmund's daughter Anna Freud returns to her father's work she implicitly criticizes his lack of attention to the specificity of adolescence. Anna Freud, unlike her father, worked directly with children and adolescents, and was keenly involved in the debates about whether, and how, children could be analyzed, whether pedagogy was necessary in the analysis of children, and how far they could enter transference. The problem of where adolescents and children fall on the scale – as subject or object of analysis – is germane. If adolescence, as a stage of development, is still waiting to be made interesting for analysis, then adolescents as potential patients are at the center of Anna Freud's work. Obviously concerned with the analysis of children and adolescents, she also needs to confront the legacy of her father's relative lack of interest in puberty. In her 1957 paper "Adolescence," Anna Freud attempts to make up for this lack of good psychoanalytic writing on adolescence.

In her paper she looks at the difficulties one encounters both in analyzing adolescents and in recovering memories from adolescence. Her model of the adolescent psyche is one that is at war with itself. The basic dynamic of the adolescent ego for Anna Freud seems to be a defensive battle between the childhood, relatively stable ego and superego, and the newly maturing and intrusive forms of the sexual drive. The old ego enters into a struggle for survival against the necessity for change (A. Freud 1969, 164–65). In adolescence, then, there is a sort of war on the ego, which puts up its own resistance to becoming adult.

Resistance is everywhere in the adolescent dynamic, but sometimes it is a resistance disguised as compliance. Adolescence is difficult to recover in analysis, Anna Freud observes, because adolescent memories, unlike infantile memories, seem to be too readily available. She writes:

> the memories of the events of the adolescent period are, normally, retained in consciousness and told to the analyst without apparent difficulty. Masturbation in preadolescence and adolescence, the first moves toward intercourse, etc., may even play a dominant part in the patients' conscious memories and, as we know well, are made use of to overlay and hide the repressed masturbation conflicts and the buried sexual activities of early childhood.
>
> (1969, 142–43)

The problem here seems to be at least partly that adolescence, unlike childhood and infancy, isn't buried deep enough to be formative; adolescence is too readily accessed, too conscious, not unconscious enough.[12] But Anna Freud goes on to claim that although the content of adolescent memories might be easily available, what is not so readily accessed is the affect that accompanied these memories:

> What we fail to recover, as a rule, is the atmosphere in which the adolescent lives, his anxieties, the height of elation or depth of despair, the quickly rising enthusiasms, the utter hopelessness, the burning – or at other times sterile – intellectual and philosophical preoccupations, the yearning for freedom, the sense of loneliness, the feeling of oppression by parents, the impotent rages or active hates directed against the adult world, the erotic crushes – whether homosexually or heterosexually directed – the suicidal fantasies, etc. These are elusive mood swings, difficult to revive, which, unlike the affective states of infancy and early childhood, seem disinclined to re-emerge and be relived in connection with the person of the analyst.
>
> (1969, 143)

Adolescent emotions seem to be strangely resistant to transference. Why might these particular feelings be so difficult to revive in transference, in comparison to infantile ones? Perhaps it's partly because the affect of adolescence, as both Freuds describe it, consists so largely of resistance; the ego resists the incursion of adult libidinal surges, the adolescent resists the strictures of the parents. There's a way in which psychoanalysis comes to define adolescence as, first and foremost, pure resistance, like the iconic teenage rebel Marlon Brando in *The Wild One*, who, when asked "What are you rebelling against?" responds, "What have you got?" In a sense the adult, who cannot revive those adolescent emotions, is taking part in a kind of transference, but the transference is actually of that adolescent resistance to authority, a kind of meta-transference of the younger self to the more compliant older self. Another way of putting this would be to say that the transference seems to occur in the fact that the emotions themselves refuse to cooperate with the adult authority that wants to coax them out.

The rest of Anna Freud's essay is largely devoted to the problem of adolescents as patients; they too resist transference. For Anna, the pitfalls of attempting to work with adolescents are many. She writes, "the analytic treatment of adolescents is a hazardous venture from beginning to end, a venture in which the analyst has to meet resistances of unusual strength and variety" (1969, 144). Interestingly she speculates that one source of adolescents' difficulty with transference is the tendency of adolescents to live entirely in the present:

> Whatever the libidinal solutions at a given moment may be, it will always be a preoccupation with the present time ... with little or no libido left available for investment either in the past or in the analyst.
>
> (1969, 147)

I will return to this "preoccupation with the present time," but in a sense, the question of why adolescent individuals make recalcitrant analysands is much easier to answer than the question of why adolescence as an unburied, consciously remembered stage of life is finally so difficult to access emotionally. "When the revolt against the parents is anticipated in the transference," Anna Freud writes, it "tends to lead to a break with the analyst, i.e., to abrupt and undesirable termination of treatment from the patient's side" (1969, 144). Adolescents, it seems, are especially good at breaking the terms of the psychoanalytic contract.

Two of Anna's father's famous cases, "Dora" and "A Case of Homosexuality in a Woman" offer abundant examples of resistance and breakage. Sigmund Freud's adolescent patients won't fall in with the transference, and often refuse to sanction the internalist readings that analysis seems to offer. Both young women come to Freud reluctantly, and both have their own non-analytic interpretations of the source of their distress – it is not psychic illness so much as social context that places Dora as an object of exchange between men, and which, in "A Case of Homosexuality in a Woman," forbids a kind of love which seems unproblematic in terms of the young woman's own psychic make-up. Freud is careful to point out that the young woman in "A Case of Homosexuality in a Woman" in fact has no neurosis about her sexuality at all – she seems perfectly happy with it, just unhappy that her beloved has rejected her (and, according to Freud's analyses, unhappy that her father has rejected her as well).[13]

Looking at these two cases, we might assume that the adolescent is likely to view her "trouble" as externally, rather than internally, produced. This is related to another cause of the lack of transference in adolescents: the problematizing of the psychoanalytic contract in terms of the cash exchange. In the case of the analysis of adolescents, the person who is paying for the cure (usually the parent) is not receiving the cure, and the person who is being analyzed may not necessarily think they need to be cured. In "A Case of Homosexuality in a Woman," the girl's father has brought her in wanting her "cured" of her desire for women. But Freud initially sees nothing to cure – she is not a "case." He writes: "the girl was not in any way ill (she did not suffer from anything in herself, nor did she complain of her condition) and ... the task to be carried out did not consist in resolving a neurotic conflict but in converting one variety of the genital organization of sexuality into the other" (Freud 1979, 375). Her lack of illness means she may have nothing repressed to uncover, and this makes any examination of her past unforthcoming: "Further, the girl had never been neurotic, and came to the analysis without even one hysterical symptom, so that opportunities for investigating the history of her childhood did not present themselves so readily as usual" (1979, 381). The young woman is a case of something (homosexuality) which, it appears, may not be a case for psychoanalytic intervention at all.

In this case there appear to be a number of reasons why transference never takes hold. One is that the girl is not sick – she and her desire are at relative peace with each other, ergo she has no symptoms, no clotted and disjointed past, nothing to sort out, no transference. Another reason is the unworkable nature of the psychoanalytic contract when it is not made with the patient but with the guardian of the patient, who has his or her own investments and definitions of what constitutes a cure. Both of these reasons for the lack of transference actually respect the adolescent patient's removal from the scene of analysis. She's not fully participating for a series of very good reasons (she's not really sick, she doesn't want to be cured, she doesn't think there's anything to cure). But by the end of the case history Freud shifts his position, insisting that there always must be some kind of transference – that distance of the sort that his patient seems to manifest is not really possible:

> For some kind of relation to the analyst must come into being, and this relation is almost always transferred from an infantile one. In reality she transferred to me the sweeping repudiation of men which had dominated her ever since the disappointment she had suffered from her father. Bitterness against men is as a rule easy to gratify upon the physician; it need not evoke any violent emotional manifestations, it simply expresses itself by rendering futile all his endeavours and by clinging to the illness.
>
> (Freud 1979, 391)

We know from what Freud said earlier that in this case he doesn't believe there is an illness to cling to. Yet in the preceding quote he succumbs both to the necessary relation between adult and adolescent and to the lure of the early – the transferential relation that is "almost always transferred from an infantile one." Freud proceeds to give this adolescent a symptomatic past when what she has revealed is no symptom at all. However, according to Freud this missing symptom may be the trickiest resistance of all, a resistance that manifests itself as total cooperation:

> The analysis went forward almost without any signs of resistance, the patient participating actively with her intellect, though absolutely tranquil emotionally. Once when I expounded to her a specially important part of the theory, one touching her nearly, she replied in an inimitable tone, "How very interesting," as though she were a *grande dame* being taken over a museum and glancing through her lorgnon at objects to which she was completely indifferent. The impression one had of her analysis was not unlike that of a hypnotic treatment, where the resistance has in the same way withdrawn to a certain boundary line, beyond which it proves to be unconquerable.
>
> (Freud 1979, 390)

The adolescent's lack of interest in Freud's theory (or more correctly her theoretical interest in the theory, rather than her emotional involvement) is infuriating to the older doctor involved in the task of explaining to her who and what she is, and why she does what she does. Freud, here, is suddenly the object in the museum, being peered at with indifference, or at best, a slight aesthetic interest; he is incapable of inspiring the emotions that he needs to produce in his patient. But it is also the adolescent's own past which is a museum object; asked by Freud to inhabit her own past and her motivations, she will only approach them as if from the safely aestheticizing, or historicizing, distance of the museum-goer. As critics have pointed out, she mirrors his role, maintaining an objective scientific interest (and Freud collected antiquities – he would have had museum pieces sitting on his desk). She is, it seems, fairly successfully living in a world in which we might surmise that a relation to him – and to her past – is not perceived as necessary. In a sense we might say that the adolescent in analysis is most threatening when he or she refuses to enter into a quasi-Oedipal relation with the analyst – she doesn't want to kill him and she doesn't want to love him. Parents and parent-substitutes are displaced by her investment in her own present circumstances.

One thing Freud's young patient accomplishes by her indifference is to force Freud back from an analysis that boldly admits that there is no necessary "case," even in the presence of homosexuality, into a defensive position, in which he needs to construct a case – a past, a symptomatology, out of what may in fact be an adolescent way of being in the world which premises itself on a radical distance from adult interpretation.

There is an aspect of this struggle between Sigmund Freud and the adolescent girl that recalls Anna Freud's speculation about the tendency of adolescents to live entirely in the present:

> Whatever the libidinal solutions at a given moment may be, it will always be a preoccupation with the present time ... with little or no libido left available for investment either in the past or in the analyst.
>
> (A. Freud 1969, 147)

Resisting his narrative strategies for her, Freud's adolescent's libido is directed elsewhere. She will not accede to a symptomatic past and the question of what kind of future she will have is open. Freud terminates the analysis quickly, obviously afraid to make the same mistakes he made with Dora. He suggests a female analyst because of what he portrays as her "sweeping repudiation of men," a symptom which seems to be brought in too late to make sense of her story. One might argue that he doesn't want to get into another battle of wills with another adolescent and wind up, once again, on the wrong side of that lorgnon. If we can see her suicide attempt as an evasion of the future (without her lover, and under the disapproving eye of her father), then she evades her past by refusing to comply with the transference.

Willa Cather's 1905 story "Paul's Case," as the title indicates, also engages with the detached language of the case. It concerns an adolescent boy with dandyish tendencies. Paul is bored by school and disgusted by his working-class home life. He only really lives in the glittering world of the theater and the concert hall, where he has a job as a theater usher. After he is taken out of school and forced by his father to quit his job, Paul steals a large sum of money from his new employer and runs away from Pittsburgh to New York, living luxuriously in a hotel until he realizes that he has run through the money and his father is coming to take him back to his deadening life in Pittsburgh. In the final paragraph of the story Paul throws himself in front of a train.

"Paul's Case" begins with the adolescent Paul being put under disciplinary scrutiny: "It was Paul's afternoon to appear before the faculty of the Pittsburgh High School to account for his various misdemeanors" (Cather 1984, 117). But an accounting is precisely what the story doesn't give us. This too is a case history that contains gaps. Although required to explain the motivations behind his petty acts of rebellion, Paul can't seem to make sense of them himself. What Paul intends, by what he says, and by his way of being in the world, is uncertain: "I don't know," Paul says when asked about what he meant by saying rude things to a teacher, "I didn't mean to be polite or impolite, either. I guess it's a sort of way I have of saying things regardless" (1984, 119). The story similarly tries to account for him, but it also hits a wall of incomprehension. What's the matter with Paul? On the one hand he is set up as a medical/criminal "case" – he shows physical signs of degeneration and deviancy: "His eyes were remarkable for a certain hysterical brilliancy, and he continually used them in a conscious, theatrical sort of way, peculiarly offensive in a boy." On the other hand, those symptomatic "hysterically brilliant" eyes are also an indicator of chosen behavior – the offensively theatrical, and significantly, *conscious* way in which he uses them. Is Paul performing something or is he just being himself? Is that something effeminacy, or an aestheticism that slides seamlessly into queerness? Judith Butler and Eve Sedgwick have explored questions of queerness, performance, identity, and identification in their readings of this story. They trace out a plethora of identifications and dis-identifications between the "mannish" lesbian, whose literary creed railed against the "artificial," and the effeminate boy whose aesthetic desires lead him unerringly towards the fake (Butler 1993; Sedgwick 1993).[14] As Cather writes, "in Paul's world, the natural nearly always wore the guise of ugliness ... a certain element of artificiality seemed to him necessary in beauty" (1984, 127). These readings are persuasive, but what if what Paul signifies, what he is consciously and unconsciously performing, is all of these things – queerness, aestheticism, theatricality, effeminacy – but also a kind of resistance to the present moment and its historical and economic conditions? Is that resistance then an adolescent one? (How would one then distinguish adolescence from homosexuality or aestheticism?)

Whatever is wrong with Paul, it provokes a disgust and a worry in his teachers which makes him "not a usual case": "Disorder and impertinence were among the offenses named, yet each of his instructors felt that it was scarcely possible to put into words the real cause of the trouble, which lay in a sort of hysterically defiant manner of the boy's; in the contempt which they all knew he felt for them, and which he seemingly made not the least effort to conceal" (1984, 118). There is something in Paul that none of them understand. His English teacher finds it insupportable when he recoils from her when she touches his hand. The fact that he wears a red carnation and bows when he leaves his disciplinary hearing only adds to their revulsion, and yet his teachers are also upset by their own feelings of antipathy towards him: "His teachers left the building, dissatisfied and unhappy; humiliated to have felt so vindictive toward a mere boy.... Some of them remembered having seen a miserable cat set at bay by a ring of tormentors" (1984, 119).

Paul is undoubtedly a Wildean aesthete figure – the carnation, the theatrical bow, and so many other details make this clear. When his teachers remember the cat attacked by a ring of tormentors it recalls the post-trial reviling of Wilde, which Cather participated in. In the last decades of the nineteenth century, Cather was strongly antagonistic to Wilde and aestheticism. In newspaper articles she lambasted Wilde for his "insincerity" and "driveling effeminacy." After Wilde's imprisonment she wrote a column denouncing the aesthetic movement and hailing Wilde's downfall as helping to bring about "the destruction of the most fatal and dangerous school of art that has ever voiced itself in the English tongue" (Summers 1990, 104–5). Critics have looked at Cather's ambivalent reworking of these feelings in this story, and have seen her developing a complex and partial identification with, and sympathy towards, Paul, which is also a sympathy for, and identification with, Wilde – that may begin to recognize a shared political/emotional terrain between the mannish lesbian and the effeminate boy.

To put adolescence into the picture is to reinforce the importance of these kinds of crossings rather than to reject them. For in a sense, Paul's youth is devoted to aestheticism, or at least one aspect of aestheticism; it is a refusal of past and future and an insistence upon the now. When he first comes to New York he looks at the snow-covered streets with a wonder that is couched in the language of Pater: "The boy set his teeth and drew his shoulders together in a spasm of realization; the plot of all dramas, the text of all romances, the nerve-stuff of all sensations was whirling about him like the snowflakes. He burnt like a faggot in a tempest" (1984, 132). Even if we leave the developing meanings of "faggot" aside, the language of spasm, sensation, and burning shows the context that Paul is entering, which is both literary – "the plot of all dramas and the text of all romances" – but also anti-literary, the burning Paterian, experiential quality of the now. It is interesting that when his teachers think he's perhaps been perverted by too much "garish fiction," the narrative voice tells us he scarcely reads at all – he "gets what he wants more quickly from music." Paul is not an artist figure; he simply consumes and consumes with a flame-like intensity.

Suddenly, in New York, Paul finds himself at home for the first time in his life. His stolen surroundings are adequate to him; they can account for him. He no longer feels the loneliness of his life in Pittsburgh: "He was now entirely rid of his nervous misgivings, of his forced aggressiveness, of the imperative desire to show himself different from his surroundings. He felt now that his surroundings explained him" (1984, 133).[15]

Cather describes Paul's striving for an adequacy to the moment that he finally achieves in the riches of New York as "his old elastic power of claiming the moment, mounting with it, and finding it all-sufficient." One might see how Paul, like the young woman in "A Case of Female Homosexuality," is incapable of the kind of transference the adult world asks from him. Transference in this sense involves a recognition of progressive time – agreeing to the possibility that you will someday be in that adult position, that you might like to have that adult power. If a desire that is directed towards futurity, and the kinds of identity that are based in temporality, is missing, then there will be no investment in your elders, no investment in your own past or your own future. Anna Freud's analysis of the resistances of the adolescent towards time seems to hold force here.

Which brings us, finally, to the troubling question of suicide, to the potential meanings of "No Future" for an earlier generation of adolescents and observers of adolescents. One might think, in Freud's case history, that the suicide attempt would be the one act of the young woman that might make "A Case of Female Homosexuality" a case, but Freud refuses to interpret it that way, despite the fact that he describes the attempt as "undoubtedly serious." The girl's father initially brings her to see Freud after she has thrown herself onto a suburban railway line, after her father has expressed his disgust at her sexuality, and her beloved has refused to see her any more because of her father's disapproval. But the upshot of the suicide attempt for her is actually that everyone gives her more leeway – her desired older woman becomes much kinder to her and her parents decide it's probably best to let her do whatever she wants. Suicide works, for her, not because it ends her life, but because it brings her closer to the pleasure principle.[16]

Mary Jacobus (1995), in her essay "Russian Tactics: Freud's Case of Homosexuality in a Woman," points towards Freud's triumphalist claim that psychoanalysis has solved the "enigma of suicide." Freud writes:

> For analysis has explained the enigma of suicide in the following way: probably no one finds the mental energy required to kill himself unless, in

> the first place, in doing so he is at the same time killing an object with whom he had identified himself, and, in the second place, is turning against himself a death-wish which had been directed against someone else.
> (Freud 1979, 389)

In his article "Mourning and Melancholia," Freud also lays out this seesaw of love and hate towards the other and self which accompanies the experience of loss. In the article, Freud describes the ways in which the loss of another (through death, or a permanent breaking off of a relationship, or even the loss of a political or religious ideal) can result in a heightened sense of despair and loss to the ego that he defines as melancholia. Unlike the normal state of mourning, which also involves feelings of intense sadness and loss, melancholics turn their sense of loss of the object in upon themselves. Their ambivalent feelings toward the lost object, towards whom they might have felt a mixture of love and hate, lead them to turn this hatred inward. The object, in a sense, seems to devour the ego. Self-hatred is really redirected other hatred (Freud 1984, 247–68; Thurschwell 2009, 87–89). In "Mourning and Melancholia," Freud also claims to solve "the riddle of the tendency to suicide," writing, "The analysis of melancholia now shows that the ego can kill itself only if ... it can treat itself as an object – if it is able to direct against itself the hostility which relates to an object and which represents the ego's original reaction to objects in the external world" (Freud 1984, 261).

What I find fascinating is the apparent lack of self-hatred – or perhaps, protection of the right to affects other than self-hatred, such as self-detachment – that both "Paul's Case" and "A Case of Homosexuality in a Woman" embody. In her article, Jacobus suggests that for Freud the first reaction to the external world is not hate, or fear, but rather "indifference," an indifference that might be reflected in the young woman's lorgnon peering, false-ringing "how interesting." Might this indifference also illuminate the specifically adolescent suicide attempt, a gesture of passion and self- and other-hatred, but also an action that reveals an indifference towards, and rejection of, the narrative trajectory the young person has been offered? Might the detached, temporally suspended structure of the "case" (both for Paul and for the young woman in "A Case of Homosexuality in a Woman") trump the more predictable plot of the *Bildungsroman*?[17] Freud's own "Contributions to a Discussion on Suicide" was published in 1910. The discussion took place at the Vienna Psycho-Analytical Society and begins specifically with a discussion of the increased rate of suicide in secondary schools.

Freud writes, "The school must never forget that it has to deal with immature individuals who cannot be denied a right to linger at certain stages of development and even at certain disagreeable ones. The school must not take on itself the inexorable character of life: it must not seek to be more than a *game* of life" (1953–74, 11:232). I want to finally suggest that we take seriously the structural and affective "games" of life and death played out in these two texts and also take seriously that "right to linger" at certain stages of development that Freud suggests here. The aesthete Paul lingers, even as he also rushes to a suicidal end.

Paul imagines his own death, the absenting of himself from his narrative, throughout the story and not just at its end. After a night ushering at a concert he comes home and crawls into his basement unbeknownst to his father, because he can't bear to enter his house with its dingy surroundings. He thinks:

> Suppose his father had heard him getting in at the window and had come down and shot him for a burglar? Then, again, suppose his father had come down, pistol in hand and he had cried out in time to save himself, and his father had been horrified to think how nearly he had killed him? Then, again, suppose a day should come when his father would remember that night, and wish there had been no warning cry to stay his hand? With this last supposition Paul entertained himself until daybreak.
>
> (Cather 1984, 124)

This dream of an enraged and murdering father seems inextricable from Paul's own unvoiced knowledge of what makes him "different" – a recognition of the abjectness of his sexuality – so that he sees himself quite literally, in Judith Butler's terms, as a body that doesn't matter, as someone or some unspeakable thing, that, to his father, would be better off dead. But that suggestive dream of murder by the father also seems relevant to a reading of the achronological, "No Future" force of adolescent desire in the story. As Paul is deciding to throw himself onto the railway tracks, he thinks: "it was a losing game in the end, it seemed, this revolt against the homilies by which the world is run" (1984, 137). When he does throw himself in front of the train, his death takes him back, briefly and longingly, into the realm of aesthetic sensation:

> When the right moment came, he jumped. As he fell, the folly of his haste occurred to him with merciless clearness, the vastness of what he

had left undone. There flashed through his brain, clearer than ever before, the blue of Adriatic water, the yellow of Algerian sands.

He felt something strike his chest, and that his body was being thrown swiftly through the air, on and on, immeasurably far and fast, while his limbs were gently relaxed. Then, because the picture-making mechanism was crushed, the disturbing visions flashed into black, and Paul dropped back into the immense design of things.

(Cather 1984, 137–38)

His last thoughts, his regrets, are for the sensations he has not experienced – the blue of the Adriatic, the vivid yellow of the Algerian sands – but not precisely for a future he will not have. In these last extraordinary paragraphs, Cather takes us almost as far inside Paul's head, and his body, as it is possible to go before we draw back from his consciousness, the moment before he stops being a "case" and drops, in that ambivalent final gesture "back into the immense design of things." I don't quite know what to make of this – is Paul's evident "unnaturalness" redeemed, at the moment of his death, by his return to a "natural" design of things? Is he finally like Wordsworth's Lucy, rolling around in earth's diurnal course? On the other hand, those gently relaxing limbs and the collapse of those "disturbing" visions into blackness seem also in tune with Paul's desires – a desire to become an "interesting" case. Are Cather and the story perhaps making a case for Paul, and for adolescence, as well as analyzing Paul as a (medical, criminal, anomalous) case? What is Paul dying for? So that he can stay, as the story puts it earlier, "the boy he always wanted to be"? Dying in order to refuse the transference that adulthood will require of him?

Both Paul and the young woman in "A Case of Homosexuality in a Woman" throw themselves in front of trains, although, of course, Freud's patient survives. This gesture might be seen to link an adolescent death drive to a certain onslaught of modernity, a form of death that allows one to relinquish control to a fast-encroaching, powerful, unstoppable, but also unbearable future that is perhaps both acceded to and refused in that moment. If twentieth-century adulthood may appear like a moving train to the adolescent resisting its approach, then throwing oneself onto the tracks may represent a double bluff – you stop the train but simultaneously, of course, the train stops you. By considering the similarities between these two psychoanalytic, psychological, fictional, medical "cases" we can begin to trace, amongst many other connections, the ways in which psychoanalysis may hit its own wall when it encounters the case of the indifferent adolescent.

Notes

1 See DeLuzio (2007) for a careful use of Foucault in thinking about the development of adolescence as a disciplinary category in the early twentieth century.

2 For a nuanced discussion of the difficulty of thinking in cases see Forrester (1996).

3 Freud suggests this in his primal myth of killing the primal father in both *Totem and Taboo* (1985b, 205ff.), and "Group Psychology" (1985a, 156).

4 See for instance Freeman (2007).

5 See Thurschwell (2013) for more on the relationship between adolescent refusal and development in relation to the *Bildungsroman*.

6 A related argument about Edelman's title and the Sex Pistols is also made by Halberstam (2006, 824).

7 See Marcus (1989) for his compelling story of the politics of adolescent rebellion as negation, which he traces through punk rock's debts to Situationism, Dada, and the Ranters, amongst others.

8 As the Foucauldian discussion of the origin of the "case" indicates, the medical case and the criminal case, particularly in the realm of homosexuality, appear to become inseparable, a case that can also be made for the simultaneous criminalization and medicalization of adolescents, especially adolescent boys. See Gilbert (2004).

9 See Thurschwell (2012). One might also argue that Freud's modernism actually leans heavily on the adolescent case – works such as "Dora" and "A Case of Homosexuality in a Woman" fragment in tension with the recalcitrant young women who only allow Freud partial and incomplete stories, and who force him to consider the partial and incomplete nature of story-telling.

10 Puberty and adolescence are distinguished by the fact that puberty refers explicitly to biological changes, while adolescence is a little more wide-ranging. Adolescence comes from the French for coming to maturity, while puberty refers to body hair, the reaching of sexual maturity. Oddly, according to the *OED*, adolescence is ordinarily considered as extending from 14 to 25 in males, and from 12 to 21 in females, which brings up the question that Freud and psychologists such as G. Stanley Hall (1925) also approach, of whether the adolescent male and female were considered, for the sake of classification, different species.

11 My article, "Freud's Stepchild: Adolescent Subjectivity and Psychoanalysis" (2012), explores the ways in which, in G. Stanley Hall's and Sigmund Freud's writings on adolescence, development is described as biological for girls, cultural for boys. See also DeLuzio (2007), and Dyhouse (2013), for cogent analyses of Hall's panic-stricken descriptions of the perceived dangers of adolescence for girls.

12 As Ian Hacking (1995) notes, in a critique of the 1990s trauma-obsessed culture of the repressed, for modern psychology and psychoanalysis, it is often the forgotten that is equated with the formative. Similarly, Winnicott took issue with Melanie Klein's always equating "most significant or deeper" with "earlier" so that the further back you went, the more likely you were to come up with the goods (Riley 1983, 80–82). You can see why this psychoanalytic yearning for first times, for origins, might necessarily make anything that happened in adolescence a rather pale and second-rate repetition.

13 See Bernheimer and Kahane (1985) and Lesser and Domenici (1999).

14 See also Nealon (2001) for a brilliant reading of the affects involved in these critics' identifications and dis-identifications with Cather and her characters.

15 For a fascinating reading of the relations between environment, queerness, and development at the turn of the twentieth century, see Mao (2008).

16 It has always struck me as a perfect example of psychoanalytic logic that for Freud an attempt at suicide is less in need of explaining than an impenetrably smooth and helpful exterior.

17 For an important recent discussion of adolescence and the *Bildungsroman* structure in relation to the uneven developments of early twentieth century colonialism see Esty (2012).

References

Bernheimer, Charles, and Claire Kahane, eds. 1985. *In Dora's Case: Freud, Hysteria, Feminism.* London: Virago.

Bruhm, Stephen, and Natasha Hurley, eds. 2004. *Curiouser: On the Queerness of Children.* Minneapolis: University of Minnesota Press.

Butler, Judith. 1993. *Bodies that Matter: On the Discursive Limits of "Sex."* New York: Routledge.

Cather, Willa. 1984. "Paul's Case: A Study in Temperament." In *The Troll Garden.* New York: New American Library

Chinn, Sarah E. 2009. *Inventing Modern Adolescence: The Children of Immigrants in Turn-of-the-Century America.* New Brunswick: Rutgers University Press.

Davidson, Arnold I. 1987. "How To Do the History of Psychoanalysis: A Reading of Freud's *Three Essays on the Theory of Sexuality.*" *Critical Inquiry,* 13, no. 2: 252–57.

DeLuzio, Crista. 2007. *Female Adolescence in American Scientific Thought, 1830–1930.* Baltimore: Johns Hopkins University Press.

Dyhouse, Carol. 2013. *Girl Trouble: Panic and Progress in the History of Young Women.* London: Zed Books.

Edelman, Lee. 2004. *No Future: Queer Theory and the Death Drive*. Durham, N.C.: Duke University Press.

Esty Jed. 2012. *Unseasonable Youth: Modernism, Colonialism, and the Fiction of Development*. Oxford: Oxford University Press.

Forrester, John. 1996. "If p, Then What? Thinking in Cases." *History of the Human Sciences*, 9, no. 3: 1–25.

Foucault, Michel. 1977. *Discipline and Punish: The Birth of the Prison*, trans. Alan Sheridan. New York: Vintage Books.

Foucault, Michel. 1990. *The History of Sexuality*, vol. 1: *An Introduction*, trans. Robert Hurley. New York: Vintage Books.

Freeman, Elizabeth, ed. 2007. "Queer Temporalities." *GLQ*, 13, no. 2–3 [special issue].

Freud, Anna. 1969. "Adolescence." In *Research at the Hampstead Child Therapy Clinic and Other Papers, 1956–65*, 138–65. Vol. 5 of *The Writings of Anna Freud*. New York: International University Press.

Freud, Sigmund. 1953–74. *The Standard Edition of the Complete Psychological Works of Sigmund Freud*, 24 vols., ed. James Strachey, with the assistance of Anna Freud, Alix Strachey, and Alan Tyson, trans. James Strachey. London: Hogarth Press.

Freud, Sigmund. 1977. *On Sexuality: Three Essays on the Theory of Sexuality and Other Works*, ed. Angela Richards, trans. James Strachey. Penguin Freud Library 7. Harmondsworth: Penguin.

Freud, Sigmund. 1979. *Case Histories II: The Rat Man, Schreber, The Wolf Man, A Case of Female Homosexuality*, ed. Angela Richards, trans. James Strachey. Penguin Freud Library 9. Harmondsworth: Penguin.

Freud, Sigmund.1984. *On Metapsychology: The Theory of Psychoanalysis: Beyond the Pleasure Principle, The Ego and the Id, and Other Works*, ed. Angela Richards, trans. James Strachey. Penguin Freud Library 11. Harmondsworth: Penguin.

Freud, Sigmund. 1985a. *Civilization, Society and Religion: Group Psychology, Civilization and Its Discontents, and Other Works*, ed. Albert Dickson, trans. James Strachey. Penguin Freud Library 12. Harmondsworth: Penguin.

Freud, Sigmund, 1985b. *The Origins of Religion: Totem and Taboo, Moses and Monotheism and Other Works*, ed. Albert Dickson, trans. James Strachey. Penguin Freud Library 13. Harmondsworth: Penguin.

Gilbert, Geoff. 2004. *Before Modernism Was: Modern History and the Constituency of Writing*. Houndmills: Palgrave Macmillan.

Hacking, Ian. 1995. *Rewriting the Soul: Multiple Personality and the Sciences of Memory*. Princeton: Princeton University Press.

Halberstam, Judith. 2006. "The Politics of Negativity in Recent Queer Theory." *PMLA*, 121, no. 3: 823–24.

Hall, G. Stanley. 1925. *Adolescence: Its Psychology and Its Relations to Physiology, Anthropology, Sociology, Sex, Crime, Religion and Education*, 2 vols. New York: Appleton.

Jacobus, Mary. 1995. "Russian Tactics: Freud's 'Case of Homosexuality in a Woman'" *GLQ*, 2, nos. 1–2: 65–79.

Lesser, Ronnie C., and Thomas Domenici, eds. 1999. *That Obscure Subject of Desire: Freud's Female Homosexual Revisited*. New York: Routledge.

Mao, Douglas. 2008. *Fateful Beauty: Aesthetic Environments, Juvenile Development, and Literature 1860–1960*. Princeton: Princeton University Press.

Marcus, Greil. 1989. *Lipstick Traces: A Secret History of the Twentieth Century*. Cambridge, MA: Harvard University Press.

Nealon, Christopher. 2001. *Foundlings: Lesbian and Gay Historical Emotion Before Stonewall*. Durham, N.C.: Duke University Press.

Riley, Denise. 1983. *War in the Nursery: Theories of the Child and Mother*. London: Virago.

Rose, Jacqueline. 1993. *Why War? Psychoanalysis, Politics and The Return of Melanie Klein*. Oxford: Blackwell.

Savage, Jon. 2008. *Teenage: The Creation of Youth, 1875–1945*. London: Pimlico.

Sedgwick, Eve Kosofsky. 1993. "Across Genders, Across Sexualities: Willa Cather and Others." In *Tendencies*, 167–76. Durham, N.C.: Duke University Press.

Somerville, Siobhan. 2000. *Queering the Color Line: Race and the Invention of Homosexuality in American Culture*. Durham, N.C.: Duke University Press.

Summers, Claude J. 1990. "'A Losing Game in the End': Aestheticism and Homosexuality in Cather's 'Paul's Case.'" *MFS*, 36, no. 1: 103–19.

Thurschwell, Pamela. 2009. *Sigmund Freud*, 2nd edn. Abingdon: Routledge.

Thurschwell, Pamela. 2012. "Freud's Stepchild: Adolescent Subjectivity and Psychoanalysis." In *History and Psyche: Culture, Psychoanalysis, and the Past*, ed. Sally Alexander and Barbara Taylor. Houndmills: Palgrave Macmillan.

Thurschwell, Pamela. 2013. "Dead Boys and Adolescent Girls: Unjoining the *Bildungsroman* in Carson McCullers' *The Member of the Wedding* and Toni Morrison's *Sula*." *English Studies in Canada*, 38, nos. 3–4: 105–28.

Warner, Michael. 1990. "Homo-Narcissism; or, Heterosexuality." In *Engendering Men*, ed. Joseph A. Boone and Michael Cadden, 190–206. New York: Routledge.

Part III

Visual Cultures

Chapter 11

Intimate *Volver*

Frances L. Restuccia

To Julia Kristeva, happiness depends on intimacy – intimacy both with oneself and with others. Intimacy with others and in turn the happiness it bestows, in fact, hinge on an initial inquiry into oneself – as one would guess, on the level of the unconscious. Therefore, with so much at stake, Kristeva, like Guy Debord in *The Society of the Spectacle*, rails against our consumerist, image-obsessed, robotizing society of the spectacle, regarding it as anathema to intimacy, as damaging to her highly cherished "culture of revolt," and ultimately as threatening to psychic life. Kristeva insists (and who can disagree?) that "The conditions of modern lives – with the primacy of technology, image, speed, and so forth, inducing stress and depression – have a tendency to reduce psychical space and to abolish the faculty of representation," which is essential for working through psychic fixations (2002, 11). We are heading rapidly, in other words, toward psychic suicide. As she elaborates in her book *Intimate Revolt: The Powers and Limits of Psychoanalysis*, Kristeva's goal is both a revived subjectivity and a reformed society, the latter depending on the former.

Kristeva outlines a psychoanalytic mode of resistance to this widespread threat of the spectacle, centered in the West but steadily creeping

A Concise Companion to Psychoanalysis, Literature, and Culture, First Edition.
Edited by Laura Marcus and Ankhi Mukherjee.

across, and in turn emptying, the globe – of subjectivity, psychic life, and meaning. As Giorgio Agamben testifies, "Guy Debord's books constitute the clearest and most severe analysis of the miseries and slavery of a society that by now has extended its dominion over the whole planet – that is to say, the society of the spectacle in which we live" (2000, 73). To defeat this so-called "society," Kristeva proposes a penetrating investigation of one's own psychic make-up, what she calls an "intimate revolt." She puts the intimate revolt she is determined to foster even more dramatically: "A synonym of dignity, revolt is our mysticism" (Kristeva 2002, 4). Kristeva's "mysticism" entails an interminable interrogation of one's being, a questioning and displacement of the past – as a function of the search for oneself. It is an "aptitude for return, which is simultaneously recollection, interrogation, and thought" (2002, 5). One unlocks meaning and in turn achieves happiness through an intimate revolt that plumbs the depths of the unconscious, since it is (only) through a profound *anamnesis* or recollection that psychical restructuring can occur. In *Intimate Revolt*, Kristeva explains that such a beneficial psychoanalytic journey involves, in fact, a *repetition* of "retrospective return" that leads to "the limits of the representable/thinkable/tenable" (2002, 7). Pushing up consistently against such radical limits, intimate revolt results in the *jouissance* essential to psychic life and thus has the capacity to fuel an unending process of re-creation, with positive reverberations throughout the social arena. The resultant freedom of the subject fosters an "energetic urge into a dynamic of meaning with the other." The subject of intimate revolt, having encountered the otherness of him- or herself in the guise of the otherness of the analyst or work of art, gains the capacity to establish "optimal connections with others" in communities that can in turn be questioned and transformed (2002, 233). This outcome, it goes without saying, militates against the isolation installed by the society of the spectacle.

Especially because intimate revolt entails accessing the abyss that constitutes the subject, Kristevan psychoanalysis extends the philosophical tradition that celebrates Being as "wrought by nothingness" or in other words "the copresence of nothingness in being" (Kristeva 2002, 8) – what exceeds the boundaries of representation, thought, and the tenable. Kristeva attaches the entire "psychoanalytic movement inaugurated by Freud" to the philosophical practice of interrogating Nothingness and negativity central to her psychoanalytic theory of intimate revolt (2002, 9). Kristeva places Freud within a tradition that features Heidegger: she concentrates on "What is

Metaphysics?" (1929) as well as Sartre's *Being and Nothingness* (1943). She also locates variations on her psychoanalytic theme of coming up against a psychical reality that threatens consciousness, exposing it to "the pulse of being," in Heidegger's work on Hölderlin, in which the philosopher captures "this near psychosis in being." A seminal psychoanalytic text in this trajectory is Freud's *Die Verneinung* (*Negation*), in which Freud explores the unbinding of the drive in the form of the symbol. The quintessential question here is how rejection and violence proper to the drive become the negativity necessary to symbolizing. Under what conditions does this transformation of the drive to symbolization occur? As Kristeva poses the question in *Powers of Horror*, "what type of repression yields symbolization, hence a signifiable object, and what other type, on the contrary, blocks the way toward symbolization and topples drive into the lack-of-object of asymbolia or the auto-object of somatization?" (Kristeva 1982, 33). The implication seems to be that a "smooth," that is, effective or productive, transition from the drive to symbolization would involve an instigating and lasting encounter with the psychotic space beyond the border on which subjectivity is founded. By putting consciousness in danger, intimate revolt threatens to dissolve subject/object borders and renders one vulnerable to an "assault of the drive" (Kristeva 2002, 9) as a way of generating the process of symbolization.

Kristeva's revolt of intimacy, then, initially involves a provisional psychosis of being. Such a black hole can be encountered not only in analysis but also in writing that has the capacity to unfold meaning on the level of sensations and drives, finding its basis in the realm of the semiotic. Kristeva attributes especially to literature the power to incite such a psychoanalytic experience for the reader. "Writing in revolt," that is, has the potential to traverse evil – defined in Kristeva as an unrepresented drive – by staging a confrontation with the abyssal core of the self, by engaging unbound realms such as "the unnamable feminine, destructivity, psychosis," in the end to articulate the drive (Kristeva 2002, 10). A semiotic text can reconcile the subject with the *Zeitlos* or timeless – the timelessness of the drive. Such an immersion and consequent hooking up with the drive, enabling its activation and representation, have the potential to give birth to a newly constituted, thriving subject, whose desire is set in motion.

This psychical "work" – well known as working-through – softens the hard kernel of trauma by inserting non-life into life. Working-through, put another way, inscribes death in "lived actuality," contracting death and life, or the timeless and time, through what Kristeva calls a "moment of grace that signals . . . the analysand's rebirth" (2002, 36). Psychic and somatic pain is transported into time. The timeless traumatic psychic material is withdrawn from the excitation, where it has been lodged for a prolonged period, and invited to "work at the heart of an expressible, conscious temporality." Resituated at the intersection of the atemporal and the temporal, the memory-trace of the psychic trouble endures. It is by no means fully extinguished. But it is spread out within the "linear time of remembering" (2002, 38). *Jouissance* ensues. After the arduous "journey to the end of the night," transmission produces joy.

"Film in revolt" can perhaps even more easily than writing index this same timelessness and thereby *work* this same magic, primarily through its staging of fantasy. In the fifth chapter of *Intimate Revolt,* "Fantasy and Cinema," Kristeva establishes that the subject is constituted through the Imaginary (where the drive may be discovered) and that fantasy serves as a passageway to this psychoanalytic register. She accepts Freud's notion of fantasy as "the intimate creation of representations" (Kristeva 2002, 63), rather than a fulfillment of desire. Such phantasmatic narratives need to be formulated and then interpreted in order to dissolve symptoms. In this way access can be gained to unconscious fantasy, to keep it from being repressed. Dreams of course are a central place where fantasies come to light, bespeaking the reality of our desire or signaling why our desire is blocked. Likewise, film can serve as a dream-space for a spectator whose psychic life resonates with the semiotic components displayed on the screen. As in all semiotic texts, here, too – that is, in certain films – we find a key crossroads between the unconscious and consciousness, drive and Symbolic formations.

Ironically, the plethora of images that bombard us today within our society of the spectacle not only fails to liberate us but also deprives us of productive fantasy spaces. Popular images may even be said to generate new maladies of the soul, which then require a curative fantasy space. Nevertheless, Kristeva maintains that the visible is the port of registry of the drive and that there is a type of cinema – what she calls the "thought specular" – that has the potential, by celebrating our identity uncertainties, to turn the spectator's aggression to filmic seduction, to help us locate the drive and transform it into desire. Despite modern man's abuse of it, the specular is "the most advanced medium for the inscription of the drive" (Kristeva 2002, 72). Kristeva looks to Eisenstein, Hitchcock, and Pasolini, in particular.

The "thought specular" opens up a fantasy space comprised of "lektonic" traces or expressibles, semiotic ingredients that have the capacity to absorb a spectator's psychic trouble. It enables a transformation of flat filmic images into containers of symptoms, putting into play primary processes. Such cinema, Kristeva believes, provides a skeleton, a logic, for the spectator's psychic material, through its themes and the rhythm of its images, as well as through laughter. The specular encodes the drive especially via its "network of lektonic elements: sounds, tone, colors, space, figures" (Kristeva 2002, 77). Yet it must be understood that "what I see has nothing to do with the specular that fascinates me" (2002, 73). The thought specular, in other words, ultimately offers the spectator an encounter with the gaze – that is, with his or her constitutive lack – as a way of immersing the viewer in that "psychotic" space conducive to psychic regeneration. Cinema seizes us at this place of the gaze: "This is its magic" (2002, 73).

Kristeva's semiotic/Almodóvar's signature

Pedro Almodóvar's *Volver* can seem to embody so many of the components of Kristeva's recent work that it may look like the quintessential Kristevan "thought-specular film." It is as though Almodóvar made the film to fulfill her theoretical dreams, both demonstrating and making legible Kristeva's theory of intimate revolt. (Almodóvar *is* known to have likened *Volver* to therapy.) That is, *Volver* can be experienced as a thought-specular film that gives rise to the spectator's intimate revolt and at the same time is *about* such a process, about the necessity of intimate revolt.

Thematically, *Volver* works through a double trauma of sexual abuse committed by the father and the psychically crippling loss of the mother that follows – in a way that accords with Kristeva's emphasis on a process of *anamnesis* that reaches all the way back to an encounter with the "dead mother." *Volver* clearly shows an "aptitude to return" that pushes up against "the limits of the representable/thinkable/tenable." Almodóvar's film pulls time into the timeless and weaves the timeless into time, befriending death in myriad ways that are analogous to the embrace of death on the part of the Spanish women villagers featured at the beginning of the film, as they clean and polish coffins in a festive Spanish cemetery in La Mancha. *Volver* champions, by putting into play, Freud's idea that "each human manifestation (act, speech, symptom)" needs to be opened "beyond consciousness, toward unconscious/prepsychical/somatic/physical continuity" (Kristeva 2002, 32). Chronos is shown to be limited. In *Volver*, the "work of the *Zeitlos* that scans it ... essentially upset[s] time's flight forward" (2002, 32). Illustrating Kristeva's theory of intimate revolt, Almodóvar's film insists on the immanence of "time unbound" within "bound living time" (2002, 33) – unbound time being what "presides over working out and sublimation" (2002, 32).

Featuring colors, images, shapes, and music, or in other words being thoroughly semiotic, replete with absorbent lektons, *Volver* has great potential to capture psychic material locked inside the unconscious of the spectator and in turn to facilitate the insertion of that non-life into representation. Moreover, *Volver* attacks the society of the spectacle for blocking such a vital movement. That is, clinching its Kristevan perspective, *Volver* even points to the society of the spectacle as what "subtract[s] this thanatology from the living." Like Kristeva, Almodóvar's film targets the society of the spectacle as the most insidious enemy of the *Zeitlos*. *Volver* returns what the society of the spectacle takes away.

Much more than a narrative about abuse and alienation, *Volver* is a postmodern explosion of color, patterns, music – sensuousness. As a thought-specular film, *Volver* operates in other words heavily, if not primarily, on the level of sensation. The film is semiotically well equipped to receive the spectator's unconscious turmoil through its dynamic lektonic traces. Like the white paper towel that slowly absorbs Paco's blood early in the film, *Volver* lektonically draws out and soaks in the spectator's psychic pain. In its opening scenes, *Volver* swoops the spectator into a splendid vision of colorful flowers and incantatory women. The camera takes time (later on) to offer shots of, or we might say to caress, seemingly random objects such as a yellow, green, and red old-fashioned tea set, with six charming cups, sugar and cream bowls, and a tea pot. Agustina's mother's collection of plastic jewelry, for another example, becomes the focal point of the camera's, and in turn our, eye. Especially Raimunda's, but Paula's colorful clothing as well, arouses our senses, as do the green, white, and red striped curtains hanging in Agustina's home, and the glistening blue and white tiles that decorate Aunt Paula's spacious entry hall.

The color red dominates. Close-ups of hot red, voluptuous tomatoes at a vegetable stand grab our attention, along with the red peppers Raimunda slices cleanly for the film-crew banquet. Raimunda wears an outstanding red and white apron and later (when she sings) a red-checked jacket; Paula sports a red and white striped shirt. The Madrid bus is red and white; Raimunda's car is unmistakably all red. Even at Aunt Paula's funeral, red and white tiles on the floor are emphasized via an overhead shot. Colorful, surreal graffiti; a multi-colored dolly used to remove the refrigerator to the restaurant and the deep freeze to the truck; a bright, rainbow-colored, tube-like decoration that Paula puts up at the restaurant; colorful straws carefully placed in the mojitos; a creamy, plump dessert turned over and plopped onto a plate encircled by colorful flowers – all of these thing-oriented shots seduce the spectator's psyche at a subliminal level.

At the very end of *Volver*, as the final credits roll, shapes and colors alone explode onto the screen, unfolding for several minutes various, mainly floral, configurations. Accompanied by heart-wrenching music, red, white, pink, and black flowers emerge and recede. Squiggly lines appear that grow more flowers. Geometrical shapes of various sorts, including red stripes, are followed by blue and red flowers as well as black, white, and red lines that form trees. Leaves evolve, and then numerous colorful circles burst forth, filling up the screen, until the film ends with black and white flowers. Just as, for Deleuze, "the broken lines and contrasting black and white structure of *Psycho*" serve as a "signed image" for Hitchcock – primary geometric shapes and colors that also appear during the credits (Deleuze 1983, 21) – here we have at the finale of *Volver* Almodóvar's signature, which picks up on many of the images (such as flowers from Raimunda's striking black and red skirt) that stood out earlier in the film. Far from being negligible, such images dominate to become the signature of the film. Almodóvar, in other words, signs his film through its lektonic traces, illustrating "Godard's formula, 'it's not blood, it's red,' ... *the* formula of colourism" (1983, 118), as *Volver* transforms traumatic blood to semiotic color.[1] Through what I am calling Almodóvar's signature – the expressibles of *Volver* that put into play primary processes via Kristeva's semiotic – the spectator's suffering is planted in the film. The sensuousness of the thought-specular film lures lektonically the spectator's (timeless) trauma, so that, through a subsequent encounter with the gaze, his or her unconscious is further moved, if not jolted, into the temporality (or atemporality) of the film. These semiotic components of *Volver*, in other words, render the spectator susceptible, at the level of the unconscious, to Raimunda's story, which then carries him or her to the end of the night.

Volver a sentir: Papa

Faithful to its title ("to return"), *Volver* rehearses extremely traumatic material. At the beginning of the film, though, Raimunda (the central, Penelope Cruz, character) appears ebullient as she is trapped in a delusion about her past – that her parents were happily married and that they died in each other's arms. "Mom was lucky," she announces gleefully to her sister Sole, "she died in Dad's arms, and she loved him more than anyone." Such a false sense of her past denies the truth of Raimunda's having been incessantly raped by her father, with the result of a pregnancy that produced her now 14-year-old daughter and sister, gorgeous Paula. The opening scenes of *Volver*, in which Raimunda greets her friend Agustina at the cemetery, with gaiety, and then, later on, visits her Aunt Paula with big smiles and effervescence, present this traumatized woman as upbeat.

However, upon seeing Raimunda's appalled reaction to a fire burning on Aunt Paula's TV (which no doubt reminds Raimunda at some level of the fire in which her parents supposedly were killed and possibly of the true conflagration that fire was caused by – her mother set the fire soon after hearing about the father's abuse of young Raimunda), we realize that there is a buried layer of trouble simmering in Raimunda's psyche. Almodóvar's *Volver* presents a working-through of all this catastrophic psychic material as the storyline centered on it is "treated" by the non-diegetic, lektonic components of the film itself. *Volver* progresses from the present in which Raimunda's trauma is repressed (Raimunda has not sung at least since the birth of her daughter and imagines that her parents died as blissful lovers, when in fact her father was a womanizer who raped Raimunda consistently during her childhood) to a new time, in which Raimunda's singing takes place as a means of confronting her past.

Raimunda's critical breakthrough into song is enabled by the killing of a father-figure. What catalyzes the film's penetrating engagement with the trauma of incestuous rape of a daughter by her father is the killing by another daughter (herself the product of that incestuous rape) of a "father" who attempts to rape her. Paco, Raimunda's daughter's (Paula's) apparent father, ogles her early in the film. We watch him eye her crotch as she lounges at home in a comfortable chair with her legs, wrapped in pink tights, spread childishly, though for Paco alluringly, before him. (That Raimunda perceives the scene as at least disturbing in itself is revealed when she orders her daughter to sit with her legs closed.) We also observe Paco glance into Paula's bedroom as she is undressing, catching the slightest glimpse of her naked young breast. Here then we have a crucial repetition. With Paco's compulsion to rape his own "daughter" (he is her non-biological father), *Volver* re-presents, repeats, returns to the original traumatic incestuous act of Raimunda's father's multiple rapes of Raimunda.

This time around, though, the victim (Paula) defends herself, by stabbing her abuser with a knife. The killing is taken seriously. When Paula tells her mother about the incident, the girl's face wrinkles up like a raisin, revealing the excruciating pain and torment she has undergone during the incident and its immediate aftermath. But this fatal violence is also methodically and thoroughly mopped up. We watch Raimunda's mop and paper towels absorb Paco's bright red blood in a way that suggests the film's own absorption of trauma into its sponge-like cinematic elements. This is of course the essential filmic activity of Kristeva's thought specular: such absorption demonstrates Kristeva's notion that "the imaginary captures fear, appeases it, and restores it to the symbolic order" (2002, 78–79).[2]

Significantly, at this point, Raimunda in a sense takes credit for the violence: "Remember, I killed him," she insists to Paula. On the one hand, here Raimunda behaves as a protective mother (taking the blame for her child), but on the other she is embracing the act psychically, as if to seize it from her daughter, as a way of grappling with her own father's abuse of her. Paco's attempted rape of Paula and its outcome restage Raimunda's trauma and thus enable her to begin the process of extracting that trauma from its encasement in timelessness and the unconscious and transplanting it in time and consciousness. Paco is psychoanalytically the scapegoat for Raimunda's father's abuse of her. His body is sacrificed, his blood mopped up, and his corpse stuffed in a deep freeze, to pay for the sins of the father. (The actual freezer in which Raimunda temporarily stores Paco's body clarifies imagistically that the death of Paco displaces the stuff of Raimunda's encryptment, that it takes the killing of Paco to begin to thaw Raimunda's psychic freezer.) Yet Paco in his own right, a beer-drinking, TV-sports addict, is nothing more than a pathetic member of the society of the spectacle. Devoid of intimacy, sex for Paco is mere "work": when Raimunda declines his invitation in bed to have sex, he volunteers to do "all the work." Then, worse, he fulfills her sense of him as a mere "pest" in flaunting his masturbatory activity as he lies close to her in bed. Killing Paco serves as a means of acknowledging the earlier abuse. It also seems tantamount to stepping on an insect, since Paco is presented as an ugly inhuman specimen of the mindless society of the spectacle that advocates through images the objectification of, and disrespect for, women and girls.

But, while men need to be killed, women's natural relation to death is celebrated. *Volver* (as mentioned) inscribes death from its very first scene, a gorgeous and, especially because of the potent east wind, animated depiction, with its abundance of flowers and cheerful singing women, attending to their as yet unburied coffins. The sensory intimacy of women, constantly giving each other loud, succulent kisses on the cheek, is unmistakable from the onset of *Volver*, along with their intimate relation to death. Here too Almodóvar overlaps with Kristeva, who also discovers in women a more sensuous, poetic, caring, supple relation to power and meaning (distinct from mastery or even significance) as well as a rapport with death. And, insofar as this is the case, both thinkers locate in the "universe of women ... an alternative to the robotizing and spectacular society that is damaging the culture of revolt" (Kristeva 2002, 5). "Their women" oppose the society of the spectacle – in which *bios* (political life) has overtaken *zoë* (natural life) – in fact, through their embrace of Kristeva's conception of the sacred, which is located at the crossroads of dichotomies such as body versus soul, life versus death, or *bios* versus *zoë*, as well as where "meaning" emerges through the inseparability of these ostensible antitheses. Kristeva regards the body of a woman in particular as "a strange intersection between *zōō* and *bios*, physiology and narration," flesh and Word (Kristeva and Clément 2001, 14).

In the opening scene, Agustina arrives at the cemetery to clean her coffin and to free herself from time: she tells Raimunda, Sole, and Paula that she often visits the cemetery to sit on her own, and "time goes by." In this way she befriends death and enters the *Zeitlos* (both of which eventually return her embrace). Plagued by cancer, Agustina in particular injects the fruits of death into *Volver*. Cleaning one's coffin, we are told, is the custom in this quaint Spanish village, although a man dusting off his coffin would seem unnatural. At Aunt Paula's funeral service, the men appear cordoned off. They look clueless, standing in a drab social space of their own. They wear gray, white, and black, reflecting colorlessness in contrast with the vibrant colors, frame by frame, that for the most part surround the women of the film, in the form of clothing, furniture, interior decor, stray props, etc., the lektonic expressibles of *Volver* that pull us in.

Aunt Paula's death follows immediately on the heels of Paco's demise, which puts a funeral, a funeral procession, and mourning at the center of this bittersweet film. On the "sweet" side: one effect of "thinking the specular" and "using the visible" to demonstrate fantasy as part of an effort to be protected from its most sadomasochistic varieties, Kristeva claims, is laughter (2002, 75). In sync with Kristeva's stress on the liberatory function of laughter in "thought-specular" films, there is a comic quality to every scene in *Volver* connected to batty Aunt Paula's passing, if not to just about every scene in the film. Laughter greets death. The grieving village women dressed in black, sitting in a circle with somber faces, while rapidly fanning themselves, resemble a swarm of agitated bees. When Sole enters the room, and the women rush up to express their condolences, the scene seems absurd, perhaps in part because of the gap between Sole's relation to her Aunt (who regards Sole as a "sourpuss") and the gloomy mood of the ritual. Next, a self-conscious, heavily stylized, stiff funeral procession creeps across the screen, led by a limo decked out in rings and bouquets of colorful flowers, with women walking behind in a straight line, the men right behind them – all of which can seem hilarious. Almodóvar's depiction of death in scenes that evoke laughter comports with Kristeva's sense that it was "inevitable ... that cinema itself should openly become the privileged place of sadomasochistic fantasy, so that fear and its seduction explode in laughter and distance" (2002, 80).

I take the funny funeral of Aunt Paula, as it follows the death of Paco, to complete the first phase of *Volver*'s process of working-through. Indolent Paco, sports-TV addict, perverse masturbator, child-molester, self-sunk to the level of a "pest," is killed off to avenge the abuse committed by the real father. As a corpse Paco is, also humorously, dragged from the household refrigerator to a deep freeze in Emilio's restaurant. He is later buried, in that freezer-coffin, in a hole in the ground that two women have the muscle to dig. Through Paco's bad deeds, his demise, and his proper burial, the trauma of the incestuous father is confronted, instead of remaining buried psychically, and brought to closure. Paco's death merges with that of Aunt Paula (Raimunda's surrogate mother), and a general funereal ambiance is comically established, making way for a more shattering confrontation.

Volver a sentir: Mama

The second phase of *Volver*'s enactment of working-through engages the central mother–daughter relation. Raimunda rejected her mother for being blind to the abuses her father inflicted upon her. After the birth of her daughter, Raimunda moved with Paco out of Alcanfor de las Infantas to Madrid and had little to do with her mother. Irene, Raimunda's mother, even announces to her granddaughter Paula that Raimunda did not love her. Raimunda put her mother away psychically, incorporating Irene in a melancholic crypt that in turn blocks Raimunda's desire. Raimunda shows no interest whatsoever in men:

Paco, needless to say; handsome Emilio, who apparently wanted her as a partner; or the young, attractive film-crew manager, who in one scene, as though mesmerized, stares at Raimunda chopping food. Now her mother returns. As I see it, young Paula's brave act of defending herself against her father-molester/monster vicariously allows Raimunda to face her rejected and now reincarnated mother. Acknowledgment of her father's abuse opens the door to recognition of the mother's role in that trauma, as Raimunda's psyche continues to undergo a gradual process of excavation. Although in the story the question is whether or not the mother is a ghost, on the psychoanalytic level of *Volver*, the mother's apparitional return indicates a further dilation of Raimunda's psyche that allows her psychic encryptment of her mother to end.

Humor again is key. Irene returns as a phantom of Raimunda's psyche, in a state between incorporation (psychic taking in) and introjection (psychic pushing out), as an externalization of the mother that is often ridiculously presented. When Sole hears her mother's voice calling from the trunk of her car ("Let me out, Sole! Let me out! I'm your mother"), a shocked Sole asserts, with excess deliberateness: "My mother is dead. ... You are her ghost or spirit." The ghost replies, "Whatever you say but get me out of here." The next shot of Irene, disheveled, in a fetal position and a bright blue dress, lying wide-eyed and cramped on her side in the trunk, has the charm to amuse every viewer. Other scenes in the film involving Irene mix the senses with humor. Raimunda detects her mother early on by smelling her flatulence. Conjoining humor with sensory intimacy, the mother's propensity to "fart" gives all the prominent women in the film a hearty laugh. And, in a scene that underlines the very point of the introjection of Irene from Raimunda's psyche, humor takes precedence. Raimunda inquires of her mother, "You're not a ghost are you? You're not dead?" Irene responds: "No love, I'm not." And Raimunda comments, "That's such a relief." Psychoanalytically, for Raimunda, it is an enormous relief. And the silliness of the exchange, the lightness with which such heavy subject matter is discussed, along with the little burst of laughter it evokes in the spectator, all demonstrate Kristeva's assertion that "evil is only representable insofar as you can laugh at it, with full knowledge of the facts" (2002, 80). A comedy about incestuous rape and a prolonged, painful alienation of mother and daughter, *Volver* fulfills Kristeva's notion, intrinsic to intimate revolt, that laughter is the most salubrious means "to achieve the distance finally entailed in working-through" (2002, 79).

Volver also demonstrates Kristeva's psychoanalytic concept of forgiveness, placing it at the center of its cinematic working-through of the mother–daughter trauma. Kristeva points out in *Intimate Revolt* that forgiveness has not been a psychoanalytic concept. She attaches it, rather, to a Christian line of thinking about guilt, which "only achieves its full meaning retroactively, in forgiveness" (2002, 15). But, in contrast to Christian forgiveness, which follows judgment, Kristeva's notion of forgiveness "suspends judgment and time" (2002, 16). Kristeva's forgiveness is offered by an-other, who must listen in a way that forgoes judgment, in the mode of an analyst rather than a priest in a confessional. "My unconscious," she explains, "is reinscribable beyond the gift that someone else is giving me of not judging my acts" (2002, 21). Kristeva's forgiveness emerges through a non-judgmental interpretation that restores the "meaning of the suffering" (2002, 16).

Psychoanalytic forgiveness has nothing to do with intellectualizing or mastery but "simply" requires the actualization of "preverbal meanings, *signifiances,* instinctual impulses, and affects," or what Kristeva calls the "semiotic" (2002, 19). Trauma is thereby absorbed in discourse as its affects are transposed into expressibles through the lektonic traces of thought-specular film. By retracing the singular genesis of ill-being, film has the capacity to put into expression unconscious material. The inexpressible becomes the expressible as an-other – *now the film* – offers forgiveness through silence and love by making "sense of the troubling senselessness" (2002, 19). In this way "complex and intraverbal experiences" are "brought to the other" – *here the film,* which draws forth and receives the spectator's psychic turmoil. The unconscious comes to consciousness to alleviate ill-being: this move (alone) entails forgiveness. Psychoanalysis then is obviously an experience of forgiveness. Sublimation likewise serves as a process of forgiveness, given that it brings preverbal material, wounded emotions and bodies, to words or other forms of expression, with the bonus of meaning. And so is *Volver*. Forgiveness in *Volver* primarily entails a metamorphosis of suffering, as the lost, yet psychically retained, desire-blocking maternal object emerges into the realm of time and consciousness.

Over soup after Aunt Paula's funeral, Agustina and Sole sit down together to converse about the return of the dead. Superstition in their Spanish town preserves the possibility of ghosts, a tradition Raimunda's mother takes advantage of, in that she is a murderer (having set fire to the hut in which her husband and Agustina's mother had just made love) on the run and fleeing justice by pretending to be a ghost, and getting away with it. (Being in the Imaginary register, everything in *Volver* takes place outside the law.) In fact, Irene (Raimunda's mother) appears in the film itself (to the spectator) as an unreal presence, looking asocially haggard, with long, grey, ugly locks, dumpy clothes, and seeming a bit (hilariously) crazed. Viewers tend to take a while before they realize she is "real." Daughter Sole assumes the supernatural identity of her mother for an extended stretch of time. This cinematic depiction of Irene as a spirit fits perfectly with a Kristevan reading of the mother in that Kristeva conceptualizes the soul as the psyche. Irene as a ghost or spirit can be read as a psychic phenomenon, an incorporated maternal object that materializes, as Raimunda, after having disavowed Irene for several years, gradually comes to acknowledge her mother's non-ghostly, real presence. Irene-as-ghost serves as Irene-as-incorporated-maternal-object returning from the dead, from unbound time, to enter into the narrative. By transporting the mother from an unconscious place of disavowal to consciousness (avowal), *Volver* enacts Kristeva's definition of forgiveness.

It is striking, in this connection, that Raimunda's mother seeks forgiveness explicitly. When Raimunda, upon seeing her mother (as "ghost") for the first time, asks her, "Aren't you dead?" Irene replies that she has returned to receive Raimunda's forgiveness – "for being blind." Irene's request, however, would seem to be for conventional forgiveness. Even as she raises the topic of forgiveness, Raimunda's mother is not presented as being involved in a process of transforming her unconscious into consciousness or timeless trauma into time (although we must credit Irene with broaching the topic of forgiveness so that it can be recognized as psychoanalytically relevant to *Volver*). But Raimunda is. Forgiveness for Raimunda transpires through the semiotic. The traumatic material embedded in her unconscious rises to the surface in a sense through the lektons that constitute *Volver*. As she becomes disentangled from past traumas, Raimunda plunges into the sensuous world of food. As soon as Paco is buried, *Volver* cuts to a vivacious scene of Raimunda carefully slicing red peppers and feeding dozens of people with appetizing meals and drinks. To slice the peppers, Raimunda uses a sharp knife that resembles the one that killed Paco, its purpose having been transformed. (Having stabbed Paco, the knife, too, is now free to chop vegetables.) Such lektons in turn provide pockets of absorption of the viewer's psychic trouble and the opportunity for the spectator's identificatory experience of forgiveness.

Although Raimunda used to sing, Raimunda's daughter, Paula, has never heard her mother's singing voice. Much is made of this fact, since it means that Raimunda stopped singing at least by the time she gave birth (to her own sister), i.e., after her father's incestuous rape produced a child. Perhaps the deepest "note" of the film is Raimunda's performance at Restaurant Emilio. In the middle of the festive, colorful film-crew banquet, Raimunda has the brainstorm of joining a small band of gypsy musicians assembling to play. (That the group Raimunda feeds and performs for is a film crew enhances the film's implication that through film, trauma can be thawed out.) Full of anticipation expressed by a wide grin on her beaming face, Paula is eager to make up for her deprivation. Raimunda then lets go, singing soulfully the lyrics of a song titled of course "Volver," whose meaning itself bears an uncanny relation to Kristeva's theory of intimate revolt.[3] Herein lie the Kristevan heart and lungs of Almodóvar's film.

The resemblance is astonishing. It is as though Almodóvar deliberately chose the lyrics to demonstrate Kristeva's theory. Raimunda has an inkling that she is on the verge of an intense experience with an earlier segment of her life. Of this she sings:

> I'm afraid of the encounter
> with the past that's coming back,
> to confront my life.
> I'm afraid of the nights
> that, filled with memories,
> enchain my dreams.

Sensing that now she is being summoned by her past, a shaken Raimunda uses her voice to experience a terrifying encounter that has the potential to release unbearable memories that have precluded her dreams from being realized. Raimunda completes the voyage to the dark night of her soul. Unlocking the sexual abuse by her father has paved the way for a renewal of relations with the mother. At this critical point in the film, the mother rolls down the window of Sole's red car (parked outside Emilio's restaurant where Raimunda sings), exposing herself, making her presence known to Raimunda, even, we might say, attempting to burst forth from Raimunda's unconscious into consciousness, to rise from the dead.

Despite her trepidation, Raimunda now feels compelled to bring her flight from her past to an end. To do so, she must first meet her past face to face. Raimunda can "see the twinkling of … lights in the distance" that "mark her return." These are the prefatory lyrics she sings that seem to well up inside Raimunda before she launches into a full expression of her need to end her disavowal:

> But the fleeing traveler,
> sooner or later,
> must come to a halt.
> And even though oblivion,
> which destroys everything,
> has killed my old illusions,
> I still retain a humble hope
> hidden away.

At this point in the song, Irene shows herself fully framed in the car window, as though the collision (of daughter and mother) is happening at this very moment, as though Raimunda's flight has now ceased. Having fled from her mother physically and having cut her off consciously, Raimunda psychically remained unconsciously glued to her. Her mother persisted in her psyche as the source of deep pain, as an obtuse, negligent, inert figure brutally ignorant of Raimunda's suffering. As she sings of her "humble hope," Raimunda gives the impression of looking beyond the restaurant, out into space, as though she senses, if not perceives, the presence of that previously buried mother. This is Raimunda's "moment of grace," the moment that "signals … the analysand's rebirth," a contracting of timelessness and time that inscribes death in "lived actuality."

The song "Volver" then proceeds hopefully, as Raimunda's encryptment continues to break up:

> And that is all
> of my heart's fortune.
> Coming back
> with a wrinkled forehead.

Framed in Sole's car window, the mother now begins to look nervous about being observed. Before entering the restaurant, Sole had warned Irene to remain in the car and to avoid letting anyone see her. Irene had replied, "No one can see me in here," insinuating that she occupies a realm of the unseen, that to grasp her presence is to embrace something beyond conventional viewing. Having lured Raimunda's unconscious, enabling Raimunda to face her – the mother retreats from the window to produce the blank site of the gaze, i.e. to leave the gaze as the residue

Figure 11.1 Raimunda sings in Restaurant Emilio. *Volver* (2006), dir. Pedro Almodóvar (New York: Sony Pictures Classics).

of her withdrawal. The next camera shot of the empty car window has the radical effect/affect of a shock, illustrating a point that Kristeva emphasizes about the thought specular: that "what I see has nothing to do with the specular that fascinates me" (2002, 73). By framing the mother's face and then following that close-up with the empty frame of the car window, *Volver* presents the psychoanalytic idea that the most magnetizing "thing" in the film (both for Raimunda and the spectator) is the Nothing lurking behind, the remainder or reminder of the now, finally, lost maternal object, in Lacanian terms, the lack of which enables the production of *objet a*, or the cause of desire.

Through Raimunda's encounter with the gaze – the Nothing that remains after separation from the maternal Thing, her constitutive lack, Raimunda carries out the psychoanalytic premise that the subject must "agree to lose" the mother to "imagine" and "name her" (Kristeva 1989, 41). Glimpsing Nothingness in the place of the mother, directly after having at long last apprehended her, enables Raimunda to continue to sing, of hope and time. Her psyche is released to enter time as she sings passionately a song that transports her past suffering into discourse. Raimunda even sings *of* this process of her quest and attempt now to name what she seeks. Beyond merely setting intimate revolt in motion for the spectator, insofar as Raimunda's experience of the gaze that enables her to commit psychic matricide is offered to the viewer, *Volver* promotes the concept:

> And the snows of time
> Silvering my brow
> Feeling
> That life is an instant,
> That twenty years is nothing,
> That the feverish eyes
> Wandering in the shadows
> seek you and name you.

Raimunda participates in Kristeva's "pardon" by "reuniting with affect through the metaphorical and metonymic rifts of discourse" (Kristeva 2002, 26). She is able to access her encrypted mother and begin to defrost her psychic trouble, to separate from her, by translating her into the semiotic poetry of song. Raimunda *re*discovers her mother in language. Kristeva knows that "psychopathological symptoms and structures" are the result of an inability "to integrate the atemporal." Hence she favors a "bringing to the fore of an unconscious time ... that encroaches on a prepsychical time and approaches the somatic" (2002, 31). Raimunda's song enacts, articulates, and celebrates that process of forgiveness and offers it to the spectator as a paradigm.

Raimunda breaks through a destructive oblivion, through years ("snows") of time, to "seek" and "name," so that she can return to a "sweet memory" rather than be plagued by a memory-trace that sabotages her desire:

> Living,
> With my soul clinging,
> To a sweet memory,
> That I weep for again.

This song "Volver" itself, especially given that the mother taught it to Raimunda as a child, is part of that sweet memory. (It is strangely as though Irene at some level had foreknowledge of Raimunda's psychic turmoil, given that she exposed her daughter to this very song about the necessity of intimate revolt.) In the midst of Raimunda's song, when she senses the presence of Irene outside in Sole's car, Raimunda experiences a provisional psychosis of being, the Nothing, the dark night of the soul. Finishing her song, Raimunda's face reflects overwhelming effort and pain; she completes the song in tears. Irene has metamorphosed from being "dead" (a ghost) to being a real presence; and because the mother immediately disappears after her appearance as that real presence, giving way to the gaze, she becomes in the end a supportive real absence. And, insofar as Irene's *subsequent* status as a real presence in Raimunda's daily life is preceded by Raimunda's intense, shattering encounter with her as a real absence, Raimunda achieves an intimate revolt.[4]

Indicting American capitalist "ethics"

Volver not only thematizes and puts into effect Kristeva's concept of intimate revolt at the level of the spectator, but Almodóvar's film also targets the society of the spectacle as the formidable threat to intimate revolt. Completely on Kristeva's wavelength, *Volver* presents intimate revolt as an antidote to the western obsession with facile images and objects of quick consumption.

Volver takes up the topic of the society of the spectacle overtly. In Sole's illegal beauty salon, her clients analyze and condemn what they call "trash TV." They note in particular its addictive quality: "Once I start watching it, I can't stop. I feel worse and worse, but I'm hooked. It's like a drug." They comment on its assault on one's sensibility, observing that trash TV keeps you from sleeping and that all the shouting "drives you crazy." Shortly after Sole's clients' explicit critique, a parodied television talk show in *Volver*, "Wherever You Are," run by Agustina's sister, Brigida, attempts to treat Agustina's relation to her mother, needless to say crudely, by bribing Agustina to speak out with the reward of a trip to a cancer-treatment center in Houston. Agustina is invited, and pressured, to sacrifice her soul to gain her biological life – what would then be a controlled "bare life." The crass talk-show host asks Agustina a series of rude, invasive questions about her mother: Was she a single parent? Was she mentally unbalanced? And who was the friend that died in the fire on the day Agustina's mother disappeared? "Wherever You Are" is fixated on what is most intimate in Agustina's life. This show is exposed in the film as cheapening that intimacy by reducing it to entertainment. The host of "Wherever You Are" expects Agustina to reveal the story of her mother's connection to Raimunda's mother – to unveil their intimate family secrets and even, we might say, to enact a superficial "intimate revolt" on television. Agustina is turned into a freak, an object of fascination for the audience and TV viewers, especially as she grows alienated by the show's rough, if not abusive, handling of her most personal issues.

In this ghastly scene, *Volver* sets up a clash between delicate psychic life and the commodification of that life in the society of the spectacle. In the interest of unveiling a murder mystery for profit, the show and its host batter Agustina with questions, pretending to be her friend. At a point of particular frustration with Agustina's unwillingness to cooperate (despite the fact that she had agreed to), the host announces that Agustina is "among friends" and urges the audience to offer "a big hand for Agustina!" The applauding audience is portrayed mechanically, as monstrously fake. The film exhibits an abyss between the applauding audience and a frail, suffering Agustina, a cancer victim lured pathetically, though understandably, by the temptation to be cured. The grotesque applause awakens Agustina to what she is doing – selling her soul to save her body. With obvious deliberation, she then marches off the live show, causing a great deal of commotion. Though in a fragile state, Agustina resists the pull of the bribe, walks humbly and honestly off the show, and in effect chooses literal death over the "death" of her psyche/soul. *Volver* lays bare the horror of the show, its cruel bribe, and the way it mangles and destroys intimate life – chiefly by supporting Agustina's last-minute decision, instead, to die, peacefully and gracefully.

Volver represents the society of the spectacle as a virtual killer, making real, natural death preferable. At supper at Aunt Paula's after the show, Sole states bluntly to Agustina: "You shouldn't have done it." Agustina returns a humiliated "I know that." Raimunda gives her approval with a nod. We watch in awe over the choice they are making. By concluding with Agustina's acceptance of literal death, the film further injects death into "lived actuality," both on the level of the figures within the film – Raimunda, Sole, Paula, and even Irene – and on the level of the spectator. Toward the end of *Volver*, Agustina becomes more and more ghostly. Her ethereal figure seems to float in a white nightgown through the domestic spaces of her home. She greets Irene as though Irene were an emissary from the heavenly realm that Agustina is on the verge of entering. However, Agustina in fact trades places with Irene, who has, at the end, living in Madrid, given up her supernatural status.

Volver is framed by Agustina's rapport with death. Agustina will soon slip into the tomb she had found solace in visiting and cleaning in the opening scene. Framing all the material of the film in this way, *Volver* conveys Kristeva's idea that death as "a temporality heterogeneous to linear time (*Zeitlos*)" must not be "subtracted" from "the logic of the living" (Kristeva 2002, 32). Leaving temporality behind, Agustina enters the *Zeitlos*, just as Irene emerges from the *Zeitlos* into time, a two-way crossing that well illustrates, and activates, Kristeva's favored intersection of life and non-life. Likewise, Irene, the mother who has emerged from the dead, plans eventually to have daily conversations with her daughter, Raimunda. When Raimunda announces to her mother that she has "so much to tell" her, Irene assures Raimunda: "I'll see you every day." Having encountered Irene at the level of the gaze and thus having pulled herself out of her psychic deep freeze, Raimunda now can engage with her on a regular basis – in time.

For all we know, at the end Irene herself may be on the verge of an intimate revolt through film. *Volver*'s final displacement of the society of the spectacle hints at this possibility. Near the end of *Volver*, the society of the spectacle seems supplanted as Irene watches Luchino Visconti's *Bellissima*. While caring for the dying Agustina, Irene takes in what appears to be a thought-specular film with the capacity to enable Irene to face her past mistakes. For *Bellissima* indirectly reflects on Irene's life. The main character, Maddelena, is abused by her husband, who has a sweet relationship with their young daughter (though it is not even implied that he abuses her). The mother too, like Irene who taught the song "Volver" to Raimunda for a "casting for child singers," teaches her daughter, Maria, a song, in the hope that Maria will be selected for a central acting part in a film.

After a great deal of duress, finally Maria is offered the role, but Maddelena, the mother, having realized the ruthlessness of this cinema world, rejects the contract she so desperately wanted at the outset. Maddelena learns that "Dreams of stardom have made many people unhappy," observes corruption (the giving of acting favors for sex and money), and experiences the crude insensitivity of the judges, who remark that her daughter is "a real dwarf." Maria, the little girl, breaks down in a heavy bout of tears during her audition. Disillusion is the only outcome of Maddelena's fierce passion to have her daughter star at Cinecittà. A meta-cinematic film, in the category of *neorealism rosa* (a sub-genre of comedy), *Bellissima* condemns the society of the spectacle or Hollywood-style cinema. Just as Agustina sacrifices a trip to Houston for cancer treatment, Maddelena sets aside her wish for a better future for her daughter rather than sell out to malignant American capitalist ethics.

By putting *Bellissima* on television at the end of his film, Almodóvar substitutes a visual attack on the society of the spectacle for that spectacle. He completes his multi-tiered Kristevan message of intimate revolt versus the society of the spectacle. The kinship between Kristeva and Almodóvar is unmistakable. Using Visconti to distinguish between films produced at Cinecittà and films like *Bellissima*, Almodóvar goes so far as to honor Kristeva's distinction between the spectacle and the thought specular – her sense that, while the society of the spectacle generates images that fail to liberate us, the visible is nevertheless the port of registry of the drive. All film is not a lost cause. Thought-specular film can, in fact, be an effective psychoanalytic counter to the threat of psychic demise posed by all its empty avatars.

Notes

1 The way *Volver* employs color to *absorb* spectatorial psychic material puts to use Deleuze's "colour-image," in *Cinema I*, which is defined by its "*absorbent* characteristic": "the colour-image does not refer to a particular object, but absorbs all that it can." Deleuze regards "colour" as "the affect itself" that has the capacity to absorb the characters, "situations," and the spectator. (In the work of film director Minnelli, "colours" are more than absorbent: "the splendour of colours" here has an "almost carnivorous, devouring, destructive ... function" [Deleuze 1983, 118–19]).

2 Calling attention to the absorption that takes place as the film engages the spectator's psyche, *Volver* contains several washing scenes: Raimunda washes dishes as well as the knife that kills Paco, both before and after it kills him; as part of her job, she cleans the spacious floor and does laundry at the Madrid airport; Sole washes women's hair and instructs her mother on how to do it properly.

3 "Volver," originally a tango by Carlos Gardel, was transformed into flamenco. It is sung by Estrella Morente; lyrics by Alfredo Le Pera.

4 *Volver* underscores the actual presence of the mother through a joke on the Eucharist. This Catholic Mystery plays an amusing role in the film through the lektonic trace of the wafers. When Paula, Sole, and Raimunda visit Aunt Paula at the beginning of *Volver*, they are served a plateful of "wafers," baked, unbeknowst to them at the time, by Irene, the "dead" mother. The tasty wafers appear, and are enjoyed periodically, throughout the film, keeping the Real Presence of the mother alive. They are a material trace of her reality, just as her odors allow her daughters to sense her real existence. Sole and Raimunda smell their mother and, in a sense, taste her, as a Catholic takes in the Real Presence of Christ during Communion. "Do this in remembrance of me," the priest utters as he holds up the host for the communicant to consume. Likewise, Raimunda's mother bakes wafers for her daughters to partake of in remembrance of her. It is all a joke. Nevertheless, the taste of the wafers ties the mother to her daughters

through sensory intimacy. Serving on behalf of working-through, the wafers insert non-life (the "dead" mother) into life. The wafers – a pun – inscribe "death into what is most alive in lived actuality" (Kristeva 2002, 36).

References

Agamben, Giorgio. 2000. *Means Without End: Notes on Politics*, trans. Vincenzo Binetti and Cesare Casarino. Minneapolis: University of Minnesota Press.

Bellissima. 1951. Directed by Luchino Visconti. Rome: CEI Incom.

Debord, Guy. 1995. *The Society of the Spectacle*, trans. Donald Nicholson-Smith. New York: Zone Books.

Deleuze, Gilles. 1983. *Cinema I: The Movement-Image*, trans. Hugh Tomlinson and Barbara Habberjam. Minneapolis: University of Minnesota Press.

Kristeva, Julia. 1982. *Powers of Horror: An Essay on Abjection*, trans. Leon S. Roudiez. New York: Columbia University Press.

Kristeva, Julia. 1989. *Black Sun: Depression and Melancholia*, trans. Leon S. Roudiez. New York: Columbia University Press.

Kristeva, Julia. 2002. *Intimate Revolt: The Powers and the Limits of Psychoanalysis*, trans. Jeanine Herman. New York: Columbia University Press.

Kristeva, Julia, and Catherine Clément. 2001. *The Feminine and the Sacred*, trans. Jane Marie Todd. New York: Columbia University Press.

Volver. 2006. Directed by Pedro Almodóvar. New York: Sony Pictures Classics.

Chapter 12

Psychoanalysis, Popular and Unpopular

Catherine Liu

In the 1956 science fiction film *Forbidden Planet*, a dashing crew of terrestrial soldiers frees a fair maiden and destroys an alien machine that can unleash the destructive power of the "id." Leslie Nielsen, playing the captain of the United Planets Cruiser C57-D, triumphs over the hubristic mad genius Dr. Morbius by forcing him to accept that the invisible monster that killed all members of his original expeditionary force was a materialization of his own "subconscious." Morbius, played by Walter Pidgeon, has been living with his daughter Alta in a modernist, biomorphic-style ranch house in a state of radical seclusion and incestuous self-sufficiency. Psychoanalytic terms like "id" were common currency in Hollywood of the 1950s: long before 1970s film theorists embraced sexual difference, the gaze, and fetishism as keys to understanding film form, spectatorship, and the ideological apparatus, the American film industry followed in the footsteps of Greenwich Village bohemian modernists by taking up the tools presented by Sigmund Freud's epochal discovery.

In narrativizing, visualizing, and taking apart the psychic apparatus on screen, Hollywood filmmakers and stars displayed their embrace of modern life: *Forbidden Planet* not only cast the psychoanalytic concept of the "id" as its villain, it was also the first feature film with a completely

A Concise Companion to Psychoanalysis, Literature, and Culture, First Edition.
Edited by Laura Marcus and Ankhi Mukherjee.

electronic score, composed by experimental musicians Lois and Bebe Baron. Dr. Morbius' home on Altair bears a striking resemblance to the intimate but modern case-study homes being built in California by a generation of idealistic architects, from Charles and Ray Eames to Gregory Ain. Its furnishings follow the biomorphic designs of Isamu Noguchi, while Robbie the Robot as futuristic butler incarnates the domestic labor-saving device in one compact, queer anthropomorphic package. Finally, under Leslie Nielsen's, or Commander John Jay Adams', insistence, Morbius acknowledges, like a good psychoanalytic patient, his dark side: he accepts that the monster is a materialization of his unconscious aggression. In order to save the world from its nefarious power, he, like the Krell technology, must be destroyed. The massive power plant, suggested by special effects produced by painted sets – implying a vast underground lair – must be laid waste, lest other creatures come into contact with its mysterious ability to realize one's unconscious aggressions. His daughter Alta is released from her incestuous sequestration and the expeditionary force can return to Earth having solved the riddle of Morbius' failure and self-destruction. The unconscious, once weaponized, can have genocidal powers: its containment is the task of a rag-tag detachment of Earth soldiers, whose respect for the chain of command allows the highest-ranking officer to win the love of the innocent daughter of an alien world. Working between high culture and pulp fiction, the film is able to refer to Shakespeare and Freud while providing an MGM showcase for Disney animators, on loan to render the monster materialized out of Morbius' unconscious.

According to Ann Douglas, Freud's career and body of work shared a "mind-set and a mood" with white urban America: "Freud and America in the modern era were not just conversationalists on a common theme, but mutual mind readers at work in an age fascinated with all forms of mind reading and mental telepathy.... As powerful arrivistes, Freud and America, more specifically New York , shared in its most acute form of adrenaline rush that was modernism" (1995, 156). Douglas' analysis of American culture of the 1920s weaves narrative strands that tie together the cultural restlessness and spirit of experimentation and invention that characterized New York and its bohemian culture. William James and Gertrude Stein, two forward-thinking Americans, emerge in her history as figures that were fascinated and repelled by psychoanalysis. Douglas describes Freud as fundamentally hostile to the energies of the young nation but his ambitions for psychoanalysis as a set of world-making and world-destroying insights inspired Greenwich Village bohemians, aspiring actresses, and men of letters. The power of his discovery of the unconscious was allegorized in *Forbidden Planet* by the Krell machine. If, according to psychoanalytic theory, resistance was the hallmark by which its proponents and adversaries measured its truth, the enthusiasm with which psychoanalytic theory was embraced in America was deeply disturbing to its founder. Popular culture as it emerged in the 1920s and 1930s had already taken up many of Freud's theories and presented them energetically in the film industry, with daring young women like movie star Colleen Moore seen reading a book by Freud in *Flaming Youth* (1923) (Douglas 1995, 123). In a letter dating from May 14, 1922, to Arthur Schnitzler, Freud writes upon the occasion of the playwright's birthday that Schnitzler had made similar discoveries in human psychology as psychoanalysis, but that he found aesthetically pleasing forms with which to communicate his insights. Apologetically, Freud closes the letter with the statement, "Forgive me for drifting into psychoanalysis; I simply can't do anything else. I know, however, that psychoanalysis is not the means of making oneself popular" (quoted in Jones 1957, 444).

In fact, MGM, the studio that produced *Forbidden Planet*, was an early adopter when it came to psychoanalysis: readers of the *New York Times* on January 24, 1925, would have found themselves scrutinizing the following headline, "Freud Rebuffs Goldwyn: Viennese Psychoanalyst Is Not Interested in Motion Picture Offer." According to the *New York Times* report, Goldwyn travelled to Vienna to ask the "master" of psychoanalysis to write a love story, but Freud refused even to meet with him. For Douglas, Freud's rejection of Goldwyn's offer was of a piece with his symptomatic dislike of American life and its popular culture: she implies that Freud's animus lay in the "hatred of small differences" that motivates narcissistic rejection of those who remind us too much of ourselves.

Freud and the American moderns like William James did diverge in their attitudes toward religion and the mind-cure therapies that emerged at the turn of the century in the United States. For Ann Douglas, James' acceptance of the practices and results of spiritualism and its exploration of the occult and the supernatural was linked to pragmatism's emphasis on practice rather than theory: in practice, mind-cure therapy was producing powerful healing effects on its patients, just as spiritualism gave succor to those who craved contact with other worlds and their lost ones. Christian Science, as pioneered by Mary Baker Eddy, was a female-oriented movement. James did not hesitate to affirm "alternative" cures and alternative knowledge produced by ordinary, often uneducated women. James rejected Old Testament austerity and the Calvinist approach to salvation, while Freud's patriarchal authoritarianism placed him in a starkly drawn genealogical relationship with impersonality and masculinist privileging of objectivity.

Like psychoanalysis, mind-cure and self-help were based upon the idea that unseen, non-organic forces shape our world and our bodies. Perhaps these movements faced a medical establishment bent on enforcing a monopoly on expertise in the healing arts, but psychoanalysis appeared exotic and foreign while self-help and mind-cure were allied to American traditions and folk cures. While compelling, Douglas' parsing of the difference between William James and Gertrude Stein, on the one hand, and Sigmund Freud, on the other, overlooks a powerful dimension of Freudian theory – its intimate relationship with the deflationary and comical worldview of Yiddish folk humor. In fact, *Jokes and Their Relation to the Unconscious* (1905) anthologizes the Jewish joke and its folk repository of popular wisdom. Freud allows us to interpret its humor as playful, infantile subversion of the pretensions of the powerful and the wealthy, even as he demonstrates that, as in the experiences of Jewish popular culture with its unflinching take on the vanity of the rich, the desire of the undesirable offers powerful examples of the power of censorship and the pleasure of nonsensical defiance. Freud's explanations of the economy of repression and its relationship to laughter can be crudely summarized in this way: a good joke allows teller and listener to save energy that we spend censoring childish associations between words (puns), aggression against the superego (displacement, nonsense, criticism), and sexual associations (dirty jokes, of which there are not many examples in the joke book). He returned over and over again to the following "Jewish joke," which he felt demonstrated the shared pleasure that jokes communicate when they present the cleverness of instinctual life defending itself from superegoic reproach:

> An impoverished individual borrowed 25 florins from a prosperous acquaintance, with many asservations of his necessitous circumstances. The very same day his benefactor met him again in a restaurant with a plate of salmon mayonnaise in front of him. The benefactor reproached him, "What? You borrow money from me and then order yourself salmon mayonnaise? Is *that* what you've used my money for?" "I don't understand you," replied the object of the attack; "if I don't have any

> money I *can't* eat salmon mayonnaise, and if I have some money I *am not allowed* to eat salmon mayonnaise. Well, then, when am I to eat salmon mayonnaise?"
>
> (Freud 1953–74, 8:49–50; translation modified)

Jewish humor embodies a subaltern people's comic vision of human vanity and social and economic inequity. In this joke, the hedonism of the poor man and his willful misunderstanding of his benefactor's reproach allow us to see philanthropy or the generosity of the rich for what it is – an exercise of power and discipline. We sympathize with the poor man's self-defense and trickery and laugh at the benefactor's hypocrisy exposed: his gift came with strings attached. A sob story and the pity evoked demonstrate that when the rich give to the poor, they do not want the poor to enjoy the good things of life. The connection between this Jewish joke and Freud's deflationary but comic view of human pretension is obscured in Douglas' otherwise magisterial account of his influence on American moderns. When she reduces Freud's interpretation of jokes to sinister vehicles for repressed violence, she is taking a cue from the melodramatic plot of popular understanding of the id as promoted by *Forbidden Planet* (Douglas 1995, 139).

Freud was without a doubt, if not an Old Testament, then an Old World patriarch, but Ann Douglas in 1995, and then David Cronenberg in his 2011 film *A Dangerous Method* represent him as particularly humorless and severe. Viggo Mortensen's Freud is an ethically upright, judgmental and brilliant man. For Douglas, Freud is a dynamic upstart. Cronenberg and Douglas perform similar acts of decontextualization by ignoring "Jewish sensibility" formed by Yiddish and its earthiness and stubborn plebeian pride (Gabler 2011, 10). Freud's book on jokes abounds with characters familiar to popular Yiddish culture: opportunistic *schädchen*, or matchmakers, desperate bachelors, Jewish beggars, Jewish millionaires, superstitious faithful and the deceitful rabbis who exploit them. As Freud describes the pleasure released when joke teller and interlocutor can share in the temporary lifting of repression, he cites the Jewish jokes and puns with which he is familiar. The comedy of unmasking "arises in the first instance as an unintended discovery derived from human social relations" (Freud 1953–74, 8:189). Neal Gabler and Harvey Pekar would agree. As Gabler concludes in his introduction to Pekar's illustrated volume on Yiddishkeit, Yiddish is capable of ripping "through formalities … prevarications – pretensions, and … dishonesty. In a world that fetishizes money and status,

Yiddishkeit shrugs at both" (Gabler 2011, 10). In the case of the joke about salmon mayonnaise, we laugh because we are given temporary reprieve from an oppressive and disciplining sense of gratitude enforced by the generosity of the powerful. In Freud's *Civilization and Its Discontents*, he casts a shadow of a doubt on his friend Romain Rolland's description of a spiritually infused "oceanic feeling of connectedness" with the shrug of Yiddishkeit's vernacular skepticism:

> So it is a feeling of indissoluble connection, of belonging inseparably to the external world as a whole. To me, personally, I may remark, this seems something more in the nature of an intellectual judgment, not, it is true, without any accompanying feeling-tone, but with one of a kind which characterizes other equally far-reaching reflections as well. I could not in my own person convince myself of the primary nature of such a feeling. But I cannot on that account deny that it in fact occurs in other people.
>
> (Freud 1953–74, 21:78)

The humor of the Jewish sensibility provided Freud with powerful examples of the depreciation of the superego in popular culture. Low Jewish sensibility communicates a critical perspective on superstition, venality, and hypocrisy, while expressing solidarity with the cunning and pleasure-seeking project of not just the ego, but also the poor, the ordinary, and the deprived.

It is striking that Douglas emphasizes Gertrude Stein's Rabelaisian appetites and carnivalesque attitude at the expense of Freud's somber and allegedly stoical pessimism, while Viggo Mortensen's Freud is essentially a humorless and resentful prig. William James and Gertrude Stein did not have to work for a living: both enjoyed family fortunes that were financially well managed. Henry James Senior was independently wealthy: William James was born at Astor House in New York City. Gertrude Stein's father, Daniel, was a railroad executive who invested in real estate. Gertrude and her brothers, Daniel and Leo, enjoyed lives of bohemian ease because of the wealth and parsimony of the family patriarch. The interest income they derived from family capital allowed them a disinterested relationship to survival that Freud could never entirely enjoy, even though by the 1920s his practice was burgeoning and he felt for the first time in his life free from the economic anxiety of a paterfamilias with six children, a wife, and spinster sisters to support. The 1920s represented a period of global economic prosperity, with the United States leading the way in forging new forms of consumerism and popular, democratic culture. The stock market soared and the principles of liberal capitalism and social mobility seemed ascendant as a rising tide of economic growth and easy credit lifted many Americans out of lives of rural deprivation into, if not lives of material ease, then at least relative urban cosmopolitanism. In the 1920s and 1930s, many of Freud's patients were Americans, like A.A. Brill who traveled to Vienna to be treated by him and paid him in US dollars, of which he began accumulating a substantial sum (Jones 1957, 147).

Douglas' historical linking of Freud, James, and Stein as the theoretical enablers of American modernity unites and divides the three figures into two groups: elitist and pluralist, with Freud alone in the first category, and James and Stein in the second. Freud's single-minded pursuit of unitary theories of psychological life can easily be characterized as dogmatic, in contrast to the eclectic, egalitarian ethos represented by the Americans in Douglas' constellation. As I have tried to show in greater detail in *American Idyll: Academic Anti-Elitism as Cultural Critique* (Liu 2011), Freud's thinking embodied the popular skepticism of an ordinary person who is capable of exercising reason and critical thinking as a matter of instinctual problem-finding and problem-solving. Pluralism and eclecticism may seem at first to be more democratic in ethos, but in psychoanalytic terms, they also demand a higher degree of sublimation and renunciation. While Freud may not have been a populist, he abhorred esoteric and mystical spiritual practices, simply because gurus and teachers of that sort did not lay out clear paths that could be followed by the exercise of reason in their disciples.

In *The Case of Sigmund Freud: Medicine and Identity at the Fin de Siècle* (1993), Sander Gilman affirms the image of a strong-minded and ambitious Freud, enmeshed in arguments about biological determinism and the pseudo-science of race and racism that characterized the medical establishment of not only the Austro-Hungarian Empire, but of the western world itself. Gilman, like most progressive academics writing and publishing in the early 1990s, was obsessed with the question of identity. For Gilman, Freud was unable to escape the dilemma presented by the rampant "medicalization of race" in late nineteenth-century Europe. He could not avoid contributing to the project of biologically defining the difference between Jews and non-Jews and yet he fought for psychoanalysis as a new science based on neutrality and objectivity in a social and cultural milieu that condemned Jews for being emotional and incapable of true reason. While Gilman does not go so far as to suggest that Freud in fact embraces an antisemitic scientific establishment, he does elaborate a theory of self and bad object that comes very close to defining Freud's ambiguous relationship to the medical establishment as a neurotic and harrowing one. Gilman seems to suggest that in choosing to be a doctor, Freud also "chose" to expose himself to more antisemitism than might have been his lot had he remained outside the field of professional medical ambition: in his words, "Freud elected to be a physician. Yet this choice heightened the meaning of his Jewish identity for he could never remove himself from the anti-Semitism that clouded his professional choice throughout his adult life. Anti-Semitism haunted the medical profession" (1993, 217). Freud's "choice," thus framed, leads Gilman to see the creation of the new science of psychoanalysis as of a piece with the Viennese doctor's "search for identity" (1993, 218). The question of identity formation in *fin-de-siècle* culture contains, according to Gilman, potential for extraordinary growth and development: "Freud's project is an example of his positive reaction to the bind of race and science he was placed in" (1993, 226). Strong-minded, assertive and positive, Freud did not just embody the traits of burgeoning modern America; he was obviously understood by Gilman as an exemplary subject, someone who made difficult choices, and who could be creative and adaptive in response to a complex set of ostensibly insurmountable obstacles. Freud was a strong individual whose search for identity allowed him to be more innovative and courageous than others around him: in choosing difference, difficulty, and complexity over homogeneity, ease, and simplicity, Freud arrived at the success of the strong-minded.

During the 1990s, many Anglo-American academics found succor in the idea of "identity" and the "search for identity": Sander Gilman's forensic analysis of Freud's relationship to his Jewish identity partakes in the intellectual climate of the time. It is not so remarkable, then, that in a book on Freud's Jewish identity written during this period of academic ferment around "identity politics," Gilman would neglect to consider the one text where Freud investigates the founding myths of Jewish identity, namely *Moses and Monotheism*.[1] This work by Freud is an extraordinary close reading of the Old Testament and an exfoliation of the greatest prophet of the Judaic tradition. Moses, Freud argues, was an Egyptian: his proof has to do with symptomatic aspects of the foundling story that betray the repressed content of Moses' foreignness to the Jews of Egypt. The foundling Moses is adopted by an Egyptian princess: he is raised as Egyptian royalty, and only later discovers his humble origins. Freud finds this reversal odd: in almost all ancient folk tales, the foundling is found by peasants or shepherds, humble people, and it is later revealed that he has royal blood. The fantasy of secret, royal origins allows us narcissistic satisfaction. If Moses' story is a secondary revision of the wish-fulfillment of the traditional folk tale, it is because the Jewish people have had to repress Moses' actual origins. Moses famously had a speech defect, and this for Freud betrayed his discomfort with the language of the Jews. According to Freud's account, which relies on Egyptologist Ernst Sellin's work, Akhnehaton ascended the throne and preached an austere form of monotheism that was rejected by the Egyptian elites upon his death. Monotheism, however, appealed to some of the most brilliant men in Egypt: according to Freud, Moses was one of these men. Upon the death of his pharaoh, he chose to leave Egypt with the Jewish people in order to preach and institute a monotheism that his chosen people found equally unbearable. In the desert, the priesthood murdered Moses, and then the guilt of his assassination and the realization of the debt of freedom that was owed to him created the elaborate series of prohibitions and proscriptions that the rabbinical elite imposed upon the tribe as collective atonement for the murder of the great man: "The Jews, who even according to the Bible were stubborn and unruly towards their law-giver and leader, rebelled at last, killed him, and threw off the imposed Aton religion as the Egyptians had done before them" (Freud 1953–74, 23:156). Freud himself never spoke about identity as an object or problem that could be either found or solved: for Freud, identification was a process, one that Jacques Lacan would later locate in relationship to mirrors and infantile delusion. When Freud talked about apparatuses and qualities, and about himself in his correspondence with his intimates, he was never anything but humorously self-deprecating. Freud as "father" of psychoanalysis continued to fascinate American thinkers, whether as an entrepreneurial strong man, austere patriarch, or conflicted, identity-seeking Jewish doctor.

Self-deprecation and devaluation may have been the emblem of the strong man of liberal capitalism, inventor, discoverer, and adventurer. It was no accident, however, that the quest for identity and self-affirmation became one of the major popular preoccupations of postwar America, a country beset by the massive social and economic changes described by C. Wright Mills in his classic *White Collar: The American Middle Classes* (2001 [1951]). Mills' analysis of the gospel of success takes off where Ann Douglas leaves off. "Self-help" and "pop therapy" would lack "the intellectual and cultural interest that James and Stein had brought to the Mind-cure tradition." By Stein's death in 1946, "It had come to be an unwritten axiom that 'theory' and 'therapy,' elite art and professionalized good cheer, were mutually and forever exclusive. Highbrow pessimism assumed low-brow optimism, and vice versa" (Douglas 1995, 143). Neither Freud, James, nor Stein was able, however, to predict the ways in which popular representations of psychic life would be reshaped and rearranged by postwar self-help movements, and the rise of new forms of popular culture and an advice industry that married self-hypnosis, self-help, the power of positive thinking, and business motivation, for a middle class confronting confusing new forms of work and leisure.

According to Mills, just as the conditions of liberal capitalism were being reshaped to suit the massive bureaucracies and corporate structures of monopoly capitalism, motivational literature sought to reinforce the psychological qualities of an entrepreneurialism that no longer suited the professional and economic progress of the salaried masses of the American postwar period:

> The way up, according to the classic style of liberalism, was to establish a small enterprise and to expand it by competition with other enterprises.... According to the old entrepreneur's ideology, success is always linked with the sober personal virtues of will power and thrift, habits of order, neatness, and constitutional inability to say Yes to the easy road. These virtues are at once a condition and a sign of success.
>
> (Mills 2001 [1951], 160)

Mills describes the evolution of the inspirational literature of entrepreneurial success: first, by bolstering individual resolve in the service of the entrepreneurial spirit; second, by justifying the cruelty of failure; and third, in the phase of monopoly capitalism and white-collar work, by encouraging "peace of mind and various physical and spiritual ways of relaxation ... by lowering the level of ambition by replacing the older goals with more satisfying internal goals.... The literature of the peace of the inner man fits in with the alienating process that has shifted men from a focus upon production to a focus upon consumption" (2001 [1951], 282–83). If fewer and fewer Americans were actually able to persevere as small business owners and self-employed entrepreneurs, the literature of success "explained" macro-economic changes in terms of individual insufficiency. If your family farm or corner grocery store could not survive a period of economic consolidation, you were not thrifty enough: you chose the easy road, unlike Freud, who allegedly "selected" the medical profession in order to present himself before the hostility of institutionalized, pseudoscientific antisemitism. On the other hand, if you were unhappy with being passed over for promotion in your white-collar job, you made yourself miserable by focusing on the external trappings of success.

Mills' analysis of the psychology of the mid-century gospel of success and inspirational literature served one end: to understand the class identity of this new American worker. Would he or she be proletarianized, as might be expected of wage workers who had no hope of enjoying inherited wealth? Or would he or she hide behind the prestige of educational credentials and office work, even if the wages were merely comparable or even occasionally inferior to those of blue-collar workers? Will they assume political power in solidarity with those below them, or in reactionary consolidation with their economic superiors? His answer is not at all clear-cut, but Mills sees the fragmentation and decentralization of political power as key in dispersing political authority across a bureaucracy or "network" as "manipulation": in an "impersonalized and more anonymous system of control, explicit responses are not so possible: anxiety is likely to replace fear; insecurity to replace worry. The problem is who really has power, for often the tangled and hidden system seems a complex yet organized irresponsibility" (2001 [1951], 349).

Although Mills' Left critique of the growth of technocratically oriented state-sponsored solutions to inequality inspired the student movement of the 1960s, his thesis about mass media, popular passivity, and "manipulation" fell out favor as a generation of post-'68 academics emerged on the cultural studies scene.[2] His class-oriented brand of qualitative Left sociology had fallen into serious disuse by the 1980s and 1990s, two decades that discarded class analysis for split selves, performativity, and identity formation. His theories of mass media manipulation and popular political indifference fall in line with his analysis of monopoly capital's thinning out of the sphere of political action: while unions and corporations seem to monopolize discussions about working conditions and two political parties divided the share of voters, the white-collar worker retreats or escapes into an inviting inner space of self-fashioning. Mills finds in the psychology behind the political indifference of the new middle class "the impasse of liberalism and the collapse of socialist hopes" (2001 [1951], 326). When a class rejects politics altogether, it no longer sees political meaning in its "insecurities or desires." The women's movement became a place where personal experience and political activity would be aligned once again, but not in ways that Mills would have recognized.

Although the hipster of the late 1950s would seem to be positioned in direct opposition to the rearguardism of Mills' white-collar workers, his stylized estrangement from political meaning and organization was articulated by Norman Mailer's 1957 essay, "The White Negro," a hipster declaration of independence from both political participation and the talking cure. Whereas, in the 1920s, to be psychoanalytically oriented was to be modern for both white and black bohemians, by the end of the 1960s analysts were "squares" and the true social and cultural rebel embraced his mental illness as a sanctified and rather problematic identification with the everyday danger faced by black Americans (Mailer 2007 [1957]). Despite or because of his bombastic tone, Mailer presaged the popular repudiation of psychoanalysis as both backward and repressive. Moreover, he attributes to the "Negro" the unique ability to live completely present to imminent destruction: hipster emulation arises not from a bohemian solidarity between white and black moderns as described by Douglas in New York City of the 1920s: Mailer's white Negro embraced the allegedly transcendent psychopathology of African Americans. While a repudiation of mental healing of any sort, "The White Negro" opens with an allusion to the unconscious and its unfathomability: "Probably we will never be able to determine the psychic havoc of the concentration camps and the atom bomb upon the unconscious mind of almost everyone alive in these years."

While psychoanalytic institutes and practices flourished in American cities in the 1970s and 1980s, Freud's science had lost its appeal to popular culture. First of all, psychoanalysis was no longer the only therapeutic instrument available to middle-class Americans hoping to find answers and cures to a spectrum of dilemmas caused by the suffering that accompanied mental illness. The counterculture that embraced the modern primitive and alternative cures, and non-traditional forms of knowledge, found Carl Jung's theories of anima and animus much more congenial to a generational quest for identity and alternatives. The search for self would animate social movements even as the intellectual arms of such movements grappled with the legacy of psychoanalysis, as both theory and therapy.

In the 1970s, psychoanalytic theory found unlikely users among a passionate cadre of feminist scholars, especially in the new field of film theory and film studies. Freud himself had puzzled over femininity and its symptoms: Jacques Lacan would later take the psychoanalytic account of castration and lack and remake it as a structural, meaning-making, but contingent mark of "difference." Sexual along with class difference were two things that feminists wanted to assert in the face of homogenizing representations of politics and political participation. Marxists like Mills had neglected the gender question: they had neglected the question of sexual difference and in doing so excluded forms of political participation and critique made possible by the identification of the oppressive powers as "patriarchal." If the women's movement declared that the "personal was the political," the objective conditions of oppression appeared apprehensible through the identification of what was unique and particular to women's experiences and women's lives. According to Daniel T. Rodgers' historical account of the early women's movement, social change was the goal of the movement's focus on raising levels of women's awareness about their identity as women:

> Consciousness raising made the personal collective and political. It gave the idea of "experience" a powerful place in the 1970s women's movement.... In the process it made solidarities: sisterhood where ... only fragmented, male-identified, household isolated and family-absorbed women had existed before.
>
> (Rodgers 2011, 148)

For feminist activists and scholars, the political significance of building feminist coalitions could not have been recognized or imagined by their male counterparts on the Left. A new worldview of politics and female experience had to be constructed from the ground up. According to Mary Ann Doane, Patricia Mellencamp, and Linda Williams, as feminist filmmakers and scholars "began to interrogate the assumptions behind a cinematic language of representation which promoted the concept of 'realism' and its effects on the construction and maintenance of sexual difference along patriarchal lines," they "began to embrace semiotic and psychoanalytic theories that seemed capable of accounting for the ways in which patriarchal ideology has elided the representation of women" (1984, 7). Although Freud had given us the tools by which to understand femininity, he was unable to completely account for the generalized cultural misogyny that had rendered femininity "the underside, the repressed of a classical or rational/conceptual discourse ... Feminism ... allied itself with the avant-garde or with any signifying practice which challenged existing discursive structures" (Doane, Mellencamp, and Williams 1984, 11).

Feminist filmmakers and activists looked for new ways of working and intervening in the art world, in the film industry, and in academia. The leading intellectuals of the movement embraced psychoanalytic theory as a powerful form of meta-criticism: the use of psychoanalytic theory provided tools by which pioneering scholars in feminist film criticism sought to introduce or smuggle new objects and new methodologies into the sphere of scholarly study. Psychoanalytic theories presented themselves as both weapons and targets for a new generation of scholars who were bringing their cultural activism into the halls of academia. The critique of realist film as male fantasy aimed at changing the world and freeing women from the straitjacket of gender. Hollywood film spectatorship was no more and no less than a form of political violence, an Althusserian exercise in ideological assertiveness. No one made the case more dramatically than Laura Mulvey in her classic essay "Visual Pleasure and Narrative Cinema" (1975), in which she uses Lacanian and Freudian concepts to dissect the ways in which the cinematic objectification of women contributes to the political suppression of women: "Woman's desire is subjected to her image as bearer of the bleeding wound. She can only exist in relationship to castration and cannot transcend it" (Mulvey 1975, 7). As figures in feminist film criticism like Laura Mulvey, Linda Williams, Tania Modleski, Kaja Silverman, and E. Ann Kaplan gained recognition in academia, their work became increasingly cited, recognized, and debated, but the goal of securing social change seemed to recede even as professional success and recognition seemed more achievable. Feminists were remarkably successful at organizing conferences and film festivals, and editing anthologies and journals in which new ideas about sexual difference and the politics of exclusion and exploitation were highlighted and criticized. In the passionate debates inspired by feminist film theory, fantasy, fetishism, and visual pleasure alternated between censure and celebration. The concepts themselves were as divorced from the practice of psychoanalysis as they were from the formulation of policy and political struggle in legislative bodies. In these familiar and tortured controversies over women's images, male gazes, and imaginary penises, a.k.a. phalluses, we see feminist film scholars using a selective language of psychoanalytic theory to present possibilities for reading, interpreting, and making film in order to remake the world itself. Christine Gledhill's 1976 essay, "Developments in Feminist Film Criticism," illustrates the problems that feminist film theorists confronted in their use of psychoanalytic concepts as ideology critique. At the beginning of her essay she writes, "there is a danger that, once the object of feminist criticism is defined solely in terms of the cinematic production of meaning, we lose the ability to deal with its relationship to women as defined in other social practices" (Gledhill 1984 [1976], 19). Gledhill's political and intellectual ambition encompasses no less than an "assault" on patriarchy using the critical tools of the avant-garde, anti-realism, Lacanian psychoanalysis, the work of Roland Barthes, and the integration of a feminist-infused form of Marxism to contest the ideologies of capitalism. It is undeniable that the 1970s were a time of political optimism for the Left, with the civil upheavals of the 1960s still fresh in everyone's memory, but Gledhill realizes as she approaches the end of her overview that something has been lost in the theoretical elaboration of poststructural psycholinguistic subject positions. "Real" women's lives, as defined by social practices, seemed to recede further and further from critical and cognitive analysis. The way out? Pointing to academic study of Harlequin romances, television, and newspaper advice columns as "unofficial discourses" by which women negotiate their relationships with dominant culture. It was during this period that poststructuralist theory became more insular and more elaborate, even as its engagements with popular cultural forms became more strident.

Psychoanalytic theory was instrumentalized as a facilitating but limited critique of patriarchy that returns the intellectual, boomerang-like, back to more study and more analysis of the repressed and the marginal, all in an airless world of dominant and marginalized discourses desperately seeking social relations in the form of real people and their experiences of spectatorship. Feminist film theory's accomplishments were many, but its mobilization of psychoanalytic theory for the purposes of cultural criticism became increasingly academic. In the meantime, on November 29, 1993, *Time* Magazine's cover featured a digitally rendered portrait of Freud's head dissolving into little puzzle pieces with the headline, "Is Freud Dead?" Along with self-help and New Age cures, behavioral and psychopharmacological therapies had increasingly replaced the Freudian cure in the practice of psychiatry with allegedly more effective and economical treatments. Freud's own "strength of mind" now appeared more as a symptom of his dogmatism and rigidity.

The famous white-collar middle class described by Mills had been thoroughly traumatized by wave after wave of corporate downsizing. Freelance work was the dignified way of understanding professional unemployment as self-employment. Blue-collar workers saw their unions decimated, their jobs transferred overseas. At the same time, 1970s feminists were disturbed by the younger generation of women's traditional choices. Even as middle-class women made their way up the meritocratic ladder, the middle class in general suffered economic setback after economic setback. The 1990s was the decade of the New Economy entrepreneur and the hacker. The rise of the Internet facilitated the study of the moving image, but undermined the importance of traditional Hollywood realist narratives; younger people had less and less experience with the realist narratives attacked by feminists and poststructuralists. The personal computer interfaced with increasingly miniaturized and mobile screens, and the on-line identities with which we accessed these spaces seemed a priori discursive, fragmented, transgressive, and unpredictable. Psychoanalysis was no longer a novelty or a scapegoat, at least in the popular imagination: almost everyone knows that sometimes "a cigar is just a cigar." A certain kind of psychoanalytic theory continues to thrive almost exclusively as an academic discourse, the history of its reception obscured by antagonisms real or imaginary with the culture that surrounded it. It is not surprising that today an obdurate but familiar indifference greets Freud's and feminism's insights regarding sexual difference and the unconscious.

Notes

1 Jan Assman's *Moses, the Egyptian* (1997) and Yosef Yerushalmi's *Freud's Moses: Judaism Terminable and Interminable* (1991) represent two different, sustained scholarly investigations of Freud's theory of the origins of monotheism.
2 See, for example, Andrew Ross' *No Respect* (1989) and Henry Jenkins' *Convergence Culture* (2006).

References

Assman, Jan. 1997. *Moses, the Egyptian*. Cambridge, MA: Harvard University Press.

Cronenberg, David, dir. 2011. *A Dangerous Method*. Sony Pictures Classics.

Doane, Mary Ann, Patricia Mellencamp, and Linda Williams. 1984. "Feminist Film Criticism: An Introduction." In *Re-vision: Essays in Feminist Film Criticism*, ed. Mary Ann Doane, Patricia Mellencamp, and Linda Williams, 1–17. Los Angeles: American Film Institute.

Douglas, Ann. 1995. *Terrible Honesty: Mongrel Manhattan in the 1920s*. New York: Farrar, Straus & Giroux.

Freud, Sigmund. 1953–74. *The Standard Edition of the Complete Psychological Works of Sigmund Freud*, 24 vols., ed. James Strachey, with the assistance of Anna Freud, Alix Strachey, and Alan Tyson, trans. James Strachey. London: Hogarth Press.

Gabler, Neal. 2011. "Yiddishkeit: An Introduction." In *Yiddishkeit: Jewish Vernacular and the New Land*, ed. Harvey Pekar and Paul Buhle, 9–10. New York: Abrams.

Gilman, Sander L. 1993. *The Case of Sigmund Freud: Medicine and Identity at the Fin de Siècle*. Baltimore: Johns Hopkins University Press.

Gledhill, Christine. 1984 [1976]. "Developments in Feminist Film Criticism." In *Re-vision: Essays in Feminist Film Criticism*, ed. Mary Ann Doane, Patricia Mellencamp, and Linda Williams, 18–48. Los Angeles: American Film Institute.

Jenkins, Henry. 2006. *Convergence Culture: Where Old and New Media Collide*. New York: New York University Press.

Jones, Ernest. 1957. *The Life and Work of Sigmund Freud, 1919–1939*. New York: Basic Books.

Liu, Catherine. 2011. *American Idyll: Academic Anti-Elitism as Cultural Critique*. Iowa City: University of Iowa Press.

Mailer, Norman. 2007 [1957]. "The White Negro (Fall, 1957)." *Dissent: A Quarterly of Politics and Culture*, http://www.dissentmagazine.org/online_articles/the-white-negro-fall-1957. Accessed November 29, 2013.

Mills, C. Wright. (1951) 2001. *White Collar: The American Middle Classes*. Oxford: Oxford University Press.

Mulvey, Laura. 1975. "Visual Pleasure and Narrative Cinema." *Screen*, 16, no. 3: 6–18.

Rodgers, Daniel T. 2011. *Age of Fracture*. Cambridge, MA: Harvard University Press.

Ross, Andrew. 1989. *No Respect: Intellectuals and Popular Culture*. New York: Routledge.

Yerushalmi, Yosef. 1991. *Freud's Moses: Judaism Terminable and Interminable*. New Haven: Yale University Press.

Chapter 13

Primetime Psychoanalysis

Ankhi Mukherjee

"Chain Reaction of Mental Anguish," episode 9 of the fifth season of the acclaimed NBC series *30 Rock*, comically shows psychic malady as a raging viral, transmitted not despite but because of commonsense "civilian" safeguards deployed against it. Liz Lemon, the eccentric scriptwriter of a fictional sketch comedy series, TGS, which is shown to be airing on NBC, has a lot on her mind – boyfriend issues with the pilot Carol that have something to do with their defunct sex life – and imperious network executive (and self-appointed mentor) Jack Donaghy issues a timely warning that she should see a therapist. Not that he would ever resort to such a thing himself, "but for lesser beings, like curly-haired men and people who need glasses, therapy can help." Liz unwisely dumps her problems on the loyal but dim-witted Kenneth, an NBC page, who, fortuitously for Liz, believes that listening is twice as important as speaking: "There's a reason God gave us two ears and one mouth." (He is distracted shortly by what he takes to be the divine purpose vested in ten fingers and runs off to poke people.) The sessions on the couch with Kenneth – all three of them – go swimmingly for Liz as she explores her issues with "men, trust." In a parody of analysis, Kenneth provides a series of formulaic (and clearly meaningless) hints and props that allow Liz to connect symptom with

A Concise Companion to Psychoanalysis, Literature, and Culture, First Edition.
Edited by Laura Marcus and Ankhi Mukherjee.

etiology and construct end narratives that cure, for instance, her longstanding disgust of eggs.

Kenneth, on the other hand, unravels from the second Liz mentions her uncle Harold. Jack Donaghy walks in on the final session to find Kenneth in a psychotic daze, scribbling "Harold" over and over again in his writing pad. "He can't handle that! Look at his head shape – he has no brain pan!" Donaghy chides Lemon. In true Jack Donaghy style, he commands Kenneth to put his mental burden in his "mind vice and I will crush it." Harold, as Donaghy had half-suspected, is not human. In fact, Harold, described by Kenneth as "the only thing I had that was like a father," used to be a farm pig. Kenneth was forced to sell him to a slaughterhouse and is convinced that it was Harold he polished off at the pig-eating contest he had entered to raise money for his ferry ride to NBC. "I ate all of him . . . I ate my father pig," Kenneth squeals in paroxysms of Oedipal guilt. Jack is pleased with himself for putting a precipitate end to this nonsense – he convinces Kenneth that the latter had given meaning and purpose to the pig's existence in that the act of filial cannibalization was instrumental in Kenneth's becoming "the lowest-level employee at the last-placed network in all America" – but the impromptu session with Kenneth stirs in Jack unresolved feelings of anger and hurt. His own writing pad is compulsively scribbled over with "Daddy" and Jack is forced to confront the memory of a school play where his father's bullying had made him fluff the lines. In an episode that suggests from the start that the "abnormal" and the culturally or sexually aberrant are the only lifestyles worth embracing, Jack retracts his cautionary advice to TGS cast member Tracy Jordan and enjoins him to continue to unconditionally love and bankroll his imposter "son" Donald (two years older than Tracy), given to preposterous business schemes with more preposterous names ("American Airlines" for a business where people call in to get air quality reports from all across the US). Jack finally talks himself out of it by the grandstanding gesture of reciting aloud his lines as "Protein" in the science play: where the child is the father of man, in the Romantic fantasy where the child self-fathers, biological fathers will cease to matter.

This episode of *30 Rock*, which aired first on December 2, 2010, raises some of the key questions I wish to interrogate in this chapter on TV representations of "treatment," often ambiguously represented as a hybrid of psychoanalysis, psychiatry, and psychotherapy. "Chain Reaction of Mental Anguish" makes it clear that mental anguish is a matter for professional intervention, and untrained, if well-meaning, gestures of containment do more harm than good. In Seminar XX, titled "Encore" (1972–73), Lacan compares the analyst to an order of discourse. As translator Bruce Fink explains in a footnote, there is a problem of grammatical structure in such a pronouncement, for "Lacan compares the analyst as a person, instead of analytic discourse, to other orders of discourse" (1975, 95). What the analyst does, according to Lacan, is differentiate the imaginary from the real and investigate the status of truth as knowledge by putting object *a* in the place of semblance. Object *a*, of course, is not symbolizable but the limit of the symbolic, standing notoriously for its failures of integrity and wholeness: "it only dissolves [*se résout*], in the final analysis, owing to its failure, unable, as it is, to sustain itself in approaching the real," Lacan adds (1975, 95). Language is inherently lacking, observes Lacan, and the subject is born through a process of radical alienation: as he states in "Position of the Unconscious," the subject is "not the cause of himself" but "bears within himself the worm of the cause that splits him" (1995, 708). Psychoanalysis does not replace the alienation brought about by the "real" with understanding, but is perhaps the language and milieu best equipped to leave the analysand better disposed toward the estrangements of their consciousness.

The *30 Rock* episode also seems to also work from the conviction that when it comes to our mental life, dysfluencies and blockages – food issues, daddy issues, and sex issues – are somehow related, and need careful untangling before they are put into recombinant forms and narratives with which we can live. It sheds valuable light on the truth of analysis, which Lacan described as a seeking after of "knowledge that is not known." As he states: "The status of knowledge implies as such that there already is knowledge, that it is in the Other, and that it is to be acquired [*à prendre*]" (Lacan 1975, 96). This chapter examines the non-linear and twisted pathways of knowledge and truth in analytic experience, further muddled and muddied in popular cultural representation and reception, Drawing attention especially to the misrecognitions and misunderstandings of TV psychoanalysis, I ask what this medium can teach us about the role of the analyst, femininity and gender, racial and cultural difference. Finally, the chapter offers a glimpse into how the analysis-interpretation of psychoanalysis in academic discourse – which Kristeva once conflated with "American university discourse" – fares against the analyst-interpreters on the little screen (Kristeva and Waller 1982).

Seasons 1 and 2 of *In Treatment*, which first aired on HBO in 2008, are remakes of Hagai Levi's hit Israeli series *Be'Tipul*. Levi studied psychology at Bar Ilan University, and is also known to have firsthand experience of therapy. The third season, which I shall selectively discuss here, boasts original characters and original scripts, not adaptations from *Be'Tipul*. Like Levi, the executive producers, Anya Epstein and Danny Futterman, have a background in psychoanalysis. Futterman's mother is a psychoanalyst and he is married to a therapist-in-training; Epstein has a psychology degree from Pepperdine University. *In Treatment* examines the classical topics of medical-therapeutic psychoanalysis, as listed by Lacan in *The Four Fundamental Concepts of Psychoanalysis* – the Unconscious, Repetition, Transference, and the Drive – through a five-nights-a-week, session-by-session record of Dr. Paul Weston's intersubjective talk therapy. Like its forerunner in Tel Aviv, *In Treatment*, the first two series of which were daily prime-time broadcasts (Monday to Friday, 9 p.m. EST), offers a choice between linear or vertical watching: one could watch all five episodes in the week, Paul's half-hour interactions with each of his four patients followed by his own therapy session, or exclusively follow the misadventures of a given character every week.

In an interview with *Los Angeles Times* (October 23, 2010), Gabriel Byrne, the Irish star of the therapy drama, says: "In the Woody Allen film 'You Will Meet a Tall Dark Stranger,' there's this line about a man who wakes up at 2 in the morning, sees eternity stretched out before him, and never sleeps again. When I saw that, I thought, 'That's Paul'." The third season, which started in 2010, sees Paul divorced, sadder, living alone in Brooklyn, and increasingly paranoid about the onset of hereditary Parkinson's. He has stopped seeing Gina, his therapist and supervisor, and is hurt and infuriated to see a thinly veiled and largely negative portrayal of his therapeutic practice in Gina's new novel. The episodes document his sessions with three patients, Sunil, Jesse, and Frances, ending each week with Paul's own patient session with his new therapist, Adele. The first, and arguably the most intriguing, patient in this season is Sunil Sanyal, a retired maths teacher and a new migrant to New York. Sunil is a 50-something widower from Kolkata (which he insists on calling by its former, anglicized name of Calcutta), who has come to live with his son and his family following the sudden death of his wife, Kamala. Sunil, essayed by the Indian thespian Irrfan Khan, is a portrait of unspoken, unplumbed melancholy and injured dignity: "He has the loneliest face I have ever seen," Paul Weston says of his new patient. If he instantly reminds readers of contemporary anglophone fiction of Jhumpa Lahiri's Pulitzer-prizewinning short stories of the Bengali diaspora, it is because Lahiri was cultural consultant to the scriptwriter, Adam Rapp. Sunil has been forcibly brought along to Dr. Weston's chamber by his daughter-in-law Julia and son Arun (now going by the American-sounding Aaron), who are increasingly concerned by the pathological turn the mourning for his dead wife seems to be taking. He doesn't eat, sleep, or shower; he hasn't left the house in two weeks. He has been prescribed Effexor by his son, a medic, and Paul Weston agrees with the young couple that psychoactive medication is efficacious when taken with talk therapy. Sunil breaks out in Bengali as his son and daughter-in-law brief the analyst, once to say that he stays home alone for the most part with the *ayah* (the domestic help), and later to respond to Julia's complaints with a cryptic "O nijeke bhoy paay" ("She is afraid of herself"). Julia, a literary agent, attractive, self-possessed, sometimes abrasive, says exasperatedly that her father-in-law makes her uncomfortable in her own home. Sunil speaks in Bengali again to produce for the record the exact number of days that have lapsed since Kamala's death, clearly incensed at Julia's blunt suggestion that there was a time limit for grief (and that he had flagrantly violated the social consensus on this one).

The producer Anya Epstein, talking to the *Los Angeles Times* about the impending Season 3 of *In Treatment*, says "We were very aware that this is the first truly American season of the show, so we wanted to talk about issues that felt very American. And for us, that meant having these characters ask, 'Who am I, really?'" (October 23, 2010). It is to the credit of the show that the commitment to American issues is untouched by triumphalism and exceptionalism, and involves instead three neurotics who represent different facets of the great American excluded: Jesse (Dane De Haan), a self-destructive gay teenager, racked with insecurities, rage, and (self-)loathing; Frances (Debra Winger), a fading movie star terrified of losing her breasts to the cancer that has claimed her mother and sister; and Sunil, a strange arrival to America whose displacement is not briskly followed by cultural rehabilitation. Not only do the characters ask "Who am I, really?" but they make Paul question his role as healer, and question also the status of psychoanalysis as a discourse of normalization, openly involved in the business of converting "delusional reality" into "objective reality," to quote Joan Copjec's terms (2000, 295).

Alone with Paul (who sends the younger Sanyals packing), and heartened by the ashtray he puts out, Sunil smokes his rolled-up cigarette and opens up slowly, ditching Bengali for English. It doesn't take long for Paul to anatomize the malady: grief and numbness brought on by bereavement; exile from homeland and repatriation in a new home that is not his; the constant culture clash with an

American daughter-in-law and a son sold to the American way of life; feelings of being superannuated, unwanted, worthless. Sunil returns the gaze with compassion: "You are not from here either." The effortless alliance between the two men deepens when Paul, in a concession to Sunil's cultural reservations against therapy, offers tea with conversation in his office. In the course of their discussions, Paul interrogates the many facets of Sunil's breakdown. For Sunil, a desert island reality show called "Survivors," where "practically naked" men and women seem willing to compromise any principle they might possess for "one million dollar [*sic*]," comes to stand for America's rampant materialism. "They do all this willingly, Paul." Sunil sees the same consumerism in his daughter-in-law, who has named her half-Indian daughter Naya after a company that makes bottled water. "Perhaps the next child will be called iPod," Sunil sighs. He is deeply disturbed by the flagrant sexuality of the female TV contestants, which he finds reflected in Julia's uninhibited physicality. Sunil is filled with inordinate rage at what he perceives as Julia's composite sexuality: her loud lovemaking, which he had once overheard alongside Kamala, her vigorous workout routines, where she looks like a "desperate animal," a hidden case of birth-control pills in her office that seems to provide incontrovertible proof of her licentiousness (Sunil believes that she and Arun are trying to have a baby), and her perceived lack of modesty around the presence of men other than her husband. "My hand turns into a fist," Paul is startled to hear Sunil matter-of-factly say.

Paul chips away at Sunil's defenses to force him to admit to the complex of terror and desire that Julia stands for. Repulsed as he thinks he is by Julia, Sunil cannot avert the scopophilic gaze. His therapist suggests that he is "intrigued, fascinated, maybe even a little jealous." Speaking of Julia and Arun's uncontrolled lust ("not acceptable behavior for principled Bengali people!"), Sunil, unbidden, brings up his college sweetheart, Malini, whom he did not finally marry, ostensibly sacrificing passion for duty. Malini was non-Brahmin; therefore, for the Brahmin Sunil, family and honor had to take precedence over personal gratification. Malini is described lyrically, sensuously – she reminded Sunil of El Greco's "Lady with a Flower in her Hair," and he would, infatuated, gaze on her for hours. Sunil later contradicts the first version of his story by saying it was Malini who ended it after an argument on the steps of the college library, impulsive Malini who walked away from the relationship wearing Sunil's coat, later found on her drowned body.

Over the course of five weeks, Sunil appears progressively deranged by his pathological suspicion that Julia is having an affair with one of her clients, Ethan Barr, popular author of *The Pale Fox*. He reports to Paul a long list of infractions, expecting the latter to confirm his hunches: Julia's lunches and dinners with "Mr Pale Fox," her gross neglect of the children in her unhealthy preoccupation with her "work," her habit of dressing provocatively, the kiss goodbye exchanged on the porch after an evening out with Barr. Sunil's uncontrollable anxiety about his son's failing marriage is caused and compounded by his deepening unhappiness with his Brooklyn life. It is galling to Sunil that the newspapers of a global, multicultural city would devote many more inches to the New York Knicks than stories of calamitous events unfolding elsewhere. "I'm outside of my life," he tells Paul, likening his predicament to the flood victims of devastating monsoons in Bengal that year. "I am as helpless to change my surrounding as those people in my country who are unable to save their houses from flood waters."

Paul Weston analyses two very disturbing dreams plaguing Sunil through what Freud called the "decoding" method, which treats dreams "as a kind of cryptography in which each sign can be translated into another sign having a known meaning" ("The Interpretation of Dreams," Freud 1953–74, 4:97). The first is about a dark-coated animal, struggling to breathe, which the dreamer finds lying at the foot of a cliff. Sunil starts to "manipulate the body" – poke and prod it – and is deterred from laying it to rest by the rising sea and the realization that "I had already buried something." Paul connects the abjected body of the dark-coated animal to Arun's labored breathing, which Sunil had mentioned earlier, wondering later if the broken body of the animal could refer to Malini's, after her fatal jump from the Howrah Bridge. Arun appears as himself in the second dream, lying unconscious on the street outside Sunil's home. A woman with long, dark hair pulls Arun's arm, which breaks off like plaster. Sunil, in the dream, knows that he wants to hurt the woman and knows also that he would need to do so to protect the grandchildren. "Perhaps it was Julia in disguise," Sunil says hopefully of the *femme fatale* of the second dream, her blonde hair colored brunette. If, as Christopher Bollas says, interpreting Freud, "the dream is an emblematic arrangement of veils articulated by the unconscious," the task of psychoanalysis is to read the discourse of the dream "by translating its iconographic utterance into the word" (1987, 64). Expressing the iconography of the dream in words, Paul suggests that the dark woman was none other than Malini, the lady with a flower in her hair. This induces a violent reaction in Sunil, who protests that he would never hurt Malini. "Ami poshu na . . . ota sapno chhilo, ota jiban noy" he exclaims in Bengali ("I am not an animal . . . it was a dream, not real life!") "What did you do when you woke up from the sleep?", asks Paul with rising concern, to be told that Sunil had subsequently checked on the children and checked on Julia's door, which had been, luckily for Julia, locked from inside.

The penultimate episode sees Julia come into Paul's office as Sunil waits outside. Julia's arm is bandaged, the result of a fracas with Sunil. "He's gotten worse," Julia says of Sunil. He chooses to be miserable, his behavior is erratic and menacing, he continues to fix Julia in a psychotic stare. When Julia announces that she is terminating Sunil's therapy, Paul advises her against it, protesting that his patient is making progress: "We're starting to build an alliance!" Julia, fraught from the ongoing conflict at home, is not willing to reconsider. "$220 a week for him to get even crazier," she remarks bitterly. In the little time that remains of that session, Paul urges Sunil to continue with the therapy, going *pro bono* if necessary. It would be a critical mistake not to do so. Sunil, who first exculpates himself by saying he had not pushed Julia with the intent to cause physical damage, but had merely pushed past her after a heated exchange, now hands over a battered cricket bat to Paul for safekeeping. He will be alone in the house with Julia when Arun leaves for yet another medical conference, and he says "I should not keep it," coolly confirming Paul's suspicion that he has imagined turning it on his daughter-in-law.

This curious analyst–analysand relationship comes to an abrupt end after Paul, on the express urging of his own therapist Adele, alerts Julia to the genuine risk posed by Sunil's avowed tendencies. The last exchange between Paul and Sunil takes place at the Varick Street Detention Center, where Sunil, rudely "voted off the island," is awaiting deportation to India. Paul realizes he was correct all along to think Sunil was not a violent man, and that Julia was not in any kind of real danger. He hadn't, however, suspected that Sunil had plotted this outcome for some time: his arrest was not merely for (Julia's) trumped-up charges, but related to his strategic refusal to show his papers to the police. "It was my only way home, Paul." Sunil's manipulation of Paul highlights what John Forrester calls the two-sided performativity of analytic speech and transference, which makes it impossible to decide "who is using and who is being used" (2000, 318). "You have been a good friend to me," adds Sunil, to Paul's utter vexation. "I'm meant to be your therapist!" "Isn't it possible to be both at once?" Sunil asks, leaving Paul in a state of shock and disbelief. As he is escorted back to his cell, he sings a Bengali song of leave-taking that he had once translated for Paul, the very song that had, somewhat undeservedly, landed him in big trouble with Julia. Goodbye and goodnight, my friend. "Bidaay bondhu bidaay."

The format of *In Treatment* ensures that we see three episodes of Paul dealing with patients in various states of emotional undress – patients who swear, act out, break down without shame or fear – and are also party to Paul's own emotional turbulence with his therapist. Some of the very objections he raises with Sunil – "You avoid answering my questions!" – are echoed in his therapist's difficulties with him, with Adele detecting in her patient the stasis, that continued state of wait-and-see, and the resistances to psychoanalysis that Paul has detected in Sunil. As did his therapist Gina in her fictionalized account of Paul, Adele faults him for that obliteration of critical distance from patients which ends up short-circuiting the dialectical process of psychoanalysis. She diagnoses in Paul a clear and debilitating "identification with Sunil": their exilic marginality, the shared predicament of having to adapt to the new world, the fact that they were both intellectual and cultivated middle-aged men leading isolated and benumbed lives, and also the coincidence that each was attracted to a younger woman unavailable to him. Paul hits out at Adele's implacable neutrality and reserve, calling her a "Freudian Ice Queen" and a "Sphinx-like doctor," but is also forced to contemplate anew the ethics of psychoanalysis. While it is true that, as Loewenberg observes, "psychoanalysts make themselves the instrument of knowledge not by suppressing their subjectivity but by employing it" (2000, 99), Paul is made to feel that he has bungled the crucial subjective aspect of psychoanalytic inquiry. Freud had sounded a relevant cautionary note about psychoanalysis, differentiating it from medical practice:

> A doctor suffering from disease of the lung or heart is not handicapped either in diagnosing or treating internal complaints; whereas the special conditions of analytic work do actually cause the analyst's own defects to interfere with his making a correct assessment of the state of things in his patient and reacting to them in a useful way.
>
> ("Analysis Terminable and Interminable," cited in Loewenberg 2000, 99)

The season ends with Paul terminating therapy, and quite possibly quitting psychoanalysis altogether.

In his last meeting with Sunil, Paul angrily dismisses the semblances of friendship in the therapeutic relationship to reiterate the following: "My job is to help you discover what you think of yourself and if you're displeased with what you discover, to help you change that." Was it all a lie, the analyses of dream and parapraxes, the transferences, the resistances, the chasing after the truth of the analysand's desire, the reconstruction of the past? Sunil, who has repeatedly called Paul a good therapist *and* a good man, doesn't think so. He thanks Paul for his help with Malini, who, we are now told, had committed suicide by leaping off the Howrah Bridge to avoid the ignominy of an illicit pregnancy. "Something inside me has opened as well," Sunil says, looking more in control and at peace than he has done previously. He says he will think of Paul as he goes to the Howrah Bridge to stare down at the water: it is impossible to know if he is hinting at a copycat suicide.

Freud's ultimate model of the unconscious "is to be on the phone," argues Laurence Rickels: "these calls belong to the deregularized competition of long distance carriers called transference (at one end of the line) and at the other, telepathy" (1990, 41).[1] Rickels reminds us that the phone call was partially responsible for the invention of TV's "liveness," and that one of television's first names was "seeing telephone" (1990, 41). Television provides an analogue of the innate mediatization of the psyche, especially in the way it pulls viewers into "a self-reflexive interior that is at once its topological surface" (1990, 45). Rickels offers further points of comparison between dream and TV registers:

> The recycling of contents and persons among sets or sitcoms, the closed-circuit co-extensivity of what takes place on and in front of the tube – the way one sees oneself as being seen or finds oneself in situations that might as well have been programmed – could all be analogized with Freud's original (telescopic) conception of the dream as the rerun of daytime trivia thus openly and simultaneously displayed or repressed.
> (1990, 45)

To watch TV is to revisit the telecommunicative and telepathic provenance of psychoanalysis itself, with the spectator assuming the place of the female subject as theorized by Freudian and Lacanian psychoanalysis. Lacan's Seminar XX explicitly proposes the formulas of sexuation, the radical split between the masculine logic of Law and the feminine logic of exception. Slavoj Žižek describes the feminine logic as one in which "there is *no* exception to the series of symptoms – that is, in which there are *only* symptoms, and the symbolic Law (the paternal Name) is ultimately just one (the most efficient or established) in the series of symptoms" (2002, 58).[2] As Beverle Houston (1984) and Laurence Rickels have argued previously, I will claim that television's plenitude of fictions and stations displaces the exclusive and sequential model of male sexuation with the simultaneity and metonymic proliferation of female sexual development as codified in psychoanalytic theory. However, while television subscribes to and advertises the feminine logic of paradoxes and the not-whole, it would be premature to celebrate TV as hypermediating femininity as the subject par excellence.

The HBO television series *The Sopranos*, produced by David Chase, which originally ran between 1999 and 2007, has been widely hailed as "a latter-day morality play in which psychotherapeutic concepts have replaced Christian ones," to quote Rob White (2008, 68). Tony Soprano (played by James Gandolfini), the head of an Italian American Mafia "family" living in New Jersey, is given to panic attacks and depression and seeks psychiatric help. TV critics and cultural historians are unanimous in seeing Tony's neurosis as a symptom of larger social pathologies, though interpretations vary: some argue that the show puts Italian American culture on the couch; others think it shows organized crime on the verge of a nervous breakdown; yet others see in the show's nexus between industry and criminality the dark side of the American dream. "This is a show about America and anyone who watches with any degree of intelligence understands that right away," Gandolfini once remarked (quoted in Hayward and Biro 2002, 211). David Simon is perhaps justified in saying that it is the many viewers of *The Sopranos* who need a psychiatrist (2002, vii).

Even the format of the show can be seen to reference the vicissitudes of the psychoanalytic scene, where linear and end-driven narrative movement is staggered by moments of stasis, silence, and breakdown. Like *In Treatment*, *The Sopranos* can be viewed as a series of discrete, self-contained episodes *or* as a series where the narrative accretes from episode to linked episode (and is a sum of its parts). Dana Polan sees in this dual structure of narrative television the opposing forces of "contraction and compression" and "endless expansion and proliferation" (2009, 32). Polan comments that this mode of narrative elaboration is undoubtedly drawn from the expansiveness of psychotherapy:

> Tony's encounters with Jennifer Melfi (Lorraine Bracco) work as both narrative and antinarrative device: the therapy sessions enable Tony to

> have moments of clarity and provide him with guidance (not all of which he interprets as Melfi would like), but the sessions also constitute a site of stuckness and silence, a rehashing of the same old arguments, an inability to move forward, a fading of ambition into self-doubt.
>
> (Polan 2009, 33)

What does Tony Soprano want? According to David Remnic, writing in the *New Yorker* on the eve of the last show of the final season, it is a Gatsby-like quest for "a renewed sense of family, heritage, coherent truths, mental health" (cited in White 2008, 68). Tony struggles to cope with the antics of his dysfunctional blood family (mother, sister, uncle, nephew), the demands and expectations of wife Carmela and their teenage kids, AJ and Meadow, and the antagonisms and treacheries of "work colleagues." His malady is linked to his distorted take on the dominant ideology of family values and futile attempts to segregate the brutalities of the family business from his suburban home life. "My rotten fucking putrid genes have infected my son's soul!" he laments in one of his sessions with Melfi (episode 17). There is also the increasing alienation of the old codes from the changing values and speeds of late capitalism. It may be the 1990s outside, but at home "it's 1954," Tony says unconvincingly (episode 11). His is the melancholia of the late-comer: "Lately I get the feeling that I came in at the end. The best is over." The sly seductiveness of the show ensures that Tony's dubious nostalgia for the self-belief, discipline, and moral certainties of the old mob families – comic when not outright offensive in its delusional articulations – can be made to relate to the vicissitudes of American masculinity itself, enjoining momentary identification and empathy, not outright condemnation, from male and female viewers alike. Take, for instance, his oft-quoted comment on Gary Cooper, "the strong silent type," in the Pilot episode.

> That was an American. He was in touch with his feelings. He just did what he had to do! Unfortunately, what he didn't know is that once they got Gary Cooper in touch with his feelings they couldn't get him to shut up! Dysfunction this! Dysfunction that! Dysfunction va fan cul!

Tony Soprano, brutal and vulnerable, primal and fiercely intelligent, larger than life yet undone by a dream of castration, could not, at any rate be expected to sell "patio furniture on Route 22," an alternative to the family business he jokingly considers in a candid discussion with daughter Meadow.

As is often the case with literary representations of psychoanalysis, in *The Sopranos* it (psychoanalysis) is not merely a panacea for the inner life of Tony Soprano but the very dynamic that posits and enhances it, giving it depth, detail, new-found clarity (as well as new conflict), language, and poetry. "Sad is good; unconscious isn't," says Dr. Melfi, and treatment proves to be a reflective and self-reflective process for both. Dr. Jennifer Melfi is played by Lorraine Bracco, who received an American Psychoanalytic Association award in 2001 for creating "the most credible psychoanalyst ever to appear in cinema or on television," and adds gravitas and pathos to the mobster–therapist relationship that is a staple of Hollywood comedy (John Cusack and his psychiatrist in *Grosse Pointe Blank* or De Niro and Billy Crystal in *Analyze This*). Is Tony, suffering from panic disorder, depression, and antisocial and borderline personality disorder, treatable? What do his treatment and eventual cure spell for the commonweal of society? She wonders if, as her colleagues mention at a dinner party, "the talking cure actually helps [sociopaths] become better criminals" (episode 20). Besides the psychoanalytic hermeneutics of transference and counter-transference, episode 30 plays out a curious case of role reversal, where Melfi, victim of a brutal rape that will probably go unpunished due to a botched police arrest of the suspect, turns momentarily to Tony for protection and avenging. True to the character, however, she does not give in. Melfi's almost robotic self-control in the sessions masks her fear and desire of this tabooed figure, the psychoanalytic drive for truth juxtaposing with the real fear of the intimacy it entails, as well as the legal and law enforcement implications of peeling away the lies. It is not always that what Hubert Damisch (2000) calls the "listening eye" of the psychoanalyst stands in for the average viewer of a TV show, but it does with Melfi, especially in the way she plays out the vagaries of audience identification. Like Melfi, the viewer is at times the subject leading the hunt and at others its vulnerable, pitiable quarry.

Melfi's femaleness – and that she is an educated Italian American woman, with a hint of a Brooklyn accent – defines and occasionally disturbs the therapeutic relationship. Unlike Tony Soprano's wife and mistress, she does not allow him to buy her love; nor does she have any patience for his infantile, impetuous outbursts and indecent proposals. The psychotherapy she offers Tony involves dream analysis and cognitive behavior techniques – as with Dr. Weston in *In Treatment*, she deftly and responsibly combines psychotropic medication with psychoanalytic method. Tony David, Professor of Cognitive Neuropsychiatry at the Institute of Psychiatry in London, observes how she deploys cognitive behavior techniques to point out her client's "negative cognitions, his tendency to catastrophize, as well as his behavioural avoidances" (2001, 1374). Patiently and skillfully, she helps Tony confront his traumatic relationship with his parents, particularly the manipulative mob mother. This makes for compelling viewing. When, for example, Melfi insinuates that Tony was attracted to Fran, his father's mistress, a woman old enough to be his mother, her patient speaks for a million viewers in his commonsense, if literal-minded, exasperation with one of psychoanalysis' structuring premises: "I did not want to fuck my mother! You should have seen her in her housedress with that hairnet." Outside the sessions, however, and in therapy with her own control psychiatrist, Dr. Kupferberg, Melfi explores her obsessive need to know the Mafia hit man above and beyond the psychoanalyst's inevitable immersion in the case material. "I've let myself be charmed by a psychopath," she says. This unusual "case" reveals to Melfi not merely the limits of her own acculturation and civilization, but the limits of psychoanalysis itself as a coping mechanism in relation to the extraordinary violence and degeneracy that Tony drags in from outside the room. Unnerved and chastened by the realization that, to quote Tony David again, "understanding the roots of certain forbidden actions does not guarantee that they will be avoided" (2001, 1374), she eventually shows Tony the door.

I end with a discussion of "Boca," the title of episode 9 of Series 1 of *The Sopranos*, which constellates a host of cultural anxieties about the confusions and failures of normative identity that the clinical practice of psychoanalysis is seen to endorse and foster. It focalizes especially the fear of a sexual difference that exceeds biological opposition and a priori symbolic schemas. "Boca" plays on the Italian word for mouth while also referring to Boca Raton, Corrado "Junior" Soprano's favorite Florida hangout. The episode gives a glimpse of the retired mob boss's love life on a holiday trip to Boca as we learn from his secret girlfriend Roberta that Tony's "Uncle Jun" is a "real artist" at cunnilingus. Corrado asks Bobbi to not breathe a word of this to the deeply misogynistic and homophobic Mafia family: "it's a sign of weakness and possibly a sign that you are a *fenucca* [Italian slang for homosexual, pronounced *fenook*]." The warning comes too late, as Bobbi has already gossiped about it at the hairdressers' and Carmela (Tony Soprano's wife) knows. In an rare display of marital harmony, Tony and Carmela laugh uncontrollably as the former lewdly describes Uncle Junior as a "bushman of the Kalahari," "whistling through the wheat field."

"Boca" sees territorial tensions between uncle and nephew come to breaking point. The episode begins with Tony Soprano's devious mother Livia at the cemetery, dourly clearing her husband's grave (we get glimpses of the Name of the Father carved in stone, playfully underscoring the theme of filial transgression) and bemoaning for Corrado's benefit the infirmities of "my son, the mental patient." Junior eventually puts two and two together – his consigliere Mikey Palmice has been spying on Tony – and resolves the mystery of Tony's twice-weekly visits to the Medical Center. In the course of the episode, each man projects onto the other his fear and loathing of feminization: while Corrado condemns Tony for "spilling his guts" in therapy, thereby violating the very code of conduct that underwrites La Cosa Nostra, Tony finds Junior debasing it by being "in the muff." To willingly submit to the "talking cure" is, for Corrado, tantamount to "singing to the feds" (Tony is the singing Soprano of the show's title). Tony, stung by a slight on his manly athletic prowess on the golf course, teases Corrado mercilessly that he is not man enough or Italian enough: "I thought you were a *baccala* [codfish] man, Uncle Jun. What are you doing eating sushi?" Corrado recovers quickly from this unexpected assault and even manages a dig at Tony's dependence on psychotherapy: "At least I can deal with my own problems." Unhappily for poor Bobbi, Corrado leaves her after this, smashing a lemon meringue pie in her face. He seethes in humiliation and rage, though taking care to mask it as concern for his "mental weakling" of a nephew who is seeing a psychiatrist ("It makes me want to cry") and concern that Tony is revealing facts about the "family" the psychiatrist might eventually be made to divulge in court testimony. Not surprisingly, the open hostilities of the golf course culminate later in Junior putting a hit on his nephew, leading to a deadly stand-off between two Mafia crews and two generations of Soprano men. "I never should've razzed him about eating pussy," a sobered Tony reflects on the family feud in episode 13: "cunnilingus and psychiatry have brought us to this." Despite knowing the deadly charges of disloyalty and betrayal that attach to his in-therapy revelations, despite the simulcast of narratives – from society, culture, psychoanalysis itself – collapsing neurosis with feminine infirmity, Tony does not quit therapy. Bobbi and Tony become unlikely substitutes of each other as the "blabbermouth cunt" Junior loves and despises. While it may be demeaning for a Mafioso to give head, Tony Soprano unwittingly proves Corrado's insinuation that there is graver and possibly incurable moral decrepitude in having one's head shrunk.

Notes

1 Diana Fuss's chapter, "Freud's Ear" (Fuss 1995), elaborates on Freud's use of media technology. For more on psychoanalysis and telepathy, see Derrida's essay "Telepathy" (Derrida 2007), and his *The Post Card* (Derrida 1987); Copjec 1984; and Forrester 1990.

2 For a detailed analysis of Lacan's formulas of sexuation, see Copjec 1995 and 2002. Bruce Fink, *The Lacanian Subject* (1995), discusses Lacan's teachings on sexuation.

References

Bollas, Christopher. 1987. *The Shadow of the Object: Psychoanalysis of the Unthought Known*. New York: Columbia University Press.

Copjec, Joan. 1984. "Transference: Letter and the Unknown Woman." *October*, 28: 60–90.

Copjec, Joan. 1995. "Sex and the Euthanasia of Reason." In *Read my Desire*, 201–36. Cambridge, MA: MIT Press.

Copjec, Joan. 2000. "The Body as Viewing Instrument, or the Strut of Vision." In *Lacan in America*, ed. Jean-Michel Rabaté, 277–308. New York: Other Press.

Copjec, Joan. 2002. *Imagine There's No Woman: Ethics and Sublimation*. Cambridge, MA: MIT Press.

Damisch, Hubert. 2000. "Bridging the Gap Between Two Scenes." In *Whose Freud? The Place of Psychoanalysis in Contemporary Culture*, ed. Peter Brooks and Alex Woloch, 93–95. New Haven: Yale University Press.

David, Tony. 2001. "Psychiatrists Get an Offer They Cannot Refuse." *British Medical Journal*, 323 (8 December): 1374.

Derrida, Jacques. 1987. *The Post Card: From Socrates to Freud and Beyond*, trans. Alan Bass. Chicago: Chicago University Press.

Derrida, Jacques. 2007. "Telepathy." In *Psyche: Inventions of the Other*, vol. 1, ed. Peggy Kamuf. Stanford: Stanford University Press.

Fink, Bruce. 1995. *The Lacanian Subject: Between Language and Jouissance*. Princeton: Princeton University Press.

Forrester, John. 1990. *Seductions of Psychoanalysis: Freud, Lacan and Derrida*. Cambridge: Cambridge University Press.

Forrester, John. 2000. "What Kind of Truth?" In *Whose Freud? The Place of Psychoanalysis in Contemporary Culture*, ed. Peter Brooks and Alex Woloch, 311–23. New Haven: Yale University Press.

Freud, Sigmund. 1953–74. *The Standard Edition of the Complete Psychological Works of Sigmund Freud*, 24 vols., ed. James Strachey, with the assistance of Anna Freud, Alix Strachey, and Alan Tyson, trans. James Strachey. London: Hogarth Press.

Fuss, Diana. 1995. *The Sense of an Interior: Four Writers and the Rooms that Shaped Them*. New York: Routledge.

Hayward, Steven, and Andrew Biro. 2002. "The Eighteenth Brumaire of Tony Soprano." In *This Thing of Ours: Investigating the Sopranos*, ed. David Lavery, 203–14. New York: Columbia University Press.

Houston, Beverle. 1984. "Viewing Television: The Metapsychology of Endless Consumption." *Quarterly Review of Film Studies*, 9, no. 3: 183–95.

Kristeva, Julia, and Margaret Waller. 1982. "Psychoanalysis and the Polis." *Critical Inquiry*, 9, no. 1: 77–92.

Lacan, Jacques. 1975. *On Feminine Sexuality*, Book XX: *The Limits of Love and Knowledge, Encore 1972–1973*, ed. Jacques-Alain Miller, trans. Bruce Fink. New York: W.W. Norton.

Lacan, Jacques. 1995. "Position of the Unconscious." In *Reading Seminar XI: Lacan's Four Fundamental Concepts*, trans. Bruce Fink. Albany, N.Y.: State University of New York Press.

Loewenberg, Peter. 2000. "Psychoanalysis as a Hermeneutic Science." In *Whose Freud? The Place of Psychoanalysis in Contemporary Culture*, ed. Peter Brooks and Alex Woloch, 96–115. New Haven: Yale University Press.

Polan, Dana. 2009. *The Sopranos*. Durham, N.C.: Duke University Press.

Rickels, Laurence. 1990. "Psychoanalysis on TV." *Substance* 19, no. 1(61): 39–52.

Simon, David R. 2002. *Tony Soprano's America: The Criminal Side of the American Dream*. Boulder, CO: Westview.

White, Rob. 2008. "No More Therapy." *Film Quarterly*, 61, no. 3: 68–69.

Žižek, Slavoj. 2002. "The Real of Sexual Difference." In *Reading Seminar XX: Lacan's Major Work on Love, Knowledge, and Feminine Sexuality*, ed. Suzanne Barnard and Bruce Fink, 57–75. Albany, N.Y.: State University of New York Press.

Chapter 14

The Art of the Symptom: Body, Writing, and Sex Change

Patricia Gherovici

Does it change our appreciation of Leonardo da Vinci's masterpiece if we know that the enigmatic smile of Mona Lisa that seems to promise "unbounded tenderness and at the same time sinister menace" (Freud 1910a, 115) may be the result of sublimated homosexual tendencies, incestuous wishes, and Leonardo's obsessive interest in the penis? Freud set a bad example when he interpreted Leonardo's life and work and indulged in a practice that in another context he would have called "wild" psychoanalysis, an approach that he found pseudo-scientific and "technically objectionable" (1910b, 226). To a certain extent, the creator of psychoanalysis was aware of the limitations of his method when it came to explaining the effect of an artwork on the spectator, as he made explicit in his analysis of the Moses of Michelangelo. Freud confessed that he was "no connoisseur in art, but simply a layman" and humbly admitted that he was "unable rightly to appreciate many of the methods used and the effects obtained in art" (1914, 211). Nonetheless, he pleaded guilty to experiencing the urge to interpret art in order to enjoy it:

> works of art do exercise a powerful effect on me, especially those of literature and sculpture, less often of painting. This has occasioned me, when I have been contemplating such things, to spend a long time before

A Concise Companion to Psychoanalysis, Literature, and Culture, First Edition.
Edited by Laura Marcus and Ankhi Mukherjee.

> them trying to apprehend them in my own way, i.e. to explain to myself what their effect is due to. Wherever I cannot do this, as for instance with music, I am almost incapable of obtaining any pleasure. Some rationalistic, or perhaps analytic, turn of mind in me rebels against being moved by a thing without knowing why I am thus affected and what it is that affects me.
>
> (Freud 1914, 211)

Understanding for Freud did not take pleasure away. On the contrary, he felt compelled to plunge into the endeavor of figuring out the source of his enjoyment in order to enhance it. Nevertheless, all along Freud knew of the futility of this task, "the apparently paradoxical fact that precisely some of the grandest and most overwhelming creations of art are still unsolved riddles to our understanding. We admire them, we feel overawed by them, but we are unable to say what they represent to us" (Freud 1914, 211). Art is bewildering and remains inscrutable, yet we cannot help feeling compelled to come up with an interpretation, perhaps as a reaction to the opaque nature of the emotions art elicits or perhaps because once we experience strong feelings of pleasure, that pleasure can be paradoxical and accompanied by pain, boredom, or disruption. Thus, we start down the path of *jouissance*[1] and we may no longer know or want to know where it will lead.

In this essay I take some distance from the usual psychoanalytic interpretation of art, one that operates on fixed keys and is prone to generalizations. I prefer the approach recommended by Freud when interpreting dreams – like Egyptian hieroglyphics, dreams are elusive, yet readable texts. My method is not a translation of meaning but rather a literal exploration of the material. I take inspiration from a comment of Freud about his Leonardo essay that he described as "partly a poetic novel" ("halb Romandichtung").[2] This does not imply that Freud denigrates the quality of his research but rather that he is aware that writing psychoanalytically entails a creative way of writing that is never too far from fiction.

Similarly Lacan insists, at the end of his life, on the links between symptoms and writing. I will use the term he uses for this conjunction, *sinthome*. I will explain the logic of this new coining in Lacan's works and apply the concept to my own corpus, which is the published memoirs of transsexuals. The chronicles of people who changed sex show that this is a new writing on the body and with which the body yields a productive understanding of art as such.

Taking into account the complex relation that transgender people have to their bodies – many often say that they are trapped in a body of the wrong (opposite) sex – I claim that an art similar to that of actual artists, if not necessarily with the genius of James Joyce, can be found in transsexual artificiality. In some cases, it gives birth to an art that, I argue, is tantamount to a *sinthome* with a structural function analogous to the role Lacan ascribed to writing, as he discovered it in the art of Joyce.

***

While Freud was well aware of the potential pitfalls involved in the application of psychoanalytic concepts to the examination of works of art, he did not escape the temptation of "psychoanalyzing" not only art works but also artists, connecting events of the artist lives with their works. Ever since, penis envy, Oedipal conflict, scopophilic drive, narcissism, and so on, have been "applied" to biographical events that offered clues into several levels of pathology to explain the creative process; life and works illustrated the theory. This is how psychoanalysis went "wild" and was derailed into the slippery field of psychobiography. One could wonder whether this type of critical production is actually psychoanalytic at all because, as Mijolla and Mijolla-Mellor observe, "there is no formulable psychoanalytical interpretation outside the psychoanalytical situation" (1996, 153), that is, outside the transference relationship established between analysand and analyst.

Lacan preferred to keep psychoanalysis closer to the couch, in fact he strongly rejected its use outside the clinical field, repeatedly attacking so-called "applied" psychoanalysis. He was vehemently opposed to it but had no qualms about using art and fiction in furthering psychoanalytic theory. It is enough to take a look at his texts devoted to the works of authors like Marguerite Duras or Edgar Allan Poe to see that he staunchly refused to psychoanalyze the author or the works and made fun of those who indulged. With understandable trepidation, most psychoanalysts have relied on a timid proposition, the well-known formula "psychoanalysis has nothing to say about art but can learn a lot from it." Lacan eventually contradicted his own declared position when he worked on James Joyce, often conflating in his analysis Joyce, the author, with Stephen Dedalus, the character. But Lacan's reading of Joyce is not an indulgent psychobiographical exercise. Like Sophocles' Oedipus for Freud, fiction offered a new and revolutionary psychic paradigm. In Lacan's Joyce, art played a central role; his writings saved him from a destiny of madness.

Lacan's year-long seminar focused on Joyce but was also a profound and extensive exploration of artistic activity as he unambiguously stated in the opening session when he summed up his project, saying that "this year will be my interrogation of art" (Lacan 2005, 22). When Lacan turned his attention to Joyce's writings, he discovered a new understanding of art and creativity. In Joyce's art Lacan found the most original definition of the symptom, one that breaks away from the medical model and brings the symptom closer to a mathematical function. From Joyce's singular (though not uncommon) situation, Lacan developed a new theory of artistic creation with implications for how we understand the relation of subject to culture and of ego to other. Lacan found a new meaning for the term "symptom" (*symptôme*) that he rewrote as *sinthome*. The word itself corresponds to an old spelling of symptom in French and is pronounced in the same way as the contemporary word for symptom. This subtle difference hints at the importance of the dimension of writing.

How productive was this coinage? This shift in terminology related the symptom to art, a *sinthome* defined as the creative knotting together of the registers of the symbolic (language, speech), the real (the mixture of pain and pleasure Lacan calls *jouissance*, the distribution of pleasure in the body), and the imaginary (images, meaning), whose interlocking sustains reality for the subject. By the time of the *sinthome*, Lacan was working in mathematical topology and knot theory, borrowing a syntax and vocabulary in an effort to offer a formalization of what he observed in the analytic experience. This shift from linguistics to topology carried major consequences. Lacan no longer thought of the symptom as something to decode, a carrier of a repressed message (a signifier) which can be deciphered by reference to the unconscious "structured like a language," but as the trace of the unique way someone can come to be and enjoy their unconscious. The symptom (*sinthome*) is an invention that allows someone to live by providing the essential organization of *jouissance*. Identification with the *sinthome* occurs when one identifies with the particular form of their enjoyment from which hangs what and who someone is. The aim of the cure was no longer to get rid of symptoms but to identify with one's unique *sinthome* in order to enjoy it. The path to follow here now was, to paraphrase Žižek's (2001) title, to "Enjoy your *sinthome*!"

The *sinthome* is inscribed in Lacan's theory of the Borromean knot; this knot is made out of the intertwining of three rings (Figure 14.1), which correspond to the tripartite structure Lacan called the real, the imaginary, and the symbolic orders. Although heterogeneous, these

Figure 14.1 The Borromean knot, three rings.

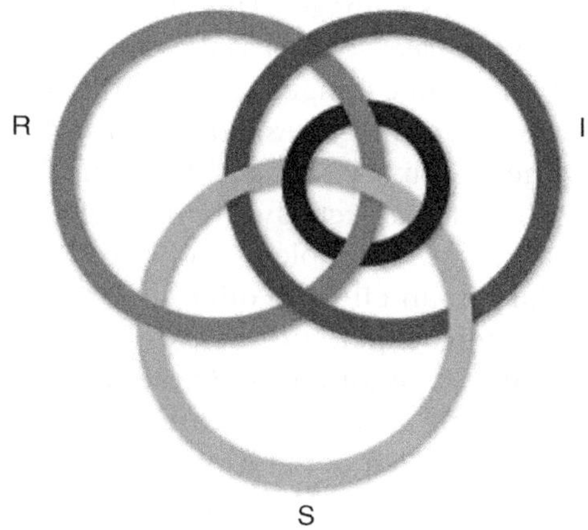

Figure 14.2 The Borromean knot, four rings.

registers can intersect and hold together. Lacan chose the Borromean knot because of its main characteristic – the rings are so interdependent that if one ring is unknotted, the other three come loose.

Nonetheless a fourth term can intervene and repair the failure in the knotting (Figure 14.2), re-linking the rings and holding together again the rings that have disentangled. Lacan called *sinthome* this fourth ring, able to remedy the unraveling of the Borromean knotting.

With his invention of the *sinthome* Lacan did not just put forward a new technical key term but opened a revolutionary theoretical avenue.

I would like to highlight that the coining was made apropos of a gifted artist like Joyce, whom Lacan claimed personified the *sinthome*. Lacan's theory of the *sinthome* applied above all to the singularities of Joyce's art but could be generalized somewhat. Taking Joyce for a "case," Lacan constructed a clinical example on the art of the *sinthome*. Lacan's idea was that Joyce's writing was a corrective device to repair a fault, a slip of the knot. According to Lacan, Joyce's enigmatic writing undid language, it became his *sinthome*, made him a name, produced a new ego through artifice and became his signature, a mark of his singularity as an artist.

My main contention will be to connect the peculiar meaning given to the concept of "art" by Lacan in his interpretation of Joyce's works with what I discovered in my clinical practice when treating transsexual patients. In Joyce's case, his art was able to compensate for a defect in his subjective structure, saving him from insanity. The *sinthome*-art grants access to a know-how which can repair faults in the psyche working as a supplement that holds together the registers of the real, the symbolic, and the imaginary in such a way that it fasten the subject in place. I will test this claim by examining some memoirs written by people who have changed sex.

***

Why do so many transsexuals write memoirs? This question has already been explored in an original manner by Jay Prosser (1998). He examined the narratives of those who crossed sexes and concluded that transsexual somatic transitions are spurred and enabled by narrative. My position is slightly different – I suggest that transsexual memoirs allow us to see the function of art in ways that affect the life of everyone, men and women, transgender and cisgender[3] alike. The transsexual's request for a physical and sexual transformation brings us close to the etymological meaning of *techné* which in Greek means both "technique" and "technology" rather than "art" in the sense of "fine arts," as Heidegger has skillfully demonstrated. Other equivalents would be "expertise," "technical knowledge," and even "science." The art of the *sinthome* is art taken in this extended sense: it is a know-how, a sort of singular tacit knowledge that cannot transfer to another person but that holds the individual, preventing them from falling apart. In the case of sex-change memoirs one could argue that writing the memoir gives the author a body that can be named. Writing elevates the unsymbolizable, the "invisible kernel, that meaningless fragment of the Real" (Žižek 2001, 12) to something that can be named.

Prosser observed that transsexuals already are involved in a writing process during their first visits to a clinician's office, where in order to be taken seriously a transsexual has to engage in a founding autobiographical act, an act of recounting a plausible story of gender trouble triggered by an institutional request or demand. This mandatory account will facilitate a certain embodiment, and this autobiography "is also a kind of second skin: the story the transsexual must weave around the body in order that his body may be read" (1998, 101.)

Prosser chooses here a very loaded word, since most transsexual persons use the verb "read" to mean "guessing somebody's anatomical identity." Being "read" often entails "to pass" or "not to pass" for other than one is. Max Wolf Valerio (2006), an American Indian/Latino poet, writer, and performer who transitioned from feminist lesbian woman to heterosexual man, chronicled in detail the first five years of his hormonal and social transformation from female to male. To his chagrin, he discovered that taking testosterone left him with an incipient receding hairline. Besides some trepidation about his sudden interest in watching hair transplant TV infomercials, Valerio welcomed this change as a potential cue for people to read him as male (2006, 324). Helen Boyd (2007) lost her husband to another woman when he became the other woman, as she put it (her husband, a cross-dressing heterosexual man, decided to consider sex reassignment surgery and become a woman). Boyd wrote, in *She's Not the Man I Married: My Life With a Transgender Husband*, "It is almost impossible for Betty to present as a feminine male because her femininity means that she [husband] is often read as a woman" (2007, 85). Valerio and Boyd use "read" differently, but they seem to agree that gender is a matter of interpretation, that gender is always a representation to be decoded. The reference to "reading" calls up Lacan's elaborations on "writing," a function he ascribed to the symptom when he called it *sinthome*.

Like Prosser, Hausman (1995) observed that the transsexual population is a well-read group for strategic reasons (1995, 143). To successfully obtain the medical treatments requested, the story of transsexuality has to match an officially sanctioned etiology. Indeed, the account has to be convincing: the very telling of the "right" story can confer legitimacy to the request for a sex change and grant access to hormone treatments and surgical interventions. Therefore the autobiographical reports delivered to the clinical experts have to conform to the constraints of a genre. Hence, published or unpublished transsexual autobiographers will follow the formal constraints of the genre quite systematically. Of course this will impose limits to the construction of transsexual subjectivity. Sandy Stone (1991) writes that the installation of an "official transsexual history" needed to obtain access to surgical and hormonal sex change treatment has produced a situation in which the potential for the "intertextuality"[4] of transsexual subjectivity is erased because the person requesting a sex change goes great lengths to appear as a "normal" transsexual. The "authentic experience is replaced by a particular kind of story, one that supports the old constructed positions." (1991, 295) A transsexual who suppresses the ambiguities and complexities of lived experience for the sake of normality is thus not very different from the patient who comes to see an analyst because the plausible story no longer efficiently lies about the past; in both cases, a symptom is endowed with the potential to start the analytic process. Yet, even when the transsexual narrative repeats the old clichés, one cannot downplay the tremendous impact that the encounter with a sex-change memoir has had for many transsexuals. Almost all the sex-change memoirs include a moment in which the author recounts reading another sex-change memoir. Often revelatory, the discovery of this type of text proves to be a defining moment anchoring the subject in the realization of an identity and often has creative and transformative functions. Memoirs of sex change are not only numerous but also often have an impressive, life-transforming effect on the future transsexuals who happen to read them – the experience of reading other people's memoirs becomes a turning point in their evolution. Those who read them before starting their process of metamorphosis tell us that encounter with the text is a completely transformative experience that reveals a truth up to then unknown, but that, once acknowledged, starts a process that is unstoppable.

In 2005, Jonathan Ames published a well-received anthology of transsexual memoirs. Ames (2005) aptly summed up the structure of sex-change autobiographies as a three-act saga: "first act: gender-dysphoria childhood; second act: the move to the big city and the transformation ... [third act] the sex change" (2005, xii). For Ames, there is one basic outline for all transsexual memoirs: "A boy or a girl very early on in life feels terribly uncomfortable in his or her gender role, and there is a sense that some terrible mistake has occurred, that he or she was meant to be the other sex" (2005, xii). Ames takes the transsexual autobiography as a *Bildungsroman* or "coming-of-age-novel" (2005, xxi). Ames observes that transsexual memoirs follow a progression in which the main characters, now aware of the "error of nature," see family and society as trying to reform them. Often, the protagonists also struggle internally, taking great pains in trying to repress their drive to become the opposite sex. Eventually, our heroes leave their hometown and venture into the outside world; they often end up in a big city. It is in this new context that they begin to masquerade as the other sex, perhaps only privately at first, but eventually more publicly. With time, the disguise and perfected ability to pass become more and more permanent and successful; this was particularly so in the second part of the twentieth century, with the increased availability of hormone treatments and surgical technologies to manipulate the body. Ablations and implants, as well as the climactic sex reassignment surgery, will finally allow the memoir's protagonist to reclaim a place of self-acceptance and peace. Ames emphasizes the literary and sociological significance of these memoirs; their appeal should be universal insofar as they deal with questions that haunt everyone, such as "Who am I?" and "What am I?"

Ames' description of the transsexual memoir as *Bildungsroman* or a novel of formation is slightly misleading, since transsexual memoirs could be described more accurately as novels of the artist, in a subgenre known as the *Künstlerroman*. There may not be such a huge difference between the two genres but this nuance is important for psychoanalytically influenced ears. On the one hand, one would have a formation (*Bildung*) of the unconscious, which means that unconscious phenomena are made visible in transsexual symptoms, while on the other hand one would come closer to art, hence to Lacan's analysis of Joyce when he presents his writing, his art, as a *sinthome*.

Following the path of pathological "formations" of the unconscious, Catherine Millot (1981) and Moustapha Safouan (1974) have claimed that the conviction with which *some* transsexuals assert that they were born in the body of the wrong sex makes them conclude that *all* transsexuals share a psychotic structure. I believe this is a misconstruction. Let us note that Millot was the first to intrude the idea that the transsexual symptom could have a function structurally analogous to that which Lacan ascribed to writing when he took Joyce as an example. I disagree with their position in terms of diagnosis. In my practice, I found evidence that not all transsexuals are psychotic. In the same way, Joyce was not psychotic, even if he was almost caught in a psychotic structure, especially in regard to what concerned his daughter. I recommend prudence when diagnosing transsexuals. I argue for a depathologization of transgenderism and thus stand back from the current pathological approach that psychoanalysis takes toward transgenderism. In my clinical practice I prefer to talk about transsexual symptoms, and they may appear in several psychic structures: neurosis, perversion, psychosis. Lacan's notion of the *sinthome* entails a new conception of verbal and textual enjoyment (the word is a quasi-Joycean coinage: it calls up the ancient spelling of the word "symptom" but it is also a pun on saint, sinner, man, Saint Thomas, and home), with important clinical consequences. Lacan's *sinthome* refers to an unprecedented type of symptom, one that has the singularity of being a creation compensating for a defect in a subject's structure. Each particular *sinthome* is a product of art that can allow someone to love, work, desire.

***

The first consequence of Lacan's theory of the *sinthome* is that it depathologizes transgenderism. If transgenderism is not an illness, a sex change cannot be either a treatment or a cure. We should, in the name of the *sinthome*, stop the systematic pathologization of the whole spectrum of transgender issues.

The second contribution of the concept of *sinthome* concerns identification and identity. We should go beyond the model of imaginary identification (Lacan's mirror stage) to understand sex changes.[5] Most commentators tend to stop at this point. This is the case of an author as gifted as Prosser. The mirror stage, Lacan hypothesized, is a stage that infants pass through in which the external image of the body (reflected in a mirror or represented by the loving gaze of the main caregiver, often the mother) is internalized as a unified body. This image, which will become the "I," is an idealized imago and will be the blueprint for emerging perceptions of selfhood. It anticipates a bodily perception of unity that does not correspond with the infant's real neurological immaturity and vulnerability. It also creates an ideal of perfection that the subject will always strive to achieve. Here we can see how the ego is dependent on an external object with which the infant identifies, how it is produced in alienation, that is, as other, as an illusion of reciprocity and a promise of wholeness, when the real experience of the body is fragmented because at this early stage the infant cannot even control its bodily movements. In the mirror stage the subject becomes an I in anticipation and alienated from itself. The dual relation of the body to the ego, which is on the basis of the body image, Lacan hypothesized, was quite different in the case of Joyce and it did not involved identification with an image but with writing. His ego was supported by his art.

When Lacan turned his attention to Joyce's art, he also discovered a new relation to the body. He observed that Joyce had a peculiar body, one that could fall, slip away, like an open envelope letting go of its contents. Lacan focused on a passage in *A Portrait of the Artist as a Young Man* (Joyce 1992), when Stephen remembers a moment of rage at his schoolmates that suddenly faded away: He had felt his anger falling from him "as easily as a fruit is divested of its soft ripe peel" (2002, 87). For Lacan (2005), such a transformation of anger was curious and revealing. According to Joyce's plans for *Ulysses*, Stephen Dedalus does not have a body, which is why Joyce stressed by contrast the strong physicality of Molly and Leopold Bloom. The idea of a mind without a very definitive body could be generalized: what Joyce proposes as a youthful being not yet fully embodied is more precisely analyzed as a body that could fall from one's self. This labile envelope is like a wrapping that does not fully hold the subject (Lacan 2005, 149). Lacan then argued that for Joyce himself, it was his writing that would have the function of "holding" the body.

The experience of slipping in and out of the body has been narrated by many transsexual authors. They also manifest the sense that there is something artificial in the construction of their new body which is tantamount to a work of art. "The art of being a sex-changed woman is precarious" (Griggs, 1998, xi). Nobody is naturally within his or her body; there is always a moment of indecision, slipping, or misrecognition. What Joyce and the transsexual manifest in a radical manner has been experienced by everyone and is illustrated by language use – one is not body but one *has* a body. The body assumption is a process made of self-division and estrangement, this is a feeling that appears vividly illustrated in transsexual narratives, as in the account of Raymond Thompson's (1995), female-to-male transsexual:

> The first time I was born, it was in a body which was other than male. By some cosmic mistake, as a budding human being I had somehow the wrong body, or the wrong body had chosen me. I am a transsexual person. … As I become more aware of myself it became more harder for me to relate to my body and it affected the way I related to the world around me …
>
> (1995, 1–2)

Thompson manages to overcome the refusal of "this ugly fragmented body of mine" (1995, 191) after a phalloplasty when his body would "become whole" (1995, 309). Thompson calls up the image of the body as a vacant shell, as an enclosure oppressing the self, a recurrent theme in sex-change autobiographical narratives. Thompson poignantly describes this experience of the body as an ill-adjusted container:

> I needed to be out of my body, to be free. It felt as if my "inner body" was forcing itself to the ends of my limbs. I was growing ever larger inside of me, making me feel I was bursting at the seams and wanting out ... out ... *out!*
>
> Because this was impossible, this process would abruptly reverse and I would start to shrink inside myself. My whole inner body shrank until I became very small inside. It was as I became so small I had to find some safe place to hide inside myself. My tiny inner body was in unfamiliar surroundings, in a place it didn't belong and I felt utterly unsafe. I became like a little shadow inside my physical body, a shadow running around everywhere trying to find somewhere inside.
>
> (1995, 200)

The sex change appears as the only possible escape from the confines of excessive *jouissance*: "I was trapped inside a living chamber of horrors" (Griggs 1998, 88). Lewins (1995) expanded this notion: "In the case of transsexuals locked inside a prison of flesh and blood, there is a constant ache for emancipation" (1995, 14). The body is experienced as a burdensome exterior layer often worn like an ill-fitting piece of clothing one is impatient to shed. This is how Diane Leslie Feinberg describes it: "I think how nice it would be to unzip my body from forehead to navel and go on vacation. But there is no escaping it, I would have to pack myself along" (1980, 20). Jan Morris reiterates a similar wish when she writes: "All I wanted was liberation, or reconciliation – to live as myself, to clothe myself in a more proper body, and achieve Identity at last" (1986 [1974], 104). Morris refers to her former body as an oppressive outer layer in which the real being, the true self, was locked; the urge to break free from it is pressing: "If I were trapped in that cage again nothing would keep me from my goal" (1986, 169).

Thus, the third advantage of the use of the notion of *sinthome* concerns the manner in which a material bodily transformation is not sufficient to change the body image. As we have seen, the body is basically fragmented and only sustained in a precarious sense of unity by imaginary relations. For Lacan, "the body, at least in the analytic perspective, is the body in so far as it creates an orifice ... that by which it is knotted to some Symbolic or Real" (Seminar XXII, session of May 13,1975, unpublished). For psychoanalysis the body is a speaking body linked with culture and a specific imaginary realm. The body is sexual, and to inhabit it we assume a sexual positioning; this is not an easy task because the body is marked by the conundrum of sexual difference, which is neither sex nor gender. One of the truths the transgender phenomenon illustrates is that body and gender coherence is a fiction that is assumed through identification (Salamon 2010). It is absurd to ascribe to anatomy the role of normalizer in a type of sexuality by focusing on the genitals or on a single prescribed act. This normalizing role has been challenged by transsexual discourse and practices. Sexual identity issues all revolve around this particular body, a body one is not born into but one that one becomes. But this identification with an image, which is like all forms of recognition a misrecognition, is not sufficient, it needs some kind of writing to anchor each subject to their body. Many people who feel trapped in a body of the "wrong" gender do experience the drive to write, to produce a text that narrates their experience, offering a testimony to their stories of transformation. It is in the writing of the sex-change memoir that a different sort of bodily transformation takes place, when the body is written. Writing a sex-change memoir does not just aim at passing from one side to the other; it has the function of tying together body and text. Writing grants a different form of embodiment in which the body finds its anchor in the sea of language. In the case of sex-change memoirs, I argue that the writing of the memoir can bring the author home to the body transformed.

It is obvious that there are unavoidable tensions in transsexual autobiographies. If the aim of the autobiography is to document the transition, for instance to show how somebody born a man becomes a woman, the purpose of the transsexual's memoir is in contradiction with the common transsexual claim that: "I was woman all along, but happened to be in the wrong body." Prosser contends that this tension between transformation and continuity in the self is inherent to the autobiographical genre (1998, 119). However, often the motivation for the transition is to accomplish a sex change that will not leave vestiges of the former sex on the body. If the transsexual wants a complete transformation to pass as a member of the new sex, the autobiography defeats this purpose. By making public the account of the steps of the transition, very often documented with photographs, the autobiography somehow exposes the decoy. And yet, by publishing the account, the transsexual who does not want to be read as a transsexual but rather wants to pass as normal will become publicly recognized as a transsexual. Prosser emphasizes this paradox and highlights the fact that while there may be sex changes accomplished by surgery and hormones, the somatic transformation is not sufficient. Writing autobiographies of sex change generates transitional moments that are "more in keeping with the flow of the story to cohere the transsexual subject." In this case, indeed, the narrative "enacts its own transitions" (1998, 123). It is therefore this last stage of the transition, that is, the narrative transition itself, that I want to emphasize. It is a transition that takes place in and through writing, at a moment when the autography seems to recapture the body, thus anchoring it through a textual embodiment. This writing has the function of nomination. Let us take again the example of Jan Morris' autobiography, *Conundrum*. Of her previous life as James, Jan explains: "I was a writer. Full as I was of more recondite certainties, I have always been sure of that too. I never for a moment doubted my vocation" (1986 [1974], 67). In writing about her writing, Morris describes her style as if it was already revealing an essential, traditional femininity, "the quick emotionalism, the hovering tear, the heart-on-sleeve, the touch of schmaltz" (1986 [1974], 133). Or again: "I often detected in myself a taste for the flamboyant ... often a compensation for uncertainty" (1986 [1974], 132). Feeling that s/he has been a writer since early childhood, Morris condenses this posture in a hedonist mode: "Creating to please my senses was certainly my own literary method" (1986 [1974], 95).

More deeply though, writing had been an attempt to make body and spirit cohere, less to please her senses than as an effort to find a strategy capable of regulating excess *jouissance*. This was achieved by way of an artifice, of a supplement (in the same way, there was the sex change but also writing about it) that allowed for an incarnation of what before had only been experienced in the real. This real corresponds to what is enacted in mystical phenomena or realized in psychosis: It is founded on the impossibility of sexual equivalence or rapport, which was at root the "sexual incongruity" experienced by Morris.

Prosser talks about "transsexual mirror stages" (1998, 101) and quotes Morris' mirror scene in *Conundrum*, minutes before going to the operating room for a sex change in Morocco. Already anesthetized, pubic hair shaven and disinfected, Morris staggers while going "to say good bye to myself in the mirror. We would never meet again, and I wanted to give the other self a long last look in the eye, and a wink for luck." The person who writes will emerge "alive and well, and sex-changed in Casablanca. ... I had a new body" (1986 [1974], 140–41). This scene is not only a transitional moment in Morris' transsexual trajectory but also the most crucial point in the transsexual narrative. As Prosser comments, this is when the "me" written about in the biography and the "I" that writes become one; they had been "so far separated by sex" and now are "fused into a singly sexed autobiographical subject, an integral 'I'" (1998, 100). Here is the place where I see the function of Lacan's ego as scriptor.

It is indeed the writing of the memoir that allowed Morris to "embody" her body. It was not enough to undergo the sex-reassignment surgery to reknot the imaginary, the real, and the symbolic. The key to why Morris woke up ecstatic from the surgery despite the sharp pain – "I found myself, in fact, astonishingly happy" (1986 [1974], 140) – is to be found in the comment of the Moroccan surgeon who performed her sex change. During the postoperative examination, Dr. B. commented in a mix of French and heavily accented broken English, nicely rendered in Morris's transcription: "*Très, très bon*, you could nevair get surgery like this in England – you see, now you would be able to *write*" (1986 [1974], 142; emphasis original). Now being "able to write," Jan Morris wrote and constructed with *Conundrum* a text that gives credibility to her being a woman. Thus, the memoir comes full circle. It opens with "I was three years old when I realized that I had been born in the wrong body and should really be a girl. I remember the moment well, it is the earliest memory of my life" (1986 [1974], 3). Since "it is only in writing this book that I have delved so deeply into my emotions" (1986 [1974], 169), it was also through writing that Morris completed the evolution toward a solution to the conundrum of her existence. The book closes with:

> if I stand back and look at myself dispassionately, as I looked at myself that night in the mirror in Casablanca – If I consider my story in detachment I sometimes seem a figure of a fable or allegory. … I see myself not as a man or woman, self or other, fragment or whole, but only as a wondering child with the cat beneath the Bluthner [piano].
>
> (1986 [1974], 174)

This is the vignette with which the autobiography begins and ends. It keeps acquiring new meaning through writing. The letter may be the same, but it reads differently. Morris, now Jan, has acquired *savoir faire*, know-how. Finally a One of body and soul has been achieved through Morris' singular *sinthomatic* identification, and it testifies to the power of transformation contained in writing.

Sex-change memoirs are meant to be read, to be interpreted. They beg for deciphering. They are as often symptoms as *sinthomes*. Does this mean that they are great literature? Perhaps not, at least not always, but they all aspire to the most essential function of literature. They are love letters to others or to oneself that somehow inscribe sexual difference. Writing a sex-change memoir does not just aim at passing from one side to the other.

In some cases, writing about one's transsexual transformation is of the order of the *sinthome*; there are many cases when the transformation achieved a reknotting of the three registers of the real, symbolic, and imaginary. Then, the *sinthome* shapes the singularity of an "art," a *techné* that reknotted a workable consistency for the subject; this movement can best be evoked by saying that it moves the subject from a certain contingency to absolute necessity. Thus, Morris describes her trajectory as inevitable, predestined, as if the sex change had always been bound to happen:

> I do not for a moment regret the act of change. I could see no other way, and it has made me happy. ... Sex has its reasons too, but I suspect the only transsexuals who can achieve happiness are those ... to whom it is not primarily a sexual dilemma at all – who offer no rational purpose to their compulsions, even to themselves, but are simply driven blindly and helplessly. ... We are the most resolute. Nothing will stop us, no fear of ridicule or poverty, no threat of isolation, not even the prospect of death itself.
>
> (1986 [1974], 168–69)

One can see why her *sinthome* was necessary: It was necessity itself. A *sinthome* is what does not cease to be written. In Morris' case, the *sinthome* has produced less a "woman" than a "woman of letters."

It is often assumed that transsexuals are marginal beings whose experiences cannot be shared by most of us; yet my contention is that their foundational uncertainty about their bodies points to a universal function occupied by art in all of our lives. Art is perhaps "artificial," but as Lacan showed about Joyce, this artifice is crucial to a knotting of the several domains making up a "whole" subjectivity. What has become a vital need and an ontological redefinition for a transsexual is in fact shared by most – but we are not aware of the fact that we are not bodies but become one, and that a degree of artificiality, and even "art" one might add, is essential in the process. There is art in transsexual artificiality. I would even argue that a transsexual who has been able to complete a true transition has become an "Ego scriptor," as Ezra Pound called himself in his *Cantos*.

Sexual difference is neither just the body (as biological substratum) nor the psychic introjections of the social performance of gender (a socially constructed role). Neither the perspective of biological essentialism nor that of social constructivism has been able to solve the problem of unconscious sexual difference. Since sexual difference is neither sex nor gender, sex needs to be symbolized, and gender needs to be embodied.

I will reiterate my claim that sex-change memoirs are a narrative form with a specific function for the subjectivity of their authors. In some cases, transsexual memoirs can function as a process of self-invention for their authors. Moreover, sex-change memoirs provide an excellent testing ground for Lacan's theory of the *sinthome* as art. Even though we know that the psychoanalytic perspective on sexual difference implies that it is not a question of anatomy but rather of its consequences, we have noted that a majority of transsexuals struggle to conform rigidly to the normative demands of a sexual identity in contradiction with their anatomical sex. While they engage in technologically assisted manipulations of their bodies, their torment seems to be the result of the limits imposed by an anatomy experienced as a tragic destiny.

Let take now the example of the book by Mario Martino, *Emergence* (1977), which the jacket copy advertised as "the only complete autobiography of a woman who has become a man." This book is presented as the account of a "painful life to live, a painful life to write" (1977, xi). Martino, a nurse, played the dual role of subject of study and clinical authority using psychoanalytic jargon, which generates some humorous self-awareness. Evoking his contempt for the father's repressive violence and his adoration for the mother, Martino comments: "A bit of Oedipus, you think?" (1977, 28). Martino describes a second phalloplasty that seemed to fail as the first one did, and the neopenis had to be surgically excised. As the tip of his new penis became black, rotted away, and necrotized, he had to sit in water every night to slowly cut away dead tissue. He comments ironically: "Talk about castration complex! Psychologically this cutting was almost impossible for me, yet it has to be done" (1977, 262). Mario broke away from the increasing distress about the inadequate results of surgery when he came to the realization that even if he wanted "a perfect phallus" he had to accept the impossibility of the wish. "So today I'm happy with what I have: a respectable phallus – three fourths perfect" (1977, 263).

The idea of imperfection is also mentioned by Renée Richards. She was asked at age 72 about the motivations for her sex change more than thirty years before. By a striking coincidence, Richards described her decision to change sex as resulting from an unyielding "pressure to change into a woman." This cannot but evoke Lacan's expression *pousse-à-la-femme* ("push-towards-Woman") used to refer to the feminization most often observed in psychosis but considered a generalized phenomenon common to several psychic structures (see Lacan 2001).

Richards also said that she wished she could have had something that could have stopped that "pressure" and prevented the surgery: "What I said was if there were a drug, some voodoo, any kind of mind-altering magic remedy to keep the man intact, that would have been preferable, but there wasn't." By then, she seemed to have regrets about something that she had felt earlier as inevitable: "Better to be an intact man functioning with 100 percent capacity for everything than to be a transsexual woman who is an imperfect woman."[6]

The notion of an "imperfect" solution relates to the etymology of the word "symptom." As we have seen, up to the late fourteenth century the spelling of word was sinthoma. This is very close to its Greek predecessor *symptoma*, which means "a happening, accident, disease." Its stem is *sympiptein* (to befall) which is a combination of *syn* (together) and *piptein* (to fall). In Greek, "symptom" literally means "falling together." The word "fall" is cognate to the word "fail." "Fail" comes from the old French *falir*, now *faillir*, "to be lacking, to miss, not succeed," from the Latin *fallere* "to trip, cause to fall." Figuratively, "to deceive, trick, dupe, cheat, elude; fail, be lacking or defective." The noun (as in "without fail") is from the late thirteenth century, from the old French *faile* "deficiency," derived from *falir*. The Anglo-French form of the verb, *failer*, came to be used as a noun, hence "failure."

This detour by way of etymology sketches a movement from failure to symptom. To quote Samuel Beckett, I would say that the *sinthome* is the art of failing better; it consists of letting the symptom fall (*falling together*) which is precisely the art proposed by the Lacanian notion of *sinthome* – failing together with one's unconscious, thus, as Beckett would say, "failing better." It was that or death, as was poignantly affirmed by several analysands. They all had a possibility of letting their bodies fall, like Stephen Dedalus, who, for Lacan, indicated Joyce's main symptom. If Stephen is, as we have seen in Joyce's scheme for *Ulysses*, a man without a body, it is because his body could not "hold him together" without art, without the artifice of writing. As one of my analysands said, "I can right/write myself through writing." For these analysands, the *sinthome* will be mandatory as it were, a necessity that nevertheless also carries along a little defect.

I want to conclude by equating art in general and the *sinthome* as the "art of failing better." The idea of failure has been explored with precision in literary criticism;[7] Walter Benjamin's observations can give us a provisional conclusion: "To do justice to the figure of Kafka in its purity and its peculiar beauty one must never lose sight of one thing: it is the purity and beauty of a failure. The circumstances are manifold. One is tempted to say: once he was certain of eventual failure, everything worked out for him *en route* as in a dream" (Benjamin 1968, 144–45). I would like to suggest that the *sinthome* should be taken as a new way of organizing *jouissance*, but via art. Art offers us a way of failing better that also allows us to live, quite simply.

Notes

1 The term *jouissance* (Lacan 1996) does not translate easily into English. Lacan himself suggested a combination of "enjoyment" and "lust." The word also is equivocal in French. Indeed, it connotes a form of enjoyment not necessarily accompanied by pleasure or joy. *Jouissance* conveys the enjoyment of an object, but an enjoyment not simply yielding advantageous returns or results; rather, it produces not a gratifying surplus benefit but a violent, climactic bliss closer to loss, death, fragmentation, and the disruptive rapture experienced when transgressing limits. *Jouissance* is a voluptuous and anxiety-provoking experience in which pain and pleasure are indistinguishable.

2 Letter to Hermann Struck, November 7, 1914; he adds: "I do not wish you to judge the validity of our other research according to the same pattern" ("Ich möchte nicht, daß Sie die Sicherheit unserer sonstigen Ermittlungen nach diesem Muster beurteilen": Freud 1960, 302). This emphasizes again the essayistic quality of his theories but does not diminish their intellectually stimulating effect.

3 "Cis" is as a prefix in Latin which means "on the same side [as]" or "on this side [of]." "Cisgender" or "cis male" or "cis female" are used to refer to those who do not identify as transgender.

4 "Intertextuality" is a term introduced by Julia Kristeva in the late 1960s. In this context it would refer to the multiple meanings of texts. For Kristeva, text is not a closed off entity but the result of an author's borrowing and transformation of prior texts as well as of the reader's attribution of meaning, which concerns not just the text in question but a network of texts invoked by the reader in the reading process.

5 The mirror stage refers to the dual relationship humans have with their own body image as illustrated by their mirror reflection. The mirror supplies an imaginary sense of "wholeness" that is in contradiction with the bodily sensations of fragmentation. Although primarily imaginary, the mirror stage also has a significant symbolic dimension. The symbolic is there when the infant recognizes herself in the mirror and supposes with great jubilation that her image is her own, and looks back to the adult holding the infant (who stands in for the big Other) looking for the approving gaze that will confirm this

image unifying the fragmented real (Lacan 2004). See also Lacan's paper, "The Mirror Stage as Formative of the Function of the *I* as Revealed in Psychoanalytic Experience" (in Lacan 2006).

6 Reported in the *New York Times*, February 1, 2007. http://www.nytimes.com/2007/02/01/garden/01renee.html?pagewanted=print&_r=0. Accessed December 13, 2013.

7 For a detailed analysis of art as failure see Ewa Ziarek's excellent book *The Rhetoric of Failure* (Ziarek 1995).

References

Ames, Jonathan. 2005. *Sexual Metamorphosis: An Anthology of Transsexual Memoirs*. New York: Vintage Books.

Benjamin, Walter. 1968. "Some Reflections on Kafka." In *Illuminations: Essays and Reflections*, ed. Hannah Arendt, 141–45. New York: Harcourt, Brace, Jovanovich.

Boyd, Helen. 2007. *She's Not the Man I Married: My Life With a Transgender Husband*. Emeryville, CA: Seal Press.

Feinberg, Diane Leslie. 1980. *Journal of a Transsexual* New York: World View.

Freud, Sigmund. 1910a. "Leonardo Da Vinci and a Memory of his Childhood." In *The Standard Edition of the Complete Psychological Works of Sigmund Freud*, 24 vols., ed. James Strachey, with the assistance of Anna Freud, Alix Strachey, and Alan Tyson, trans. James Strachey, vol. 11, 57–138. London: Hogarth Press.

Freud, Sigmund. 1910b. "'Wild' Psycho-Analysis." In *The Standard Edition of the Complete Psychological Works of Sigmund Freud*, 24 vols., ed. James Strachey, with the assistance of Anna Freud, Alix Strachey, and Alan Tyson, trans. James Strachey, vol. 11, 219–28. London: Hogarth Press.

Freud, Sigmund. 1914. "The Moses of Michelangelo." In *The Standard Edition of the Complete Works of Sigmund Freud*, 24 vols., ed. James Strachey, with the assistance of Anna Freud, Alix Strachey, and Alan Tyson, trans. James Strachey, vol. 13, 209–38. London: Hogarth Press.

Freud, Sigmund. 1960. *Briefe 1873–1939*, ed. Ernst L. Freud. Frankfurt am Main: Fischer.

Griggs, Claudine. 1998. *S/HE: Changing Sex and Changing Clothes (Dress, Body, Culture)*. Oxford: Berg.

Grosz, Elisabeth. 1994. *Volatile Bodies: Toward a Corporeal Feminism*. Bloomington: Indiana University Press.

Hausman,, Bernice. 1995. *Changing Sex: Transsexualism, Technology, and the Idea of Gender*. Durham, N.C.: Duke University Press.

Joyce, James. 1992. *A Portrait of the Artist as a Young Man*. New York: Penguin.

Kristeva, Julia. 1980. *Desire in Language: A Semiotic Approach to Literature and Art*. New York: Columbia University Press.

Lacan, Jacques. 2001. "L'Étourdit." In *Autres écrits*. Paris: Seuil.

Lacan, Jacques 2004. *Le Séminaire*, Livre X: *L'angoisse*, ed. J.A. Miller. Paris: Seuil.

Lacan, Jacques 2005. *Le Séminaire*, Livre XXIII: *Le sinthome 1975–1976*, ed. J.A. Miller. Paris: Seuil.

Lacan, Jacques 2006. *Écrits: The First Complete Edition in English*, trans. B. Fink. New York: Norton.

Lewins, Frank. 1995. *Transsexualism in Transsexuals*. Melbourne: Macmillan.

Martino, Mario. 1977. *Emergence: A Transsexual Autobiography*. New York: Crown.

Mijolla, A., and S. Mijolla-Mellor. 1996. *Fundamentos del psicoanálisis*. Madrid: Síntesis.

Millot, Catherine. 1981. "Un cas de transsexualisme féminin." *Ornicar?*, 22/3: 167–76.

Millot, Catherine. 1990. *Horsexe: Essays on Transsexualism*, trans. K. Hylton. New York: Autonomedia.

Morris, Jan. 1986 [1974]. *Conundrum*. New York: Holt.

Prosser, Jay. 1998. *Second Skins: The Body Narratives of Transsexuality*. New York: Columbia University Press.

Safouan, Moustapha. 1974. Contribution à la psychanalyse du transsexualisme. *Scilicet*, 4: 137–59. Republished in *Le Champ freudien: Études sur l'Oedipe*, 74–97. 1974. Paris: Seuil.

Salamon, Gayle. 2010. *Assuming a Body: Transgender and Rhetorics of Materiality*. New York: Columbia University Press.

Stone, Sandy. 1991. "The Empire Strikes Back: A Posttransexual Manifesto." In *Body Guards: The Cultural Politics of Gender Ambiguity*, ed. J. Epstein and K. Straub, 280–304. New York: Routledge.

Thompson, Raymond, with Kitty Sewell. 1995. *What Took You So Long? A Girl's Journey to Manhood*. New York: Penguin.

Valerio, Max Wolf. 2006. *The Testosterone Files: My Hormonal and Social Transformation from Female to Male*. Emeriville, CA: Seal Press.

Ziarek, Ewa. 1995. *The Rhetoric of Failure: Deconstruction of Skepticism, Reinvention of Modernism*. New York: State University of New York Press.

Žižek, Slavoj. 2001. *Enjoy Your Symptom! Jacques Lacan in Hollywood and Out*. New York: Routledge.

Chapter 15

The Desert of the Real

Todd McGowan

The imaginary trap

The cinema enacts a constant struggle between plenitude and excess. Or, to put it another way, cinema provides an experience of imaginary wholeness for the spectator but also makes possible an encounter with the real that is impossible within the symbolic structure. The symbolic order is the order of signification where signifiers constitute a lacking and thus desiring subject. Absence in the symbolic order leads the subject to turn toward the imaginary, an order of images, for the illusion of completeness that it lacks in its symbolic identity. But the failure of symbolic identity also leads the subject to the real, which escapes all representation and knowledge.[1] There are thus two competing forms of enjoyment – an imaginary enjoyment and an enjoyment in the real. Cinematic fantasies become ideological when they privilege the former, and they cease to function as an ideological supplement when they privilege the latter. Historically, however, psychoanalytic theory has not been quick to recognize this second possibility.

The problem is that the cinematic viewing situation seems to privilege – and almost render impossible any alternative – an imaginary enjoyment. This is why the first psychoanalytic film theorists stressed

A Concise Companion to Psychoanalysis, Literature, and Culture, First Edition.
Edited by Laura Marcus and Ankhi Mukherjee.

the danger of always lurking in the cinema. Christian Metz, for instance, notes:

> The unique position of the cinema lies in this dual character of its signifier: unaccustomed perceptual wealth but at the same time stamped with unreality to an unusual degree, and from the very outset. More than the other arts, or in a more unique way, the cinema involves us in the imaginary: it drums up all perception, but to switch it immediately over into its own absence, which is nonetheless the only signifier present.
>
> (1982, 45)

Cinema immerses us in an imaginary plenitude that hides the working of the (ideological) signifier. By keeping ideology present only through its absence, films provide the perfect fantasmatic supplement for ideology.[2] Spectators experience them as respite from the demands of ideology precisely at the point when these demands exercise their full force.

Metz sees the task of psychoanalytic film theory "as an attempt to disengage the cinema-object from the imaginary and to win it for the symbolic, in the hope of extending the latter by a new province" (1982, 3). The danger of cinema, as Metz rightly sees, lies in the predominant role that the imaginary plays within it. Cinema propagates various fantasies that create a sense of wholeness for the spectator, and the theorist can make evident the symbolic structure that underlies and produces this wholeness. In doing so, the theorist offsets the power of the cinematic imaginary with signifiers, but signifiers are not free of ideological taint themselves.

In spite of the cogency of Metz's critical theorization, what has become increasingly evident is its glaring omission of Lacan's third category of experience – the real. For Metz and the psychoanalytic theorists that followed in his wake, cinema presents a struggle between the imaginary and the symbolic, between the object itself and its theorization, in which the real has no place. The spectator's captivation by the imaginary in the cinema is so extreme that it leaves no possibility for a real encounter to occur. The most that the thoughtful spectator can do is to gain awareness of the symbolic structure at work amid the experience of imaginary plenitude.

While Metz is certainly correct to note how the cinema marginalizes the symbolic at the expense of the imaginary, the fundamental cinematic struggle isn't the theorist's attempt "to disengage the cinema-object from the imaginary and win it for the symbolic," but between the imaginary and the real. The central conflict in the cinema exists between the lure of imaginary plenitude and the encounter with the real excess that the spectator's cinematic immersion makes possible. Plenitude is thus not just the great danger of the cinema but also its possibility for redemption. Contra Metz, the task of the psychoanalytic theorist does not involve detailing the symbolic structure that underlies the cinema's illusory imaginary plenitude. It involves instead distinguishing between this plenitude and the excessive disruptions of it.

The conflict between plenitude and excess is a conflict between two different forms of enjoyment or *jouissance*. In Jacques-Alain Miller's article "Paradigms of *Jouissance*" (2000), he differentiates between six conceptions of enjoyment that Lacan develops chronologically over his career as a thinker. The first form, according to Miller, is imaginary, and this imaginary enjoyment has no other function than to disrupt the symbolic circuit in which the subject finds itself articulated. Early in Lacan's career, imaginary enjoyment is a stumbling block within the symbolic order, a stumbling block that the analyst must struggle against. As Miller puts it, "imaginary *jouissance* stands as an obstacle or barrier vis-à-vis the symbolic development" (2000, 14). The imaginary register provides enjoyment, but it does so only insofar as it blocks the path through which the subject attains symbolic recognition and takes up its symbolic identification. The plenitude of the imaginary is thus a danger to the functioning of the symbolic order in this early conception of enjoyment.

In the later paradigms of *jouissance*, Miller, following Lacan's theoretical development, dissociates it completely from the imaginary. It becomes located either somewhere in signification itself or in some form of the real (what is irreducible to signification). In the third and sixth paradigms of *jouissance*, Miller links enjoyment not to the imaginary interruption of the symbolic circuit but to the real transgression or interruption of this circuit. The real becomes the site of enjoyment, either in the form of the impossible Thing from Seminar VII (in the third paradigm) or the absence of the sexual relation in Seminar XX (in the sixth paradigm). Even though these two forms of enjoyment differ radically, what they have in common is their association of enjoyment with the real, a real that interrupts the process of signification in a different way than imaginary enjoyment does in the first paradigm.

Though Miller thinks through the paradigms of *jouissance* in terms of the chronological development of Lacan's thought, one can put them in a synchronic relation with each other, so that rather than competing with each other, they exist in a supplementary fashion. The imaginary enjoyment of the first paradigm does not become outmoded when Lacan, to use Miller's formulation, "installs the non-rapport between *jouissance* and the Other" (2000, 41) in the sixth paradigm. Instead, imaginary enjoyment comes to compete with real enjoyment. The imaginary form of enjoying interruption comes at the expense of its real form, even though Lacan does not discover this real form until much later. In the cinema, the competition between these two types of enjoyment manifests itself at all times. Both of these forms of interruption function in the cinema under the guises, respectively, of plenitude and excess.

Cinematic plenitude acts as an imaginary interruption of the real interruption of the symbolic structure. That is to say, the experience of plenitude presents the symbolic order as seamless and hides its real fissures. When spectators immerse themselves in plenitude, they cannot see how the symbolic order fails. Through an investment in this plenitude, spectators miss the excess that disturbs their symbolic identification. In this sense, plenitude actually works to reinforce the symbolic structure, and Metz's name for the cinema – the "imaginary signifier" – is just as much a signifier as it is imaginary. Though Lacan saw imaginary plenitude as an obstacle to symbolic identification very early in his thought, the cinema reveals how this plenitude can play a vital role in sustaining symbolic identification by keeping any real interruption at bay. Lacan (1961–62) himself makes this point obliquely in his unpublished "Le Séminaire IX: L'Identification," when he notes, "the libidinal structure, in as much as it is marked by the narcissistic function, is what for us covers over and masks the relation to the object" (session of June 13, 1962). Imaginary plenitude – the result of the narcissistic function that Lacan describes here – disrupts the relation to the real object.

The imaginary disruption can occur in many forms, and almost all of them are present in the cinema. As Lacan suggests above, the imaginary relation can take the form of narcissism, in which the subject finds its own ego in the place of its object. This is one of the primary ways that cinematic identification works: the spectator identifies with the all-seeing perspective of the camera and the quasi-omnipotent hero as an ideal ego. But this imaginary disruption also occurs through the idea of the complementary sexual relationship, a relationship that apparently disrupts the symbolic structure only in order to undergird it. Sexual complementarity provides the spectator with a sense of wholeness that outstrips even that of the most heroic ideal ego. An isolated but seemingly whole John Wayne pales in comparison with Billy Crystal running to profess his undying love for Meg Ryan. The idea or ideal of the complementary sexual relationship is the sine qua non of cinematic plenitude, and it keeps the encounter with real excess at bay.

The problem is not simply the fact that so many films end with the complementary romantic union but that the image of enjoyment present in this union dissociates enjoyment from loss and associates it instead with the overcoming of loss. By doing so, the cinema consigns spectators to an imaginary enjoyment and deprives them of the real. But the relationship between imaginary and real enjoyment is not simply an either/or. As the cinema makes clear, real enjoyment can often emerge out of the image, and conversely, imaginary enjoyment remains enjoyable only to the extent that it has a basis in the real. The image of enjoyment is nothing but an image, and it alone cannot satisfy the cinematic spectator.

Cinematic plenitude makes possible the cinematic encounter with excess. If the trip to the cinema didn't remove spectators from the distractions of the everyday world and immerse them fully in an imaginary world, excess would have no opportunity to appear. Spectators are readied for the encounter with excess because, as in a dream, their firm symbolic identifications and allegiances are at a lessened state of alert. But by the same token, the enjoyment that cinematic plenitude provides for the spectator – the experience of submitting to the visual and aural image – depends for its part on the excess that the cinema produces. In the end, imaginary enjoyment is only imaginary, and in order for a film to captivate a spectator, it cannot rely simply on plenitude but must also call on excess. To modify Metz a bit, the task of the psychoanalytic film theorist involves identifying the real enjoyment, the enjoyment of excess, which lurks behind the image of enjoyment or the enjoyment of plenitude.

Cinematic plenitude emerges not as a natural outgrowth of the cinematic apparatus or the viewing situation but as an attempt to contain or derail the possible encounter with excess that the cinema provides. This encounter does not just manifest itself with trains coming toward the screen as in the famous Lumière Brothers' actuality but primarily in the enjoyment of those moments when the screen makes evident the spectators' involvement in what they see. The distance between the screen and the spectator does not inhibit the proximity that film can create, a proximity that does not exist elsewhere (as on the stage, for instance). Enjoyment arrives when film erases the distance between screen and spectator, and through this erasure, deprives spectators of the security inherent in their symbolic identity. Here, cinema exceeds the limitations of the screen and produces an enjoyment in the real.

Historically, psychoanalytic film theory has viewed the spectator's enjoyment at the cinema as a problem. Enjoyment comes at the expense of thinking, and thought about the spectator's political situation is requisite, or so the theory went. Laura Mulvey (1985) gave this idea its most concise formulation in her description of the political intention underlying her famous article "Visual Pleasure and Narrative Cinema." Toward the beginning of the essay, she notes,

> It is said that analysing pleasure, or beauty, destroys it. That is the intention of this article. The satisfaction and reinforcement of the ego that represent the high point of film history hitherto must be attacked. Not in favour of a reconstructed new pleasure, which cannot exist in the abstract, nor of intellectualised unpleasure, but to make way for a total negation of the ease and plenitude of the fictional narrative film.
>
> (1985, 306)

Here, Mulvey sees plenitude as identical to the "fictional narrative film," when in fact plenitude makes its appearance as a defense against the encounter with excess that the spectator of the narrative film risks. To go to the cinema necessitates an experience of its plenitude, but understanding our enjoyment of the cinema requires seeing this plenitude as a secondary response to an originary excess.

Understanding our enjoyment involves rereading our response to the cinema. One must see how the imaginary enjoyment that closes the film depends on moments of real excess. The detour of imaginary enjoyment has the effect of blinding spectators to the role that these moments play in the enjoyment of the film, and one must make clear this interdependence. This appears in its simplest version in the formulaic romantic comedy. In the typical film from this genre, we see two people at odds with each other who gradually overcome their opposition in order to form a complementary whole in a romantic union. Perhaps the pioneer of this genre is Frank Capra's *It Happened One Night* (1934). As Linda Mizejewski points out in her book on the film, "*It Happened One Night* has many literary and cinematic precedents, but it's usually considered the foundation of the romantic comedy film genre produced and refined in its classic period, the 1930s and early 1940s" (2010, 17). What gives Capra's film its foundational status is the complete opposition that it sustains throughout most of the film between the romantic leads, Peter Warne (Clark Gable) and Ellie Andrews (Claudette Colbert), which their final union overcomes.

Warne belongs to the working class, embodies its values, and displays a strong masculinity, while Andrews is a member of the nobility, displays a sense of high fashion, and constantly performs her femininity. Even this extreme opposition must give way to the power of the concluding romance, a romance whose ideological power derives from the sense of complementarity that it ultimately provides to the seemingly intractable oppositions that animate the film.

Though spectators associate – and even experience – enjoyment with the concluding romantic union, this enjoyment is only imaginary. They enjoy the image of wholeness that the couple provides, but this enjoyment can only be imagined. If it were to come into being, its failure would become evident, which is why *It Happened One Night* (and other films of the genre) must end with the coupling and not with what follows. The real enjoyment of the film lies not in its concluding image but in the real antagonism that occupies most of the film's running time.

Lacan famously rejects the possibility of the sexual relationship, which means that the romantic union cannot successfully transform sexual opposition into complementarity. As Joan Copjec points out, Lacan theorizes both a male and a female form of the failure of complementarity. Copjec claims that whereas an exception (the primal father) constitutes male identity as clearly defined, female identity has no corresponding ideal and thus no clear definition. In contrast to male subjects, the status of female subjects is undecidable, and as a result, the two sides do not come together to form a complementary whole. In *Read My Desire*, she says, "Rather than defining a universe of men that is complemented by a universe of women, Lacan defines man as the prohibition against constructing a universe and woman as the impossibility of doing so" (1994, 235).[3] The key idea behind Lacan's conception of sexual difference, according to Copjec, is that each sex embodies a different form of the failed sexual relation. The impossibility of reciprocity stems from the fact that sexual difference entails two different structures that conceive the same terrain in radically disparate ways. As Lacan conceives it in Seminar XX, enjoyment does not consist in overcoming this opposition – one simply cannot do so, except through an imaginary short-circuit – but through the non-relation itself. The subject enjoys its failure to relate to the Other, its specific mode of non-relation.

The spectator's real enjoyment of a film like *It Happened One Night* occurs not during the final resolution but in the series of failures of Warne and Andrews to relate to each other. One enjoys Warne's exposure of the pretensions of Andrews, and, alternately, the insults that Andrews hurls at Warne. When one experiences the film, one tends to interpret these failures as the prelude to their overcoming: the partiality of real enjoyment paves the way for the wholeness of the imaginary enjoyment that arrives with the concluding romantic union. The conventions of the genre are so well established that there is little room for narrative surprise, and spectators know almost exactly the form that the concluding image of enjoyment will take, which is what enables them to anticipate it while experiencing the various failures of the sexual relation throughout the film. That is to say, we typically read the film retrospectively, from a perspective that takes the imaginary enjoyment of the ending as an unsurpassable culmination.

But a proper understanding of the relationship between imaginary and real enjoyment enables us to reverse this method of reading and to see the dependence of imaginary enjoyment in the cinema on an enjoyment of the real. Though it seems as if the enjoyment of the failed sexual relation depends on the image of its ultimate success, the reverse is actually the case. One enjoys *It Happened One Night* in the real, and the concluding imaginary enjoyment serves only to make this real enjoyment palatable for the spectator. The various modes of failure that the sexual relation takes on during the film allow the spectator to enjoy in the real, to submit to an enjoyment that transcends their own self-experience.

The only possible access to enjoyment consists in the failures and conflicts that the imaginary enjoyment of the romantic union attempts to obscure. The enjoyment of the romantic union does not stem from the overcoming of the conflicts that precede it but subsists as their residue. The only enjoyment that the subject has involves opposition and conflict – or what we see prior to the conclusion of *It Happened One Night*. As Colette Soler points out, "Since an infinite jouissance has been excluded, the speaking being is condemned to conflicts of jouissance. There are no other conflicts. Everyone thus spends his time sacrificing one thing to another: the family to ambition, love to one's profession, happiness to knowledge, the child to the beloved man, the poor woman to the rich woman" (2006, 82). The conflicts of *jouissance* or enjoyment appear to be transcended in the typical filmic romantic union, but the transcendence of these conflicts implies the death of enjoyment rather that its ultimate fulfillment.[4] This is why the enjoyment that the spectator experiences at the end of the film is actually the culmination of the enjoyment produced throughout. In order to enjoy in the real, the spectator must encounter failure and opposition, and this failure underlies the imaginary success of every concluding romantic union. One enjoys success because of failure rather than enjoying failure because of the promise of an ultimate success.

Imaginary enjoyment depends on the image of plenitude. It appears is the self-sufficiency of the ideal ego, the apparently omnipotent figure of authority, or the complementarity of the romantic couple. In each case, there is no gap within the image, and the wholeness provides subjects with an image of enjoyment. Enjoyment here depends on overcoming loss and reconstituting a wholeness. The problem is that wholeness can only provide the image of enjoyment, not real enjoyment. The satisfaction of wholeness is always illusory: once the subject attains it, one immediately looks for what one has missed. Wholeness, in other words, sparks the desire for what wholeness lacks, even though it lacks nothing.

The distinction between imaginary and real enjoyment stems from the ability to see this nothing that wholeness lacks as something. The image of wholeness cannot include the nothing that it lacks, and this nothing is the cause of the subject's desire. It is nothing that has the effect of something. Real enjoyment centers on this nothing that wholeness cannot include. The subject accesses the nothing not by realizing its desire for an object but by breaking up the image of wholeness with an object that embodies nothing. Through this creative act, the subject enjoys the nothing that it produces.

In his Seminar XXIII, Lacan associates the enjoyment of the real with masochism. He notes, "it is clear that enjoyment of the real involves masochism, which Freud perceived. Masochism is the main enjoyment that the real gives" (2005, 78). The enjoyment of the masochist is not simply another in a catalogue of perversions. Lacan sees it as central to enjoyment as such, enjoyment of the real. This is because masochism uses the act of self-wounding to shatter the imaginary wholeness of the body (and imaginary enjoyment) in order to create an object that embodies nothing. This object of nothingness is the only source of enjoyment. We can only enjoy nothing. It captures the singularity of the subject without reducing this singularity to a signifier or to an image. Through the masochistic act, the subject lacks the object, but the object also adheres to the subject as an excess that the subject cannot evade.

This masochism is the key to the enjoyment that occurs in cinematic spectatorship. Spectators enjoy the cinema because it repeats the shattering of the subject's imaginary wholeness at the moments when the distance between screen and spectator breaks down. This connection to masochism is formal, but the depiction of the masochistic act in the content of a film makes the formal connection evident. When spectators see characters wound themselves, the self-wounding of every trip to the cinema comes to the fore.

Two modes of self-destruction

Two Oscar-nominated films from 2010, *Black Swan* (Darren Aronofsky) and *127 Hours* (Danny Boyle), both seem to privilege an enjoyment of the real. A masochistic act occurs near the conclusion of each film, and each one organizes the narrative structure around this act. Despite the similarity of the two films, a juxtaposition of them actually reveals the difference between the possibility for real enjoyment in the cinema and the standard form of imaginary enjoyment that most films offer. *Black Swan* provides an enjoyment in the real, while *127 Hours* proffers a fantasy of imaginary wholeness, a fantasy consistent with Hollywood cinema since its earliest moments.

127 Hours begins with a series of images of enjoyment. In the very first shot of the credit sequence, a crowd wildly cheers in an image that occupies the left third of the screen. The middle third of the screen is quickly filled with another, closer, shot of a different crowd clapping, while the right third then displays a credit line denoting the production companies responsible for the film. These opening images are followed by others depicting different forms of enjoyment – religious rituals, sporting events, the floor of the stock market, and a populated sunny beach. Then, the film shows similar images in the split screen of people beginning to run a race, and the split in the image seems to disappear amid the running masses. The image of enjoyment here appears to heal the split in the image and to create a whole out of the three separate sections of the screen. The visual image of enjoyment in the beginning of the film has an audio supplement. When the images of the runners seem to come together, the voice on the soundtrack chants, "There must be some fucking chemical, chemical in your brain, makes us different from animals, makes us all the same." Though enjoyment is not a chemical, it is, as the soundtrack suggests here, what differentiates the subject from the animal and what all subjects share (even if they all enjoy in their particular fashion).

After returning to the split screen, the film introduces the protagonist, Aron Ralston (James Franco). At first, we see Aron coming into his apartment and preparing for his journey, juxtaposed with people on the other thirds of the screen heading to work. Here, the film contrasts Aron's focus on enjoyment (which it associates with the cheering crowds and the runners) with the ordinary person's commitment to work. Even the way that Danny Boyle shoots Aron's preparation suggests that he is already enjoying, even before he arrives at the site of the hike. But this enjoyment is imaginary, stemming from a wholeness that those around him lack. Initially, Aron occupies just a third of the screen as he enters his apartment, and then a cut extends his image to include another third. Finally, Boyle eliminates the working people altogether and gives the whole image over to Aron preparing for his adventure. The composition of this sequence suggests the wholeness of Aron and his enjoyment, an enjoyment that is able to overcome the divisions of the screen itself for the spectator.

While Aron assembles his supplies for the trip in a series of fast moving shots, we hear a telephone call from his sister in which she urges him to call his worrying mother. Despite hearing this message, Aron evinces no concern for the caller or for his mother. He exists as a self-sufficient whole. After he leaves his apartment, Boyle cuts to him traveling to the desert and again resorts to the split screen. This time, he juxtaposes shots of Aron driving in isolation with the numerous cars on the Los Angeles highways. This makes clear that Aron stands out in his isolation, but the film does suggest the falsity of this wholeness when Boyle uses a third of the screen for a close-up of the dripping water faucet in Aron's home where he filled his water bottle. This shot foreshadows the lack of water that will imperil Aron when he becomes trapped and underlines the absence that haunts his imaginary completeness.

The vision of Aron as a figure of complete enjoyment continues during his trip to the desert. The rapid series of shots of him biking in the desert connote an enjoyment untrammeled by the restrictions of the social order. Here in the desert, Aron is free to enjoy fully. Even when he encounters others, they simply partake in his enjoyment rather than constraining it. While hiking in the desert, he meets Kristi (Kate Mara) and Megan (Amber Tamblyn). Though one might expect some sexual tension between the two women and Aron, there is none. He simply introduces them to a hidden form of enjoyment known to him and – one might assume – a few initiates. They climb through a narrow crevice in a mountain, and then Aron lets himself drop down into a beautiful pool of water. The women then do the same, and they all repeat the activity. The film presents this as a pure enjoyment of the body interacting with the beauty of the natural world, but it also presents it as an asexual enjoyment. The scene concludes with Aron and the women parting and without sexual reaction on Aron's part. Despite his attractiveness, he enjoys his wholeness at this moment in the film, and this makes him incapable of desiring the women.

In the midst of Boyle's depiction of Aron's enjoyment that follows his departure from the women, he falls into a crevice and a large rock pins his arm against the crevice wall. The rock traps Aron in the middle of the desert with little food or water and no one to hear his cries for help. He remains trapped for days as his water supply dwindles and his death becomes imminent. Because he has only a cheap knife, Aron has been unable to free himself by slicing through his arm and cutting his hand off. But finally he arrives at the idea of breaking his arm in order to circumvent the problem of cutting through bone with a dull knife. Boyle renders this act graphically, and it is the moment in the film where Aron's imaginary wholeness completely falls apart.

The sequence begins with scenes of Aron fantasizing about his childhood, but then Boyle shows a close-up of Aron's face as he strains to break his own arm. Boyle cuts from the pain registered on his face to a shot of his arm just as the snap of the bone becomes audible. After a close-up of his expression of pain, the film cuts to a scream of enjoyment, the enjoyment that stems from his ability to break free from the constraints of his own body. Boyle depicts Aron cutting off his arm in a series of close-ups illustrating expressions of pain on his face and the gruesomeness of the act itself. But this act is one moment when Aron is able to overcome his sense of imaginary wholeness, and it is always the moment around which all the spectator's enjoyment of the film centers. When he finally frees himself, the film's loud soundtrack stops abruptly and the remainder of his arm – as a partial object – becomes visible in a long shot. The suffering that Aron endures is at once freedom from an inexorable constraint – and this is precisely the status that real enjoyment has.

The conclusion of *127 Hours* depicts Aron's new life without his right hand, but at the same time, it shows him restored to the imaginary wholeness that the beginning of the film associated with him. The final montage sequence shows Aron returning to the bodily activities that provide him enjoyment – swimming, hiking, and so on – in order to show that the loss of his hand has not destroyed his capacity to enjoy. His relationship to enjoyment has changed, though not in the way that we might expect. Rather than sustaining the enjoyment in the real that occurs at the moment of self-mutilation, his finds someone to provide the imaginary wholeness that he had on his own at the beginning of the film.

127 Hours ends with a shot of the actual Aron Ralston, his wife, and their newborn child. It then cuts back to James Franco playing Aron in a reverse shot looking at the family as they constitute an imaginary whole. After a cut back to the family, a final shot of Aron hiking in the snow concludes the film, and it includes the title, "He always leaves a note to say where he has gone." This conclusion shows that Aron has exchanged one form of the imaginary enjoyment – that of the isolated ego – for another more common form – that of the complementary couple. The film locates the spectator's enjoyment in the final image of complementarity, but what stands out is the moment when Aron breaks from the wholeness of the imaginary. Aron cuts off his hand in order to survive, and survival here creates an alibi that covers the enjoyment that the act provides. For the first time in the film, Aron's act of self-destruction transforms him into a subject capable of real enjoyment, which is why this is the pivotal scene in the film, the one to which spectators gravitate.

The self-mutilation of Nina Sayers (Natalie Portman) in *Black Swan* has nothing to do with survival. Like the narrator (Edward Norton) in *Fight Club* (David Fincher, 1999), this mutilation is sublime and frees her from the body and concerns about its survival. At the end of the film when the wounding reaches its zenith as she stabs herself in the midsection before the finale of *Swan Lake,* it is unclear if her body survives at all. Self-destruction in this film serves the cause of enjoyment rather than survival, and Aronofsky, in contrast to Boyle, does not conclude with an image of wholeness.

Throughout the film, Aronofsky ties Sayers' self-destruction to the enjoyment of her art. At the beginning of *Black Swan,* Sayers does not display the requisite passion for the starring role in the new production of the ballet *Swan Lake.* But as we witness her descent into an apparently psychotic self-destruction – replete with delusions and paranoid speculation – we see her at the same time become a passionate dancer. As Aronofsky depicts it, the more that she destroys herself, the better the dances. Our enjoyment of Sayers and the ballet itself depends on her self-destruction.

Sayers' self-mutilation only becomes apparent at the conclusion of the performance. When she dances with her partner and he lifts her, the wound is apparent for a brief moment. Then, just before her character jumps to her death, Sayers runs up the ramp on the stage. In the long shot of this act, a spot of red becomes visible on her midsection. As she turns to face the audience, a close-up on this spot shows the blood expanding and the evidence of her self-wounding becoming clearer. The camera pulls back quickly from the wound itself to a full image of Sayers dancing the final number. This camera movement connects her self-destruction to the performance and shows that they are inextricable from each other.

Just before she jumps to her death in character, Aronofsky shows her looking at her mother in a shot/reverse sequence. Whereas shot/reverse shot has traditionally connoted an imaginary wholeness in the cinema, here the film uses it to make clear how Sayers' self-wounding – which is also the self-wounding of the spectator – breaks this imaginary bond. She is no longer within the complementary relation with her mother because she has destroyed the imaginary wholeness of her own body. A slow-motion shot depicts her diving onto the mattress on the side of the stage, and the film shows the company running to congratulate her. They notice the bloody wound, but Sayers insists on her own enjoyment, which the self-destruction makes possible. Aronofsky concludes the film with a close-up of her face as she whispers, "It was perfect," and then the film fades to white with the cheers of the crowd in the background. Enjoyment here derives from the intrusion of the real cut into the image of wholeness. Unlike the conclusion of *127 Hours*, *Black Swan* ends with the correlation of real enjoyment and the necessity of the spectator's embrace of self-destruction in order to access that enjoyment.

When contrasting the difference between imaginary and real enjoyment, it is not so much a matter of rejecting certain films and celebrating others. It is more the construction of a different way of relating to the cinema, a way that contrasts with that of the first psychoanalytic film theorists. For them, the imaginary danger of the cinema had to be fought with symbolic efforts, attempts to register the symbolic structure of the cinematic situation and the filmic endeavor. But the distinction between the imaginary and the symbolic is, in an important sense, not a distinction at all. As Lacan says as early as his first seminar, the imaginary relation always occurs within a symbolic context. He claims straightforwardly, "The symbolic will shape all those inflections which, in the life of the adult, the imaginary commitment ... can take on" (1988, 219). The fundamental distinction occurs between the symbolic/imaginary and the real. The enjoyment that occurs with the former always depends on that that occurs with the latter. The key to cinema spectatorship is identifying the source of our enjoyment. We enjoy the moments at which the cinema takes a bite out of us, not those where we find the image of an illusory wholeness.

Notes

1 See Lacan (1988) and Leupin (2004) for an explanation of Lacan's tripartite division of experience into symbolic, imaginary, and real.

2 The early psychoanalytic theorists of the cinema tended to stress identification much more than fantasy. As a result, they largely overlooked the possibility of the encounter with the real in the cinema. Whereas identification highlights the role of the imaginary order, fantasy brings the symbolic, the imaginary, and the real all into play.

3 When Copjec defines man through prohibition and woman through impossibility, she implicitly conceives male subjectivity as a retreat from female subjectivity, which is necessarily prior. The impossibility of the symbolic order comes first, and we construct prohibitions in order to conceal this impossibility. In the same way, male subjectivity and its ideal provide respite from the undecidability of female subjectivity.

4 For a thorough discussion of *jouissance* in Lacan's thought, see Fink (1995).

References

127 Hours. 2010. Directed by Danny Boyle. Los Angeles: 20th Century Fox, 2011. DVD.

Black Swan. 2010. Directed by Darren Aronofsky. Los Angeles: 20th Century Fox, 2011. DVD.

Copjec, Joan. 1994. *Read My Desire: Lacan Against the Historicists*. Cambridge, MA: MIT Press.

Fight Club. 1999. Directed by David Fincher. Los Angeles: 20th Century Fox, 2000. DVD.

Fink, Bruce. 1995. *The Lacanian Subject: Between Language and Jouissance*. Princeton: Princeton University Press.

It Happened One Night. 1934. Directed by Frank Capra. Los Angeles: Columbia, 1999.

Lacan, Jacques. 1961–62. "Le Séminaire IX: L'Identification, 1961–1962." Unpublished manuscript.

Lacan, Jacques. 1988. *The Seminar*, Book I: *Freud's Papers on Technique, 1953–1954*, ed. Jacques-Alain Miller, trans. John Forrester. New York: Norton.

Lacan, Jacques. 2005. *Le Séminaire*, Livre XXIII: *Le sinthome, 1975–1976*, ed. Jacques-Alain Miller. Paris: Seuil.

Leupin, Alexandre. 2004. *Lacan Today: Psychoanalysis, Science, Religion*. New York: The Other Press.

Metz, Christian. 1982. *The Imaginary Signifier: Psychoanalysis and Cinema*, trans. Celia Britton, Annwyl Williams, Ben Brewster, and Alfred Guzzetti. Bloomington: Indiana University Press.

Miller, Jacques-Alain. 2000. "Paradigms of *Jouissance*." *Lacanian Ink*, 17: 8–47.

Mizejewski, Linda. 2010. *It Happened One Night*. Oxford: Wiley-Blackwell.

Mulvey, Laura. 1985. "Visual Pleasure and Narrative Cinema." In *Movies and Methods*, ed. Bill Nichols, vol. 2, 303–15. Berkeley: University of California Press.

Soler, Colette. 2006. *What Lacan Said about Women: A Psychoanalytic Study*, trans. John Holland. New York: The Other Press.

Chapter 16

"One of the Most Obscure Regions of Psychoanalysis": Defamiliarizing Psychic Economy

Anna Kornbluh

Summoned to testify before the U.S. Congress about the causes of the current financial crisis, Federal Reserve Chairman Bernanke pled lack of expertise: "Senator," he said with a smile, "You ask me my opinion as an Economist, but unfortunately this is a matter for psychology" (quoted in Reddy 2008). Bernanke's displacement of the roots of the crisis from unstable financial instruments to unstable "animal spirits" reminds us that psychology offers not only a set of tropes for economic phenomena (mania, panic, depression), but also a matrix of causality within which the vertiginous vacuity of fictitious capital, collateralized debt obligations, credit default swaps, and naked short sales can be arrested by the solid rock of the psyche. Encompassing both right-wing market fundamentalists (irrational exuberance drives the economy) and liberal skeptics (greed makes the world go round), this prevailing displacement from fictitious capital to fickle subjects – let us call it "psychologism" – can be traced back at least to the nineteenth-century co-emergence of finance capital and the discipline of psychology.[1] Within this paradigm, the notion of "psychic economy" is no rhetorical flourish, but rather a literalistic instantiation of the causal continuity between desire and money, the mind and the market.

A Concise Companion to Psychoanalysis, Literature, and Culture, First Edition.
Edited by Laura Marcus and Ankhi Mukherjee.

Within more critical discourses, ranging from sociology to literature, "psychic economy" is first among proper names for substantifying the workings of desire, sexuality, the psyche, and even the conscious mind, finally designating the foundational structure of psychosocial life, and putatively authorizing theoretical insights into a specific mode of economy, namely, capitalism. But even in psychoanalytic circles, there remains surprisingly little theory of what this thing is, despite the fact that Sigmund Freud used the term, evidently certifying its conceptual rigor. As a prolegomena for such a theory, this essay returns to Freud's formulations, finding no consecrated concept of psychic economy.

When the Freudian event ignited psychoanalysis as something else than psychology, psychologism too was transcended, with the consequence that psychic economy in Freud's discourse bears little resemblance to what came before or what has come after. At face value, Freud's economic metapsychology departs from the Victorian-Bernankean rubric by virtue of Freud's total restraint from floating claims about capitalist economy as the fulfillment of human nature. More strikingly, a radical distinction emerges from Freud's unwavering emphasis on the figurative tenor of his economic thought. Against the *longue durée* of ideological literalizations, Freud's economic thought makes explicit that "economy" is merely a figure for the psyche – in principle, one potential figure among others. The following pages trace the vicissitudes of that figure. For Freud's closest reader, Jacques Lacan, Freud's thought inheres in his twists and turns, reformulations and new topographies, and thus "the poetics of Freud's work" open "the first entryway into its meaning" (Lacan 2007, 261).[2] In the wending and winding inspirations and revolutions of Freud's economic language rest what Abraham and Torok refer to as "uncommonly strange semantic phenomena": Freud's self-consciously experimental thinking "designifies" "psychic economy," estranging all easy referents of "psyche" and of "economy."[3] In so doing, Freud's evocations of "psychic economy" performatively disclose the essentially open, antagonistic, and dynamic nature of any given economy. It is this idea, I propose – and not Freud's alleged naturalization of "investor psychology" – which constitutes the seminal psychoanalytic contribution to the critique of political economy. By emphasizing the openness of economy and the contingent constitutions of economic life, psychoanalysis elaborates the *political* dimension of political economy, the impossibility that any particular mode of economy is immanent to the psyche.

The economic base

Some idea of "economy" absolutely anchors Freud's wide-ranging thought: it provides conceptual architecture for his first attempts to outline psychoanalysis, it buttresses major revisions to the principles of psychoanalysis, and, most fundamentally, it furnishes the cornerstone of his project. Freud built it up, grading "the economic" essential to his "metapsychology." Along with the "topographic," which maps regions of the psyche (conscious, unconscious, preconscious, and later, id, ego, superego), and the "dynamic," which models repression (regulating the expression of psychic ideas in and across the different topographic regions), the "economic" is the third of Freud's metapsychological hypotheses, metaphorizing the "distribution" of psychic resources. Among these three, the economic serves almost as a *meta*-metapsychology, for it conditions the other two: psychic topography and psychic dynamism are both based upon the central structuring function of psychic equilibrium. This infrastructural function manifests in the determinate priority for the economic – we might even say, in Freud's "economic determinism" – from the first to the last instance: the inaugural *Project for a Scientific Psychology* (1895) all the way through to the ultimate *Civilization and Its Discontents* (1934) equally stipulate fixity of psychic resources and systematic psychic organization. Despite the undeniable centrality of the economic hypothesis to Freudian psychoanalysis, it remains rather challenging to determine what "economy" signified for Freud. Scholarly accounts have regularly historicized one or another vector of economic hypothesis – Freud's enrollment in physics courses, his enmeshment in bourgeois Vienna – while generally failing to take stock of the shape of his economic rhetoric as a whole (see Bennett 2011; Birken 1988; Breithaupt 2005).

From the very beginning, in 1895, when a young Freud set out to devise a radical alternative to psychology, he esteemed "the economic" precisely as rhetoric. He wrote in a letter to Fliess: "I am tormented [*mich quälen*] … to discover what form the theory of psychical functioning will take if a kind of economics [*eine Art Oekonomik*] … is introduced into it" (Freud 1986, 130). As generative as this importing of economics might be for the nascent theory, for the incipient theorist the import seems both cause and effect of disquiet, "torment." Qua cause, this torment registers the constitutive irony that all science, whether physics, chemistry, biology, or psychology, must employ what Freud called "figurative language" (*Bildersprache*) for "we could not otherwise describe the processes in question at all, and indeed we could not have become aware of them" (1953–74, 18:60). "It is only from analogies," Freud asserts, "that we shall find the courage to set up the hypotheses necessary for throwing a more penetrating light upon" psychic life (1953–74, 15:65). In psychoanalysis as in science, figurative language is indispensable and perhaps even desirable: since the unconscious speaks in figures, theorizing the unconscious best proceeds through figures.

Out of its primal demand to name the unnamable, psychoanalysis appropriates "a kind of economics" (see Freud 1953–74, 1:282 and 14:151; Freud 1940–52, 11:389). But under the urgency of that demand, torment persists, unsettling almost every reference to the economic. Torment betrays the insufficiency of the economic, the way the qualifying "kind of" surveys the insurmountable chasm between what is wished for and what is attained. Freud held open this gap, warning that the economy image only amounted to "a rather vague expression," and constantly marking the image with self-reflexive confessions, qualifications, adverbial circumlocutions (like "so to speak" [*sozusagen*], "so called" [*sogenannte*]), and scare quotes.[4] Freud couples his economic expressions with consistent and considered indication of the speech acts that generate them. All this conscientious circumspection dissolves the coherence of "psychic economy" consecrated by Victorian psychologists and political economists, and puts to shame the casual evocations that abound in contemporary discourse. We epigones have long since settled into a colloquial comfort with psychic economy, but we would do well to mark the vexation, conscientiousness, and complexity that attend Freud's formulations.

For our project to defamiliarize the metaphor of "psychic economy," the first thing to note is that this vexation and its attendant thought experiments destabilize the thingliness of psychic economy. Indeed, quite strikingly, the Freudian syntax features the noun "psychic economy" exceedingly rarely – perhaps five times in the entire oeuvre.[5] James Strachey's translations have considerably muddied matters, for he rather insistently inserts the English noun "economy" in numerous instances in which Freud stakes other holdings. To take just two examples, in *Dora: An Analysis of a Case of Hysteria,* Freud uses "psychic household" (*psychischen Haushalt* [Freud 1940–52, 5:203]) but Strachey opts for "domestic economy of the mind" (Freud 1953–74, 7:42); in the essay "Libidinal Types" Freud writes "household of the soul" while Strachey overwrites "libidinal economy" (1953–74, 21:220).

In the context of Freud's relentless caution with economic language, Strachey's hasty consolidations seem problematically insensitive and misleading.

Notwithstanding the overarching importance of the economic hypothesis to the metapsychology, no nominative "psychic economy" predominates. What, then, is the referent of "economic"? Far more often than to a concept or thing, Freud's appeal to "the economic" refers to a "point of view" (*Gesichtspunkt*), a consideration (*Betrachtung*), a perspective, a prism.[6] The economic signals a way of seeing, a "figurative language" with which to describe and to know – but a figure born of a torment, a figure that holds at a distance what it also brings into focus. "The economic," Freud repeatedly cautions, "leads us to one of the most important, but unluckily one of the most obscure, regions of psychoanalysis" (Freud 1953–74, 16:355).[7] Ferried by metaphor into obscure realms, Freud even has a dream of finding himself on a train, moving confusedly between different cars, unable to determine whether he is the owner of a copy of Adam Smith's *The Wealth of Nations*. In *The Interpretation of Dreams*, that dream is strangely reported and left only partially interpreted, powerfully conveying the ongoing enigma of unaccountable crossings under the seminal sign of Political Economy.[8] As a point of view, as a figurative language, as a disoriented guide on shaky transport to obscure regions, "economy" obscures as much as it elucidates, dissimulates as much as it conceptualizes.

Where for the Victorian psychological tradition and the hegemonic paradigm it installs, "psychic economy" designates a natural object, "the economy" heralds desire as its cause, and capital serves as the unique and adequate signifier of desire, for Freud "economy" is inextricably bound up with obscurity and torment, with denatured objects and inadequate figures. If this means that psychoanalysis offers no immediate insights into economics, no sanctification of the Marginal Utility Revolution's desire theory of value, and no accounting for the intransigence of capitalism, this is so much the better for the psychoanalytic contribution to the critique of political economy. To get at that contribution, we must read Freud's economic images in the manner he himself demands they be read: figurally. Around the signifier "economy" circulate manifold modalities that cannot be reduced to "market" or "capitalism." As we shall see, at alternating junctures the language of economy evokes: the *nomos* of the *oikos*; the law of the arrangement of life; a closed equilibrium; fixed material resources; a "system of writing"; and the disequilibrium of drive. It is to this very complexity and evasiveness of the figure of economy that we must look for Freud's greatest economic insights. The diversified economic figures in the Freudian portfolio attest to the fundamental polyvalence of "economy," what Marxian thought hails as economy's essentially *political* character. Freud's various formulations perform the essential deferral of the grounding of economy: *there is no given economy*; no hypostatized – or literally capitalized – Economy.[9] The economic hypothesis leads to "one of the most obscure regions of psychoanalysis" because economy as such is obscure; any instantiated economy must be made, designed, planned.

Households of the soul

One connotation of economy stands out in Freud's thought – not for its simplicity or fundamentality, but for his unhesitating invocation of it:

> The motive of human society is in the last resort an economic one [*Das Motiv der menschlichen Gesellschaft ist im letzten Grund ein oekonomisches*]; since it does not posses enough provisions to keep its members alive unless they work, it must restrict the number of its members and divert their energies from sexual activity to work. It is faced, in short, by the eternal, primeval exigencies of life [*die ewige, urzeitlich … Lebensnot*], which are with us to this day.
>
> (Freud 1953–74, 16:311; for the German, see 1940–52, 11:322)

So many temporal adjectives underscore the immutability of the economic. In this instantiation, "economic" demarcates the insuperable base of existence, the cause of human sociality – as Freud remarked in a letter to Roman Rolland: "I myself have always advocated the love of mankind not out of sentimentality or idealism but for sober, economic reasons: because in the face of our instinctual drives and the world as it is I was compelled to consider this love as indispensable for the preservation of the human species as, say, technology" (Freud 1961, 374). Over the course of his career, Freud returns several times to this unqualified, untormented reference to "the economic," indexing this ineluctable materiality that must be encountered, managed, formed into any particular economy – a formation that is always the object of political antagonism.[10] In this way Freud recalls the Aristotelian conception of the *oikos* as the arena of eating and drinking, dwelling and laboring, whose every constitution under a *nomos* is contingent.[11]

It is this necessity–contingency polarity that galvanizes the enigmas of existence and enjoyment. "Economy" in this instance names the necessary fact that there is economy – a fact in excess of any predicates.

When Freud then repeatedly conjures a "psychic household" (*psychischen Haushalt*), his image entails not only a mental space in which "work" is carried out and the "stuff of life" (*Lebensmittel*) is managed, but also an analogously inexorable and contingent arrangement of the psychic: there is no immanent order of the mind.[12] This idea of arrangement buttressed by the household image is the fundamental framework of Freud's notion of the psyche, which is why "household" is his preferred noun. As Lacan observes:

> If the psyche has any meaning, if there is a reality which is called psychic reality, or, in other words, if living beings exist, it is in so far as there is an internal organization [*organisation interne*] which up to a certain point tends to oppose the free and unlimited passage of forces and discharges of energy, such as we may assume to exist, in a purely theoretical way, intercrossing in the inanimate reality.
>
> (Lacan 1991, 60)

If life must be made from available materials and happy accidents, then so must the psyche. Libido is "something that should be differentiated – an amount of affect, a sum of excitation – something having all the attributes of a quantity, although we possess no means of measuring it" (Freud 1953–74, 3:59). Because this material is the stuff of the psyche, because psychoanalysis is an account of the sexed materiality of everyday life, but because psychic matter is never present without a form or channel or container, one way of classifying diverse material manifestations is by a kind of economics: "production, increase or decrease, distribution and displacement," "investments" and "withdrawals" are the processes that constitute classes.[13] The initial clinical encounter with hysteria and obsession inspired this "quantitative conception," which was "derived directly" from the problems of "excess" that such pathologies evince: psychic energy manifesting as hysterical excess must have been displaced by repressive subtraction elsewhere in the topography of the subject.[14] If "a kind of economics" provides a conceptual architecture for the emergent libido theory, this provision is entirely analogical: it is, in the interest of accounting for the systematicity of an as yet unidentified system, a loan of the vocabulary and relationships of another system. In turn, by providing an interpretive procedure for economic dynamics in the psyche, psychoanalysis might offer itself as a model of a structural analysis of any particular given economy.[15]

One of the most common errors leading to the confusion of Freud's economic thought with a naturalization of capitalism is the translation of *Besetzung* as "investment." Strachey proposed "cathexis" but most regularly used "investment," a highly ideological translation that has played no small role in the reception of Freud as a universalizer of a particularly capitalist subjectivity.[16] To re-approach Freud's slippery term, we can start with the arrangement of resources drafted by the household image. The appeal of the verb *besetzen* is precisely its domestic ubiquity, its manifold quotidian denotations. It encompasses "to put," "to place," "to cast," "to occupy," and many other open-ended functions. Freud deliberately opted to root his idea in this polysemous verb, activating an unusual noun to substantialize an everyday, everywhere, ongoing process of organizing, putting something to use in a certain way.[17] That deliberate choice explains numerous facts of textual and translation history. He resisted Strachey's invention of "cathexis," and did not even use the word *Besetzung* anywhere in the paper from which Strachey took one of his main connotations, an "electric charge."[18] He declined to ever fix the definition of the term. He mobilized diverse, context-dependent expressions when making English translations of his own work, selecting verbs like "colored" or "toned" where Strachey uses "cathected" or "invested."[19] All of these factors comprise Freud's repeated affirmation of the intrinsically dynamic character of *Besetzung*. It was an economic tenet for him: material must be put to use, but how that use is valorized remains an open question. If there is an economy of the psyche, it is the arena not of any particular mode of production, but of vivacious, adaptive use. Both the homogenization of "cathexis" and its standard incautious translation into "investment" totally eclipse Freud's careful convictions about the complexity of psychic functions, egregiously inflating the capitalist economic parallels. Under the sway of these translations, it becomes very difficult to hew rigorously to the complexity of Freud's insights and the polysemy of his language. But close scrutiny of the corpus simply shows that "investment" occludes the complexity of processes at work; characterizing the Freudian subject as an "investor" and thus a typical bourgeois agent of finance dangerously reduces the complexity of Freud's ideas (Bennett 2010).

Substitutive representations

Alongside his interest in arrangement and relative intensity, Freud experimented with the "working hypothesis" of "quantity," a heuristic for experimentally apprehending this material and "intensity" (1953–74, 3:103). At times, Freud suggested that "quantitative" might be a preferable synonym for "economic" in his thought, and quantity jumps to the forefront in those discussions of the economic metapsychology which seek to explain Freud's economic language as a reflexive mirroring of his scientific education in the works of Fechner and Helmholtz.[20] Here, too, that explanatory gesture under-reads the dynamic and generative aspects of Freud's conscientiously figurative language. Freud adamantly maintained not only that "quantity" was a figure, but that it was an instrumental figure, a useful figure, to which he gave the unusual compound name *Hilfsvorstellung,* a "helping image" (like a "helping verb" [Freud 1953–74, 3:60]).[21] The insufficiency of this help never falls out of focus: Freud deems quantity a figure for something else, "something which possesses all the attributes of a quantity though we have no means of measuring it" (1953–74, 3:59). Terms like "increase" or "decrease," "yield" or "withdrawal" belong to this experimental framework, adding further dimensions even as they propagate its inexactitude. Hence Freud's caution that such quantifiers connote something "relative" rather than absolute.[22] A wary eye always appraises the approximate, insufficient timbre of these images, and Freud asserts repeatedly that quantity is merely a proxy for the qualitative determinations that remain utterly elusive.[23] He writes almost plaintively, in *The Economic Problem of Masochism,* for instance, of the unsuitability of quantity:

> Pleasure and unpleasure therefore cannot be referred to an increase or decrease of a quantity ... they depend, not on some quantitative factor, but on some characteristic of it which we can only describe as a qualitative one. If we were able to say what this qualitative characteristic is, we should be much further advanced in psychology. Perhaps it is the rhythm, the temporal sequence of changes, rises in falls in the quantity of stimulus. We do not know [*Wir wissen es nicht*].
>
> (Freud 1953–74, 19:159)

Quantity is a tool, a helping image of last resort, a figure in the service of grasping at what "we do not know." Later critics often cling to quantity as the basic meaning of Freud's economic thought, referring it to the thermodynamic and physical models Freud studied in his youth, and citing it as a foundational analogy attesting to a fundamental continuity. In the words of Deleuze and Guattari, "Just as Ricardo founds political or social economy by discovering quantitative labor as the principle of every representable value, Freud founds desiring-economy by discovering the quantitative libido as the principle of every representation of the objects and aims of desire" (2004, 329). But the nature of the thought-experiment was that helping images could be used, tested, and rejected, and so Freud took creative license with physics allusions, and then discarded conservation models as early as 1905.[24] "We have long since abandoned the most obvious and simplest view of this economy," he wrote in reference to the conservation image. Freud's insistence on the dynamism symbolized and performed by his economic language allows for this conceptual flux and agility.

To the extent that "quantity" augurs finite intensities, what it helps to image is not scarcity but the lump sum: the psyche insists on its own complete integrity. Its will to make itself known compels it, where complete expression is internally or externally prohibited or prohibitive, to seek out substitute expressions. Dreams, parapraxes, fantasies, and symptoms all come to be thought as "substitutive representations" (Freud 1953–74, 19:150).[25] The psyche possesses a materiality that insists on itself, but cannot directly present itself – it must be reckoned with through representation.[26] Significantly, Freud conceived this representation as a "system of writing" which he opposed to a "language," elevating the pictorial, graphic, and material dimensions of representation above its referential or signifying function.[27] And just as the psyche commissions successive figurative expressions to make itself know, psychoanalysis crafts figurative language to make itself known – a figurative language that, Freud's tireless reservations about metapsychology remind us, is always in flux.[28] Thus, in 1925, Freud expands "the economic factor" to exceed "quantity" and incorporate this agency of insistent substitutive figuration – and he retroacts this expansion all the way back to *Studies on Hysteria*.[29]

Indeed, Freud had already obliquely formulated "economy" as a forum of "substitutive representations" with his analogy between obsession and currency in "Notes on a Case of Obsessional Neurosis" (1909). I want to linger over this case of the Rat Man, one whose insights Freud suffers more than narrativizes, and which we have yet to assimilate. Surprisingly, the Rat Man is not addressed by major critical works on Freud's economic thought such as Goux's *Symbolic*

Economies (1990) or Lyotard's *Libidinal Economy* (1993). In *The Post Card*, Derrida alludes to this unaddressable quality of the Rat Man, registering in his initial section of postal messages (which he recommends be read "as the preface to a book that I have not written") the density and dream-like quality I am referring to: "Yes, I was speaking to you of the Rat Man. Nothing about it has been understood yet, or so I feel ... the passage is essential, constitutive, irreducible. Not a step of Freud's which does not come back to it" (1987, 68, 3). For all this essential importance, then, the case of the Rat Man remains strangely underencountered. One of the great enigmas of Freud's archive, his singular act of retaining the Rat Man's original case notes (it was his habit to destroy raw material after working through it), attests to this unencountered status as an ur-feature of the problem (Freud 1953–74, 10:162). The Rat Man, let us recall, is a patient who experiences obsessional fantasies about rats – specifically, the enactment of a military torture regime. In his fantasies, his father and his fiancée are subjected to the torture, suffering anal penetration by rats. Analysis of the fantasies educes associations of rats with torture and authority, with vermin and filth, with offspring and penises, and, finally, with money, loans, debts, and compounds. Within the case study, this sheer proliferation ensnares analysand and analyst alike, for Freud not only hunts the rats in the Rat Man's own language, such as his upcoming marriage (*Heirat*), he also burrows around in a wealth of associations in his own analytic language. Fantastically playing with verbs, gerunds, adjectives, and nouns with "Rat" at their root, he calls the case a *Rätsel* (riddle) and deems the process by which "Rat" has acquired so many associations *hinzutraten* (accumulating). No wonder then that the Rat Man himself, remarking the homophone between *Ratten* (the plural "rats") and *Raten* (the plural "rates") and *raten* (the verb "to counsel"), arrives at a formula for the analytic exchange: "so many florins, so many rats" (Freud 1953–74, 10:212). The Rat Man comes to analysis *to work*, and for that privilege he pays, twice, in florins and in rats – and receives, in return, only more rats.[30] For his part, Freud notes that in this transaction the Rat Man purchases (*erwerben*) ever more associations for "Rat", and he concludes that through the logic of his neurosis the Rat Man "had coined a regular rat currency" ("eine förmliche Rattenwährung eingesetzt") (Freud 1953–74, 10:212; 1940–52, 7:433). Freud's ratting around in puns betokens the particular formation of economy at stake in this case: however much "Rat" symbolizes to the analysand, to the analyst "Rat" symbolizes above all else the sheer possibility of symbolization itself.[31]

Economy may be incarnated as a system for symbolic substitution, conjuring the abstraction "value" to ground exchange, coining currency to symbolize value, commissioning paper to substitute for precious metal. The psyche may be understood as a forum of substitutive mechanisms – as indeed Freud had already elaborated in his interpretation of dreams, symptoms, and parapraxes. With the Rat Man case and the currency metaphor, Freud analogizes these two modes of substitution. In this case, then, Freud introduces yet another connotation of "economy" into his overall discourse. At the same time, his thought here opens onto the possibility that psychoanalysis, as the theory of symbolic substitution, might apprehend structures of substitution beyond the subject. The repetition of formal structures in multiple aspects of human social life (in, say, the unconscious as well as in capitalism) becomes an object of inquiry for psychoanalysis, which vigilantly restrains itself from accounting for this repetition as a naturalization of capitalism. Quite to the contrary, in discovering the structures of exchange dispersed throughout human culture, psychoanalysis helps illuminate how capitalism needs not monopolize differential symbolization. Capitalism, everyone from nineteenth-century financial journalists to twentieth-century philosopher-critics might say, is inextricable from symbolization (see, paradigmatically, Goux 1990). In the Rat Man case and beyond, Freud authorizes a radical qualification of this argument: while capitalism presents itself as coeval with symbolization, symbolization has priority.

Freud's quick quipping currency analogy functions here much more as a symptom than an analysis, a rat chasing its own tail. Much like the torment that inspires psychoanalysis, the analogy between neurosis and currency in the Rat Man gnaws at Freud. That unsettling opacity powerfully manifests that something in this mode of economy qua perpetual symbolization proves recalcitrant to accounting – an incisive point about capital if ever there was one.[32] And it equally confirms that not all of Freud's economic thought can be assimilated to economy qua symbolic substitution, that not all of what Freud grasps under the sign "economy" is continuous with capital.

Capital analogies

We must tender the same observation apropos the most notorious moment of economic language, Freud's analogy between a wish and a capitalist. Seeking to explain the role of conscious experience (daytime thought) as dream fodder, Freud differentiates between the idea in a dream and what he italicizes as the *force of the drive* (*Triebkraft*) which makes the dream:[33]

> The position may be explained by an analogy. A daytime thought may very well play the part of *entrepreneur* for a dream; but the entrepreneur, who, as people say, has the idea and the initiative to carry it out, can do nothing without capital; he needs a *capitalist* who can afford the outlay, and the capitalist who provides the psychical outlay for the dream is invariably and indisputably, whatever may be the thoughts of the previous day, a *wish from the unconscious*.
>
> (Freud 1953–74, 3:560; emphasis original)

Let us tease out the actual logic of the analogy. A daytime thought has an idea it wants to express, a vision it wants to realize, but this thought is insufficient to make the dream ("the worry alone could not have made the dream"). A driving force is required – a driving force which the analogy first likens to "capital" itself, capital which stands un-italicized, until the register shifts after the semi-colon, opposing "capitalist" to that capital. The italic emphasis on the "capitalist" underscores the agency of this driving force: it is not just stuff or matter, not just energy or power, but a personification of that force. The wish from the unconscious is not itself the capital (nor even itself analogized to capital); it is rather like the capitalist, the one with the power to realize ideas, the agency that asserts itself into representability. This mapping of unconscious dream-making onto economic dream-making, as the most intimate connection in the Freudian oeuvre between the psyche and capitalism, signals nothing about desires for entrepreneurship or desires for accumulation. It signals only something about the pulsating force that seeks expression. Freud's analogy therefore recapitulates Marx's emphatic exploration of personification as central to the manifestation of the workings of capital, and Marx's complicated centralization of drive as the "inner nature" of capitalism. In so doing, his economic language in this particular instance invites analysis of psychic economy through the looking glass: not the desire for capital, but the desire of capital, not the innate capitalism of the psychological subject, but the psychic structure of the subject Capital.

The weirdness of these traversed formulations lends them the air of the unformulatable. They are something so novel that Freud must re-encounter them, even repress them, and submit them to working over. Alongside the enigma of retaining the Rat Man case notes rests another archival oddity that presents Freud's suffering of his own insights. Freud committed quite bizarre unadorned self-citation of this *Triebkraft*–capital(ist) analogy on two occasions, acknowledging a kind of compulsion to repeat:

> I have made one or two observations in my *Interpretation of Dreams* on the relation between the waking thoughts which are continued into sleep (the 'day's residues') and the unconscious wish which forms the dream. I will quote them here as they stand, for I have nothing to add to them [*die ich hier unverändert zitieren werde, denn ich habe ihnen nichts hinzuzufügen*].
>
> (Freud 1953–74, 7:86; 1940–52, 5:249)

> I have made use of an analogy for the relation of the day's residues to the unconscious wish, and I can only repeat it here [*den ich hier nur wiederholen kann*].
>
> (Freud 1953–74, 15:225; 1940–52, 11:231)

Crystallizing the vexation of the helping images of economy, the compulsive repetition of this analogy challenges as much as it confirms. Beneath the veneer of aptitude lies an obduracy that cannot be confronted. This is no confident, triumphant suture of psyche and capital, but a strange stutter. Something – it tries to say – *something* of a relation between capital and dreams exists. In the end, it is the compulsory repeating of the image that tells us more about the idea than the image itself: dreams, like capital, like repetition compulsions, are substitutive image engines.

Unlike that of his predecessors and wayward progeny, Freud's economic language did not work to ground economic phenomena in the psyche. Rather, by maintaining a strictly analogical relationship, and by proceeding from the clinic outward to the metapsychology, Freud tentatively worked to explain economic phenomena as structures. By refusing psychological causality and instead illuminating economic structurality, the metapsychology renders an analysis of economic modes. In this illumination of economy, Freud's economic hypothesis begins to sketch an alternative, critical psychic economy construct that ought be forcefully opposed to the reification of psychic economy qua naturalization of capital. It is to the thought of drive that we must look for this radical alternative.

(D)riven economies

Freud often reverentially limns the opacity and complexity of the drives, deeming them "mythical entities, splendid in their indefiniteness" (Freud 1953–74, 22:95). Essential but opaque, inevitable but variable, drives share the radical ontological openness of economy. The language of economy around drives captures this. Thus when Freud discovers the death drive, his first choice for how to frame the discovery is as an economic mystery. Indeed, the opening paragraphs of *Beyond the Pleasure Principle* reiterate that the economic metapsychology's emphasis on quantity and constancy is the closest Freud's thought can come to "the obscurest and least penetrable region of psychic life," the definition of pleasure (Freud 1953–74, 18:10). But as heuristically valuable as quantity and constancy have been up to this point, it has emerged from analytic experience that however much the subject has a goal of pleasure, "the tendency toward the goal does not imply the attainment of it, and in general the goal is only approximately attainable" (Gustav Fechner, cited in Freud 1953–74, 18:10). The book elaborates this approximation of goals, attributing for the first time a structure of "short circuit" and "circuitous routes to a direct and substitutive satisfaction" – that is, introducing the topos of circuit to the paradigm of substitution Freud deems "currency" (Freud 1953–74, 18:10, 37, 38). As *Beyond the Pleasure Principle* works to become a theory of circuits, of how "the organism wishes to die only in its own fashion," this concept of indirection enfolds the pleasure principle itself into a more overarching "death drive," and expands economy from a closed system to an internally riven, spastically driven anti-system (Freud 1953–74, 18:38). The economy of drive is disequilibriate because drive names the excess in the subject beyond its systematicity, beyond its self-interest, beyond its own life. Drive is the enigmatic impulsion out of stasis and into dynamism, but its enigma entails the ineluctable inertia back toward stasis, death, inorganicity. Capitalism endeavors to turn excess to account, whereas the ultimate motion of the drive is ontologically unaccountable.

The death drive, "a function whose business it is to free the mental apparatus entirely from excitation or to keep the amount of excitation in it constant or to keep it as low as possible" (Freud 1961, 76), mandates a return to an inorganic state. Here again we find cause for concern with Strachey's scientizing translation of *Trieb* as "instinct" rather than as "drive," for it has occluded an essential Freudian distinction. While instinct is directed outward, toward an external object that would satisfy it, drive is directed inward and remains objectless. In contrast to instinct, drive finds satisfaction through its very movement, the excessively repetitive circuit that yields still more excess. Without drive, there is no enjoying subject, but the enjoying subject is not the drive's product (strictly speaking, drive has no product) so much as the *residue* of its movement. As this indirect circuit, the death drive paradoxically denominates the momentum of life, even though this is not its goal. That effect reverberates in the narrative rhythm of *Beyond the Pleasure Principle*, whose argument progresses by staging three successive examples of failures of the principle (traumatic war neuroses, *fort-da* game, negative therapy), thereby performing the motion of circuitry: each incomplete idea gives way to another reiteration that is itself still incomplete. *Beyond the Pleasure Principle* thereby becomes a text whose recursive structure formalizes the topology of the "short circuit" that it identifies in psychic life. It opens with a discussion of the importance of the "economic" (set off by quotation marks also in the original). Freud's interest in stretching the signifier "economic" to encompass this discovery is evident in his commencing of the theory of circuits with a strangely recalibrating citation of Fechner: "the tendency toward the goal does not imply the attainment of it, and in general the goal is only approximately attainable" (Freud 1953–74, 18:10). Freud claimed a reassessment of the economic axis as the occasion for that text, whose avowedly "speculative" gestures introduce the topos of "short circuit," those "circuitous routes to substitutive satisfaction" that the psyche follows instead of simply attaining its goals directly (Freud 1953–74, 18:10, 37, 38). For our purposes, it is important to note that these insights inhere aesthetically, not just deictically. The theory of drive emerges more in the metaleptic structure of the text than in its enunciations – Freud does not rest with the articulation of the repetition compulsion; the disturbance compels him to ever more formulations, subverting every attempt to specify it completely. The inadequacies of the successive examples of the repetition compulsion stir Freud to theorize drive, but the very inability to formulate the theory completely is already implicated in the structure of the drive itself. The topos performed by the argument presents the economic as a system that maintains itself "after its own fashion," circuitously, indirectly, through paradoxically generative failures. This text formalizes the disequilibrium of economy, the suspension of successive figures, the inevitably circuitous achievement of ends. Every *oikos*, because of its necessary and contingent *nomos*, will pursue its ends "in its own fashion," "after its own way."

Discovering that repetition compulsion lends a circuitous topos to enjoyment and a "short circuit" topos to life, Freud also discovers that disequilibrium is a truer form of economy. *Beyond the Pleasure Principle*'s narration of "repetition compulsion" complements the earlier notion of an economic tendency toward constancy by another economic quality, that of continuous repetitive circuits. From a notion of an efficient, self-contained equilibrium, the economic hypothesis shifts to entail a suspensive oscillation between excitation and release, expansion and contraction, excess and efficiency, what Freud terms a "vacillating rhythm" (1961, 49). Freud's understanding that "the aim of all life is death" is leavened with the formulation that "the living organism struggles most energetically against events (dangers in fact) which might help it to attain its life's aim rapidly – by a kind of short circuit" (1961, 47). The figure "short circuit" opens the closed conception of economy qua equilibrate system, installing instead the conception of economy qua disequilibrate, paradoxically productive failure. Freud framed the discovery of drive as a revaluation of his economic point of view, and any utilitarian resonance of the purposeful pursuit of pleasure is dissipated by the form of "circuitous routes" the subject follows instead of attaining its goals directly.[34] Drive therefore animates another register of the economy figure: the suspensive oscillation between the pleasure principle and the movement beyond the pleasure principle. We might ask why economy is the name for this disequilibrium, and for that one would need to turn to that other theorist of drive, Karl Marx. But for now let us just take this additional valence of economy to conclude that no simple expository project operates through the figurative language of economy; no unitary concept is enshrined. Therein lies the force of psychoanalytic economic thought. The sheer density and polyvalence of Freud's economic figures – the household, the closed system, the network of substitutions, the disequilibrium of drive – discloses the radical openness of economy, and the antagonism that founds every contingent economic order.

Freud's economic thought advances figuratively: "economy" itself functions as a figure, a figure whose referent cannot be reliably determined, a figure that divulges just how much referential unreliability is crucial to economic relations. Psychologism occludes this antagonism and forecloses this contingency, forsaking structural analysis of financial leverage for obfuscating platitudes about insatiable desire, reifying "psychic economy" to forcibly naturalize the capitalist mode of economy. What is proper to Freud, by contrast, is the torment that incites psychoanalysis, the helping images with which it develops its revolutionary inquiry, the radical questioning by which psychoanalysis transcends psychology, and the condensation of all of these things in the economy that knows itself as figure.

Notes

1 Alexander Bain, Samuel Smiles, Herbert Spencer, George Henry Lewes, and William Stanley Jevons, fathers of psychology and modern economics both, authored their own economic hypotheses in which the language of

exchange, distribution, and money described the mental functioning which comprised the macroeconomic desire theory of value. "Psychic economy" for these thinkers secured the ground of the otherwise ungrounded economy during the tumultuous process of financialization. For exploration of this historical context, see Kornbluh (2013).

2 In his own close reading of Lacan, Fink (2004, 67) is a vigilant reminder of this insistence.

3 "Let us take any term introduced by Freud, whether he coined it or simply borrowed it from scientific or colloquial language. Unless one is deaf to its meaning, one is struck, as soon as it is related to the unconscious Kernel, by the vigor with which it literally rips itself away from the dictionary and from language. It is the allusion to the non-reflexive and the unnamed which, in fact, induces this uncommonly strange semantic phenomenon. The language of psychoanalysis no longer follows the twists and turns (tropoi) of customary speech and writing. Pleasure, Id, Ego, Economic, Dynamic, are not metaphors, metonymies, synechdoches, catachresis; they are, through the action of the discourse, products of de-signification and constitute new figures, absent from rhetorical treatises" (Abraham and Torok 1994, 85).

4 In one of the early usages, in his essay in French on the "Heredity and Aetiology of Neuroses," he refers to the image of "l'économie nerveuse" as a "rather vague expression" ("l'expression un peu vague") (1953–74, 3:150; 1940–52, 1:414). For "What we may call an economic" and just a few of the circumlocutionary gestures, see Freud 1953–74, 15:274, 355, 377, *passim*.

5 Freud 1953–74, 12:236, 18:391, 20:149, 232, 21:218. Posthumous essays published only in English tend to use the noun formulation an additional three or so times.

6 See Freud 1953–74, 18:228, 18:7, 23:226, 21:161, 16:374. For *Betrachtung*, see Freud 1953–74, 16:274.

7 See also the caution that "we now have a suspicion of an economy in the far more comprehensive sense of psychical expenditure in general; and we must regard it as possible that a closer understanding of what is still the very obscure concept of "psychical expenditure" (Freud 1953–74, 8:117).

Freud's disquietude about the metapsychology materializes in his archive, from which mysteriously disappear seven of the twelve papers on metapyschology from 1915.

The first use of "psychoanalysis" is in "L'Hérédité et l'étiologie des névroses," *Revue Neurologique*, March 30, 1896.

8 "I was suddenly in another compartment, in which the upholstery and seats were so narrow that one's back pressed directly against the back of the carriage. I was surprised by this, but I reflected that I might have changed carriages while in a sleeping state. There were several people, including an English brother and sister. A row of books was distinctly visible on a shelf

on the wall. I saw 'The Wealth of Nations' and 'Matter and Motion,' a thick volume and bound in brown cloth. The man asked his sister about a book by Schiller, whether she had forgotten it. It seemed as though the books were sometimes mine and sometimes theirs" (Freud 1953–74, 4:55).

9 On the historically specific hypostatization of "the" economy, see Appleby 1978.

10 See also "okonomie des Menschenlebens" (Freud 1953–74, 14:276; 1940–52, 10:325), and "satisfaction (of the instinctual dispositions) is the economic task of our lives" and "laws of economic necessity" (Freud 1953–74, 21:95, 103).

11 See Aristotle (1996). Perhaps not coincidentally, Freud's most direct commentary on economic systems, his discussion of Soviet communism in *Civilization and Its Discontents*, strongly makes this point about the ineluctability of antagonism in social relations (Freud 1953–74, 21:112). See also Arendt 1998.

12 He used the formulation "psychic household" or variations "household of the soul," or "libido household," regularly, in contrast to the rare use of "economy" as a noun that I have already noted (see, for example, Freud 1940–52, 5:203, 8:37, 14:500, 511, 512, 15:88, 105).

13 We thus reach the idea of a quantity of libido, to the mental representation of which we give the name ego-libido, and whose production, increase, or diminution, distribution, and displacement should afford us possibilities for explaining the psychosexual phenomena observed in Freud (1953–74, 7:217). See also the idea of libidinal increases, *Libidosteigerung*, where *steigerung* is the economic name for sales increase, or production increase (1953–74, 10:210; 1940–52, 7:436). On "the great reservoir" see Strachey's explanatory note, (Freud, 1953–74, 19:62).

14 As Freud writes in the *Entwurf*: The quantitative conception "derived directly from pathological clinical observation especially where excessively intense ideas were concerned – in hysteria and obsessions, in which, as we shall see, the quantitative characteristic emerges more plainly than in the normal." (1953–74, 1:294)

15 This would be a variation on Žižek's (1989) elemental point about the "homology" of procedure between Freud and Marx.

16 See for example Birken (1988), Bennett (2011), Zaretsky (2005). Notably, none of these authors cites Freud's German. For a rebuttal of such arguments, see Gay (1985, 78–115).

17 His first usages of it involve scare quotes (see Freud 1940–52, 1:215).

18 Strachey (1963) acknowledges his invention of the term in "Obituary for Joan Riviere." The electric charge image occurs in the 1894 "Neuropsychoses of Defense" (Freud 1953–74, 3:41–60). On the term in an Austrian context and its distortion by Strachey, see Ornston (1985, 392).

19 See for example: "eines mit Affekt besetzen seelischen," translated as "a mental process which is emotionally colored" or "eine Gruppe von

zusammengehörigen, mit Affekt besetzen Vorstellungselementen," translated as "a group of ideas which belong together and have a common emotive tone" (Erwin 2001, 72).

20 "The economic, or, if you prefer, the quantitative factor, which is intimately linked to the pleasure principle, dominates all its processes" (Freud, 1953–74, 22:73).

21 "Ich will endlich mit wenigen Worten der Hilfsvorstellung gedenken, deren ich mich in dieser Darstellung der Abwehrneurosen bedient habe" (Freud, 1940–52, 1:73).

22 "The outcome of such situations will entirely depend upon economic considerations – of the relative magnitudes of the trends which are struggling with one another" (Freud 1953–74, 19:152).

23 Derrida has commented on this elusiveness of the qualitative as part of the "speculative," and therefore not philosophical, tenor of Freud's thought (1987, 279 *passim*).

24 On the inconsistency of Freud's references to physics, see Bass (1997).

25 This idea recurs regularly. See, for just a couple of examples, "the multiplicity of developmental dispositions which give repressed impulses the opportunity of breaking through into substitutive structures" (Freud 1953–74, 13:174). Or "Repressed impulses ... succeed in making their influence felt in the mind by circuitous paths, and the indirect or substitutive satisfactions of repressed impulses thus achieved are what constitute neurotic symptoms" (Freud 1953–74, 20:267).

26 Freud maintained that the substitutes, as representations, were not able to dispose entirely of the substance they represent: "In our discussion so far we have dealt with the repression of an instinctual representative, and by the latter we have understood an idea or group of ideas which is cathected with a definite quota of psychical energy (libido or interest) coming from an instinct. Clinical observation now obliges us to divide up what we have hitherto regarded as a single entity; for it shows us that besides the idea, some other element representing the instinct has to be taken into account, and that this other element undergoes vicissitudes of repression which may be quite different from those undergone by the idea. For this other element of the psychical representative the term quota of affect has been generally adopted. It corresponds to the instinct in so far as the latter has become detached from the idea and finds expression, proportionate to its quantity, in processes which are sensed as affects. From this point on, in describing a case of repression, we shall have to follow up separately what becomes of the idea, and what becomes of the instinctual energy linked to it" (Freud 1953–74, 14:152).

27 "If we reflect that the means of representation in dreams are principally visual images and not words, we shall see that it is even more appropriate to compare dreams with a system of writing than with a language. In fact the interpretation of dreams is completely analogous

to the decipherment of an ancient pictographic script such as Egyptian hieroglyphs. In both cases there are certain elements which are not intended to be interpreted (or read, as the case may be) but are only designed to serve as 'determinatives,' that is to establish the meaning of some other element. The ambiguity of various elements of dreams finds a parallel in these ancient systems of writing; and so too does the omission of various relations, which have in both cases to be supplied from the context. If this conception of the method of representation in dreams has not yet been followed up, this, as will be readily understood, must be ascribed to the fact that psycho-analysts are entirely ignorant of the attitude and knowledge with which a philologist would approach such a problem as that presented by dreams" (Freud 1953–74, 13:176). For a formidable discussion of the consequences of this distinction, see Derrida (1972).

28 See for instance "In the total absence of any theory of the instincts which would help us to find our bearings, we may be permitted, or rather, it is incumbent upon us, to start off by working out some hypothesis to its logical conclusion, until it either breaks down or is confirmed. ... But I shall be consistent enough [with my general rule] to drop this hypothesis if psycho-analytic work should itself produce some other, more serviceable hypothesis about the instincts." (Freud 1953–74, 14:77).

29 In *An Autobiographical Study* Freud clarified that the "economic factor" ("einen ökonomischen Faktor") arose conceptually from early clinical "regard (for) the symptom as the product or equivalent of an amount of energy which would have otherwise been employed some other way." He added in parentheses directly thereafter: "This latter process was described as conversion" (Freud 1953–74, 20:22). The very idea of quantity is subordinated to the idea of conversion, substitution.

30 Dany Nobus (2009) has a remarkable project in progress on this conception of psychoanalysis as paying for the privilege of working.

31 However much he emphasizes the similarities between dreams and symptoms, Freud also maintains a distinction between them, precisely, as Lacan points out, on economic grounds (where "economic" connotes the insistence of integrity): "there is an absolutely fundamental economic difference between the symptom and the dream. All they have in common is a grammar. That's a metaphor, don't take it literally. They are as different as an epic poem is from a work on thermodynamics. The dream makes it possible to grasp the symbolic function at play, and it is, on that account, capital for understanding the symptom. But a symptom is always part of the overall economic state of the subject, whereas the dream is a state localized in time, under extremely specific conditions" (1991, 122). Goux has formidably argued that the psychic and monetary logics of substitution amount to one and the same "global mode of symbolizing ... reproduced in each register" (1990, 139).

32 We might even ask whether, when confronted with a displacement machine, metalanguage is desirable or even technically feasible. Karatani makes a formidable observation: "It is absolutely impossible to control capitalism from the meta-level, because capitalism itself is deconstructive" (1995: 67). In the case of psychoanalysis, we might say that psychoanalysis refuses to operate as metalanguage, because it seeks a form adequately open to, rather than structurally closed against, its object, the unconscious.

33 Strachey renders *Triebkraft* as "motive force."

34 This utilitarian connection is offered by Goux (2011).

References

Abraham, Nicolas, and Maria Torok. 1994. *The Shell and the Kernel*, ed. and trans. Nicholas T. Rand. Chicago: University of Chicago Press.

Appleby, Joyce Oldham. 1978. *Economic Thought and Ideology in Seventeenth-Century England*. Princeton: Princeton University Press.

Arendt, Hannah. 1998. *The Human Condition*. Chicago: University of Chicago Press.

Aristotle. 1996. *The Politics*. Cambridge: Cambridge University Press.

Bass, Alan. 1997 "The Status of an Analogy: Psychoanalysis and Physics." *American Imago*, 54: 235–56.

Bennett, David. 2010. "Introduction: Psychoanalysis, Money, and the Economy." Introductory Address, Conference Proceedings, Freud Museum, London.

Bennett, David. 2011. "Money is Laughing Gas to Me: A Critique of Pure Reason in Psychoanalysis and Economics." *New Formations*, 72: 1–19.

Birken, Lawrence. 1988. *Consuming Desire: Sexual Science and the Emergence of a Culture of Abundance, 1871–1914*. Ithaca, N.Y.: Cornell University Press.

Breithaupt, Fritz. 2005. "Homo Oeconomicus: The Rhetoric of Currency and a Case of Nineteenth-Century Psychology." *Nineteenth-Century Prose*, 32: 6–26.

Deleuze, Gilles, and Félix Guattari. 2004. *Anti-Oedipus: Capitalism and Schizophrenia*, trans. Robert Hurley, Mark Seem, and Helen R. Lane. London: Continuum.

Derrida, Jacques. 1972. "Freud and the Scene of Writing." *Yale French Studies* 48: 74–117.

Derrida, Jacques. 1987. *The Post Card*. Chicago: University of Chicago Press.

Erwin, Edward, ed. 2001. *The Freud Encyclopedia: Theory, Therapy, and Culture*. London: Routledge.

Fink, Bruce. 2004. *Lacan to the Letter: Reading Écrits Closely*. Minneapolis: University of Minnesota Press.

Freud, Sigmund. 1940–52. *Gesammelte Werke: Chronologisch Geordnet*, 17 vols. With the assistance of Anna Freud and Maris Bonaparte. London: Imago.

Freud, Sigmund. 1953–74. *The Standard Edition of the Complete Psychological Works of Sigmund Freud*, 24 vols., ed. James Strachey, with the assistance of Anna Freud, Alix Strachey, and Alan Tyson, trans. James Strachey. London: Hogarth Press.

Freud, Sigmund. 1961. *The Letters of Sigmund Freud*, ed. Ernst Freud. London: Hogarth Press.

Freud, Sigmund. 1986. *Briefe an Wilhelm Fliess, 1887–1904*, ed. Jeffrey M. Masson. Frankfurt am Main: Fischer Verlag.

Gay, Peter. 1985. *Freud for Historians*. New York: Oxford University Press.

Goux, Jean-Joseph. 1990. *Symbolic Economies: After Marx and Freud*, trans. Jennifer C. Cage. Ithaca, N.Y.: Cornell University Press.

Goux, Jean-Joseph. 2011. "Pleasure and Pain: At the Crossroads of Psychoanalysis and the Political Economy." *New Formations* 72: 117–30.

Karatani, Kojin. 1995. *Architecture as Metaphor: Language, Number, Money*. Cambridge, MA: MIT Press.

Kornbluh, Anna. 2013. *Realizing Capital: Financial and Psychic Economies in Victorian Form*. New York: Fordham University Press.

Lacan, Jacques. 1991. *The Seminar of Jacques Lacan*, Book II: *The Ego in Freud's Theory and in the Technique of Psychoanalysis*, ed. Jacques-Alain Miller, trans. Sylvana Tomaselli. New York: Norton.

Lacan, Jacques. 2007. *Écrits: The First Complete Edition in English*, trans. Bruce Fink. New York: Norton.

Lyotard, Jean-François. 1993. *Libidinal Economy*. Bloomington: Indiana University Press.

Nobus, Dany. 2009. "What Are Words Worth? On Value for Money in the Psychoanalytic Economy." Keynote Address, Association for the Psychoanalysis of Culture and Society Annual Conference, Rutgers University, New Brunswick.

Ornston, Darius Gray. 1985. "The Invention of 'Cathexis' and Strachey's Strategy." *International Review of Psychoanalysis*, 12: 391–98.

Reddy, Sudeep. 2008. "Does Treasury Need $700 Billion All At Once?" *The Wall Street Journal*, September 24.

Strachey, James. 1963. "Obituary for Joan Riviere." *International Journal of Psychoanalysis*, 44: 228–30.

Zaretsky, Eli. 2005. *Secrets of the Soul: A Social and Cultural History of Psychoanalysis*. New York: Vintage.

Žižek, Slavoj. 1989. *The Sublime Object of Ideology*. London: Verso.

Part IV

Transformations

Chapter 17

Chronolibido: From Socrates to Lacan and Beyond

Martin Hägglund

The debate between philosophy and literature begins over the question of desire. When Socrates addresses Homer's poetry in Plato's *Republic*, the crucial issue concerns the fate of desire.[1] Socrates' main charge against Homer is that his poetry leaves us in the grip of the desire for mortal life. The dramatic pathos in the *Iliad* is generated when the heroes cling to what they will lose and cannot accept the death that awaits them. Even the bravest heroes, such as Hector and Achilles, lament the fact that their lives will have been so short. When this pathos is transferred to the audience, it opens a channel that allows the spectators to come into contact with their own grief. "You know," says Socrates, "that even when the very best of us hear Homer imitating one of the heroes who is in grief, and is delivering a long tirade in his lamentations, that we then feel pleasure and abandon ourselves and accompany the representation with sympathy and eagerness" (Plato 1961, 605d). A few lines further on, Socrates specifies that this fascination with tragedy stems from the part of our soul that "in our own misfortunes was forcibly restrained and that has hungered for tears" (606a). To be taken in by mimesis is thus to be overtaken by the vulnerability and the desire for mortal life that the philosopher should overcome. Indeed, Socrates argues

A Concise Companion to Psychoanalysis, Literature, and Culture, First Edition.
Edited by Laura Marcus and Ankhi Mukherjee.

that the problem with mimesis is that "it waters and fosters these feelings when what we ought to do is to dry them up" (606d). The true philosopher does not cry, according to Socrates, since he knows that "nothing in mortal life is worthy of great concern" (604c). The philosopher should not let himself be "disturbed" by the loss of mortal beings; he should rather turn his desire toward the immutable presence of the eternal.

The issue of desire is the deepest motivation for Socrates' demarcation of poetry from philosophy. The former engages the desire for a mortal life that can always be lost. In contrast, the task of philosophy is to convert the desire for the mortal into a desire for the immortal that can never be lost. To be sure, Plato's denigration of poetry has been subjected to centuries of critique. Yet defenders of poetry have traditionally not pursued Plato's insight into the link between the affective power of aesthetic representation and the investment in mortal life. Rather, epiphanies of aesthetic experience tend to be explained in terms of an intimation of eternity, and even modernist literature continues to be read in terms of a desire for immortality.[2] My aim here, however, is not to provide a historical account of the persistence of Platonism in aesthetics. Rather, I want to call attention to a Platonic axiom that is still operative in our understanding of desire, namely, that the aim of desire is to repose in a state of being where nothing can be lost. This logic of desire is succinctly formulated by Socrates in the *Symposium*. Socrates argues that temporal objects do not answer to what we really desire. The proper destination of desire is rather an eternity that "neither comes into being nor passes away" and thus transcends temporal finitude (Plato 1961, 211a).

Two major consequences follow from Socrates' premise. First, desire is understood as the desire for what *is* in itself. Second, everything that is not in itself is understood as the *lack* of fullness. It would be hard to overestimate the influence of this notion of lack. In contemporary literary studies, it comes to the fore in what is arguably the most influential model for reading the problem of desire: the psychoanalytic theory formulated by Jacques Lacan. While Lacan clearly recognizes that there is no fullness of being, he holds that we *desire* to reach such fullness and that our temporal being is a lack of being. For Lacan, the lack of being is not derived from an object we once had and subsequently lost. As he explains in Seminar II: "It is not the lack of this or that, but the lack of being whereby being exists" (Lacan 1988, 223). Even though Lacan often describes the absent fullness in terms that may seem to invoke a lost object (such as "the Thing") it is important to understand that it cannot be equated with any object whatsoever. What is desired under the heading of "the Thing" is a state of absolute fullness to which no object can ever be adequate. The lack of such fullness is for Lacan the *cause* of desire, since it is precisely because desire cannot be fulfilled that there is desire.

If the notion of lack seems persuasive, it is because it apparently adheres to an impeccable logic. As Socrates argues, the movement of desire is predicated on a constitutive difference, since we can only desire to be what we are not. The one who really *is* wise or happy cannot desire to be wise or happy, since there is no reason to desire to be what you already are. The decisive question, then, is how one should read the constitutive difference of desire. Traditionally, the constitutive difference of desire has supported the inference that desire testifies to an ontological lack. Because desire cannot be fulfilled – because it cannot repose in itself or in what it desires – it answers to a lack of being in itself. Consequently, in order to challenge the logic of lack one must provide another account of the constitutive difference of desire. It is such an account that I seek to develop as the notion of *chronolibido*.

The notion of chronolibido traces the constitutive difference of desire to the condition of time. For one moment to be succeeded by another, it cannot *first* be present in itself and *then* cease to be. A self-present, indivisible moment could never give way to another moment, since what is indivisible cannot be altered. The succession of time requires not only that every moment be superseded by another moment, but also that this alteration be at work from the beginning. Every moment must negate itself and pass away *in its very event*. If the moment did not negate itself there would be no time, only a presence forever remaining the same.

The condition of time thus allows one to account for the constitutive difference of desire without interpreting it as an ontological lack. It is indeed true that desire cannot coincide with its object, but not because the object of desire is a timeless being. On the contrary, both the subject *and* the object of desire are from the very beginning temporal. They can thus never be in themselves, but not because they have lost or aspire to reach a being-in-itself. Rather, they can only be themselves by not coinciding with themselves. This constitutive difference is what makes it possible to desire anything in the first place. Without a temporal delay there would be no desire, since there would be no time to reach out toward or aspire to anything whatsoever. Even if I only desire myself, autoaffection presupposes that I do not coincide with myself – otherwise I could never affect or be affected by myself. The point is thus not that desire cannot be fulfilled. Rather, what is at stake is to rethink fulfillment as essentially temporal. Even the most ideal fulfillment is necessarily inhabited by non-fulfillment – not because fulfillment is lacking but because the state of fulfillment itself is temporal and thus altered from within. Even at the moment one *is* fulfilled, the moment is ceasing to be and opens the experience to loss.

Returning to the *Symposium*, we can trace the logic of chronolibido in Socrates' own account of desire. The key to such a reading is a logical conundrum to which Socrates calls attention. Why do we desire to be happy even when we are happy, given that we cannot desire to be what we already are? The classical answer is that we continue to desire happiness because we *lack* the ideal state of full happiness. The constitutive difference of desire is thus interpreted as the difference between the imperfect and the perfect. The happiness we experience is *actually* imperfect but we continue to desire happiness because we strive toward its perfection, which is *potential* in us. What is remarkable, however, is that Socrates also provides a quite different explanation of why we desire to be what we already are. This explanation occurs at the beginning of Socrates' dialogue with Agathon. It is inserted to make sure that they are on the right track, but in fact it derails Socrates' entire trajectory:

> If, Socrates continued, the strong were to long for strength, and the swift for swiftness, and the healthy for health – for I suppose it *might* be suggested that in such cases as these people long for the very things they have, or are, already, and so I'm trying to imagine such a case, to make quite sure we are on the right track – people in their position, Agathon, if you stop to think about them, are bound here and now to have those very qualities, whether they want them or not; so why should they trouble to want them? And so, if we heard someone saying, "I'm healthy, and I want to be healthy; I'm rich, and I want to be rich; and in fact, I want just what I've got," I think we should be justified in saying, "But, my dear sir, you've *got* wealth and health and strength already, and what you want is to go on having them, for at the moment you've got them whether you want them or not. Doesn't it look as if, when you say you want these things here and now, you really mean, what you've got now, you want to go on keeping?" Don't you think, my dear Agathon, that he'd be bound to agree?
>
> (Plato 1961, 200b–d)

Even though Socrates does not acknowledge it, the logic of his argument is incompatible with a metaphysical logic of lack. The man in Socrates' example is healthy and wants to be healthy, but not because he is lacking perfect health. Rather, in his very experience of health there is an apprehension that his health will not last; otherwise there would be no need to "keep" it for the future. This temporal sense of keeping or persisting is even more evident in the Greek text. What is here translated as the desire to "go on" having or being something is literally the desire to have or to be something "also in the time that follows [*kai eis ton epeita chronon*]."[3] In and through the very experience of being healthy, the man is seized by the desire to go on being healthy, precipitated by the sense that his health may cease to be in the time that follows. This anticipation of loss and the concomitant desire to persist are unthinkable unless the experience of health is always already temporal. If the man were simply reposing in perfect health, he would never have the sense that his state of being could be followed by another and that his health may be lost. Indeed, if the man were reposing in perfect health he would not care about his health in the first place. The condition for desiring health, then, is that health can be lost.

The point to underline here is that Socrates does not say that the man wants to repose in perfect health. On the contrary, he wants to go on being what he is – to *live on* in time. Socrates' own argument thus articulates how temporality is intrinsic to the fulfillment of desire. An integral part of being healthy is the desire to *continue being healthy*, which is both animated and agonized by the sense that the state of fulfillment will not last. Fulfillment is not a static completion but a state in which one wants to linger, which is necessarily intertwined with the apprehension that the state of fulfillment is passing away. Without such exposure to time, there would be no desire to sustain the experience of health – and no impetus to linger in its quality – since there would be no risk of loss that could make one care to linger.

Thus, the precarious experience of time is not only a negative peril but also the positive possibility of coming into being, living on, and sustaining desire. Indeed, we will see how the desire to live on – to survive – is incompatible with the desire for immortality, since it wants to hold on to a life that is inherently temporal. The reason why the desire for survival never reaches a timeless state of immortality is not because the latter is unattainable, but because the desire for survival is not oriented toward such a state.

The distinction between survival and immortality can be traced in the text of the *Symposium* itself. Socrates presents his argument in favor of immortality by recounting a speech by Diotima of Mantineia. This speech is the canonical source for the conception of desire as a desire for immortality. Yet when Diotima sets out to prove her thesis that all creatures are driven by the "passion for immortality" (Plato 1961, 208b), she in fact shows that all creatures are driven by the passion for survival:

> Mortal nature [*physis*] does all it can to live forever and to be immortal. It can only do this by reproduction [*gēnesis*]; it always leaves behind another, new generation to replace the old. This point applies even in the period in which each living creature is described as alive and the same – for instance, someone is said to be the same person from childhood till old age. Yet, for all we call him the same, every bit of him is different, and every day he is becoming a new man, while the old man is ceasing to exist, as you can see from his hair, his flesh, his bones, his blood, and all the rest of his body. And not only his body, for the same thing happens to his soul. And neither his manners, nor his disposition, nor his thoughts, nor his desires, nor his pleasures, nor his sufferings, nor his fears are the same throughout his life, for some of them grow, while others disappear. ... This is how every mortal creature perpetuates itself. It cannot, like the divine, always be the same in every respect; it can only leave behind new life to fill the vacancy that is left behind in its species by obsolescence. Through this device [*mēchanē*], Socrates, the mortal partakes of immortality, both in its body and in all other respects; there is no other way. And so it is no wonder that every creature prizes its own offspring, since the whole creation is inspired by this zeal, this passion for immortality.
>
> (Plato 1961, 207d–208b; translation modified)

Diotima here demonstrates that the movement of survival is operative not only in the passage from one generation to another but also in the passage from one moment to another in the life of the same temporal being. A temporal being is constantly ceasing to be and can only perpetuate itself by leaving traces of the past for the future. Accordingly, Diotima emphasizes that a temporal being has to sustain itself through reproduction (*gēnesis*) and that this condition "applies even in the period in which each living creature is described as alive and the same." Indeed, "for all we call [someone] the same," Diotima points out, "every bit of him is different, and every day he is becoming a new man, while the old man is ceasing to exist," in a process of temporal change that Diotima extends to the soul as well as the body. "This is how every mortal creature perpetuates itself," she emphasizes, "It cannot, like the divine, always be the same in every respect; it can only leave new life to fill the vacancy that is left behind." This temporal process is the movement of survival that transcends a particular moment of finitude and yet is bound to finitude as a general condition. To survive is never to repose in a timeless presence. Rather, to survive is to remain after a past that has ceased to be and before a future that may not come to be. The experience of survival is thus always haunted by loss, both in relation to what has ceased to be in the past and what may cease to be in the future. The "offspring" that allows a temporal being to live on despite its own passing away is no less subjected to temporal finitude than its predecessor, since it has to give way to a successor that may erase the trace of what has come before.

The survival of a mortal being is thus quite different from the immortality of an eternal being. If mortal being "partakes of immortality" through the movement of survival it is only by temporalizing the notion of immortality. This is why the supposed "passion for immortality" turns out to be a passion for survival. On Diotima's account, the desire to have children, to be famous, or to be commemorated, is an expression of the desire for immortality. Yet, following her own description, we find that these desires are *not even oriented toward immortality*. Rather than aiming for a timeless state of eternity, they seek to extend the legacy of a finite life and in so doing they remain exposed to death. To live on thanks to one's children or one's reputation is not to become immortal; it is to live on through others who themselves are mortal. The children that resemble one or the admirers that remember one are themselves mortal and offer no safe haven from oblivion. The desire to survive that is expressed through them is thus not a desire for immortality. If one desires to have children or to be remembered one is rather seeking to *live on* as a mortal being for oneself and/or for other mortal beings.

To be sure, Diotima holds that the desire to survive ultimately is driven by the desire to be immortal. According to her own analysis, however, proper immortality would require a state of being that is "always the same in every respect" (Plato 1961, 208a) and "neither comes into being nor passes away, neither flowers nor fades" (211a). As is clear from this definition, the timeless state of immortality would eliminate any form of survival. In a state where nothing comes into being or passes away *nothing survives*. It follows that the desire for survival – which Diotima analyzes in terms of a desire for reproduction (*gēnesis*) that animates and sustains our temporal being – cannot be driven by the desire for immortality. Indeed, the desire to perpetuate a temporal being is incompatible with the desire to be immortal, since immortality would not allow anything to live on in time.

One may nevertheless ask why the temporality of survival cannot – at least on the level of the imaginary – be reconciled with immortality. The Greek gods, for example, are said to be immortal but nevertheless live on in time. My claim, however, is that Diotima has good reasons not to align the life of the gods with a proper state of immortality. Even if one removes organic deterioration and death, the temporal finitude of survival is still operative in anyone who is susceptible to a temporal change in his or her disposition, since such change minimally entails that a thought, feeling, or desire comes into being while another passes away. This is exactly what Diotima demonstrates in the speech quoted above. With remarkable precision she defines a "mortal creature" not primarily in terms of organic death but in terms of the temporality of survival, which entails a structural relation to loss even in the persistence of the "same" being across time.[4] Every moment of living on necessarily involves a relation to what does *not* live on and this negativity already constitutes a minimal relation to death. If one survived wholly intact – unscathed by the alteration of time – one would not be surviving; one would "always be the same in every respect." By the same token one would not be susceptible to any form of change, since nothing could happen to one. Insofar as the gods are subject to change – insofar as they have thoughts, feelings, and desires that respond to what happens – they are therefore "mortal," even if they do not organically cease to be.

Diotima's discourse thus allows us to articulate the distinction between survival and immortality, which is central to the notion of chronolibido. To survive is to live on in a temporal process of alteration. In contrast, to be immortal is to repose in a state of being that is eternally the same. While Diotima maintains that the latter state is the desired end of the former, her own account allows us to call into question this teleology. The desire to live on through reproduction cannot aim at transcending time, since temporality is intrinsic to the state of being that is desired. What I want to emphasize, then, is not only that the temporal finitude of survival is an inescapable condition but also that the investment in survival animates and inspires all the forms of care that Diotima analyzes. Without the sense of the beloved passing away there would be no desire to reproduce it or to care for its sustenance. Indeed, the notion of chronolibido seeks to show that it is *because* of temporal finitude that one cares about life in the first place.

If life were fully present in itself – if it were not haunted by past and future, by what has been and what may be – there would be no reason to care about life, since nothing could happen to it. Even a being free from organic death would have to remain susceptible to loss – the affective "death" of what he or she wants to keep – in order to care. Inversely, a being exempt from such death could not sense the value of caring for anything at all.

The desire for survival, then, should not be understood exclusively or primarily in terms of a biological drive for self-preservation but includes all "spiritual" commitments to living on in time. It is because one is invested in the survival of temporal life that one seeks to save anything from death, since only temporal life can be threatened by death. Yet the state of immortality cannot answer to the survival that is desired. Rather than allowing a temporal being to live on, it would put an end to the time of life in favor of a state of eternity where nothing comes into being or passes away. Being in a state of eternity would therefore require that one renounce all care and become completely indifferent to the fate of survival. That is why it is consistent to emphasize (as many religious sages do) that detachment is the ultimate condition for attaining the state of eternity. Only by detaching oneself from the care for temporal life can one embrace the timelessness of immortality.

The chronolibidinal argument is that such an ideal of detachment dissimulates a preceding investment in temporal life. The latter is the source of both what one desires and what one fears, both the desirable and the undesirable. As an *effect* of this double bind one can come to embrace the desire for absolute fullness/absolute emptiness. The point, however, is precisely that this desire is an effect and not an originary cause. The desire for absolute fullness/emptiness is not the truth of desire but rather a self-defeating attempt to deny the investment in temporal life that is the source of all care. Far from being an external refutation of the desire for immortality, the logic of chronolibido thereby seeks to read it against itself from within.

The key argument here concerns the co-implication of *chronophobia* and *chronophilia*. The fear of time and death (chronophobia) does not stem from a metaphysical desire to transcend temporal finitude. On the contrary, it is generated by the investment in keeping a life that may be lost. It is because one is attached to a temporal being (chronophilia) that one fears losing it (chronophobia). Care in general, I argue, depends on such a double bind. On the one hand, care is necessarily chronophilic, since only something that is subject to the possibility of loss – and hence temporal – can give one a reason to care. On the other hand, care is necessarily chronophobic, since one cannot care about something without fearing what may happen to it.

The philosophical tradition offers two different prescriptions for curing the chronolibidinal condition of care, one deriving from Plato and the other from Epicurus. The Platonic prescription seeks to eliminate chronophilia: to detach one from the care for mortal life in favor of an immortal state of being. Accordingly, Socrates argues that if one desires immortality one has no reason to fear death, since death will bring about the end of mortal life. As he maintains in Plato's *Phaedo* (1961, 68b–c), if you see a man who is afraid of dying you can be sure that he is not a philosopher (that is, a lover of wisdom) but a lover of the mortal body. The Platonic diagnosis, then, is that we will overcome the fear of death if we overcome the desire for mortal life and learn to desire immortality in a proper philosophical fashion.

In contrast, the Epicurean diagnosis is that we fear death *because* we desire immortality. Rather than eliminating chronophilia, the Epicurean prescription seeks to eliminate chronophobia: to convince one to accept death as the natural end of mortal life and not entertain vain hopes of living on. Through this operation, Epicurus proposes both to stimulate chronophilia (the enjoyment of mortal life) and to cure the chronophobic fear of death. As he argues, "the correct recognition that death is nothing to us makes the mortality of life enjoyable, not by adding on a limitless time but by removing the longing for immortality. For nothing is fearful in life to the person who is genuinely convinced that there is nothing fearful in not living" (Epicurus 1994, 10.124). If we remove the desire for immortality, we should therefore be able to remove the fear of death and learn to savor "not the longest time but the most pleasant" (1994, 10.126). As we have seen, however, the fear of death does not stem from a desire for immortality but from a desire for survival. If one fears death, it is not because one wants to be immortal but because one wants to live on as a mortal being. Consequently, when Epicurus argues that there is no reason to fear death because *death is nothing to us* – it is not something we can experience because our death excludes our existence – he misconstrues what is at stake in the fear of death. To fear death is not to fear the state of being dead (which indeed will be nothing at all to the living being who is afraid of dying) but to fear the loss of what one wants to keep. The fear of death is thus not limited to the care for one's own life or to the fear of actual physical death. Rather, the fear of death is operative in relation to everything one cares about, including "the most pleasant time" that one is savoring.[5]

For the same reason, being invulnerable to the fear of death (whether by virtue of Platonic immortality or Epicurean *ataraxia*) would amount to being completely indifferent. Both Socrates and Epicurus seek to cure the condition of chronolibido by eliminating the care for survival. What I analyze as the *constitutive* care for survival, however, makes clear that the condition of chronolibido is incurable. Contra Epicurus, chronophilia cannot cure chronophobia but is rather the cause of it. Inversely, contra Socrates, chronophobia cannot be cured by the promise of a deliverance from time. The promise of an eternal state of being cannot even hypothetically appease the chronophobic fear of death or satisfy the chronophilic desire to live on. Rather than redeeming death, the state of immortality would *bring about* death, since it would terminate the time of mortal life.

Accordingly, we can distinguish between the two propositions concerning death and the afterlife that Socrates makes toward the end of the *Apology*. On the one hand, Socrates appeals to the desire for survival by appealing to our desire for mortal life to continue beyond death (for example, the hope that we will be able to spend time with Homer, Hesiod, and others who have passed away). On the other hand, Socrates appeals to the desire for death itself, which is incompatible with the desire for survival. As he argues, if death is a total annihilation that entails "no consciousness but only a dreamless sleep" then "death must be a marvelous gain" (Plato 1961, 40d). My point here is that Socrates promotes death *for the same reason that he promotes immortality*, namely, that it cancels out the condition of temporality. Indeed, the dreamless sleep of total extinction is claimed to be desirable "because the whole of time [*ho pas chronos*], if you look at it in this way, can be regarded as no more than one single night" (40e).

Distinguishing between immortality and survival, we can now specify the difference between chronolibidinal reading and Lacanian psychoanalysis. While Lacan emphasizes that immortality is an illusion, he maintains that we are driven toward and desire such fullness. The Lacanian reading thereby stops short of questioning the *structure* of the traditional narrative of desire. The fullness of immortality is deemed to be an illusion but the *desire* for such fullness is itself taken to be self-evident. On a structural level, the Lacanian account thus conforms to the conception of desire that has been handed down to us from the Platonic tradition: we are temporal, restless beings but desire to repose in the fullness/emptiness of timeless being.

It is here instructive to consider Lacan's own reading of Plato in Seminar XI. With a reference to the *Symposium*, the experience of survival – of the life that lives on by *not* being immortal – is described as the experience of an ontological lack. We are thus treated to a clear account of what Lacan understands as the fundamental lack of being, which is worth quoting at length:

> Two lacks overlap here. The first emerges from the central defect around which the dialectic of the advent of the subject to his own being in relation to the Other turns – by the fact that the subject depends on the signifier and that the signifier is first of all in the field of the Other. This lack takes up the other lack, which is the real, earlier lack, to be situated at the advent of the living being, that is to say, at sexed reproduction. The real lack is what the living being loses, that part of himself *qua* living being, in reproducing himself through the way of sex. This lack is real because it relates to something real, namely, that the living being, by being subject to sex, has fallen under the blow of individual death.
>
> Aristophanes' myth pictures the pursuit of the complement for us in a moving, and misleading, way, by articulating that it is the other, one's sexual other half, that the living being seeks in love. To this mythical representation of the mystery of love, analytic experience substitutes the search by the subject, not of the sexual complement, but of the part of himself, lost forever, that is constituted by the fact that he is only a sexed living being, and that he is no longer immortal.
>
> (Lacan 1998a: 204–5)

Lacan begins by outlining his doctrine that our dependency on language answers to an alienation, here described as the "central defect" of being dependent on a signifier that cannot be controlled by the subject. This notion of language presupposes that the necessity of mediation – the necessity of relating to ourselves via the alterity of time and language – is experienced as a lack of being. Lacan goes on to say that the ultimate source of this lack is that the subject is *no longer immortal*. This may appear to be a startling statement, but Lacan has anticipated his point a couple of pages earlier, when arguing that all objects of desire are "representatives" of "immortal life, or irrepressible life, life that has need of no organ, simplified, indestructible life. It is precisely what is subtracted from the living being by virtue of the fact that it is subject to the cycle of sexed reproduction" (1998a, 180). The temporal process of survival – here exemplified by sexual reproduction – is thus opposed to a proper immortality. As living beings subjected to generation and corruption we can never be immortal: we can only *live on* through reproduction – whether this reproduction is sexual, linguistic, or dependent on some other form of mediation. This movement of survival will never yield a proper immortality, since whatever lives on through reproduction is itself subject to corruption and death. If one assumes that we seek a proper immortality – an absolute self-sufficiency – one must therefore conclude that the experience of survival is one of ontological lack, since the movement of survival compromises any self-sufficiency from its first inception. The aim of what Lacan here calls "analytic experience" is to make us recognize this fundamental lack at the core of our libidinal being. In contrast to the experience of love, which makes us believe that the relation to another can fulfill us, analytic experience would make us recognize that what we are *really* seeking in seeking love is an absolute self-sufficiency that is forever lost and inaccessible to us as mortal beings.

Whether there ever was a state of self-sufficiency is equivocal both in Lacan's text and in the established commentaries. According to Joan Copjec's detailed interpretation, libidinal objects are "representatives" of an immortal life that has been lost, but the status of the lost immortality is unclear. On the one hand, Copjec asserts that "immortal, indestructible life has been subtracted from us" (2003, 52) and that "the body and satisfaction have lost the support of the organic body and the noumenal Thing" (2003, 37), which implies that there once was an immortal life or a noumenal Thing. On the other hand, she asserts that the self-sufficiency of immortal life is a myth of something that never existed. Copjec's contradictory assertions culminate when she writes that "pure and total self-sufficiency does not now and never did exist (or: there is no original plenum), yet something nevertheless remains of that never-existing, mythical time and self-sufficiency" (2003, 52). One is thus left to wonder how something can remain from what never existed.

A defender of Lacan could certainly avoid the inconsistency by strictly maintaining that the supposed loss of immortality is nothing but a retrospective projection and that Lacan only analyzes it as the fundamental fantasy of the subject. Yet this qualification does not affect the premise with which I take issue, namely, that the "truth" of desire is the lack of immortality. In Lacan's terms, there is a constitutive difference between the *jouissance* expected (full enjoyment) and the *jouissance* obtained (temporal enjoyment), since no object of experience can answer to the desired Thing. As he puts it in Seminar XX: "'That's not it' is the very cry by which the jouissance obtained is distinguished from the jouissance expected" (Lacan 1998b, 111).[6] For Lacan, the *jouissance* expected is not inaccessible for contingent reasons that can be overcome. On the contrary, it is inaccessible due to the ontological lack of being. Following Seminar XI, this ontological lack should ultimately be understood in terms of the fact that we are mortal. The absent Thing is proper immortality and the impossibility of ever attaining such an absolute self-sufficiency – the impossibility of ever transcending the temporal finitude of survival – is the repressed "truth" of desire that Lacan aims to elucidate.

This assumed "truth" of desire has two major consequences. First, the fantasy of the absolute is diagnosed as the cause of our inability to come to terms with reality. The reason why we develop neuroses, phobias, and resentful aggression is ultimately because we sustain the fantasy of an absolute enjoyment (the transcendent Thing) that no actual object or real human being ever can provide. Second, this diagnosis assumes that *if* we were able to let go of the fantasy of absolute enjoyment we would be able to come to terms with reality. Lacanian analysis therefore sets out to dispel the idea that there is a Thing out there that can be obtained by the subject. The moment of "authenticity" in Lacanian analysis is the moment when one recognizes the lack of being that nothing can fill and assumes the "symbolic castration" that constitutes one's subjectivity. By "traversing the fantasy" of absolute enjoyment the analysand is supposed to arrive at the insight that nothing can satisfy his or her desire – that nothing can be *it* – and learn to live with this absence of the Thing.

In contrast, chronolibidinal reading seeks to show that the ontological lack of being is not the repressed truth of desire. On the contrary, the idea of an ontological lack *is itself a repression* of the constitutive bond to mortal life. The experience of loss does not stem from the mourning of a Thing we never had but from the mourning of a temporal being who is ceasing to be from the beginning. The fundamental problem of desire is not that mortal life cannot answer to the immortality we desire, in accordance with Lacan's formula *that's not it*. Rather, the fundamental problem of desire is that *this is it*: the bond to mortal life is the condition for everything we desire and everything we fear.

The thinking of chronolibido thus returns us to the problem that Socrates analyzes in Homer. If one is bound to mortal life, the positive can never be released from the negative. Indeed, as Socrates points out, the investment in mortal life leads one to hold "contrary opinions at the same time about the same things" so that there is "division and strife of the man with himself" (Plato 1961, 603c–d). This internal division articulates the double bind of chronolibido. It is because one wants to hold on to a mortal life that one is devastated by the extinction of this mortal life and cannot come to terms with death. The source of what one desires – the mortal life one wants to guard and keep – is also the source of what one fears. It follows that there is chronophilia at the heart of every chronophobia and chronophobia at the heart of every chronophilia. The notion of chronolibido seeks to provide the framework for thinking this double bind and thereby open a new way of reading the dramas of desire as they are staged in philosophy and literature.

Notes

1 To speak of "literature" with regard to the Platonic dialogues is of course anachronistic, since there is no equivalent term or category for literature in ancient Greece. I use the term literature as shorthand for what Plato criticizes in terms of poetry, tragedy, and mimesis more generally, to underline the relevance of the debate for modern understandings of the relation between philosophy and literature. For incisive analyses of the stakes of the Platonic critique of poetry and tragedy, see Nussbaum (1986) and Staten (1995).
2 For an elaboration of this claim, see Hägglund (2012), where I pursue the practice of reading outlined in this essay.
3 This locution is repeated twice in 200d.
4 Although my argument does not depend on it, one may here note that the "device" (*mēchanē*) through which the mortal perpetuates itself is a term that Plato employs for the Greek gods as well. As Stanley Rosen (1987, 255) has observed, the term *mēchanē* (which he translates as "contrivance") "appears in various key passages throughout the dialogue; it is used to describe the cunning of Orpheus, Zeus, Eros, and now of the mortal generally. One may wonder whether Plato thereby links the Olympian gods to the daimonic poetry of mortals. They may be alike because they are bound by genesis, in contrast to the truly divine."
5 For an immanent critique of Epicurus and Lucretius, which establishes the intrinsic link between care and the fear of death with exemplary rigor, see Nussbaum (1996, ch. 6).
6 The French original reads: "*Ce n'est pas ça* – voilà le cri par où se distingue la jouissance obtenue, de celle attendue" (Lacan 1975, 101).

References

Copjec, Joan. 2003. *Imagine There's No Woman: Ethics and Sublimation*. Cambridge, MA: MIT Press.

Epicurus. 1994. "Letter to Menoeceus." In *The Epicurus Reader*, ed. and trans. Brad Inwood and L.P. Gerson. New York: Hackett.

Hägglund, Martin. 2012. *Dying for Time: Proust, Woolf, Nabokov*. Cambridge, MA: Harvard University Press.

Lacan, Jacques. 1975. *Le Séminaire de Jacques Lacan*, Livre XX: *Encore, 1972–1973*, ed. Jacques-Alain Miller. Paris: Seuil.

Lacan, Jacques. 1988. *Seminar II: The Ego in Freud's Theory and in the Technique of Psychoanalysis*, ed. Jacques-Alain Miller, trans. Sylvana Tomaselli. New York: Norton.

Lacan, Jacques. 1998a. *Seminar XI: The Four Fundamental Concepts of Psychoanalysis*, ed. Jacques-Alain Miller, trans. Alan Sheridan. New York: Norton.

Lacan, Jacques. 1998b. *Seminar XX: Encore, On Feminine Sexuality, The Limits of Love and Knowledge*, ed. Jacques-Alain Miller, trans. Bruce Fink. New York: Norton.

Nussbaum, Martha. 1986. *The Fragility of Goodness*. Cambridge: Cambridge University Press.

Nussbaum, Martha. 1996. *The Therapy of Desire*. Princeton: Princeton University Press.

Plato. 1961. *The Collected Dialogues of Plato*, ed. Edith Hamilton and Huntington Cairns. Princeton: Princeton University Press.

Rosen, Stanley. 1987. *Plato's Symposium*, 2nd edn. New Haven: Yale University Press.

Staten, Henry. 1995. *Eros in Mourning*. Baltimore: Johns Hopkins University Press.

Chapter 18

Psychoanalytic Animal

Maud Ellmann

> Four-year-old Harry (not his real name) grew up with all the privileges one might expect from doting, dual-income parents in Los Angeles: great toys, a spacious apartment, lots of attention. But at a very early age he suffered from separation anxiety. When he was particularly distressed, often in response to loud noises, he would race about, hide in closets and sometimes even jump out the window of the family's ground-floor apartment. His loved ones knew Harry needed therapy and consulted several experts before finally choosing one they liked. Now, after a steady regimen of psychotherapy and antidepressants, Harry no longer alarms his family by leaping out of windows. Even better, he's lost his compulsion to bite strangers.

Harry, as the reader may have gathered, is a German Shepherd. This anecdote comes from an article called "When Fido Gets Phobic," published in *Time* magazine in 1999, which reports that "the latest twist in the $21 billion pet-care industry is an expanding range of alternative treatments and drugs aimed at Fido's psychological well-being." As a result, "dogs are learning to get along with their fellow schnauzers and pinschers at doggy day-care centers, having their troubles massaged away at spas, getting acupuncture to alleviate behavior problems, and taking herbal medicines like St. John's Wort to

A Concise Companion to Psychoanalysis, Literature, and Culture, First Edition.
Edited by Laura Marcus and Ankhi Mukherjee.

lift their mood" (Barovick 1999). Evidently this industry treats the dog as the problem rather than the owners, as if it were abnormal, for example, for a dog cooped up alone all day to protest by howling, tearing at the furniture, or shitting on the carpet. Yet regardless of owners' delinquencies, it's the dog who is expected to mend her ways, aided by a growing arsenal of pharmaceuticals.

Inevitably, there are limits to this anthropomorphic regimen. To vary an old proverb, you can lead a dog to the couch, but you can't make her free associate. Yet several of Freud's later patients, including the poet H.D., recall that dogs played a memorable role in psychoanalytic treatment at Berggasse 19, the Freuds' home in Vienna; indeed H.D. complains that "the professor" was sometimes more interested in his chow Jofi than in her story (H.D. 1985, 162).[1] In the following pages I discuss some of these canine interventions. After the Freuds' dogs, I turn to Lacan's boxer bitch, Justine, to open up the question of the psychoanalytic status of the animal. If the unconscious is structured like a language, as Lacan (1998, 15, 21, 48) claims, does this mean that animals have neither language nor unconscious? This chapter examines how several thinkers have responded to this question and its implications, including Derrida and Agamben.

Freud, in contrast to Lacan, tends to emphasize the continuity between the human and the animal by stressing the persistence of animal instincts in the civilized mind. The kinship that small children feel towards animals, Freud argues, corresponds to the phase of totemism in the childhood of humankind. A discussion of Freud's account of the "return of totemism" in animal phobias is followed by a speculative conclusion, which considers some possible consequences of Freud's (Darwinian) view that "man's adoption of an upright posture" is responsible for civilization and its discontents.[2] In particular I investigate how the metaphorics of upright and prone, vertical and horizontal pertain to the question of writing and textuality in psychoanalysis. Deleuze and Guattari (2004, 264–65) have pointed out that psychoanalysis tends to overlook the multiplicity of species that crop up in patients' discourse by identifying every animal with the Oedipal scenario. This suppression of zoological diversity, I suggest, is bound up with an anxiety about the horizontal materiality of writing.

* * *

So far as we know, Freud never tried to analyze his dogs. On the other hand, he did enlist their services in the consulting room, where they collaborated in the treatment by nosing out patients' moods. If the patient was calm, Jofi the chow would lie down near the couch, but would retreat across the room if the patient was anxious. Jofi also helped to time the sessions, rising to her feet as soon as the analytic hour had expired (Coren and Walker 1997, 78; see also Gay 1988, 540).

However, Jofi's timing could sometimes be perverse, as if she were campaigning in advance of Lacan for varying the length of the analytic session. Roy Grinker, an American doctor who was treated by Freud in 1932, remembered that Jofi would sometimes interrupt the session by scratching at the door. Freud would get up to let her out, explaining that "Jofi doesn't approve of what you're saying." Later, when Jofi scratched at the door to get back in, Freud would comment, "Jofi wanted to give you another chance." These jokes may contain an element of countertransference, with Freud projecting his own ambivalent reactions towards the patient onto Jofi's restlessness. On the transferential side, Grinker admits that he used to scold the dog in lieu of criticizing Freud (Grinker 2001, 39).

Grinker also had to contend with Anna Freud's dog, a giant Alsatian called Wolf, who would bark furiously when the doorbell rang and thrust his jaw into the trembling visitor's genitals. "I entered Freud's office," Grinker said, "with a high degree of castration anxiety." Anna Freud tried to reassure the patient that Wolf, who used to eviscerate sheep, had now matured into a harmless pooch, so that Grinker need only pull his tail to stop him barking. Grinker replied that there was not the faintest chance that he would touch that ferocious hellhound (Grinker 2001, 39). While many psychotherapists today claim that dogs exert a calming influence on troubled patients, the Freuds' dogs seem to have produced the opposite effect, arousing rather than assuaging anxiety. In their analytic capacity, these dogs therefore bear more affinity to Klein, whose methods aim to bring anxiety to the surface, than to today's animal-assisted psychotherapy, which tends to favor reassurance over confrontation with unconscious terrors.

Although dogs can serve as allies of the analyst by arousing and detecting patients' fears, they cannot verbalize their observations. But this is not because dogs can't talk, according to Lacan, who insists that his boxer bitch, named Justine in homage to Sade, possesses "without any doubt the gift of speech." In contrast to many human beings, however, Justine speaks only when she needs to speak, at moments of emotional intensity, communicating in the form of "little guttural whimpers." What distinguishes these whimpers from human speech is not that they fail to convey meaning or elicit the desired response, but that the dog never fails to recognize her interlocutor. Human communication, by contrast, is founded in misrecognition. "Contrary to what happens in the case of man in so far as he speaks," Lacan insists, Justine "never takes me for another." For the dog, "there is only the small other," whereas the human subject necessarily mistakes the small other for "the Other with [a] big O." By investing his dog with this unfailing power of recognition, Lacan is invoking a tradition that goes back to Homer's *Odyssey*, where the ancient dog Argos has no difficulty seeing through (or rather smelling through) his long-lost master's disguise. It is this unambiguous "relation to identity," Lacan contends, that differentiates the canine from the human speaker (Lacan 1961). Incidentally Gertrude Stein makes a similar claim in her mischievous reformulation of the cogito: "I am I because my little dog knows me" (1984, 149).

Derrida would probably object that Lacan, by denying the big Other to the dog, perpetuates the longstanding "carnophallogocentric" chauvinism that defines the animal by what it lacks. "Speech, reason, experience of death, mourning, culture, institution, politics, technique, clothing, lying, feigned feint, effacement of the trace, gift, laughter, tears, respect, etc. – the list is necessarily indefinite, and the most powerful philosophical tradition in which we live has refused *all of that* to the 'animal'" (Derrida 2009, 130). To my knowledge, Derrida never addresses Lacan's remarks about Justine; instead, he focuses his critique on Lacan's paper "Position of the Unconscious," especially on a cryptic passage suggesting – in Derrida's words – that "the animal cannot have its own unconscious" (Derrida 2009, 114). What Lacan actually proposes, a propos of analytic training, is characteristically elusive:

> In the introductory phase, one can illustrate the effect of enunciation by asking a student if he can imagine the unconscious existing in animals, unless they have some degree of language – human language. If he indeed agrees that this is the condition that would allow him to at least consider the possibility, you have verified that he distinguishes between "unconscious" and "instinct."
>
> (Lacan 2006, 707)

Derrida homes in on the first sentence, which he takes to mean that "the animal has neither the unconscious nor language, it does not have the other, it has no relation to the other as such, except by an effect of the human order, by contagion, appropriation, domestication" (Derrida 2009, 114). It is true that Lacan's argument relies on the arguably anthropocentric doctrine that the unconscious is structured like a language, but the point of this passage is to differentiate the unconscious from instinct. Besides, Lacan leaves a tantalizing loophole for speculating that an animal with access to "some degree of language – human language" might thereby be possessed of – or possessed by – an unconscious. If language can be passed on to animals through interspecies cross-contamination, does this imply that the unconscious is equally contagious?

Science has shown that animals – at least some animals – can dream, which attests to their unconscious mental processes. Whether these processes amount to "an unconscious," in the psychoanalytic sense, is another question. Experiments have proved that laboratory rats dream about the mazes that they navigate during their waking hours, replaying every twist and turn of their trajectories (MIT News 2001). In some cases the correlation is so close that researchers claim to be able to reconstruct the sleeping rat's exact position in the maze, and to determine whether the animal is dreaming about running or hesitating at a junction. These findings imply that the rat's dream consists of a mimetic reproduction of its waking experiences. If so, the dream-life of the rat lacks (or does away with) the symbolic dimension of the Freudian dream, a dimension that arises from the struggle between wish-fulfillment and censorship. Free of superego, the rat has no need to disguise its dream-wish – the same wish that motivates its hungry journey through the maze – and therefore no reason to resort to oneiric subterfuge.

In *The Interpretation of Dreams*, Freud admits:

> I do not myself know what animals dream of. But a proverb, to which my attention was drawn by one of my students, does claim to know. "What," asks the proverb, "do geese dream of?" And it replies: "Of maize." The whole theory that dreams are wish-fulfilments is contained in these two phrases.
>
> (Freud 1953–74, 4:131–32)

If this proverb were true, lab rats would dream about their food-reward, rather than reliving their labyrinthine journeys to this prize. But lab rats dream of mazes, not of maize. In this sense their dreams bear more resemblance to the nightmares of trauma victims than to the supposedly straightforward wish-fulfillment dreams of children. It seems that sleeping rats are gripped by the compulsion to repeat, like the shell-shocked veterans of World War I whose recurrent nightmares persuaded Freud to hypothesize the death drive (see Freud 1953–74, 18:32). Like lab rats' dreams, these combatants' nightmares consisted of literal re-enactments of traumatic events, undisguised by symbolic substitution. If the human is distinguished from the rat by the capacity to dream in tropes, does this mean the traumatized are less than human?

Although this question borders on absurdity, it follows from the premise that human dreams are governed by the logic of symbolic substitution. What's at issue here is not whether animals can talk, dream, or symbolize, but whether these powers are "proper" or integral to the human. Since all these powers can be lost, diminished, or disrupted, they cannot be guaranteed as inalienable properties of human minds. For this reason, Derrida argues that "what is attributed as proper to man does not belong to him in all purity and all rigor; and ... one must therefore restructure the whole problematic" (Derrida 2009, 56). Language, for example, is usually regarded as unique to human beings, although it is evident that other animals, such as Lacan's dog, both understand and participate in human speech. Yet however eloquent her whimpers, or effective in procuring human care, Justine would make a poor analysand: she could not be treated by the talking cure.

Even so, the same could be said of many (or perhaps the majority of) human beings, especially infants, autistics, or the so-called Muslims (*Muselmänner*) of Auschwitz – those "drowned" human beings, as Primo Levi described them, for whom the ethical principles of dignity, respect, and mutual recognition no longer hold (Levi 1989; see also Agamben 1999, 41–86). If *Homo sapiens* is a talking animal, this does not mean that every human being talks, let alone communicates with others. On the contrary, Giorgio Agamben contends that infancy, meaning the inability to speak, should be seen as the distinctive experience of human life.

In *Infancy and History*, Agamben proposes that infancy is not merely "something which chronologically precedes language, and which, at a certain point, ceases to exist in order to spill into speech." Infancy is not a paradise lost, which we leave forever when we learn to speak, but coexists in its origins with language. Indeed infancy is constituted by language, which constantly expels infancy in order "to produce the individual as subject" (Agamben 1993 [1978], 48). Animals, by contrast, "do not enter language, they are already inside it" (1993 [1978], 52). Nor can animals lose language, as befell the *Muselmänner*, whose state of infancy or speechlessness, brought on by hunger, cold, exhaustion, and despair, caused them to be shunned by fellow prisoners. These ruined beings, whose bare life brings to a crisis the distinction between human and non-human, were expelled by the living through the same reflex that expels infancy from speech.

This expulsion underlies what Agamben (2004, 33–38) elsewhere calls the "anthropological machine," by which the category of the human is created in contradistinction to the animal. In earlier phases of western societies, Agamben argues, this machine has operated by humanizing animals, so that slaves, barbarians, and savages were seen as animals in human form; more recently it has operated by animalizing human beings, so that detested populations are classified as less than human, such as the victims of the Nazi Holocaust. In either case the anthropological machine establishes the human by driving out the beast within, whether in the form of human beasts or bestial humans. To overcome this lethal mechanism, Agamben contends, it is necessary to recognize that "human beings are human insofar as they are not human," or more precisely that "human beings are human insofar as they bear witness to the inhuman'" (1999, 121).

Agamben's theories have provoked much controversy, whose stakes are too complex to scrutinize in this short chapter.[3] Yet it could be argued that psychoanalysis anticipates Agamben's challenge to witness the inhuman in the human by emphasizing the persistence of animal instincts in civilization. It's this emphasis, according to Freud, that accounts for the widespread resistance to psychoanalysis, causing its theories to be perceived as an "assault on the dignity of the human race" (1953–74, 19:218).

Jean Laplanche, however, has argued that Freud's appeals to animal instinct, which escalate in the course of his career, serve as a defense against the more unsettling insights of psychoanalysis.[4] Freud (1953–74, 17:140–41) boasted that psychoanalysis had administered the third and final blow to human narcissism, following those of Copernicus and Darwin. Yet Laplanche contends that Darwin's theory of evolution exercised a dangerous magnetism for Freud, deflecting the founder of psychoanalysis from his "Copernican" decentering of human consciousness. According to Laplanche, whenever the otherness of the unconscious becomes too spooky, as in the repetition compulsion investigated in *Beyond the Pleasure Principle*, Freud retreats into biologism, reducing what is alien within the psyche to the resurgence of animal instincts. The effect of this animalization is to dispel the strangeness of both the human and the animal, since the animal is thereby domesticated and installed at the core of the human psyche. Rather than a foreign body invading the psyche from without, "instinct" represents the animal within, a secret self, and therefore serves to re-center the psyche in its putative biological inheritance. For this reason the progressive instinctualization of the drives, which takes place in the course of Freud's development, entails a growing insistence on the kinship of the human and the animal. This doctrine of kinship disavows the alien in both the human being and the animal, transforming all species into fellows and familiars.

***

One of Freud's most famous assertions of this kinship occurs in *Totem and Taboo*, where he argues that children, like "savages," show "no trace of the arrogance which urges civilized men to draw a hard-and-fast line between their own nature and that of all other animals":

> Children have no scruples over allowing animals to rank as their full equals. Uninhibited as they are in the avowal of their bodily needs, they no doubt feel themselves more akin to animals than to their elders, who may well be a puzzle to them.
>
> (Freud 1953–74, 13:126–27)

This passage implies that the adult is more enigmatic to the child than the animal. Laplanche has taken up this implication to argue that the otherness of psychic life derives from the "enigmatic signifier" of the adult, as opposed to the irruption of animal instincts.[5] Freud himself, however, doesn't linger on the strangeness of the adult. His point, instead, is that children treat animals as siblings, much as "savages" worship them as forefathers.

As Freud points out, this belief in animal descent has worried anthropologists, who have developed several rationalizations to account for it. "Nominalist theories," for example, argue that the totem originates in a system of nomenclature in which the names of animals were chosen to distinguish clans from one another. Julius Pikler, in a passage quoted by Freud, proposes that "once savages bore the name of an animal, they went on to form the idea of kinship with it." According to this theory, the animal ancestor is retroactively invented to justify the name, the origin of which has been forgotten, thus implying that totemism is a "misunderstood form of ancestor worship" (quoted in Freud 1953–74, 13:110–11). Freud, by contrast, proposes that the kinship children feel towards animals signals a "return of totemism." To account for this return, Freud constructs what one reviewer called a "just so" story to explain the origins of the totemic animal (Marrett 1920, 205–6).

This famous narrative construction, as James DiCenso has pointed out, "is created mainly by linking Darwin's primal horde with Robertson Smith's account of the totem meal" (1999, 71). In the primal horde, Freud speculates, the brothers banded together to rebel against the ruling patriarch, whom they murdered and devoured in order to appropriate his women. Yet this "tumultuous mob of brothers were filled with the same contradictory feelings which we can see at work in the ambivalent father-complexes of our children and of our neurotic patients" (Freud 1953–74, 17:143). The brothers loved their father, even though they also hated him, but they could not eat their father and have him too. Once they had devoured him, satisfying their hatred and their desire for identification with him, they were stricken with guilt. In penitence they imposed prohibitions against incest and parricide, laws that bear witness to the prehistoric crimes that they forbid. Subsequently both the guilt and the hostility associated with the primal murder were displaced from the father to the totem animal. This displacement implies that the animal serves as the first symbol, established in its metaphoric afterlife by means of the murder of its referent. According to Freud, a taboo was imposed against killing or eating this totem, except on certain ceremonial occasions when the forgotten violence against the father was re-enacted on his animal substitute.

In accordance with the principle that ontogeny recapitulates phylogeny, Freud argues that the present-day child re-enacts this archaic struggle with the father in the form of phobias towards animals. The common fear of being bitten, for example, represents the terror of castration at the hands of the vindictive father. Yet because the father is both loved and hated, phobias are usually attached to "animals in which the child has hitherto shown a specially lively interest." For children living in towns, the choice of animal tends to be restricted to "horses, dogs, cats, less often birds, and with striking frequency very small creatures such as beetles and butterflies." Yet these fears may also extend to animals encountered by the child in "picture books and fairy tales," such as those that terrified the juvenile Wolf Man (Freud 1953–74, 13:127). These phobias result in an embargo on touching the creature in question, comparable to the taboos associated with the totem animal.

Animal phobias figure prominently in Freud's clinical works; in fact his most famous patients, the Wolf Man and the Rat Man, have come to be known by the names of their respective phobia-inducing animals. Other theriophobes include little Hans, who is entitled to be called the Horse Boy, or Leonardo to be known as the Vulture Man. Similarly Little Árpád, a child discussed by Ferenczi who features in *Totem and Taboo*, might have been renamed the Chicken Boy. And Schreber's *Memoirs of My Nervous Illness*, which Freud used as the basis for his case study of the author's florid psychosis, abounds with persecuting animals. These include familiar fauna of the cityscape, such as horses, dogs, cats, and spiders, in addition to exotic creatures such as scorpions and lungworms. Among the animals "miracled" into existence to torment him, Schreber writes, "the commonest are insects of all sorts, particularly flies, gnats, wasps, bees, bumble-bees, ants, earwigs, butterflies, night-moths, moths, etc., etc." (2000, 218).[6] As these multiplying etceteras imply, it is the riotous proliferation of these miraculous births, as opposed to any particular species, that fuels Schreber's paranoia.

Freud, however, pays little heed to Schreber's menagerie. Instead he focuses on Schreber's fantasy of becoming-woman in order to pursue an unconvincing link between paranoia and latent homosexuality. This blindness to animals persists among Freud's followers, despite the "vertiginous array of fauna" (Marder 2010, 121) to be found in psychoanalytic writing. In Klein's *Narrative of a Child Analysis* (1998), for instance, her account of her four-month treatment of a 10-year-old boy called Richard during World War II, animals crop up in almost every session. Bobby, the family spaniel, with whom Richard seems to have engaged in sexual play, takes a starring role, in addition to a bestiary that includes aquatic creatures such as lobsters, goldfish, starfish, trout, salmon, and whales; birds such as swans and cygnets, hens, cocks, chicks, canaries, budgerigars, and robins; insects such as bees, beetles, bluebottles, butterflies, and moths; mammals such as monkeys, horses, hedgehogs, mice, pigs, rabbits, rats, cows, and sheep, along with creepy-crawlies such as worms and spiders. (This catalogue is facilitated by Klein's remarkably exhaustive index, which includes such memorable entries as "'Job, big' (*see also Faeces*).")

Klein, however, pays no attention to this zoological diversity, but interprets all these species as parents, siblings, or part-objects – particularly penises. Nor are animals distinguished from the military imagery that features so prominently in this wartime analysis; if starfish are penises, so are submarines, while all the warring nations of the world are identified with Mummy, Daddy, or their rivalrous sons. What is striking is that such a cornucopia of imagery – animal, vegetable, and mineral – is so remorselessly reduced to the stark geometry of the Oedipal triangle. For example, whenever Richard shows an interest in the dog-pictures decorating the playroom where the analysis takes place, these animals are instantly conscripted into the family plot. In one of these pictures featuring two dogs, Klein identifies the animals with Mummy and Daddy, as well as with Mrs. Klein and Mr. Klein, the absent father in the analytic triangle. Richard's interest in another picture, of two dogs flanking a puppy, is imputed to his supposed wish to be the baby that comes between the parents. Bobby the spaniel, meanwhile, is identified at times with Richard, at other times with his father and his brother, shuffling among the various positions in the family as in a game of musical chairs. In fact this dog literally ousts the father from his chair: Richard tells Klein that "when Daddy got out of his chair by the fire Bobby would jump into it and take up so much room that there was only a tiny bit left for Daddy" (1998, 32–34). Predictably, Klein interprets this anecdote in terms of Richard's desire to take his father's place, but this dog seems to have Oedipal ambitions of his own, not only symbolizing Richard's desire to unseat the father but performing this insurrection on his own behalf.

While Klein's *Narrative of a Child Analysis* abounds with animals, Kelly Oliver (2009, 247) claims to have spotted more than eighty species in Freud's *Gesammelte Werke*, including apes, wolves, beetles, caterpillars, crayfish, donkeys, emus, foxes, frogs, giraffes, gnats, herring, jaguars, kangaroos, lizards, moths, opossum, oysters, porcupines, ravens, snails, starfish, tigers, toads, wasps, and whales. Similarly, Elizabeth Marder has pointed out that the Wolf Man, who has come to be associated with a single species, offers his analysts "a veritable bestiary," containing in addition to the famous wolves such animals as "sheep, sheep dogs, flies and beetles, caterpillars, snakes, horses, a wasp, goats, a fledgling bird, a giant caterpillar, a snail, and finally a swallowtail butterfly that, we discover, is the second animal incarnation of the same [castration] anxiety that produced the famous wolf dream" (2010, 121). Yet the extensive psychoanalytic commentary on this case follows Freud's lead in disregarding the bestiary in favor of the wolf, and the wolf in favor of the father. This tendency to overlook the diversity of animals coincides with a tendency to masculinize them.

It is striking that most of the animal phobias discussed by Freud occur in males, including the Wolf Man, the Rat Man, little Hans, and even Leonardo, whose childhood memory of being assaulted by a vulture forms the kernel of Freud's psychobiographical study. Furthermore the animals themselves are masculinized by Freud, who interprets them as stand-ins for the father. Even Leonardo's vulture, which Freud at first connects to the artist's unmarried mother, citing an ancient tradition that all vultures are female, undergoes a sex-change in the course of Freud's analysis. "While I was in my cradle," Leonardo reported, "a vulture came down to me, and opened my mouth with its tail, and struck me many times with its tail against my lips" (quoted in Freud 1953–74, 11:82). Freud acknowledges that this memory evokes breast-feeding – in Kleinian terms, this monstrous bird would represent the worst of all bad breasts – but Freud goes on to phallicize the vulture, insisting that its tail represents the penis that the mother does not possess. Consequently the vulture attack is understood as a fellatio fantasy, symptomatic of Leonardo's passive homosexual desires. Through this interpretation, the vulture is turned into a human being, the female turned into a male, while the vulture – qua vulture – recedes from view, exorcised by these symbolic metamorphoses – as if psychoanalysis were a hermeneutic form of pest control.

By contrast, Freud's case history of his female patient Dora features no tormenting beasts, except for those in human form. To track down theriophobes among Freud's female patients, it is necessary to go back to the pre-psychoanalytic *Studies in Hysteria*. Here Josef Breuer's patient Anna O refuses water after seeing a dog drink from a glass, despite suffering "tormenting thirst" (Freud 1953–74, 2:34–35). Furthermore Freud's hysteric patient Frau Emmy von N suffers from a veritable *Tiergarten* of animal hallucinations.[7] Animals attack her in her dreams: "The legs and arms of the chairs were all turned into snakes; a monster with a vulture's beak was tearing and eating at her all over her body; other wild animals leapt upon her, etc." (Freud 1953–74, 2:62). This telltale "etcetera" suggests that Emmy's "attacks of zoöpsia [animal hallucinations]" have something in common with Schreber's miracled animals, those swarming persecutors whose multiplicity bespeaks the disintegration of the self (1953–74, 2:63). Yet Emmy's animals come both in single spies and in battalions; she remembers one occasion on a walk when a single toad jumped out at her; on a subsequent walk, the entire path was writhing with toads (1953–74, 2:62, 74). At another time an "enormous mouse" whisked across her hand – a hand that she was often loath to extend to other people lest it should turn into a dreadful animal, "as had so often happened" (1953–74, 2:72, 74).[8] On a further occasion she encountered a mischief of mice (to enlist a mouse-dedicated collective noun) sitting on the branches of a tree (1953–74, 2:72): a vision that looks forward to the Wolf Man's famous dream about the wolf-infested walnut tree.[9] Evidently Emmy is afraid of vermin, but her fears are not fixated on a single species; it is the animal's capacity for sudden ambush and intrusion that alarms her, along with its propensity to pullulate. One morning, for instance, while taking her prescribed bran bath, Emmy begins to scream, having mistaken the bran for wriggling worms (1953–74, 2:72–73).

At this early stage of his career, Freud attempts to relieve Emmy's symptoms with hypnosis, the technique pioneered by Charcot and Breuer in the treatment of hysteria. During her hypnotic trances, Freud asks Emmy to tell him "more animal stories," attempting to dissipate her fears by tracing them back to their traumatic origins (1953–74, 2:74). As in a demonic exorcism, each of these animals has to be invoked in order to be fumigated from the psyche. In the course of the treatment, Freud is obliged to "wipe out" a colorful assortment of species, including bulls, rats, dogs, lizards, horses, bats, leeches, and American Indians dressed up as animals (see, for example, 2:59, 74n2, 78).[10] What he finds is that these pests come back unless the patient makes a full confession of every memory associated with the animal in question. These recovered memories, however, often sound as delusional as Emmy's hallucinations. For instance, the patient associates her horrifying vision in the bath with a pretty pincushion, stuffed with bran, which had been given to her as a present, but turned out to be crawling with worms. "(A hallucination? Perhaps a fact)" – Freud parenthetically interpolates (1953–74, 2:74). In another implausible memory, Emmy explains "why the small animals she saw grew so enormous" by recalling a theatrical performance where a gigantic lizard had appeared on stage (1953–74, 2:63). Asked by Freud why she is so easily frightened, Emmy confesses that when she was 5 years old her siblings used to pummel her with dead animals (1953–74, 2:52).

It is likely that an older, more suspicious Freud would have treated these associations as fantasies or screen memories, designed to cover up unconscious conflicts. In this pre-psychoanalytic case history, however, Freud attributes Emmy's fears to "the primary phobias of human beings," those aroused by the "vermin of which Mephistopheles boasted himself master" in Goethe's *Faust*:

> The lord of rats and eke of mice,
> Of flies and bedbugs, frogs and lice.

Although Freud goes on to argue that these primal phobias have been reinforced by "traumatic events" in Emmy's life, he rarely questions the accuracy of her memory (1953–74, 2:87). Nor has he yet developed a theory of the transference that might account for the extravagance of Emma's "animal stories." Today such a patient might be sectioned, or at least prescribed a regimen of antipsychotics. But Freud's view that her delusions were relatively mild may have been closer to the mark, since it is likely that Emmy was trying to captivate her handsome young hypnotist: "She entertained me, in an apparently quite normal state, with gruesome stories about animals," Freud reports (1953–74, 2:51). In Emmy's case, the enticements to transference – not to mention countertransference – must have been intense, given that Freud's treatment involved both mesmerism and massage.[11]

Freud's footnotes to this case history, written at later dates, indicate dissatisfaction with his early methods, particularly his failure to uncover the symbolic import of his patient's fantasia (see, for example, 2:62n2). In contrast to later psychoanalytic cases, such as the Rat Man and the Wolf Man, none of Emmy's animals is phallicized by Freud – not even the small animals that grow enormous. Nor are these creatures "Oedipalized" or identified with members of the patient's family, partly because Freud has not yet developed the theories that would authorize such imputations. But it's also possible that Emmy's animals resist symbolic exegesis. Their sheer proliferation makes it difficult to see them as one-to-one equivalents for something else. One toad may represent the father but a swarm of toads exceeds this correspondence; similarly one worm may represent the penis but this equation fails to account for the seething vermicelli of Emmy's bath. To counter this objection, Freud would probably invoke "the technical rule according to which a multiplication of penis symbols signifies castration," which he elsewhere adduces to explain the nest of snakes on the Medusa's head (1953–74, 18:273). In Emmy's case history, however, Freud draws no such inferences, and although castration terror may have fueled this patient's animal delusions, their zoological fecundity challenges Freud's "technical rule." Emmy's animals are too prolific, various, and startling to be reduced to the castration complex; their tendency to pounce suggests a traumatic violation, while their capacity to multiply resembles Schreber's talking birds and swarming insects, redolent of psychic fragmentation.

It is these swarms and multiplicities, according to Deleuze and Guattari, that the theory of the Oedipus complex is designed to stifle. Through Oedipalization, the many-headed monsters of Schreber's deliria are condensed into a single father-figure, an impoverishment similar to that which Freud describes in *Moses and Monotheism*, whereby the multitudinous spirits of the pagan world were swallowed up into a single patriarchal godhead. To resist this impoverishment, Deleuze and Guattari adopt Schreber's phantasmagoria as the basis of their anti-Oedipal philosophy. Most of their key terms, such as "becoming-woman" and "the body-without-organs," along with "multiplicities" and "intensities" (comparable to Schreber's "rays"), come from the pages of *Memoirs of My Nervous Illness*.

In a much-cited passage of *A Thousand Plateaus*, Deleuze and Guattari claim that psychoanalysis understands only "individuated animals, family pets, sentimental, Oedipal animals each with its own petty history, 'my' cat, 'my' dog." Against this view, the authors insist that "every animal is fundamentally a pack, a band" (2004, 264–65). The lone wolf is a contradiction in terms; wolves always form a "rhizomatic multiplicity" (2004, 37), comparable to the "jeunes filles en fleurs" that Proust's narrator encounters at the Balbec seaside, the "little band" of girls that condenses into Albertine, only to break apart in the kaleidoscope of Albertines invented by her lies (Proust 2005). According to Deleuze and Guattari, Freud constantly brushes up against such bands and prides and drifts and shoals and plumps and murmurations (the English language is curiously rich in collective nouns for animals), such as the "five or six" wolves in the Wolf Man's dream, or the Rat Man's teeming rat-currency. To these well-known examples might be added Anna O, who mistakes her fingers for writhing snakes, together with Emmy von N's verminous hallucinations, or the miracled insects of Schreber's deliria. Deleuze and Guattari object that psychoanalysis ignores the plurality of these assemblages, reducing the wolf pack, for example, to "the Oedipalized wolf or dog, the castrated-castrating daddy-wolf, the dog in the kennel, the analyst's bow-wow" (2004, 32; see also Genosko 1993, 605, 613–17).

Although there's much to be said for Deleuze and Guattari's spirited critique of Freud, I would argue that they overlook the rhizomes of *intertextuality* out of which the phobic animal arises like a mushroom out of its mycelium. As Freud observes in the case history of the Wolf Man, "the anxiety-animal was not an object easily accessible to observation . . . but was known to [the patient] only from stories and picture-books" (1953–74, 17:32). Thus the multiplicity that Deleuze and Guattari neglect is the spotty surface of the written page, a surface comparable to their own description of the Wolf Man's pimpled nose, its skin "prickling with bumps and pustules, and . . . dwarfish black heads emerging from pores grimacing and abominable," a "field of tiny rhinoceros horns" where "little scars in the pores, little ruts in the scar tissue, ceaselessly dance, grow, and diminish"; a "field of anuses" or "flying vaginas" (2004, 33, 30, 34, 36).

I'll return to the pockmarked page at the end of this chapter, but first I want to focus on the nose, an organ that plays a crucial role in Freud's theory of the rise of man, and the concomitant expulsion of the inhuman. Recently I wrote a paper called "Noses and Monotheism" that focuses on two notorious footnotes to *Civilization and Its Discontents* (Ellmann 2010).[12] In these footnotes Freud, adopting Darwin's view that the cultural dominance of vision stems from "man's adoption of an upright posture," argues that the erect male forfeited the sexual stimulus of scent, which is best appreciated on all fours, in favor of the vertical stimulus of vision. Standing upright exposed the genitals to view, requiring them to be protected and concealed. As a result of this verticality, the periodic sexual stimulus of smell was subordinated to the perpetual stimulus of sight (Darwin 1871, 17–18; Freud 1953–74, 21:99n1). According to Freud, "the deepest root of the sexual repression that advances along with civilization is the organic defence of the new form of life achieved with man's erect gait against his earlier animal existence" (1953–74, 21:106n3). In Tennyson's words, "Move upward, working out the beast, / And let the ape and tiger die" (*In Memoriam* CXVIII).

One consequence of this "move upward" is the taboo against menstruation; another is a general depreciation of the sense of smell, extending to an embargo against all bodily odors. Although Freud doesn't say so in these footnotes, it could be argued that this evolutionary process is recapitulated in childhood when the infant learns to walk, rising from a crawling to an upright posture. In the same period of infancy, toilet training reinforces the denigration of the world of odors by association with the taboo smell of excrement.

Freud also proposes that this process of repression and defense "is repeated on another level when the gods of a superseded period of civilization turn into demons" (1953–74, 21:99n1). The example he probably has in mind is the Furies, relics of a prior matriarchal order suppressed by the cult of Apollo. This suppression laid the foundations of monotheism, a development attributed by Freud in *Moses and Monotheism* to the rise of imperialism in the ancient world, which established the hierarchy of oneness over multiplicity by banishing the plural spirits of the pagan universe. This argument implies a chain of equivalences whereby the human = standing upright = vision = patriarchy = monotheism = oneness = separation = homogeneity, as opposed to the subordinate chain in which the animal = horizontality = smell = matriarchy = polytheism = multiplicity = merger = heterogeneity.

As David Howes (1999) has pointed out, the idea that olfaction is animal whereas vision is human, or that men look whereas women smell, is based on ideology rather than biology. Furthermore Freud's denial of nasality may be traced back to his falling out with Wilhelm Fliess, their friendship having come to grief over a nose. In a book entitled *The Relationship between the Nose and the Female Sexual Organs* (1897), Fliess published his notorious theory that the nose contains genital spots, which swell up with sexual substances that course around the body in periods of twenty-three days for men and twenty-eight days for women. Masturbation, condoms, and coitus interruptus cause these substances to circulate too furiously, producing hysterical disorders. The only permanent cure for hysteria therefore consists of an operation on the turbinate bones on the nose, reinforced by abstention from masturbation.

Freud was sufficiently convinced by Fliess' theory of the naso-genital relationship to become obsessed with his own nose, filling his letters to Fliess with details of its inflammation and discharge. He also embraced Fliess' "laws of periodicity" to the extent that he worried himself sick about the forecast date of his own death, and other "critical periods" predicted by Fliess' numerological calculations. In 1895 Freud arranged for Fliess to perform his trademark nasal operation on Emma Eckstein, a patient suffering from stomach pains and menstrual problems that Freud attributed to excessive masturbation. Some days after the operation the patient suffered a massive nasal hemorrhage, filling two bowls with pus, and her nose began to emit a fetid odor. The wound continued to hemorrhage until another specialist pulled out of her nose a long string of purulent gauze, which Fliess, in an egregious act of medical negligence, had forgotten to remove (Appignanesi and Forrester 2000, 119–20).

This episode lurks behind Freud's famous dream of "Irma's Injection," with its strange scene of Freud and another doctor "Otto" gazing down a female patient's throat in a laryngeal/gynecological examination. The Eckstein debacle compelled Freud to detach himself from Fliess and to reject his collaborator's fanciful theories about periodicity and the nasal etiology of hysteria. The two famous footnotes to *Civilization and Its Discontents*, which connect the rise of man to the suppression of the nasal and the periodic, project onto the evolution of the human species Freud's own rejection of Fliess' naso-genital hypothesis.

***

It is appropriate that these footnotes, which discuss the suppression of the prone, should be relegated to the lower regions of the page in the

Standard Edition of Freud's works. Their position means that Freud's references to the animal, the horizontal, and the naso-genital origins of sexuality literally underlie the text, much as the renounced four-footedness of humankind supposedly underlies the edifice of civilization. These textual dynamics of the upright and the prone also play a crucial part in the case history of the Wolf Man. It is important that this patient's wolf-phobia was drawn from literature, not from life, specifically from a picture of an upright wolf, rather than a living, horizontal animal. Found in a book of fairy-tales, this illustration showed a wolf standing up on his hind legs, thereby assuming the erect posture attributed by Freud and Darwin to the rise of man from his four-footed origins. The Wolf Man's sister Anna used to flash this illustration at her little brother in order to provoke his screams.

The obvious inference is that the wolf represents the phallus erect. Freud argues that the picture also reactivated memories of the primal scene, in which the upright father penetrated the prostrate mother from behind in animal fashion (*a tergo more ferarum*). Spectacular though it is, this interpretation overlooks the bookish nature of this wolf, whose terror cannot be dissociated from its literary context. What scares the child is not the animal per se, but the drawing where the vertical wolf looms up out of the horizontal page, a page tilted upright by his naughty sister. What I'm suggesting, then, is that the Wolf Man is afraid of literature, of the capacity of drawn or written marks to rise up from the page as monsters. If the uncanny (in Freud's words) is that which should have remained hidden but which has come to light, the phobic wolf stands for everything that should have remained horizontal but which has risen upright – the human animal, the printed word, the illustrated page.

At this point I'd like to compare the dynamics of the upright and the prone in Freud to those explored by Michael Fried in his study of the painter Thomas Eakins and the writer Stephen Crane. In this study, *Realism, Writing, Disfiguration* (1987), Fried argues that painting and writing are associated with the upright and the prone, respectively. In Eakins' painting *The Gross Clinic* (1875), the master-surgeon stands upright, holding a gory scalpel like a paintbrush between his blood-stained fingers, while other surgeons look down at a prostrate body, the principal assistant probing an open wound. Fried proposes that the master-surgeon could be seen as a double of the painter, standing upright, while his assistant, who inscribes the flattened body with his blade, emblematizes the horizontal arts of drawing and writing. For this reason the painting could be seen either as an effort of containment – in which the vertical canvas incorporates drawing and writing, thereby overcoming the horizontality of both those arts – or as the failure of containment, since images of writing and drawing infiltrate the painting, adulterating the domain of verticality. Fried then compares Eakins' painting to Stephen Crane's writing, arguing that Crane's recurrent images of upturned faces, staring blankly or disfigured, reflect the blank page staring upwards and disfigured by the inky scalpel of the pen (Fried 1987, 13, 81, 93–101).

To retrace Fried's detailed and compelling argument would require more than my allotted space. But it's worth considering how Fried's case for the correspondence between writing and the horizontal bears on Freud's conception of the horizontal origins of humankind. This primordial horizontality is never fully overcome: the riddle of the sphinx reminds us that man is the animal that walks with four feet in the morning, two in the afternoon, and three in the evening, so that his verticality is restricted to the hours between noon and dusk. Furthermore every human infant has to re-enact the struggle of its ancestors by renouncing a crawling for an upright posture, thus foregoing the stability of hands and knees for the tottering state of bipedalism. Even adults, supposedly erect, spend much of their existence lying down in semi- if not fully recumbent postures. In death, as in sleep, the human body is usually laid out in a supine pose (apart from some archaic societies in which warriors were buried upright), which means that the horizontal is associated with mortality. It's also associated, as Freud implies, with the passive position in sexual intercourse, whether *more ferarum* or flat on one's back.

Examples could be multiplied, but it's clear that the human species – like the supposedly vertical phallus – is much more often down than up. As soon as human beings rose up on their hind legs, they also condemned themselves to falling down. Their upright stance is sabotaged by infancy, old age, and constitutional infirmity, much as the transcendence associated with the realm of speech is constantly subverted by the prostrate materiality of writing. We speak with our noses in the air, but we write with our noses pointing downwards to the pitted, pockmarked, spotted page.

Agamben emphasizes that the Latin etymology of infancy denotes the inability to speak. Yet infancy also implies the inability to walk or stand upright, an inability enshrined in Oedipus' name, which means swell-foot. If writing, like infancy, is associated with the speechless and the prostrate, this suggests that writing could be understood as the infancy of speech – a provocative suggestion, since we usually think of speech as the infancy of writing. Mute and flat – like the prostrate, speechless infant – writing could be seen as the horizontal ghost that haunts the vertical domain of speech, just as the prostrate body in Eakins' *The Gross Clinic* haunts the vertical domain of painting.

To pursue this connection between writing and prostration it's instructive to turn Samuel Beckett's writing. For the cripples and geriatrics who populate these works are constantly defeated in their struggle to keep up the proud stance of *Homo erectus*. At best they walk on three legs in the evening, supported by canes or comparable prostheses; at worst they resort to rolling in the muck, like the nameless creatures slithering in primeval slime in *How It Is* (1964 [1961]). These fables of limping and paralysis may also be understood as allegories of writing, in which crutches and walking-sticks double for writing implements: "I shall not say this again, when not mentioned my stick is in my hand, as I go along," says the writer in *From an Abandoned Work* (Beckett 1995, 161). Similarly, *How It Is* may be interpreted as "the crawling slog across the lines of an exercise book," as Phil Baker (1997, 166) has observed. Hunched or prone, Beckett's hobbling, crawling scriptors imply that writing entails the collapse of verticality. Far from upright, these derelicts end up toeless, legless, or floundering on the quaking sod, as if writing had reduced them to the horizontal state of animality. The last words of *The Unnamable* – "I can't go on, I'll go on" – reveal that going on, impossible as it may be, is more conceivable than going *up* (Beckett 2009, 407).

I've already discussed Deleuze and Guattari's view that psychoanalysis Oedipalizes animals by reducing the infinite variety of fauna to the nuclear family. In denying multiplicity to animals, psychoanalysis may also be attempting to repress the horizontality of writing, the swarming letters of the pimpled page, or the footnotes that rise up against the body of the text, subverting the hierarchies of above and below, before and after. This horizontality aligns writing with the debased chain of equivalences suggested by the footnotes to *Civilization and Its Discontents*, in which the animal = horizontality = smell = matriarchy = polytheism = multiplicity = merger = heterogeneity.

This chain in turn suggests that writing is akin to animality. This kinship is not so unlikely as it seems if we consider that writing is a means of making tracks, inscribing prints – an activity we share with many of our prone and horizontal ancestors.[13] Although writing is usually seen as exclusive to the human species, indeed the very pinnacle of human exceptionalism, it is possible that writing, rather than the instincts, is the place to look for the persistence of the animal in humankind.

Notes

1 Other dog encounters occur on pp. 98, 148. Freud offered H.D. one of Jofi's puppies, a gift eventually refused but causing considerable embarrassment for both the poet and her partner Bryher, whose pet name was Dog (H.D.'s was Cat). See Friedman (2002, 200, 230, 235, 235n15, 31) and Sarah Jackson (2010).

2 The fourth chapter of Freud's *Totem and Taboo* (1913) is entitled "The Return of Totemism in Childhood" (1953–74, 13:100–61). See also Charles Darwin's *The Descent of Man* (1871, 17–18) and Freud's *Civilization and Its Discontents* (1953–74, 21:99n1).

3 See, for example, Bernstein (2004).

4 The following discussion of Laplanche is indebted to Nicholas Ray's (2012) skillful analysis.

5 While Laplanche's insistence on the intersubjective dimension of the unconscious could be seen as another form of human exceptionalism, Nicholas Ray (2012, 63) makes the convincing argument that the "anthropo-decentrism of Laplanche's work is not simply a reconfigured humanism, since it is oriented toward resisting at the level of formal theory those constitutive myths of the animal-in-man which, beyond their superficial audacity, function primarily to insulate the category of the human."

6 See Deuteronomy 14:19: "And every creeping thing that flieth *is* unclean unto you: they shall not be eaten."

7 This patient's real name was Fanny Moser (see Appignanesi and Forrester 2000, 91–103).

8 Breuer reports that Anna O, when attending her father's deathbed, suffered from a similar hallucination that her fingers had turned into snakes (Freud 1953–74, 2:38).

9 See also Schreber (2000, 80): "At times cats with glowing eyes appeared on the trees of the Asylum's garden."

10 Freud admits that he overdid this wiping out, leaving his patient with troublesome amnesias involving "the most important moments of her life" (1953–74, 2:61n1).

11 To be precise, the regimen consisted of "warm baths, massage twice a day, and hypnotic suggestion" (Freud 1953–74, 2:51).

12 The title was a gift from the late Eve Kosofsky Sedgwick.

13 Derrida (2008, 33) makes a similar point.

References

Agamben, Giorgio. 1993 [1978]. *Infancy and History: The Destruction of Experience*, trans. Liz Heron. London: Verso.

Agamben, Giorgio. 1999. *Remnants of Auschwitz: The Witness and the Archive*, trans. Daniel Heller-Roazen. New York: Zone Books.

Agamben, Giorgio. 2004. *The Open: Man and Animal*, trans. Kevin Attell. Stanford: Stanford University Press.

Appignanesi, Lisa, and John Forrester. 2000. *Freud's Women*. London: Penguin.

Baker, Phil. 1997. *Beckett and the Mythology of Psychoanalysis*. New York: St. Martin's Press.

Barovick, Harriet. 1999. "When Fido Gets Phobic." *Time*, February 1. http://www.time.com/time/magazine/article/0,9171,990113,00.html. Accessed November 30, 2013.

Beckett, Samuel. 1995. *The Complete Short Prose, 1929–1989*, ed. S.E. Gontarski. New York: Grove Press.

Beckett, Samuel. 2009. *Three Novels*. New York: Grove Press.

Bernstein, J.M. 2004. "Bare Life, Bearing Witness: Auschwitz and the Pornography of Horror." *Parallax*, 10, no. 1: 2–16.

Coren, Stanley, and Janet Walker. 1997. *What Do Dogs Know?* New York: Simon & Schuster.

Darwin, Charles. 1871. *The Descent of Man*. London: John Murray.

Deleuze, Gilles, and Félix Guattari. 2004. *A Thousand Plateaus: Capitalism and Schizophrenia*, trans. Brian Massumi. London: Continuum.

Derrida, Jacques. 2008. *The Animal That Therefore I Am*, ed. Marie-Louis Mallet, trans. David Wills. New York: Fordham University Press.

Derrida, Jacques. 2009. *The Beast and the Sovereign*, vol. 1, ed. Michel Lisse, Marie-Louise Mallet, and Ginette Michaud, trans. Geoffrey Bennington. Chicago: University of Chicago Press.

DiCenso, James J. 1999. *The Other Freud: Religion, Culture and Psychoanalysis*. London: Routledge.

Ellmann, Maud. 2010 "Noses and Monotheism." In *Back to the Future: A Festschrift for Tadhg Foley*, ed. Maureen O'Connor, 165–76. London: Peter Lang.

Freud, Sigmund. 1953–74. *The Standard Edition of the Complete Psychological Works of Sigmund Freud*, 24 vols., ed. James Strachey, with the assistance of Anna Freud, Alix Strachey, and Alan Tyson, trans. James Strachey. London: Hogarth Press.

Fried, Michael. 1987. *Realism, Writing, Disfiguration: On Thomas Eakins and Stephen Crane*. Chicago: University of Chicago Press.

Friedman, Susan Stanford, ed. 2002. *Analyzing Freud: Letters of H.D., Bryher, and Their Circle*. New York: New Directions.

Gay, Peter. 1988. *Freud: A Life for our Time*. New York: Norton.

Genosko, Gary. 1993. "Freud's Bestiary: How Does Psychoanalysis Treat Animals?" *Psychoanalytic Review*, 80: 603–32.

Grinker, Roy R., Jr. 2001. "My Father's Analysis with Sigmund Freud." *Annual of Psychoanalysis*, 29: 35–47.

H.D. 1985. *Tribute to Freud: Writing on the Wall and Advent*. Manchester: Carcanet.

Howes, David. 1999. "Freud's Nose: The Repression of Nasality and the Origin of Psychoanalytic Theory." In *Nose Book: Representations of the Nose in Literature and the Arts*, ed. Victoria de Rijke, Lene Østermark-Johansen, and Helen Thomas, 265–82. London: Middlesex University Press.

Jackson, Sarah. 2010. "Touching Freud's Dog: H.D.'s Tactile Poetics." *Angelaki*, 15, no. 2: 187–201.

Klein, Melanie. 1998. *Narrative of a Child Analysis*. London: Vintage.

Lacan, Jacques. 1961. "Seminar 3." In *The Seminar of Jacques Lacan, IX: Identification 1961–1962*, trans. Cormac Gallagher. http://www.valas.fr/IMG/pdf/THE-SEMINAR-OF-JACQUES-LACAN-IX_identification.pdf. Accessed November 30, 2013.

Lacan, Jacques. 1998. *The Seminar of Jacques Lacan*, Book XX: *Encore, On Feminine Sexuality, The Limits of Love and Knowledge*, ed. Jacques-Alain Miller, trans. Bruce Fink. New York: Norton.

Lacan, Jacques. 2006. *Écrits: The First Complete Edition in English*, trans. Bruce Fink. New York: Norton.

Levi, Primo. 1989. *The Drowned and the Saved*, trans. Raymond Rosenthal. New York: Random House.

Marder, Elissa. 2010. "The Sexual Animal and the Primal Scene." In *Sexuality and Psychoanalysis: Philosophical Criticisms*, ed. Jens De Vleminck and Eran Dorfman, 121–37. Leuven: Leuven University Press.

Marrett, R.R. 1920. "Psycho-Analysis and the Savage." *Athenaeum*, 4685: 205–6.

MIT News. 2001. "Animals Have Complex Dreams, MIT Researcher Proves." *MIT News*, January 24. http://web.mit.edu/newsoffice/2001/dreaming.html. Accessed November 30, 2013.

Oliver, Kelly. 2009. *Animal Lessons: How They Teach Us to be Human*. New York: Columbia.

Proust, Marcel. 2005. *Within a Budding Grove*, trans. C. K. Scott Moncrieff. Adelaide: eBooks@Adelaide. http://ebooks.adelaide.edu.au/p/proust/marcel/p96w/. Accessed November 30, 2013.

Ray, Nicholas. 2012. "Psychoanalysis and 'The Animal': A Reading of the Metapsychology of Jean Laplanche." *Journal for Critical Animal Studies*, 10, no. 1: 40–66.

Schreber, Daniel Paul. 2000. *Memoirs of My Nervous Illness*, trans. Ida Macalpine and Richard A. Hunter. New York: New York Review Books.

Stein, Gertrude. 1984. *Look at Me Now and Here I Am: Writings and Lectures 1909–45*, ed. Patricia Meyerowitz. Harmondsworth: Penguin.

Chapter 19

On the Right to Sleep, Perchance to Dream

Ranjana Khanna

Insomnia

In 2005, the UK-based chapter of the Red Cross commissioned an art exhibition entitled *Insomnia* for its Refugee Week. The exhibition took its name from a concept found in the work of philosopher Emmanuel Levinas, who was attempting to understand the relationship between the inside and the outside of hospitality, human interactivity, alterity, and what it is that keeps us awake when in principle we desire to sleep. The exhibition provides a starting point to discuss philosophies of hospitality as they relate to asylums, human and state "right," repose or sleep, agitation or risk, and the way in which we understand and experience otherness psychoanalytically and otherwise.

The organizers of the conference presented sound, photography, and sculptural installations, as well as video art and a short film that addressed spatial relations through cinematic space, sculptural occupation of space, and installations. The works in the 2005 Red Cross exhibit did not overtly represent recognizable images of refugees.[1] Anna Sherbany's durational video piece, for example, depicts a bed, and then a woman lying in it, sleeping and not sleeping, restless, and alternately taking up no space and then lots of space. It is unclear in the video if

A Concise Companion to Psychoanalysis, Literature, and Culture, First Edition.
Edited by Laura Marcus and Ankhi Mukherjee.

she is alone in the bed, though she seems to be at least physically, as the sheets form their own patterns around her as she moves and occupies space. Hers is the most literal of the renditions of the word "Insomnia" that gave the exhibition its title.

The exhibition, as I have said, took its title from the twentieth-century Lithuanian Jewish philosopher Emmanuel Levinas, who first started writing on the topic of "Insomnia" when he was in a forced labor camp during World War II, a war in which his family in Lithuania was killed. His book *Existence and Existents* hails from this moment. "Insomnia," "when sleep evades our appeal," he writes, manifests "[t]he impossibility of rending the invading, inevitable, and anonymous rustling of existence" (Levinas 2001, 61). Insomnia, which holds the subject hostage in sleeplessness, is an attack on the consciousness of the subject and its ability to be unconscious or asleep. Some otherness grips the subject and dissolves it. Insomnia is, then, an attack on being by something beyond the control of being. It is a resistance to the giving up of consciousness in sleep, and yet it does not allow for full consciousness.

Besides using the language of hostage-taking, Levinas posits insomnia in relation to anonymity and placelessness. The otherness to which one becomes subject in insomnia does not have an identity and is not situated, but it has a menacing existence that cannot be described; it is, as Levinas puts it, "a dissipation of personages" (2001, 63). If it could be described, it would in principle be staging a person, and insomnia calls for something beyond that – something that is inhuman. Wakefulness is not experienced by a subject, it dissolves subjective life, and in dissolving it, suggests another register of experience that does not happen to "anyone."

For Levinas, sleep is a suspension of physical and psychic activity, one that psychoanalysis might understand as a psychic *location*:

> The summoning of sleep occurs in the act of lying down. To lie down is exactly to limit existence to a place, to position.
>
> A place is not an indifferent "somewhere," but a base, a condition. Of course we ordinarily understand our localization as that of a body situated just anywhere. That is because the positive relationship with a place which we maintain in sleep is masked by our relations with things. Then only the concrete determinations of the surroundings, of the setting, and the ties of habit and of history give an individual character to a place which has become our home [*le chez-soi*], our hometown, our homeland, the world. When detached from its atmosphere, localization is generally taken to be presence in an abstract extension, like that of a

> star in the infinity of space. Sleep reestablishes a relationship with a place qua base. In lying down, in curling up in a corner to sleep, we abandon ourselves to a place; qua base it becomes our refuge. Then all our work of being consists in resting. Sleep is like entering into contact with the protective forces of a place; to seek after sleep is to gropingly seek after that contact. When one wakes up one finds oneself shut up in one's immobility like an egg in its shell. This surrender to a base which also offers refuge constitutes sleep, in which being, without being destroyed, is suspended.
>
> (Levinas, 2001, 66–67)

Sleep, for Levinas, is emblematic of the safety and security of a place of refuge we understand as home. The centrality of being linked to place, and linked to a place one begins to understand as home and as refuge, presents an idea of the solidity of the subject that is constituted through an idea of belonging. For Levinas, there is no consciousness, then, without attachment to a place or refuge, where one can first have consciousness, and then, in repose, have sleep.

Levinas resists this idea of belonging linked to being as the foundational ontological basis of philosophy. He seeks rather to put, in the place of ontology – or a theory of being – a model of ethics understood as a relation to otherness, or a relation of hospitality. In other words, the modern form of Being and subjecthood is a problem because it acknowledges inadequately how it assumes the importance of belonging to a place. Insomnia, for him, becomes one way of understanding this restlessness in relation to something other than Being that imposes itself on the subject, undoing it, and taking it hostage, forcing it into wakefulness when it would rather sleep. Rather than acquiring the self-same consolidation of conscious Being through refuge such that Being may be suspended in repose, then, Levinas provides a model for thinking relationally, less through an idea of homeland than through one of hostage formation or occupation by the unknown at the border between being awake and being asleep. In the case of insomnia, this occupation is a restlessness that seems to come from elsewhere. It is a restlessness that cannot be assimilated into consciousness or into the suspension of consciousness – i.e. sleep.

If we accept Levinas' reading, the right to sleep, then, is the right to refuge, to a base, to a place, to home, homeland, or to a global or astral location from which one may dream. It coincides also with the right to consciousness or thought that has a location or at least a point of departure. This tight connection between Being and belonging, and belonging and property in the modern period is one of the obstacles to hospitality. Insomnia, precisely, disrupts consciousness, subjectivity, and home by an unrecognizable and anonymous intrusion that may indeed manifest itself as emotion, delirium, madness, or the absence of a master in control of consciousness. Insomnia is the arc through which Levinas establishes a notion of an affective pre-consciousness opened by the other.

Levinas' theory of insomnia would appear to demand a psychoanalytic reading. However, Levinas himself was extremely skeptical of psychoanalysis, and indeed thought of himself as a non-psychoanalytic thinker as he suggests in his paper on dreams – "Quelques réflexions talmudiques sur le rêve" – for the 1980 conference in Montpellier which posed the question, "La psychanalyse est-elle une histoire juive?" (Levinas 1981). In *Entre Nous*, he would criticize psychoanalysis for being unable to attend to notions of alterity that have not already been previously conceived within a certain secular post-Enlightenment setting mixed with a nostalgic reliance on the fabular:

> Questioning the position of the thinker suggests a psychoanalysis. Psychoanalysis is, in its philosophical essence, the end point of rationalism: it places the same demands on reflection that reflection placed on naively thinking thought. The non-philosophical end result of psychoanalysis consists in a predilection for some fundamental, but elementary fables – the libido, sadism, or masochism, the Oedipus complex, repression of the origin, aggressivity – which, incomprehensibly, alone would be unequivocal, alone in not translating (or masking or symbolizing) a reality more profound than themselves: the end terms of psychological intelligibility.
>
> (Levinas 2006, 27)

In its affinity with history, psychoanalysis "culminate(s) with the destruction of the *I*" (Levinas 2006, 21). It is nonetheless in affinity with the topic of desubjectivation that psychoanalysis would seem to have something to offer to Levinas' model, and it is indeed in the theory of dreams and sleep that Levinas understood Freud to have a talmudic background (Levinas 1981).[2] For Freud, however, we can understand this taking hostage – and the encounter with the foreign – in relation to the feminine, on the one hand, and trauma on the other.

Freud offers at least two versions of the function of the dream in sleep. Most famously, in *The Interpretation of Dreams*, "Dreams are the guardians of sleep and not its disturbers" (Freud 1953–74, 4:233). The necessity of sleep makes dreams not only wish-fulfillments of sleep itself, but also wish-fulfillments of the dreaming subject's adult life.

However, in addition, one can find at moments in *The Interpretation of Dreams*, and also later in the war neurosis text *Beyond the Pleasure Principle*, a version of dream that is more distantly related to wish-fulfillment – the dream that causes a breakdown in sleep – a dream resulting in wakefulness:

> The study of dreams may be considered the most trustworthy method of investigating deep mental processes. Now dreams occurring in traumatic neuroses have the characteristic of repeatedly bringing the patient back into the situation of his accident, a situation from which he wakes up in another fright. This astonishes people far too little. They think the fact that the traumatic experience is constantly forcing itself upon the patient even in his sleep is a proof of the strength of that experience: the patient is, as one might say, fixated to his trauma. Fixations to the experience which started the illness have long been familiar to us in hysteria. Breuer and Freud declared in 1893 that "hysterics suffer mainly from reminiscences". In the war neuroses, too, observers like Ferenczi and Simmel have been able to explain certain motor symptoms by fixation to the moment at which the trauma occurred.
>
> I am not aware, however, that patients suffering from traumatic neurosis are much occupied in their waking lives with memories of their accident. Perhaps they are more concerned with *not* thinking of it. Anyone who accepts it as something self-evident that their dreams should put them back at night into the situation that caused them to fall ill has misunderstood the nature of dreams. It would be more in harmony with their nature if they showed the patient pictures from his healthy past or of the cure for which he hopes. If we are not to be shaken in our belief in the wish-fulfilling tenor of dreams by the dreams of traumatic neurotics, we still have one resource open to us: we may argue that the function of dreaming, like so much else, is upset in this condition and diverted from its purposes, or we may be driven to reflect on the mysterious masochistic trends of the ego.
>
> (Freud 1953–74, 18:13–14)

Freud would go on to formulate the death drive and its manifestation in repetition such that it becomes clear that traumatic repetition in dreaming that recalls, in the example, an accident, can lead to wakefulness – "he wakes up in another fright" (Freud 1953–74, 18:13) In this instance, it appears that dreams are far from the guardians of sleep as they appear to be in *The Interpretation of Dreams*, which, as Jacqueline Rose (2003) has noted, is itself an extremely ambiguous text on the topic of sleep.

Bertram Lewin, writing on Freud's dream theory in relation to wakefulness and insomnia, considers the mechanisms of the wish-fulfillment theory as it pertains to infants. Infants wish first and foremost for sleep, he argues, and this comes after oral satisfaction, most particularly in drinking from the breast. If, in later life, dreams have all the myriad of pre-conscious associations to populate them and then be organized by complex unconscious forces that shape the dream, in infancy the child has very little to bring into the dream other than the "blankness" of the breast. Lewin writes of how this forms a "dream screen" and the blank screen represents the wish to sleep following oral satisfaction and is constituted out of the flattened breast. In infancy, according to Lewin, this form of sleep following oral satisfaction confirms to the child that there is little distinction between mouth and breast, and thus that there is a porous relation between mother and child such that its needs will always be fulfilled: "it reproduces the fusion of the ego and the breast" (Lewin 1946, 420).

Subsequently, the ego may rest during sleep, but there are more complex wishes that interfere with this desire to sleep expressed in the dream content. The ego, now differentiated from the mother, has its own exposure, its own wishes, and therefore its own dream content, which may indeed be projected onto the dream/blank/breast screen but may also conflict with the basic desire to sleep. Indeed, insomnia, as we have also understood from Freud, could even result from the fear of disturbing dreams. But like the peacefulness of an infant's sleep and the oral satisfaction that precedes it at the breast, the retrospective desire for the pre-Oedipal is also a manifestation of the death drive, and potentially represents, in the depressive state, the desire for death itself. As Lewin writes,

> In mania, to cite Rado (1928), the ego fuses with its superego in an intrapsychic reproduction of that fusion with the breast which takes place at nursing. In going to sleep, many have remarked (since M.J. Eisler's original exposition in 1921), the ego repeats a process like the first infantile falling asleep: a fusion with the breast at nursing. Except for the topography and the two mental end states, these remarks are identical: an intrapsychic fusion repeats the baby's psychic experience at the breast and leads in one case to mania, in the other to sleep. Freud, in *Group Psychology and the Ego*, compared sleep and mania because of the disappearance in both of a part of the personality. In sleep the ego disappears, rejoining the id, and comparably in mania the superego disappears, rejoining the ego. Referring to the Saturnalia, carnivals and other feasts, Freud thinks of a possible periodic biological necessity for both types of psychological dedifferentiation.
>
> (Lewin 1946, 419)

The fear of merging with the mother, or the adult's retrospective desire to merge with the site of origin, carries simultaneously the desire to merge and the fear of loss of the ego. This could be a source of insomnia as much as the fear of disturbing dreams, such that wakefulness fears the wish-fulfillment of return to origin. "The wish to sleep is opposed then by other wishes, the unconscious and pre-conscious wakers and disturbers, which with greater or less distortion form the manifest content of later dreams" (Lewin, 1946, 420). Dreams, then, at times, seem to be anything but the guardians of sleep, and often, as in the traumatic dream, muddy the borders between sleep and wakefulness. Freud has shown us that the mind is incredibly active in sleep; Kant has gone so far as to tell us that dreams are what keep us from death. Levinas reframes insomnia as a hostage formation in which the sentient being who transcends consciousness, is plunged into a kind of madness and a kind of traumatism, to use a word Simon Critchley (1999) dwells on to pose the question concerning Levinas' relationship to the psychoanalytic. Over and again, Levinas' language for the transcendence of Being that occurs first through sentience is dark, is a kind of unreason, and a destabilization.

Levinas brings together the psychic, the political, and the sentient to elaborate on his notion of hospitality to the foreign, the feminine, the divine, and the unrecognizable alterity that presents the greatest challenge to hospitality, the entity that is yet to be either anthropomorphized or substantiated into recognizability. Psychoanalysis may understand this as the yet-to-be-realized feminine, and perhaps Levinas' metaphor of the egg gestures toward this: "Sleep is like entering into contact with the protective forces of a place; to seek after sleep is to gropingly seek after that contact. When one wakes up one finds oneself shut up in one's immobility like an egg in its shell. This surrender to a base which also offers refuge constitutes sleep, in which being, without being destroyed, is suspended" (Levinas 2001, 67). Insomnia may, then, be a rejection of the feminine understood as a return to the maternal. It is the ur-repression that shapes further relations to alterity in psychoanalysis, even as a certain psychoanalysis may reject the bond with the maternal as a retrospective repression, acknowledging that the feminine is always already fractured.

Both for Freud and for Levinas there is insight that comes with the territory of not being able to sleep, of being neither bound to place nor to the pre-Oedipal. There is, of course, in literary terms, a long history of insomniacs whose madness, or whose lack of self-mastery in the face of such affective disruption, has led to insight that reveals the tenuous distinction between reason and madness. They are both writers, such as Proust or Kafka, and literary characters, such as Hamlet, or the allegedly mad domestically incarcerated wife in Charlotte Perkins Gilman's *The Yellow Wallpaper*, or, from *1001 Nights*, Scheherazade, her sister Dinarzade, and King Sharyar, who collectively keep the virgins of the kingdom alive through insomniac storytelling and listening. In a stunning short story, Saadat Hasan Manto's "Toba Tek Singh" (1997), we hear of a dilemma facing the governments of India and Pakistan, when, a few years after the partition of India in 1947, the states decided they must redistribute those who were in mental asylums. One such inmate, who dies on the border that has yet to be consolidated and who does not know where he belongs, exposes the farce of belonging and the madness of having to make such a decision. It is rumored that he had not slept for fifteen years.

For psychoanalysis, insomnia is a symptom usually associated with depression, trauma, or the forms of manic behavior one may see in a melancholic. All these symptoms are of the taking hostage of the subject by otherness such that consciousness cannot absorb or assimilate that otherness into itself. The institutions of belonging, that exist in Levinas' terms, are suggestive (within the psychoanalytic terminology) of a displacement of the first home – the encounter with the feminine or the porous relation to the maternal. The blank dream or dream screen could then be displaced off the feminine and rendered within the history of western philosophy as homeland, belonging, or even death.[3]

The idea of a right to sleep in a place of refuge attached to home assumes an ability to reside, and a consciousness undisturbed by insomnia, melancholia, or trauma. Insomnia, then, becomes a means through which Levinas develops his philosophy of ethical relation, and it is a philosophy of hospitality – the opening of oneself to the other with all the risk that is implied in that gesture.

Hospitality

Hospitality, or the response to the stranger, is a concept that has many mythical instantiations in different cultural contexts. Famously, Zeus carries the epithet Xenios, the protector of strangers. The ancient Greek laws of hospitality demanded certain appropriate gestures in relation to hospitality on the part of the guest and on the part of the host. To violate those laws was not a rudeness or a mishap, but it was religious transgression that the gods would punish. We see the consequences in

Homer for the transgressions of hospitality, which may involve, as they do in the case of those who violate the hospitality given at Odysseus' home, for example, fleecing the house, raping the maids, or courting the wife. Odysseus, calling these violators dogs, kills them, and within the logic of the text is quite justified in doing so. The hospitality provided to those of the same class, however, made one vulnerable to such violations, and particularly, as many have pointed out, made women vulnerable as appendages of the host.

Such ancient rights to hospitality form a framework historically for the manner in which asylum is conceived in international law. As we know, the first theorists of international law were philosophers and jurists. Vitoria, in the early sixteenth century, developed a theory of the natural right to travel, reside, trade, use common property, and accept expulsion from the land. He also protected in principle the indigenous right to own property, expel someone from the land, and not accept mistreatment from foreign visitors. As he understood these as natural rights, however, he failed to show how they could be implemented in laws. They were moral demands and obligations rather than legal practices, and even as they in principle protected the rights of the foreigner or the non-citizen, they did not provide any legal or institutional means for demanding or protecting those rights. They also naturalized an idea of belonging to land through property.

Scholars of early international law like Gideon Baker (2013), Georg Cavallar (2011), Anthony Anghie (2007), and Ileana Porras (2012) further elaborate on the manner in which jurist philosophers like Grotius in the early seventeenth century sought to justify morally the exploits of Dutch colonialism through the natural right to hospitality and trade. By the time we reach the writings of Immanuel Kant in his *To Perpetual Peace: A Philosophical Sketch from 1795*, the term cosmopolitan was invoked to temper the sovereign power of states on the one hand, and support the European colonial market economy on the other. This well-known treatise on hospitality across borders articulated these ideas within the contradictory terms thrown up by hospitality – the international command to perform it, and the local sovereignties that protected their right to dismiss or accept the stranger at the gate. In place of the moral structure of natural right, Kant inserted a notion of cosmopolitan right that guided principles for the right to travel, trade, and reside temporarily or permanently in a foreign state; the right to expel; and the right to self-governance. Fundamentally, this right of movement and commerce that he found to be so important would be the backbone of the constitution of laws of peace, a "league of peace," of ideas of friends and enemies (theorized at least since 1650 by Richard Zouch, writing on the *jus inter gentes*), because, as Kant wrote, the "spirit of trade cannot coexist with war." (Kant 1795, 125). In other words, the notions of both belonging and movement across borders were linked to property and trade, the movement of capital; and ideas of the sovereign self also emerged in conjunction with these.

I have elaborated on this trajectory of the philosophies of hospitality in international law in order to situate Levinas in a line of theorists of hospitality who have guided principles on, for example, the right of a foreigner to reside in or to be expelled from a site and to place this discussion in the context of the history and development of international trade and European colonial venture, concepts that were circulating once again during the period when Levinas wrote. Levinas sees the trajectory of his own thought in terms of the history of talmudic philosophy, that stands in contrast to what he sees as the Christianized forms of western philosophy that assume a notion of the subject that is produced through Eurocentric dominance. His radical understanding of hospitality nonetheless highlights the antinomies between natural and cosmopolitan law.

Levinas' notion of an ethics as hospitality toward another stands in contrast to Kantian ideas of ethics and the sovereign subject. The subject, as we have seen in Levinas' description of insomnia, is, by definition, welcoming of the other, opening itself to occupation by the other. This opening to the other is an opening to risk. But it is also, if we follow the logic of sleeplessness, uprooting oneself from an idea of Being linked to place, home, property, or even world. In Jacques Derrida's reading of Levinas' ethics and the subject, we see this idea of hospitality brought to bear on the contemporary situation of the persecution of hostages, such as foreigners with or without papers, exiles, refugees, those without a country, the stateless, and the displaced internally or globally. For Derrida, Levinas' thinking concerning hospitality as the dissolution of the subject as a Being in place leads the way to an alternative international right, the politics of borders, humanitarian or ahumanitarian politics, beyond the interest of nation-states. If the philosophers of hospitality and international law sought to protect state interests, Derrida looks to find in Levinas an alternative to the domestic and propertied sleeping sovereign subject. In so doing, we see Levinas as a philosopher of ethics as hospitality with all the risks that go along with it. The subject in dissolution is always of the other – it is the other who demands of the host, who occupies the host. In Derrida's funerary speech for Levinas, later published as *Adieu to Levinas*, he writes that "if the at-home with oneself of the dwelling is an 'at-home with oneself as in a land of asylum or refuge,' this would mean that the inhabitant dwells there also as a refugee or an exile, a guest and not a proprietor" (1999, 72).

In *La Ronde de Nuit* (*Night Patrol*), a play performed by the traveling theater company Aftaab, and created in collaboration with the experimental director Ariane Mnouchkine at the Théâtre du Soleil outside Paris, we are presented with the theatrical space as set. The caretaker of the theater, which is an old, fragile structure, shows around a man from Afghanistan. The theater, she tells us, contains an archive of all that has occurred there. Both the man and the police who come by to do night patrols of the building guard and care for that archive. The caretaker has already told us of the other temporary residents of the theater who make appearances – the prostitute from across the street, the woman who has nowhere to live, the tramp who comes to use the bathroom. Voices from afar also occupy space in the theater through Skype connectivity, which brings the world into this unofficial archive of temporary residents. As the night moves on, the man receives a phone call from a friend, whom he discourages from visiting him. The friend nonetheless turns up, and then many more come, men and women.

As they set up sleeping mats on the floor, each tries to sleep, perchance to dream. Yet each has troubled, unrestful sleep, frightening dreams of the violence from which they have escaped and sought temporary refuge from in this temporary residence. They wake from their dreams, and are restless insomniacs, traumatized and unable or unwilling to narrativize and thus substantiate or give a name, a structure, or an identity to their troubles, which they cannot assimilate into consciousness, on the one hand, or repose on the other. The police outside do their patrols, as do the prostitutes that work in that area, until the freezing weather becomes the great equalizer that causes all to seek refuge in this theater space. The theater becomes the site of non-location, or non-permanence, of an archive of people passing through. In other words, like Levinas' insomniac who neither has nor makes claim to place or property where s/he can sleep, the host is as much a guest as is the other who is welcomed. The calm sleep of belonging, then is not available to the restless figure who remains guest and host, temporary residents passing through on this planet, as they welcome each other through an ethical opening.

Ranjana Khanna

Asylum

The term "asylum" brings together the philosophical, the psychical, and the political and connects the ideas of refuge, insomnia, border, and hospitality that all function with a notion of the subject that both psychoanalysis and Levinasian philosophy challenge. The challenge to the sane national reasonable rights-bearing liberal citizen-self that constitutes the ontological basis of philosophy is revealed by the most vulnerable to be the source itself of fear and insomnia.

Asylum as a space is a site of sanctuary offering apparently unconditional hospitality even though determined by ecclesiastical, "divine," and sometimes royal parameters. The term designates too an institution and a building for the mentally unstable, or those labeled thus. Asylum is the right of a state to grant refugee status, residency, or citizenship to a persecuted foreigner; the right neither to deport nor to extradite. What kind of a concept is it? Religious, medical, spatial, political, juridical, local, global, androcentric or anthropomorphic, philosophical, or anti-philosophical? And if the latter, is it a concept at all?

Extending insights concerning one form of asylum's institutional setting (the mental asylum) to its most expansive version (the nation) highlights the manner in which asylums, including nations, are bound not only by borders but also by strict rules. The space of asylum suggests the rights of institutions over living bodies, rather than the rights of citizens emerging into different spaces. Asylum, through figures of sovereignty and subjectivity, highlights the forms through which the sovereign intervenes in lives to formulate concepts of the human, the valuable, the propertied, the citizen, the subject, and the disposable.

Today, "holding facilities" and prisons, like the "mental asylums" of the nineteenth century, restructure and capitalize on the notion of safe space, and alter received norms concerning the treatment of difference, the practice of hospitality, and the regulation of labor. Feminist scholarship has demonstrated the differential violence women encountered in "mental asylums" through the treatment of hysteria, and the incarceration of non-compliant women by fathers, brothers, sons, doctors, and, in some instances, female family members also.

With the increased medicalization of asylum claims and the demand for diagnoses of trauma and post-traumatic stress disorder symptoms, increasingly psychiatrics and other mental health professionals have roles in providing information as expert witnesses in cases on the decision to grant asylum (Fassin 2013). Many write of the difficulties faced by analyst and analysand alike in the context of the analytic/advocate role played by the analyst, especially one that considers the advocacy role only as the first step of the therapeutic relationship.

But psychoanalytic theory poses questions concerning our figure underneath the sheet with whom we began in terms of the relationship to alterity and to the feminine. If Levinas' theory of insomnia gives us a troubled figure in search of refuge but resistant to it, it imagines this figure as being caught and held hostage to otherness much in the way that psychoanalysis conceives anyone who is unable to sleep. In *The Interpretation of Dreams*, Freud writes of another figure under a sheet:

> I will give the explanation of a vision that was described to me by another hysterical patient (a woman of forty) as having happened before she fell ill. One morning she opened her eyes and saw her brother in the room, though, as she knew, he was in fact in an insane asylum. Her small son was sleeping in the bed beside her. To save the child from having a fright and falling into convulsions when he saw his uncle, she pulled the sheet over his face, whereupon the apparition vanished. This vision was a modified version of a memory from the lady's childhood; and, though it was conscious, it was intimately related to all the unconscious material in her mind. Her nurse had told her that her mother (who had died very young, when my patient was only eighteen months old) had suffered from epileptic or hysterical convulsions, which went back to a fright caused by her brother (my patient's uncle) appearing to her disguised as a ghost with a sheet over his head. Thus the vision contained the same elements as the memory: the brother's appearance, the sheet, the fright and its results. But the elements had been arranged in a different context and transferred on to other figures. The obvious motive of the vision, or of the thoughts which it replaced, was her concern lest her little boy might follow in the footsteps of his uncle, whom he greatly resembled physically.
>
> (Freud 1953–74, 4:545)

The hysterical woman, in fear lest the child become insane like her uncle who pretends to be a ghost, that is, repeatedly pretends to be an instantiation of death, hides the vision from her child by binding him to the breast – i.e. covering him with a sheet. In other words, in seeking to protect him from insanity and the death drive, she ultimately returns him to that porous relation to herself, binding him to her in sleep underneath the sheet. Seeking refuge for him, she effectively repeats the gesture, and covers him in the sheet.

One can understand from this the demand to repeat the gesture of attachment to place, to nation, and to belonging as psychic spaces.

And yet the attachment to the site of the feminine hysteric here is of protection from what is known by the woman in sentient form but cannot be substantiated. If Levinas sought the ethical relation precisely in the form in which Being breaks down such that one is porous and hospitable to the Other, psychoanalysis gives a way of showing how ambiguous that notion of refuge and place is, as sites of horror and death as much as comfort. Psychoanalysis figures that knowledge through the feminine maternal, and the figure of the foreigner would always constitute a secondary manifestation in the example of that foreign visitor who knocks on the door.

Levinas will certainly at times speak of alterity as feminine, and yet the feminine and the foreign at times become interchangeable manifestations of the divine. In psychoanalysis, the feminine is not interchangeable in this way, because it becomes the as yet unthought, such that hospitality to the other would always be with the knowledge of non-being always already violated by being. If the propertied self can be hospitable, it is with the knowledge historically and mythically, even biblically, of putting the woman-as-property at risk. Antigone, Lot's daughters, and the Sabine women come to mind.

Once we acknowledge the sovereignty of the state as the arbiter of life and death for those trying to enter, we see also the population that thinks it belongs through the instruments of social contract, property, citizenship, and the documented proper name. The idea of the healthy, untraumatized, propertied, and rights-bearing citizen who passionately defends their homeland and thus underscores their sense of belonging is entirely consistent with a narrative of state protection that is more fragile than one might assume. Those who have until recently been excluded from rights of full citizenship may bear the scars of such vulnerability, as did the mythical victims of hospitality and belonging to what the Universal Declaration of Human Rights calls the human family, like Lot's daughters, the Sabine women, or Antigone.

Having failed to stop the struggle between men for sovereignty over the state, Antigone protests in the only way she can – first, through an act of defiance against her uncle Creon, by mourning the body of her brother who has not been allowed state burial rights, and then through suicide, which in many ways is the only way to thwart the sovereign Creon's control over her life and death. Like the Sabine women, Antigone is destined to live with the knowledge of her violent inception that will leave her perpetually melancholic (unable to adequately mourn). Insomnia is a restless rejection of the narrative of being and belonging in favor of not belonging. Belonging creates, after all, its own corrupt system of sovereignty in which it becomes clear that woman is an anomaly for the state, and, like asylum seekers, bears the trace of being less than human in its terms. In saying this, I do not want to pathologize political difference or dispossession, but rather suggest that the narrative of belonging is always a fiction, indeed, a legal fiction. If the blank screen, like the stage of *Night Patrol*, provides an arena for the performance of refuge, the archives stored there provide for the sleepless knowledge of the feminine.

Notes

1 http://www.annasherbany.com/video.html. Accessed November 30, 2013.
2 In addition to Levinas, others have considered the sources of Freud's dream interpretation in talmudic thought. See e.g. Frieden (1990). On the question of the relationship between Jewish thought contemporary with the development of psychoanalysis, see also Rose (2005).
3 Luce Irigaray (1985) makes an argument about the repressed first home of western philosophy as the uterus in her discussion of Plato's cave.

References

Anghie, Anthony. 2007. *Imperialism, Sovereignty and the Making of International Law*. Cambridge Studies in International and Comparative Law. Cambridge: Cambridge University Press.

Baker, Gideon, ed. 2013. *Hospitality and World Politics*. London: Palgrave Macmillan.

Cavallar, Georg. 2011. *Imperfect Cosmopolis: Studies in the History of International Legal Theory and Cosmopolitan Ideas*. Cardiff: University of Wales Press.

Critchley, Simon. 1999. "The Original Traumatism: Levinas and Psychoanalysis." In *Ethics, Politics, Subjectivity: Essays on Derrida, Levinas and Contemporary French Thought*, 183–97. London: Verso.

Derrida, Jacques. 1999. *Adieu to Levinas*, trans. Pascale-Anne Brault and Michael Naas. Stanford: Stanford University Press.

Fassin, Didier. 2013. "The Precarious Truth of Asylum." *Public Culture*, 25:1 69: 39–63.

Freud, Sigmund. 1953–74. *The Standard Edition of the Complete Psychological Works of Sigmund Freud*, 24 vols., ed. James Strachey, with the assistance of Anna Freud, Alix Strachey, and Alan Tyson, trans. James Strachey. London: Hogarth Press.

Frieden, Ken. 1990. *Freud's Dream of Interpretation*. New York: State University of New York Press.

Irigaray, Luce. 1985. *Speculum of the Other Woman*, trans. Gillian C Gill. Ithaca, N.Y.: Cornell University Press.

Kant, Immanuel. 1795. "To Perpetual Peace: A Philosophical Sketch." In *Perpetual Peace and Other Essays*, trans. Ted Humphrey. Indianapolis: Hackett, 1983.

Levinas, Emmanuel. 1981. "Quelques réflexions talmudiques sur le rêve." In Jean- Jacques Rassial, *La Psychanalyse est-elle une histoire juive?*, 114–31. Paris: Seuil.

Levinas, Emmanuel. 2001. *Existence and Existents*, trans. Alphonso Lingis. Pittsburgh, Pa.: Duquesne University Press.

Lewin, Bertram. 1946. "Sleep, the Mouth and the Dream Screen." *Psychoanalytic Quarterly*, 15: 419–34.

Manto, Saadat Hasan. 1997. "Toba Tek Singh." In *Mottled Dawn: Fifty Sketches and Stories of Partition*, trans. Khalid Hasan, 1–10. New Delhi: Penguin.

Porras, Ileana. 2012. "Liberal Cosmopolitanism or Cosmopolitan Liberalism." In *Parochialism, Cosmopolitanism, and the Foundations of International Law*, ed. M.N.S. Sellers, 118–48. Cambridge: Cambridge University Press.

Rose, Jacqueline. 2003. "On Not Being Able to Sleep: Rereading the Interpretation of Dreams." In *On Not Being Able to Sleep: Psychoanalysis and the Modern World*, 105–24. Princeton: Princeton University Press.

Rose, Jacqueline. 2005. "'Imponderables in Thin Air': Zionism as Psychoanalysis." In *The Question of Zion*, 58–107. Princeton: Princeton University Press.

Chapter 20

Freud on Cultural Translation

Robert J.C. Young

What relation has Freud to translation? Not only in terms of how we translate Freud, but also how Freud himself deploys translation as a concept and as a practice? While there has been a lot of discussion, even books written, on the question of Freud and translation, the vast bulk of material has been concerned with the translations of Freud. The discussions and critiques of the somewhat formalizing translations by James Strachey in the Standard Edition pioneered by Bruno Bettelheim have resulted in the recent retranslations of the new Penguin Freud, edited by Adam Philips, where Freud's German reappears in a more conversational and idiomatic mode. Some of the translators of this new edition spend a lot of energy detailing the various faults ascribed to the hapless yet still majestic Strachey. The preoccupation within the psychoanalytic and literary communities with the problems of translating Freud plays out against the larger question of interpreting Freud, which at some level it must always involve. What is interesting in these debates is that the issue is generally discussed without drawing in the question of what principles Freud himself used in his own translation work – he himself translated five books, by J.S. Mill, Charcot, Bernheim, and others, in addition to a number of other texts, into German. Freud himself translated on fairly relaxed principles,

A Concise Companion to Psychoanalysis, Literature, and Culture, First Edition.
Edited by Laura Marcus and Ankhi Mukherjee.

producing a relatively free translation that turns the original text into a German idiom, blithely oblivious to the principle of fidelity, and making his own translations somewhat at odds with the scrupulous translations made of Freud himself today (Mahoney 1982). The debates about the translations of Freud also typically avoid any discussion of the degree to which Freud himself was not only a practitioner but also a theorist of translation. Freud in fact quite often discusses questions of linguistic translation, which come into his accounts of hysteria, his explanations of dream-work, of everyday parapraxes, jokes, and the uncanny. His discussions emphasize the degree to which we inhabit a translational space, suggesting that the psyche is multilingual, alert to the constant possibility of using translation as a mechanism of displacement in the face of repression. An everyday social practice of this sort, as he points out, is the use of polite euphemisms in another language, when direct expression would be embarrassing, such as *ménage à trois*, or *derrière*, or, as Freud puts it himself in a paradoxical but suggestive euphemistic expression in his discussion of Dora, "*j'appelle un chat un chat*" (Freud 1977, 82). What Freud shows is that this linguistic displacement through languages is a fundamental part of our psychical apparatus, not something that is only the specialized practice of experts, and that such translation itself could be thought of less as a form of "carrying across" than as a form of displacement, dislocation, even derangement, that it itself forms a practice of diaspora from one language to another – for languages are always migrating, beginning with the different registers within any particular language.

But rather than pursuing that Derridean route, I want to look instead at Freud's use of translation as a metaphor, or analogy: the practice of psychoanalysis, says Freud the translator, is itself a form of translation. Arguably, the later theory of transference will increase the extent to which this is so (Ingram 2001). Going even further, Freud describes psychic life itself as a process of translation that operates in a dialectical relation with what he tantalizingly calls not cultural translation but "cultural transformation" (*kulturelle Wandlung*) (Freud 2005, 224). This amounts to a radical theory of cultural translation that has never been considered within the realms of translation theory.

Patrick Mahoney, who along with fellow analyst Jean Laplanche is one of the few who have explored the question of translation in Freud in depth, argues that Freud should be seen as one of the "great thinkers and innovators in the domain of translation" (Mahoney 1982: 63). He may be right, but it is easy to see why Freud has not been celebrated in this way in the realm of translation theory. What Freud performs is rather a translation of translation theory, or perhaps more accurately, but still working within the range of meanings of the word *Übersetzung* in German (translation, setting above, transposition, transference), a transposition of the concept of translation. Psychoanalysis itself is a practice that effects a form of translation says Freud, but it is more complicated than that. Because if it does so, this is because the psyche has already been busy translating things into a foreign language that is unreadable to the individual subject him or herself.

Hysteria and translation

Let's consider then some examples of Freud's use of the concept of translation. We can find them straightaway in the case histories in Freud and Breuer's *Studies on Hysteria* (2004 [1895]). Their theory of the hysterical symptom as a form of conversion, which Freud defined as "the transformation of psychical excitation into chronic physical symptoms," brings hysteria close to a practice of physical bodily translation (Mavrikakis 1998). Hysteria, Freud observes, is fundamentally a form of bilingualism, and can take that form literally at times (Freud and Breuer 2004 [1895], 132). So Breuer's Anna O at one point expresses herself by the following symptom: she switches into speaking only in English, without realizing that she is doing so (2004 [1895], 29); if asked to read French or Italian aloud "she would sight-read an excellent English translation with astonishing rapidity and fluency" (2004 [1895], 30). In some sense, psychoanalysis itself will mimic this translational facility, converting one language to another. In the case of psychoanalysis, however, this translation will not follow the classical model of translation between European languages.

In Freud's own case history of "Katharina," which reads as much like a short story as a case history, Freud relates the dialogue that took place between himself and Katharina 6,000 feet up on a mountain top in the Austrian Alps. None of the English versions attempts to capture the Austrian country dialect that the country girl Katharina uses and which in the original German text Freud scrupulously retains:

> "Fräulein Katharina, if you could remember now what was happening in you at that time, when you had your first attack, what you thought about it – it would help you."
>
> "Yes, if I could. But I was so frightened that I've forgotten everything."

> (Translated into the terminology of our "Preliminary Communication," this means: "The affect itself created a hypnoid state, whose products were then cut off from associative connection with the ego-consciousness.")
>
> (2004 [1895], 131)

This statement represents one fundamental mode of translation in psychoanalysis for Freud, the kind of translation that Jakobson would characterize as intra-lingual. Today, after Foucault, we would also talk about it in terms of the registers of different discourses. Freud's translation is certainly between two languages, but he is not producing an equivalent in another ordinary language but a translation of dialectical German into a different discursive regime. Freud translates the girl's colloquial remark into his own terminology, the "scientific" or medical language of psychoanalysis through which psychoanalytic understanding is achieved: so, "I was so frightened that I've forgotten everything" becomes "The affect itself created a hypnoid state, whose products were then cut off from associative connection with the ego-consciousness." (I am quoting from the new Penguin translation, which cannot obviate the extreme degree of this psychoanalytical transposition which ideologically, à la Bettelheim, it seeks to deny.) What happens in this translation or transposition from one discourse to another, apart from a move into unintelligibility for the ordinary reader, beginning with the girl herself? Her sentence is depersonalized, and her experience moved into the universal structure of mental functioning that psychoanalysis produces as its form of theoretical understanding. "I was so frightened" is translated into "the affect itself created a hypnoid state," while "I've forgotten everything" is transposed into a breaking of associative connection with the ego-consciousness. At one level this represents the fundamental form of the talking cure. The cure is effected through the subject's own speech, but that speech is submitted to a form of translation of a language which, in more complex cases, the patient herself will come to understand, if not speak. The particular experience of the individual is translated into the scientific discourse that enables that experience to be understood as a function of the psyche or the body as it is understood in the realm of medical science. The individual's experience is depersonalized into a universal theoretical framework, one which in Freud's case was in fact being perpetually modified in response to new experiences that he encountered. The question that this raises, however, is to what extent this psychoanalytic translation is more than a translation: to what extent does psychoanalysis offer real understanding or explanation as opposed to a translation into its own specialized idiom, setting the one above the other? This is the classic question for psychoanalytic literary criticism, and one that continually plays back into psychoanalysis itself: to what extent is it *nothing but* a translation? At one level this does seem to be the case – except that it is a very complicated kind of translation.

The transposition of ordinary language into psychoanalytic discourse, or translation as transposition, is undoubtedly one of the most common ways in which Freud invokes the term translation. This is hardly an original use of the practice of translation – we have the original, the girl's words, which are then subsequently translated by Freud into his own specialized psychoanalytic language. In making this move, in fact, Freud is performing nothing less than the characteristic translation of philosophy of the real world into terms of abstraction which Marx would decry in Hegel. At the same time, Freud is also reversing the human subjective experience so that its attributes become the attribute of something that he has created (the psyche), in the very mode of religion that Feuerbach, and Marx after him with respect to philosophy, would seek to retranslate or more accurately de-translate back into the realm of human agency. What's interesting is that while the language of psychoanalytic theory performs the first kind of translation, the second Feuerbachian/Marxian strategy comprises the manner in which Freud deploys the concept of translation in *The Interpretation of Dreams*, where translation is put into reverse.

The Interpretation of Dreams: reverse translation

The word *Übersetzung* in various formations appears at least forty-five times in the *Interpretation of Dreams*. Here again, Freud uses the concept of translation in different ways. Of more minor interest is his use of the term translation to describe the interpretation of symbolism in dreams: some symbols are so constant in their recurrence and their meaning, he says, that they can be translated easily into specific meanings. Freud calls these "stable translations" (1953–74, 15:151) – they operate rather like what the Russian linguist Valentin Volosinov calls "signals" (Volosinov 1973: 68). In other words, their interpretation is not ambiguous. Such symbols have a relatively fixed translational equivalent, as in "hat" for *chapeau*, for example, or in Freud's case, "hat" for "male genitals." Such "symbol-translation" (Freud 2006 [1899], 373) as Freud calls it, is, however, too easy and misses the point: "I should like to issue an emphatic warning against overrating the importance of symbols so far as interpreting dreams is concerned – limiting the work of dream-translation to translating symbols, for instance, and abandoning the technique of making use of the dreamer's ideational associations" (2006 [1899], 373). The work of what Freud calls "dream-translation" is altogether more complicated. What is involved?

The first instance will be the translation of unconscious expressions into conscious rational motives or wishes. What makes this more than just translation into another discourse at this point, however, is that psychoanalysis is here translating the unknown. As Freud puts it in his discussion of *Hamlet*, wonderfully oblivious to the fact that he is discussing a fictional character: "Here I have translated into consciousness what in the hero's mind has to remain unconscious" (2006 [1899], 279). He thus very frequently summarizes an action or a dream by offering its rationalized meaning as his translation. This is relatively easy with the symptom, or even the articulate literary text, but altogether harder with respect to the dream.[1]

At the opening of chapter 6 of *The Interpretation of Dreams*, "The Dream Work," Freud begins by contrasting his method with previous accounts of the meaning of dreams that in one way or another simply interpret what he calls "the manifest dream-content," or more simply, the dream as such. Freud's innovation is to move dream interpretation into the realm of translation. The manifest dream-content is a translation of something else, and that, including the relation between them, is the meaning of the dream. So he sets up his model of the relation of the manifest dream content to the "latent dream-content or dream-thoughts": the dream-work is the means by which the former are transformed into the latter. It is this relation, he argues, that is one of translation.

> Dream-thoughts and dream-content lie before us like two representations of the same content in two different languages – or, rather, a particular dream-content appears to us as a version of the relevant dream-thoughts rendered into a different mode of expression, the characters and syntax of which we are meant to learn by comparing the original with the translation.
>
> (Freud 2006, 293)

Unlike the earlier instances that we have seen, here it is dreams themselves, rather than the analyst, that engage in forms of translation. The dream-content is simply a translation into another language of the dream-thoughts "rendered into a different mode of expression."

However, dream interpretation cannot involve simply returning from language B (target language) to rediscover the original language A (source language), since language A is unknown, consisting of "a different mode of expression" whose characters and syntax we can only learn by comparison with the translation. Freud's first claim therefore is that the dream-thoughts and content are simply the representation of the same content in different languages, but this is immediately modified to a second claim that the dream-content is a version of the dream-thoughts rendered in a different mode of expression, whose "characters and syntax," that is whose text, "we are meant to learn by comparing the original with the translation." But we don't know the original: the dream-thoughts are in an unknown language that we can only decipher on the basis of the translation.

The situation that Freud describes, as he was perhaps aware though unexpectedly for someone so interested in antiquity he nowhere mentions it in all his writings, is remarkably similar to that of the Rosetta Stone, where the Egyptian, demotic, and Greek texts are placed in parallel beside each other – which famously enabled Champollion to decipher hieroglyphics for the first time. Freud makes frequent comparison of dream-content to hieroglyphs. "Dream-content is embedded, as it were, in a hieroglyphic script whose characters need to be translated one by one into the language of the dream-thoughts" (Freud 2006, 293). Why hieroglyphs in particular? Because they suggest an unknown language that requires decoding and deciphering, as was the case with Egyptian hieroglyphs until 1822. And secondly because, although primarily phonetic, hieroglyphs still retain elements of a picture language – they are made up of a combination of phonetic and ideographic signs. It's a language that, like dreams, shifts between the linguistic and the pictorial in its representations.[2] This is an idea that he developed as far back as the *Studies in Hysteria*, where he compares hysteria to an unknown pictographic script, *Bildersprache*, picture speech, at one point in the case of "Katharina": "We had frequently compared the hysterical symptomatology with a pictographic script which we were able to read once we had discovered a few cases of bilingualism" (Freud and Breuer 2004 [1895], 132).

With hysteria, the pictographic script is there on the surface, often on the surface of the body itself. All that is required is that the analyst reconverts it back into the symptom. In the case of dream-translation, however, the hieroglyphic language hides the dream-thoughts that have to be deduced from the dream-content. In this case, it is impossible to compare the original with the translation on the Rosetta Stone model because the original is not there to be read: it can only be inferred. This would therefore more closely resemble the situation with the Harappan script of the Indus Valley civilization, which remains undeciphered even today since no bilingual inscription exists. Psychoanalysis finds the meaning of dreams not in dreams themselves but in their invisible origins. In dreams we have only the translation: the patient's and analyst's job is to translate the incomprehensible dream-content back into its original, and then to analyze and repeat in reverse the work of translation which has transformed the first into the second. Dream interpretation, therefore, as Jean Laplanche (1992) has suggested, is more a question of de-translation, trying to de-translate the dream back into an occulted original. This is where and why the work of interpretation through association must come into play: breaking the dream-content down into its constituent parts one by one, and working through the dreamer's associations, analyst and dreamer engage in the laborious work of de-translating the dream-content back into its original dream-thoughts. These, when identified, offer comprehensible, distortion-free, rational sentiments as the meaning of the dream.

Psychoanalysis thus becomes a kind of reverse translation, translating the dream back into its unconscious original text, mimicking the dream-work, which has carried out the original translation that produced the dream itself. The latter, however, is not a proper translation in the way that it would normally be thought of in terms of the transposition from one language into another, for it is, in a sense, a willfully bad translation, in which the ego tries to disguise the meaning of the dream-thoughts altogether, subjecting them therefore to distortion, condensation, displacement, and all the other mechanisms of repression – it's a nightmare translation, the kind translators only meet with in bad dreams. The manifest dream-content is a willfully obscured, bad translation, so that the de-translator not only has to translate the dream back into its original, but according to a procedure of the reversal of the particular mechanisms of repression. It is this bizarre process of translation that the patient has to turn around in order to achieve psychic health. But how easy will that be, given that she has to rediscover an original that she never knew from a translation that has willfully obscured its relation to its original? Freud is unabashed, and remains confident: once he has isolated the four major mechanisms of the dream-work, then the dream "does nothing but translate the relevant dream-thoughts in accordance with the four conditions prescribed" (Freud 2006, 459). Without a knowledge of these consistent conditions, then, the work of de-translation would be impossible. Unlike conventional translation, it may be observed, in de-translation there is no real hierarchy between the different texts because although the original dream thoughts may be "the primary text," they are only made evident through the process of de-translation in which they are restated by the analyst in his own transposed language of psychoanalysis. We never, in a sense, get to the original as such, only to a third text, the analyst's rephrasing of its meaning.[3]

If psychoanalysis therefore operates on a model of translation and de-translation, it is a translation like no other. Freud's model of translation in psychoanalysis is as idiosyncratic as psychoanalysis itself. How useful, though, is this model of translation for other kinds of translation? There are, after all, few instances where we have the translation but not the original, and an original, at that, that the translation has willfully distorted precisely so that it does not obviously correspond to its original, and requires a labor of interpretive detective work in order to track it back down to its origin. This is no doubt why Freud, however radical as a translation theorist, has not made a major impact on translation theory as such. But as a theoretical paradigm it remains infinitely suggestive. It offers, for example, a possible way of reading the invisible, the subaltern, those whose forms of public representation distort their fundamental being, where the invisibility or repression of subalterns in official discourses and documents from the past require a de-translation exercise to make them visible in their own terms. Or it could be used in the context of ideology, which according to Marxist theory deliberately distorts the conditions of the real. We might also find an analogy with the situation of having an unknown mother tongue, which Derrida describes in *Monolingualism of the Other* (Derrida 1998 [1996]). Or as Freud himself points out elsewhere, his position comes close here to that of Kant, the difference being that while Kant says not knowing the thing-in-itself doesn't matter, for Freud getting to the originating dream-thoughts is precisely what matters (Freud 1953–74 14:171; Cavell 1987, 27; Altman and Coe 2013, 8–26). His method of getting there, however, remains Kantian, namely by constructing the categories through which we process the original data.

Meanwhile the paradox of Freud's own use of translation could be said to be that psychoanalysis as a discursive practice translates experience into the register of abstraction at the same time as it seeks to de-translate the displaced or abstracted thoughts of its patients back to the reality of their repressed originals. Freud, we could say, has developed a theory of double or doubled translation, and it is this dialectical form, at once moving forwards and backwards, that constitutes the heart of his theory of cultural translation.

The uneasiness of cultural translation

Freud describes the process of psychic life as a form of translation. He then develops this into an idea of sublimation which amounts to a kind of cultural translation that anticipates its modern use, though with rather different implications. Though he does not use the term as such, Freud's focus on issues of translation and of culture has the effect of putting the two together in the doubled, dialectical form that I have just described.

Freud summarizes his general thesis in this area in his 1932 letter to Albert Einstein, "Why War?," in this way:

> Since time immemorial, mankind has been moving through the process of cultural evolution. (I know that there are those who prefer the term civilization.) It is to this process that we owe the best that we have become, and a great deal of that which causes us suffering.
>
> (Freud 2005, 231)

The ambivalent "cultural evolution" that mankind has been moving through is recapitulated in the individual life of the human being where "a cultural suppression of the instincts" (Freud 1984: 425) effects the translation of the individual from the state of the child to that of the adult.[4] In Freud, cultural translation is the result of the denial, suppression, renunciation, or repression of the instincts. It works in two ways at once: good for civilization or culture, but not so hot for the individual.

Though it was not to be fully developed until the 1930s, we find anticipations of this idea of translation as renunciation and transformation very early in Freud. In a letter of December 6, 1896, to his great friend and confidant Wilhelm Fliess, Freud sketches out an early idea of the stages of psychic life as a structure of "successive transcripts." He divides psychic life into four epochs, and describes the transition between the "successive epochs" as moments of "translation." Neurosis, he argues, results from a failure of translation, leaving an anachronism, or as he puts it in the anthropological language of E.B. Tylor, untranslated "survivals" of phenomena from earlier periods. These are at once cultural and psychic. Freud's schema runs as follows: "successive registrations represent the psychical achievement of successive epochs of life. At the boundary between two such epochs a translation of the psychical material must take place." Freud thus sketches out a chronology of the different epochs of the psyche, in which the subject moves from one stage to another, across a boundary or frontier that lies between them. The term translation is used both metaphorically and literally to describe the transition periods of the movement across the mental frontier. It involves a carrying across from one stage to another, in the course of which the components of the libido are themselves transformed and reordered, so that the "excitatory process" or sexual energy is drained off, at which point a successful translation takes place. The "peculiarities of the psychoneuroses," on the other hand, are explained "by supposing that this translation has not taken place in the case of some of the material, which has certain consequences." In this instance, where a "memory-trace" from an earlier phase has not been translated, "an anachronism persists: in a particular province, *fueros*,[5] are still in force, we are in the presence of 'survivals'." Neuroses, in this account, therefore result from what Freud describes as

> A failure of translation – this is what is known clinically as "repression." The motive for it is always a release of unpleasure [*Unbehagen*] that would be generated by a translation; it is as though this unpleasure provokes a disturbance of thought that does not permit the work of translation.
> (Freud 1985, 208)

Repression here thus amounts to a failure of translation, where the psyche rejects the release of unpleasure that the translational process generates. We might expect the opposite, that is, for translation to be identified with repression of some kind. In fact, the word here translated as repression is not the usual term translated as repression, *Verdrängung*, but rather *Versagung*, which means denial or refusal or countersaying. This repression is a refusal that rejects and forestalls the working-through that will allow the work of translation across successive phases of the psyche to produce the normative pattern that enables psychic health, even though it generates unpleasure. Freud thus offers an account of the etiology of the human being moving through consecutive epochs of psychic life, translating his or her psychical material into that of a further stage, or alternatively refusing the process because of the unpleasure that it brings, failing to translate, and therefore carrying forward survivals from the past. Translation produces psychic health, failure of translation, neurosis. Neurosis will take the form of the denial of a memory-trace which "has not yet been translated" but which then nevertheless gets translated otherwise through conversion into hysterical symptoms.

This early idea of "psychic life as the work of a series of successful translations that generate unpleasure" occurs in a different form many years later in *Civilization and Its Discontents* (1930), except that here the etiology of such a process, though still repressing or translating sexuality, is ascribed to the effects of culture: culture represses sexuality while repressed sexuality is sublimated into cultural production. Civilization, and all its achievements such as art and technology, arise from what is both lost and gained in translation.

The word Freud uses here to describe the movement through successive stages of the repression of sexual drives in the individual psyche from infant to adult is no longer translation but sublimation, no longer *Übersetzung* but *Sublimierung* (Freud 2002 [1930], 59). The meaning of these two words is strikingly close: while *Übersetzung* means placing or setting above, *Sublimierung* or sublimation means an "elevation to a higher state or plane of existence; transmutation into something higher, purer, more sublime" (*OED*). Sublimation is therefore the process of putting or moving something above, translating it in the sense now reserved for saints such as Elijah who are translated straight from earth to heaven, or in German also sending it lower – to the depths, the sub of the subterranean.[6] The two words remain provocatively close: the transmutation of sublimation, like translation, pushes the instincts onto a higher plane, though by repressing them in the process, sending them lower, it produces unpleasure and leaves a malaise or discontent in its wake.

So much for translation. But what about culture? True to his preference for idiomatic translations, Freud was happy with the iconic title of the English translation of this book, *Civilization and Its Discontents*, but it is significant that its original 1930 title was *Das Unbehagen in der Kultur*, which translates as "the uneasiness, discomfort or malaise, (literally *unpleasure*), in culture" (Freud 1930). The interesting question here is why the German *Kultur* was translated as civilization, not culture. Civilization would have probably been the more obvious word to use in English in the nineteenth or first half of the twentieth century, as in Henry Thomas Buckle's *History of Civilization in England* (1857–61), a work which in certain respects provides a precursor to Freud's. Today by contrast, "civilization" is not a word that we use unselfconsciously in English, given the legacy of the colonial civilizing mission according to which civilization was what was supposed to distinguish European from non-European cultures in the colonial racio-cultural hierarchy. We might now feel much more comfortable with the word culture, especially since, in English, the broader anthropological meaning of culture has supervened upon its alternative meaning of the arts, refined high culture: as an *OED* quotation from the *Financial Times* of 2001 puts it, "in 15 years, culture has moved from the most sublime performances of opera, dance and classical music to street parties, social inclusion, and fun." As the *FT* quotation might indicate, a literal translation of Freud's title, "The Uneasiness in Culture," would be somewhat perplexing today. Why should we be uneasy in our culture of fun, music, theater, sports, and the like? In the 1920s and 1930s, by contrast, there were many tracts, poems, and books written about the widespread sense of western culture having become unbearable and unlivable – think T.S. Eliot or D.H. Lawrence. Today this lives on in the lugubrious nostalgia of New Age thinking and other quests for the civilizational fantasy of primitivism. Lawrence and the New Ageists would agree with Freud's description of the common view in 1930 that "much of the blame for our misery lies with what we call our culture [civilization], and that we should be far happier if we were to abandon it and revert to primitive conditions" (Freud 2002 [1930], 24–25). But the particular historical discontent with civilization or hostility to culture in the 1920s and 1930s, which was largely the result of the extravagant imperialist nationalism which produced World War I, is not the only reason why today discontent with "culture" seems somewhat anachronistic.

In Freud's day, the word "culture," in English or German, had itself an aura that today it has lost. In the 1920s and 1930s, the common view was that there were two rival European cultures or civilizations, often characterized as Anglo-French civilization vs. German *Kultur*. This distinction was a product of the ideology of World War I, and continued up into the Nazi era and even beyond. The word *Kultur* even became an English word, and can be found in the *OED*, where its meaning is given as "civilization as conceived by the Germans; especially used in a derogatory sense during the 1914–18 and 1939–45 wars, as involving notions of racial and cultural arrogance, militarism, and imperialism." "*Kultur*," *The Times* opined in 1915, "in fact, has become the exact opposite of 'culture'" (cit. *OED*). *Kultur*, to the British, represented a brute Prussian militarism that lacked all ethics: so Rudyard Kipling wrote in 1918 that "It is the peculiar essence of German Kultur, which is the German religion, that it is Germany's moral duty to break every tie, every restriction that binds man to fellow-men, if she thinks it will pay" (cit. *OED*). German treatment of prisoners and civilians in the Great War, or the practice of taking revenge actions against entire cities, such as the destruction of the Belgian city of Louvain in 1914, meant that John Buchan, in his *History of the Great War* (1921–22), already characterized German *Kultur* as responsible for a "holocaust" (Buchan 1923, 1, 241). For this reason, the resonances of *Kultur* in English, however foreign from Freud's usage, meant that the better equivalent for *Kultur* was the more anglicized "civilization." Although the word *Zivilisation* does exist in German, Freud never uses it in his text. He uses the term *Kultur* exclusively and indeed, as we have already heard, in the Einstein letter published the following year, while acknowledging the existence of the term civilization, he says that he prefers culture. In Germany, *Zivilisation* was in turn associated with the qualities identified in English with *Kultur* – for in Germany, the understanding of *Kultur* was almost the exact opposite of that in England: elevated German *Kultur* was regarded as the very opposite of Anglo-American philistine commercialism.

Given, however, our contemporary reservations about civilization, amnesia with respect to the English associations of *Kultur*, and the transmutation of the meaning of the word culture in English, what if we were to rethink Freud's text today in terms of its being about culture rather than civilization? What if we followed the, in this case unadopted, principles of the new Penguin Freud and retranslated Freud's title as *Unpleasure in Culture* and substituted the word culture for civilization throughout? I shall now proceed to do this.

Freud's description of *Kultur* first comes in part 2, devoted to questions of human happiness. The word culture, he writes, "designates the sum total of those achievements and institutions that distinguish our life from that of our animal ancestors and serve the dual purpose of protecting human beings against nature and regulating their mutual relations" (2002 [1930], 27). The progress of culture, Freud suggests, produces all that is finest in human existence, but the sublimation of the drives which it demands is achieved at some considerable personal cost. Freud then proposes a parallel between the process of culture and the libidinal development of the individual, both of which involve the sublimation of the drives, collectively or individually. Culture is a process of translation for the individual where each one learns to control and/or displace their erotic and aggressive drives. "Sublimation of the drives," Freud writes, "is a particularly striking feature of cultural development which makes it possible for the higher mental activities – scientific, artistic and ideological – to play such a significant role in cultural life" (2002 [1930], 34). "Sublimation is a fate that culture imposes on the drives" Freud continues, while it is at the same time sublimation that produces culture. This leads to the darker insight of the book that culture "is built up on renunciation" and non-satisfaction of the sexual drives through repression. One effect of culture's restriction of the sexual life is to produce what Freud calls "cultural frustration" (2002 [1930], 34). "Cultural frustration" is how *Kulturversagung* (p. 59) is generally translated, but *Versager* in German generally means failure or refusal and here we return to the *Versagung* of translation in the Fliess letter, whereby the subject refuses the translation of the drive or memory trace because of the unpleasure (*Unbehagen*) or disquiet that it provokes. The unpleasurable sublimation, or translation, that culture requires therefore paradoxically produces cultural denial and refusal, just as translation could fail in the Fliess letter if (the prospect of) its unpleasure (*Unbehagen*) provoked its repression or refusal. The uneasiness of culture that Freud describes in 1930 is therefore paradoxically the product of its successful cultural translations. It is cultural translation that inducts us into civilization's iron cage (Weber 1992 [1904–5], 123).

What does this theory mean for translation? For Freud, at one level culture involves a process of sublimation that produces psychic translation. For the individual and for society, therefore, culture is nothing less than a process of repression that produces translation through its mechanisms of sublimation; translation for its part is thus nothing less than a procedure of sublimation in which the original sexual drives are renounced. What is distinctive about this process of cultural translation, however, is that, in Freud, the translated elements of sexuality in particular never disappear even in the translated person – for they reappear retranslated in dreams, and, for those whose translations have not been entirely successful, in the symptoms of hysteria and neurosis. So it is not a question of translation as in moving from text A to B, leaving text A behind, but rather moving to text B by making text A unconscious, repressed, but with A still haunting text B as its shadow and liable to reappear in disguised form at any moment. Cultural translation, in Freud, therefore, is not a process by which the former text or elements are ever entirely left behind, but one in which the new text always remains doubled and haunted, its translations always remaking themselves, the translated text perpetually seeking to revert to its original, like a ball held under water. The different languages, as in the dream, remain forever present. In some sense, therefore, according to Freud we live in two or more languages at once. This bi- or multilingualism in which, as it were, like Anno O we read one language but translate it simultaneously into another, can illuminate how, in this model, the general sense of loss in translation modifies its gain – for while in cultural terms much is gained, in the individual this gain produces at the same time a constant sense of unease, of dis-ease, malaise, of "cultural frustration," cultural denial, or as we might say today, of cultural dislocation, of nostalgia for the past that has been suppressed, and, Freud suggests at the end of the book, guilt.[7]

In this situation, while initially Freud draws on the older terms of sexuality, sublimation, and repression, increasingly he moves towards a dialectical account of the translational relation being one of perpetual struggle, or ambivalence. The malaise of contemporary culture or civilization in Freud's day comes from too successful a history of sublimation, or, we might say, cultural translation. The more successful it is, then paradoxically the more ambivalent individuals feel about it and the more inclined they are to reject it. At this point Freud comes closer to Marx, with his theory of alienation, than to Hegel, for whom culture is the objective expression of the subjective spirit (Hegel 1991 [1820]).

In contrast to Hegel, therefore, in Freud the development of culture also produces an increasing tension or dissensus between the community and the individual. For Freud, cultural translation as sublimation is thus something about which at best we can only feel ambivalent. Its community gains are also the losses of its individual members. "The patient may be psychically conceived as an accumulation of translations," writes Patrick Mahoney (2001: 837). For its part, culture is not just a process of translations but represents a form of translation in itself, one whose effect will always be doubled because it works simultaneously in two directions. Just like the discourse of psychoanalysis in fact, which mimics the repressive hierarchical transpositions of culture by translating the primitive speech of the subject into the elevated language of scientific knowledge while at the same time attempting to de-translate the subject's speech back into its lost, irretrievable original.

And cultural translation? If culture involves a process of translation, how then, it might be asked, can cultures themselves be translated except as the translations of translations? Unless we articulate and highlight its dialectical structure of a two-way doubling, then if culture is always a form of translation, the phrase "cultural translation" would in a sense always be a tautology. Perhaps this explains why, for all his many uses of the words culture and translation, and his analyses of the complex dialectical play between them, Freud never actually uses the phrase "cultural translation" (*kulturelle Übersetzung*).

Notes

1 Cf. Weber 1982, 60–62, 81–85.
2 At the same time, Freud often moves quickly from hieroglyphs to the idea that dreams are more like a picture-puzzle or rebus, in which the value of each image needs to be replaced by a word or syllable that indicates its meaning, which seems to imply an understanding of the nature of hieroglyphics prior to their decoding by Young and Champollion. In general Freud contrives to maintain the sense of interpreting from both language and pictures at once.
3 As Todorov (1982) observes, this reverses the normal hierarchy: here the commentary is the ingenious work of art, the original a flat and lifeless piece of incomprehensible text.
4 Cf. Freud, "'Civilized' Sexual Morality and Modern Nervous Illness" (1908): 1953–74, 9:177–204.
5 Spanish: an ancient feudal law guaranteeing traditional privileges for a city or region.
6 If we look back to the Fliess letter, we can see that there Freud is using *Übersetzung* in the sense later reserved in psychoanalysis for sublimation, whose meaning is defined as "the refining of instinctual energy, especially that of the sexual impulse, and its manifestation in ways that are socially more acceptable" (*OED*).
7 The guilt that translation produces helps to illuminate why Freud was so fond of quoting the famous witticism about the unavoidable cost of translation, *traduttore, traditore*!

References

Altman, Matthew C., and Cynthia D. Coe. 2013. *The Fractured Self in Freud and German Philosophy*. Basingstoke: Palgrave Macmillan.

Buchan, John. 1923. *History of the Great War (1915–19)*, 4 vols. Boston: Houghton Mifflin.

Buckle, Henry Thomas. 1857–61. *History of Civilization in England*, 2 vols. London: John W. Parker.

Cavell, Stanley. 1987. "Psychoanalysis and Cinema: The Melodrama of the Unknown Woman." In *Images in Our Souls: Cavell, Psychoanalysis and Cinema*, ed. Joseph H. Smith and William Kerrigan, 11–43. Baltimore: Johns Hopkins University Press.

Derrida, Jacques. 1998 [1996]. *Monolingualism of the Other, or the Prosthesis of Origin*, trans. Patrick Mensah. Stanford: Stanford University Press.

Freud, Sigmund. 1930. *Das Unbehagen in der Kultur*. Vienna: Internationaler Psychoanalytischer Verlag.

Freud, Sigmund. 1953–74. *The Standard Edition of the Complete Psychological Works of Sigmund Freud*, 24 vols., ed. James Strachey, with the assistance of

Anna Freud, Alix Strachey, and Alan Tyson, trans. James Strachey. London: Hogarth Press.

Freud, Sigmund, 1977. *Case Histories I. "Dora" and "Little Hans"*, trans. James Strachey. Pelican Freud Library 8. Harmondsworth: Penguin.

Freud, Sigmund. 1984. "The Economic Problem of Masochism." In *On Metapsychology. The Theory of Psychoanalysis*, trans. James Strachey, 413–26. Pelican Freud Library 11. Harmondsworth: Penguin.

Freud, Sigmund. 1985. *The Complete Letters of Sigmund Freud: Letters to Wilhelm Fliess, 1887–1904*. Cambridge, MA: Harvard University Press.

Freud, Sigmund. 2002 [1930]. *Civilization and Its Discontents*, trans. David McLintock. London: Penguin Books.

Freud, Sigmund. 2005. *On Murder, Mourning, and Melancholia*, trans. Shaun Whiteside. London: Penguin.

Freud, Sigmund. 2006 [1899]. *Interpreting Dreams*. trans. J.A. Underwood. London: Penguin Books.

Freud, Sigmund and Breuer, Josef. 2004 [1895]. *Studies in Hysteria*, trans. Nicola Luckhurst. London: Penguin.

Hegel, Georg Wilhelm Friedrich. 1991 [1820]. *Elements of the Philosophy of Right*, trans. H.B. Nisbet. Cambridge: Cambridge University Press.

Ingram, Susan. 2001. "Translation Studies and Psychoanalytic Transference." *TTR: Traduction, terminologie, rédaction*, 14, no. 1: 95–115.

Laplanche, Jean. 1992. *Seduction, Translation and the Drives*, ed. John Fletcher and Martin Stanton. London, Institute of Contemporary Arts.

Mahoney, Patrick. 1982. "Towards the Understanding of Translation in Psychoanalysis." *Meta: journal des traducteurs*, 27, no. 1: 63–71.

Mahoney, Patrick. 2001. "Freud and Translation," *American Imago* 58:4, 837–40.

Mavrikakis, Catherine. 1998. "L'Hystérique face aux symptômes de la traduction." *TTR: Traduction, terminologie, redaction*, 11, no. 2: 73–93.

Todorov, Tzvetan. 1982. *Symbolism and Interpretation*, trans. Catherine Porter. Ithaca, N.Y.: Cornell University Press.

Volosinov, V.N. 1973. *Marxism and the Philosophy of Language*, trans. Ladislav Matejka and I.R. Titunik. New York: Seminar Press.

Weber, Max. 1992 [1904–5]. *The Protestant Ethic and the Spirit of Capitalism*, trans. Talcott Parsons (1930). London: Routledge.

Weber, Samuel. 1982. *The Legend of Freud*. Minneapolis: Minnesota University Press.

Chapter 21

Psychoanalysis and Pedagogy: Narratives of Teaching

Isobel Armstrong

> I am sick and tired of hearing psycho-analytic theories – if they don't remind me of real life they are of no use to me. An application of a theory ... is no good to me unless it reminds me of something which I can see at any time in the world in which I live.
>
> (Bion 1978, 44)

I can still remember my exhilaration when I first learned some of the basic principles of Freudian and Lacanian thought concerned with gender and sexuality. They lifted a troubled feminism, beset with blame, anger, and puzzlement, into another world of thought. An ongoing inquiry into the construction of sexual difference seemed to be the project of both feminism and psychoanalysis, and there were times when I probably identified one with the other. The beauty of psychoanalytical models of, for example, phallic loss, or the symbolic order, was that they described deep, organizing structures in the self and in society that constituted not so much a totalizing explanation as an account of formative forces at work in culture. They provided complex reasons for women's oppression and its history. They released one from a politics of anger into a politics of analysis. I wanted to pass on this excitement to my students. But I'm not at all sure that I did. I begin by explaining why.

A Concise Companion to Psychoanalysis, Literature, and Culture, First Edition.
Edited by Laura Marcus and Ankhi Mukherjee.

I sometimes wonder how our students on our Masters program at Birkbeck, "Gender, Society and Culture," survived on the grim psychoanalytical fare we presented them with in the 1990s. We may have taught the pleasure principle, but we certainly did not practice it. The concentration of psychoanalysis came in an intensively taught optional half-unit of about six weeks, and consisted of six texts by six authors, then considered to be canonical, presented to the students raw, in roughly historical order, without the help of adjacent literary or cultural texts. This was partly because we were suspicious of any attempt to "apply" psychoanalysis to texts, and partly that the project of the course was theoretical. We did not want to use texts as mere illustrations of psychoanalysis, a process that actually makes both texts reductive, and sets up a pattern of master discourse and subsidiary discourse. We wanted to inquire into the constitutive power relations of gender construction. We were discussing the way sexual difference was conceptualized through different phases of psychoanalysis, historicizing these discourses, and seeing them as historical documents. But we were certainly searching for answers.

All our students encountered Freud's work, *Three Essays on the Theory of Sexuality*, in an introductory course that included a number of historical, sociological, literary, and political texts. In the optional unit I taught we returned to Freud with "Fragment of an Analysis of a Case of Hysteria" together with "Female Sexuality," but only after we read a founding document of feminist thought, Simone de Beauvoir's *The Second Sex* of 1949. (Nowadays a more likely choice would be her lover Sartre's 1939 book, *The Emotions: Outline of a Theory*.) We followed these with essays by Jacques Lacan, Julia Kristeva, Luce Irigaray, and Judith Butler. They constituted together an incessant attempt to define sexual difference, as if psychoanalysis were concerned with nothing else.

From de Beauvoir's great work we set the first part of Book One, "Destiny." This section in particular prepares us for the famous statement at the start of Book Two, "One is not born, but rather becomes, a woman." De Beauvoir's massive intellectual ambition, the comprehensiveness of her research, and her grasp of and inwardness with a range of disciplines, particularly psychoanalysis, are still stunning today, and for this reason alone I am glad that we started out with her. Some of her research has dated, some has not. (De Beauvoir must be among the earliest feminists to pick up on the importance of Lacan's mirror stage.) What is striking is her compulsive need to critique psychoanalysis and an equally compulsive need to use it in the service of an account of woman's indoctrination into her "vocation" as second sex. For her it is the patriarchal mode of Freudian psychoanalysis itself that is instrumental in creating the western woman as other even when it constitutes an explanation of that otherness. It is indispensable to her. She resents it and relies on it. Psychoanalysis confirms her narrative of the culturally made nature of women's oppression because it is itself a product of patriarchal culture but she uses it for some of her foundational arguments. She agrees that "the whole sexual drama is more complex for the girl than for her brothers"(1997, 72) but denies the validity of the central premise, the punitive castration theory that gives women the status of second sex: in speaking of phallic power and phallic loss, Freud based female sexuality on a masculine model of male libido that persuades the girl that she has been mutilated, she argues. Freud's determinism ("All psychoanalysts systematically reject the idea of *choice* and the correlated concept of value" [1997, 76]), and his literalizing of the penis ("this weak little rod of flesh" [1997, 73]), preoccupy her. Yet she enters into dispute with Freud precisely in these terms. The penis, the vagina, the clitoris, and later in Book Two, penile urination, female micturation (women like watering with hoses as compensation for the projectile power they lack), a welter of sexual body parts, overwhelm her discussion.

Through de Beauvoir we discussed the issue of determinism and literalism in psychoanalysis. But what I see now in de Beauvoir is an irritability, an anger, an impatience with her own dilemma. She at once asserts the coercive power of empirical gender discrimination – this with a painful, accusatory asperity – and denies the explanatory force of Freudian models of gender formation while flying to them as a moth to a candle. The result is that she begins to hate women – and herself – for being what they are. She is the first post-World War II feminist, the first female misogynist. But what it is important to note now is that she set up in us exactly the same pattern of accusatory irritability and compulsive admiration that Freud evoked in her. And, I think, exactly the same pattern of resentment and reliance on the Freudian model of gender formation. This pattern seems endemic to the teaching of psychoanalysis – at least in this kind of course. The result is that the teacher becomes an apologist (and the master) instead of a collaborative explicator, constantly justifying the text in order to put a stay on the students' foreclosure of judgment. One solution, of course, is to tell them what is happening. But that cannot be the end of the matter. It is important for students to know you take seriously what is for many of them a first-time reader response, while trying to make reading a speculative and exploratory collective enterprise instead of a rush to judgment. Students will be angry through sheer interpretive frustration: they will joke to deal with the bewilderment of unfamiliar thinking. I hesitate to describe this response as a "resistance" that can be smoothly overcome and incorporated into psychoanalytic discourse (saying no when yes is intended), because this procedure ignores the felt urgency of students' responses.

We looped back to Freud, Dora, and "Female Sexuality" after de Beauvoir, followed by Lacan's "The Meaning of the Phallus" and Kristeva's "Stabat Mater" (1986) – all well-worked but difficult texts. Irigaray's (1985, 226–40) chapter, "Volume-Fluidity" from *Speculum of the Other Woman* followed, and we concluded with Judith Butler's (1990, 43–72) critique of Lacan and Freud in *Gender Trouble*. It is a familiar genealogy. Re-reading these texts now, I am still struck by their supreme intellectual richness as well as by their exacting and sometimes charmless theoretical virtuosity. All these texts are concerned with the repercussions, the reverberations, of castration theory, the prohibitive intervention of the father, and the girl's discovery, as Freud puts it, "of her own deficiency" and sense of "misfortune" in lacking a penis (1977, 380). They constitute an exhaustive poetics of the phallus even when they attempt to replace the Oedipal moment with something else. Looking back there was something obsessive, fixated, about this phallus-centered configuration of texts.

Here I will discuss responses to just two of these texts – Freud's analysis of Dora and Lacan's essay – and what we did to open them up.[1] I will ventriloquize the students' voices, for often impulsive and seemingly basic critiques recall one in a raw way to essential problems, problems that a practiced and sophisticated reader of psychoanalytic texts might ignore.

What does Freud want?

> I get this, the multiple signification of the symptom, this is neat. The way Dora's cough transfers the pressure of Herr K's erect member from the lower body to the upper body, the way the her Dad's fellatio with Frau K. focuses on the throat, the connection between the parents' catarrh of the lower body (gonorrhea) and the catarrh in Dora's throat.
>
> ("A symptom is the representation of a sexual phantasy ... a symptom has more than one meaning and serves to represent several unconscious mental processes simultaneously" [Freud 1963, 64].)
>
> But why always, always, always a sexual phantasy – why not other kinds of pain and fear?

This is a psychodrama – too many people in love with too many people, as if the unconscious levels out every relation and assigns an equal value to it. Bad luck for the unconscious I say.

This man is a bully, a patriarchal bully. Dora has been "handed over" to him. He forces her to accept she is in love with Herr K, forces her into the paradigm of the jealous hysterical woman, forces her into the guilt of masturbation and bed-wetting. He knows everything (what he won't see is that Dora is trapped) and conducts everything in an authoritarian way. "Wait and see," he says, when she wonders how her mother gets into the first dream, and then adds a note saying Dora has violated the "rules" of dream interpretation like a disobedient schoolgirl.

("I don't in the least know how mother gets into the dream" ... "I will explain that to you later" ... Footnote 9: "This remark gave evidence of a complete misunderstanding of the rules of dream interpretation, though ... Dora was perfectly familiar with them" [1963, 86–87].)

Man, this is abuse, not bullying.

There is a problem with the dream – Freud always footnotes or sidelines the mother. She is an obsessive housewife, Dora's father "gets nothing" from her, no sex, Dora hates her, we are told, so she doesn't matter. Yet she is *in the dream*. And we are specifically told that Dora tells *her mother* about Herr K's proposition in the wood by the lake, though Freud elides this into "parents."

Why should the mother's castration matter?

Why does the dream have to be univocal, to represent an unfulfilled wish, when the symptom can be multivocal?

And if everything can be turned around to its opposite, why is Freud selective about the items he chooses to read inversely? The father could be saying, "I consent to let my [not our but maybe "your"] two children be burnt for the sake of your [the mother's] jewel case." If the mother is "really" Frau K, this is what he is doing. But Freud ignores this because every dream has to be an unfulfilled wish.

We decided to look afresh at the first dream, to see if there were other possibilities within the psychoanalytical paradigm.

("A house was on fire" [1963, 81].) Not "the" house but "a" house, a generalized house that seems to have been subjected to an act of arson.

It sure was on fire: even if we turn it around and say it was flooded, as Freud turns fire round to its opposite, both lead to sexual activity. A house in the conflagration of erotic feeling, in flagrante, or flooded with the wetness of sex. Her father, Frau K, Herr K, the governess (we learn later), and maybe Dora's own sexual feelings. They are all at it and all lying. Is she overwhelmed by this overdetermined sexual life? The "something" that might happen in the night is not an "accident," the bed wetting (Freud uses the word "accident," not Dora) – it's sex [Freud 1963, 88].

Freud substitutes Herr K for the father (with reason), but the fact remains that the father is the prime mover in this conflagration. It is he who wakes her to sexual life if we trust the Oedipal moment.

He wakes her to sexed life but the mother wakes her to sexual life earlier because she has the phallus.

OK. But the overwhelming wish of the dream is what Freud says, to get away.

But to get away with what? The mother *wants her jewel-case*, just as she wanted those pearl earrings, the droplets of sex, that her husband denied her (instead chaining her with a bracelet about which she was furious, we hear). Freud says that Dora wants to "give" her jewel case to the father, to Herr K. But what if the dream is speculating on the father's denial of genital/sexual life to the mother, the sacrifice? Might she be like the mother, living with loss, if she does not retrieve her jewel case and its promise of fulfillment? This looks like conflict, not an unfulfilled wish. The mother is much more important than Freud says, whatever we decide.

That's when Eros becomes death, when the jewel case is left to burn. The jewel case is the nexus of condensation, as Freud [1963, 96] says, but might it have additional and opposing significations? Sexual life and its negation.

The dream may want her mother to save her rather than the father – or maybe the dream is wondering how each parent might both save and let her down.

She is hurried downstairs. In other parts of Freud's writing, to go downstairs is to make a move to the lower body, whereas to go upstairs is to move beyond it. She is hurried into the arena of sex, not actually rescued

> from it. It is a dream about fear of sex and desire for it, ambivalence about sex?
>
> All dreams are messy, not neat like Freud says.
>
> But he doesn't say they are neat: he says contrary impulses cohabit in the unconscious and contrary meanings run on different tracks in the dream.

Whatever we felt about these challenges and questions, the students learned to begin to read Freud. They learned the art of questioning, demystifying, and the close reading of images and statements. They learned to follow a chain of connections and began to see the complexity of gender identifications as Freud describes them.

What does Lacan want?

Turning to "The Meaning of the Phallus," Lacan evoked intense dislike in the students, not only because of the difficulty of the essay, but also because of its content and tone. There are five complex phases to this condensed and elliptical essay, to say nothing of Lacan's detachment – paring his fingernails – from the "comedy" of gender and sexuality, and the constant peripeteia of the argument.[2]

> "It speaks in the Other." Why this mystification? Why this religiosity? Can't he *name* the Phallus? Why re-enact its "veiled" mystery for us? He is imitating the word of God. What's going on?
>
> And why is castration and desire central to all relations? Why must we be in a state of privation? Why is the phallus the master signifier? What hubris.
>
> This is theology.

"It speaks in the Other" (Lacan 1982, 79). Different questions emerged when we had unpacked this "theological" sentence (in fact a key sentence), which comes quite late in the discussion, worked back from it, and looked at the details of the five phases of this essay. "It," the phallus, the universal "it," is intelligible through difference and creates difference. The "Other" is not de Beauvoir's excluded object or "other" but the founding alterity entailed by the oppositional play of signification itself, which we find in the very structure of language. The linguistics of Saussure, requiring the creation of meaning through diacritical marks, obviously speaks in Lacan's phallus. All language, and in parallel, all sexual relations, all subject–object relations, are organized through alterity. The fundamental "Other," the site of difference, is the unconscious. The phallus is the primordial signifier because it signifies the structure of signification itself, the possibility of meaning …

> OK. Stop there. Why the emphasis on language and the unconscious as a language? The realities of sexual difference are very remote from all this.
>
> If the unconscious is structured like a language, what is the status of "real," conscious language? I don't get it.
>
> Maybe it's like the dream? A manifest language and a latent language?
>
> And why is there this "passion" [1982, 78] of the signifier?

The structure of signification is founded on the stable form of signifier/signified. It constitutes the law, the symbolic order that ordains meaning. But the order of signification is itself unstable, founded on the split between signifier and signified. It is this constitutive splitting and the unstable elements of language – metaphor, the pun, the homonymic clash, the ambiguity, "combination and substitution," as Lacan puts it (1982, 79), which makes possible the activity of repression (when one meaning has to disappear to make another function intelligibly), so that we are always subject to the conscious/unconscious split. The "passion" of the signifier comes in here. The "passion" means to be acted upon, to suffer. For the signifier is not only the omnipotent determinant of signification: it is *subject to splitting* by virtue of the signifier/signified duality. Splitting is the very form of castration. Thus the phallic fate of castration is built into language: it is the deep formative structure that the signifier signifies. We could say that castration creates language, and language creates castration. It is built into our communications. Underlying this system is not the threat of castration but its privation.

> So this is determinism, a tragedy, not a psychodrama like Freud. So why does he call it all a comedy?
>
> *I don't feel* that I suffer from castration – I refuse it.

> What have need, demand, and desire to do with all this and with sexual difference?
>
> What does it mean to have and to be the phallus?
>
> Why is having assigned to the male, being to the female? Can't it switch?

We struggled through the two last phases of the essay embodied in these two questions to engage with the formative and inevitable asymmetry that constitutes gender relations. It was when we reached an account of this asymmetry, someone (there is always a joker in the class) burst out –

> This is like a comic strip. He says that there's a no win situation because each side of the couple wants to incite desire in the other (first frame). No one wants to betray need or appetite, no one wants to be the passive object of love, no one wants to be the recipient of love (second frame, stalemate). So, we divide up forms of possession of the phallus, which is both real and not real (third frame, here, not here, I go, I come back). For the guy, who *has* the phallus, he keeps the unreality of the phallus going to protect its unreality and to cover its castration (fourth frame, the emperor's new clothes). For the woman she is in deep trouble – she signifies the desire of the Other (which isn't "really" there anyway), reflecting his phallic power. But that phallic power is in fact lack. She wants, anyhow, to abandon the masquerade of being the phallus and to be loved for not having it (fifth frame, three ways of being not there). Last frame, there's nothing there. But all the same, it takes two phalluses to fandango.

Given this theater of the absurd, we tried to get away from Beckettian drama by going back to need, demand, and desire. Lacan's neat formulation seemed to make need, the concrete appetites, disappear into repression by being re-described as absolute demand for unconditional love, the wanting in excess of need. Desire, the residue of longing left over from the subtraction of need from desire, and the position from which *both* sides of the couple start. That is to say, phallic lack takes up its residence in desire. This seemed a valuable addition to the lexicon of analysis, a way of thinking through the vagaries of the conscious and unconscious. Though these seemed hitched to the phallus as it were, rather arbitrarily, in effect desire is a form of phallic lack.

But we reached a stalemate with this text. Its abstraction, its coercive detachment, were real problems. We tried to solve this by going back to Freud and seeing how Lacanian positions could be mapped on to Freud's Dora narrative. Lacan (1990), of course, wrote about this text. But we were less interested in his specific interpretation than in the ways this particular essay might illuminate Freud's text, or the ways we might contest his thinking, or indeed the ways it might alter his Lacan's own thinking. So we re-described Freud, and here are some observations:

What does Dora want?

So we don't need to see Freud as just the inexplicably all-powerful patriarchal father figure. He *has the phallus*. He is the signifier, the maker of meaning. It is he who understands the constitutive split of the unconscious when its language is betrayed. That means he is in charge of castration.

("He that has eyes to see and ears to hear may convince himself that no mortal can keep a secret. If his lips are silent, he chatters with his fingertips; betrayal oozes out of him at every pore. And thus the task of making conscious the most hidden recesses of the mind is one which it is quite possible to accomplish" [Freud 1953–74, 7:96].)

Dora's father thinks he has the phallus too, certain he knows that the encounter with Herr K was a fantasy. He wants Dora to desire him and to collude with him in his affair with Frau K. I guess his disavowal of the phallus – he lets it be known he is impotent – masks his libido, which again masks phallic absence?

Maybe the way to think about this is through the heavily populated scene of desire: everyone wants to be the cause of desire in others. They want to have the phallus while someone else *is* it, endorsing the person who has it and reflecting back their power. Or else they want to be the phallus while someone else has it. Freud wants Dora to accept his hysterical reading – she wants to kiss him, he suggests. Herr K wants Dora to want to kiss him. Dora's father wants her to want him (or at least his explanations and prevarications). Frau K wants Dora to want her. Frau K wants Dora's father to want her. Dora's father wants Frau K to want him. While Freud sees all desire as emanating from Dora, Lacanian theory would see Dora as the focus of the desire of the

Other. Trapped. She would be *in* a structure, not the center of a self-created network of relations.

Does this alter Freud? What does Dora want? Dora seems to opt out of the chain of desire. She displays an atavistic need for survival rather than the desire that is expected of her in Lacanian theory. A need for literalism – she confronts Herr K and Frau K with the truth of their betrayal of her as she sees it – and an archaic attachment to the mother, characterize her responses. Not allowed her phallic jewelry the mother is without, a person of lack. But, contra Lacan again, being without may grant a certain freedom even if it leads to privation.

And the dream?

Everything is on fire, yes, but the conflagration is the fire of desire, which has an equal importance with literal sexual activity.

The father's appearance is the appearance of the phallus, power, the man who has, but the man who is weak, impotent, he says.

Dora dresses herself hurriedly. Is she donning phallic being, the clothes of masquerade, under duress? Her being to his having? To prop him up?

The mother wants the phallus: she wants to go back for her jewel case, to preserve it.

But her preservation is the father's (and the children's) destruction. Hence the interdict. The mother must be in a state of desire in order to create the logic of lack that enables that essential having of the phallus.

("for each partner in the relation, the subject and the Other, it is not enough to be the subjects of need, nor objects of love, but they must stand as the cause of desire" [Lacan 1982, 81].)

Dora wants out from all of this, to regress to need, the mother. Forget about desire and demand.

But maybe she has lesbian desires?

But is she in mourning? Is she refusing masquerade for the death wish?

Must it all be lack, lack? Lack, Lacan, manqué.

What does a teacher want?

Some students become fascinated by the theory and practice of psychoanalysis. There is no need to argue with them, as happens sometimes, that it is important to teach psychoanalysis because it represents one of the new knowledges of the twentieth century, and that, along with Marxism, it is historically important as a mode of inquiry: that to explore this mode of inquiry in as much complexity as is possible is a pedagogical necessity. Such students become convinced of this without persuasion. But there will always be the student who cannot accept work on psychoanalysis: "To spend time reassessing the Oedipus complex may well be interesting but most women who are struggling, bored and dissatisfied with their lot could well see it as a debate doing nothing to help them ... there is a lot more practical work changing laws and conditions which may be more vital" (quoted in Armstrong 1989, 88).

I am not sure that there is anything to be said to such a student. If the course fails to engage curiosity and excitement one can only respect that, with disappointment. "What psychoanalysis can teach us is to substitute the art of listening for the seizure of meaning," Maud Ellmann (1984, 11) wrote in her *Psychoanalytic Literary Criticism*. With its attention to the subtleties of chains of signification, to condensation, to ambiguity and linguistic composites, to the functioning of metaphor and metonymy in the dream and in discourse, psychoanalysis is hyperconscious of those very elements of language that structure both speech and writing. This attention runs parallel to the attention of the literary critic. Indeed, on some occasions, as Ella Freeman Sharpe's (1950) systematic grammar of psychoanalysis suggests, textual analysis and psychoanalysis go hand in hand (see also Armstrong 2001). Freud was a brilliant textual critic, and thus his work can donate to the literary critic invaluable methodological practices. These generate meaning and material from a text's language. Attention to *The Psychopathology of Everyday Life* (1901) and *The Interpretation of Dreams* (1900) will elicit a range of interpretive practices, from parapraxes to the taxonomy of dreams, which invite the literary critic to develop them through linguistic and formal analysis. When students ask how they might "use" psychoanalysis, it is often apposite to appeal to these practices as hermeneutic tools that the student can employ, hermeneutic tools that are imaginatively liberating and productive. They are equally illuminating for readings of prose fiction and poetry.

But it is not quite enough to stop there. For to plunder a methodology from psychoanalysis without attending to its content speaks a formalism that circumvents the demands of psychoanalysis itself. For Freud as for Lacan, the unconscious speaks in language, and to proceed without recognizing this is to leave psychoanalysis behind.

What psychoanalytical material, then, would we seek to put before the student now? Ellmann's collection of essays amply demonstrates the richness and depth of psychoanalytic literary criticism. This is a collection of classic essays. The first group of essays remains with the Oedipal problem; others, such as Žižek's account of desire in film noir, revise Lacanian principles of masquerade and the negation of "the woman." Jacqueline Rose's virtuosic account of Sylvia Plath's "Daddy," feminine fantasy, fascism, mourning, and metaphoric language, is an exemplary discussion of identification and its complexity.

This collection terminates in the early 1990s, the era that accepted Lacan's dismissal of an "appeal to the concrete, which is so pathetically conveyed by the term 'affect'" (1982, 79) and did not challenge his contempt for what he termed "nurse-analysts" (1982, 81), the psychoanalysis of object relations that deals with children (though he had a great respect for Melanie Klein). But it is this material, the work derived from object relations, which has begun to emerge in accounts of literature and psychoanalysis. The scene of reading and teaching has changed. The syllabus I described had an almost theological aspect to it. The overwhelming move towards affect and the study of the history of the emotions has surged over the last decade, altering the axis of teaching and writing.

An example of this new direction is Nancy Yousef's prize-winning essay of 2010, "Romanticism, Psychoanalysis and the Interpretation of Silence." The phallus-centered work I once taught does not make an appearance here. Christopher Bollas, D.W. Winnicott, Michael Balint, and Masud M. Khan are the interlocutors in this essay. The emphasis is less on psychoanalytical explanation than on the total analytic relationship and its intersubjective complexity. In a note, Yousef quotes Jeanne Wolff Bernstein's recognition of a revisionary shift in psychoanalytic thinking as a "new royal road to the unconscious": "Attention to the analyst's affective responses is indicative of the radical transvaluation of countertransference in recent decades. The concept once used to name a failure of analytic technique and a breach of neutrality is now commonly viewed as a vital source of insight, a 'new royal road to the unconscious'" (2010, 671). Yousef builds this revaluation of the analyst's status from a figure of impersonality to an intersubjective presence into her revaluation of a number of central Romantic poems, Coleridge's "Frost at Midnight," Wordsworth's "Tintern Abbey," and the narrative of the "Discharged Soldier" in Book IV of *The Prelude*. Such poems, frequently read as examples of Romantic solipsism, and carrying with this reading a political criticism of the isolated Romantic artist, are now explored in and through processes of intersubjective attunement. The subtle and constant rebalancing of the existential priorities and needs of the subject and its other (and here the other is the other side of the pair) enacted in these poems becomes the field of critical investigation. The phenomenology of meditation, generative silence, the solitude that takes place against a relational background, the necessary presence of the other as a container of the subject's reverie, the possibilities of a nurturing "spiritual idleness" (Yousef 2010, 658), all these belong to relational states for Yousef. She considers the ebb and flow of psychic responsiveness in "Frost at Midnight," as the poet researches into his own interiority to understand the figures of his past, the guardian presences he lacks, his own child and its intersubjective future: "The sense that self-involvement precludes, or seeks to evade engagement with communal or civic life only duplicates the rigid opposition between solitude and sociality that a poem such as 'Frost at Midnight' interrogates" (2010, 657). Encounters with the self, she argues, are the ground of politics. She stresses that Romantic poems are not concerned with an easy response to what Christopher Bollas (1987, 13–29) has called the "transformational object" (that which transforms selfhood), and traces the psychic hesitancies, disturbances, and failures of intersubjective exchanges, such as she finds in the "Discharged Soldier" narrative in *The Prelude*.

This essay offers a wholly new way of thinking about psychoanalysis and the text. It is over-simplifying to say that this form of criticism represents a move from the phallus to the breast, from the father to the mother, from structure to nurture, but certainly Winnicott's "good enough mother," Christopher Bollas' aesthetic of mothering, and, more distantly, Wilfred Bion's account of the breast as the ground of knowledge, as well as the work of Melanie Klein on the mother's body, constitute a tradition that stands behind this essay.

What would a psychoanalytical syllabus for literary students look like today? There are two ways of looking at this. One way is to compile a course that responds to these newly introduced texts. I don't think it is necessary to set up a conflict between earlier "phallic" texts and this new material. It does suggest, however, a reconfiguring of the content of our teaching. The second way is not to create a distinctively psychoanalytical syllabus at all, but to study literary texts alongside a range of critical and historical materials that includes a psychoanalytic perspective.

What does the student want? A syllabus?

Here is a possible revisionary syllabus that attends to the new directions that Yousef's essay signals.

One would surely begin with Freud's foundational *Three Essays on the Theory of Sexuality* of 1905. Jean Laplanche's gloss on this text, the first chapter in his 1970 *Life and Death in Psychoanalysis*, "The Order of Life and the Genesis of Sexuality," which attends to "the extraordinary broadening of the notion of sexuality occasioned by psychoanalysis" (1985, 25), could be read side by side with Freud. Laplanche's emphasis on "*maternal fantasies*" (1985, 24) that are tied to sexual excitation associated with a new internal entity would be a good way of modifying father-related texts. It would be a bridge to Lacan's work, which I would decisively want to retain. He is a canonical figure. "The Meaning of the Phallus" is so central to his work and to the linguistic turn of psychoanalysis that it is still crucially important reading. However, it is important to include work by the "nurse analysts" he speaks of. Melanie Klein is the analyst he most respects here, and chapters from *Love, Guilt and Reparation* would be an appropriate transition, possibly "Early Stages of the Oedipus Conflict" (1988, 186–98). The essay challenges Freud's dating of the Oedipus complex and locates it at an early stage in the child's development, but it is less a quibble about dates than an exploration of the importance of "*not knowing*" (1988, 188), or epistemophilia, to the child, adding a whole new category to the Freudian model. A move to Julia Kristeva's *Powers of Horror: An Essay on Abjection*, and the chapter "Something To Be Scared Of" also reveals connections between knowing and language, but in the context of the phobic object and "the instability of object relation" (1982, 32–55). Kristeva moves into the sphere of object relations here, but sees them as inevitably pathologized, a "horror of being" that is the other side of the religious, moral, and ideological codes that ordain the social order.

Here we need to loop back to earlier work on object relations, that of Wilfred Bion, D.W. Winnicott, and their contemporary follower, Christopher Bollas. All psychoanalytical readings involve a two-sided relationship, but for this group the relational element in identity formation and the maternal holding capacity is paramount. Bion has described the principal addition to psychoanalytic theory on which this work is founded: describing "projective identification" he says:

> I don't think there is much to be said beyond Melanie Klein's version – what she called an omnipotent phantasy; a phantasy that a person can split off feelings, thoughts and ideas he does not want and evacuate them into another person, more particularly into the mother, and more particularly still at a primitive state of existence, namely, at the breast itself. Of course the infant doesn't *do* anything; nothing happens. But the infant *feels* as if he could do that, and *feels* that it gets rid of some characteristic which it doesn't like and then becomes afraid that that same characteristic is directed towards it by the other person – originally by the mother, or by the breast into which it projects it. The theory was not intended as a substitute for already existing psycho-analytic theories, but as an addition to them.
>
> (Bion 1978, 1)

Bion describes an addition to psychoanalytical thinking – the mother for the father, the breast for the phallus, and, instead of *desire*, the paramount emotion is *fear*: fear of the avenging other, fear of not knowing, fear of the void. The corollary of this is that there is an intense emphasis on what will assuage fear. Consequently, the potency of the earliest mothering, and the arousal and satisfaction of epistemophilia, receive an attention not present in the earliest psychoanalytical thought. Here I would offer the student chapters of Winnicott's *Playing and Reality*, concerned as it is with both nurturing and the "transitional object," that protean entity of early life that is neither subject nor object, a piece of blanket or a toy, for instance, that for the child negotiates the space between itself and the world, the relationship with the mother and externality (Winnicott 1971, 118). Several of Bion's essays in *Second Thoughts*, notably "A Theory of Thinking" (1984, 93–109) and "Attacks on Linking" (1984, 110–19), explore fear and thought, and the importance of the breast in precipitating thought. Finally, the opening chapters of Christopher Bollas' *The Shadow of the Object*, with their emphasis on the mother's aesthetic of care and the search for a "transformational object," that which will alter the imagination, would bring this syllabus up to the present.

It would be appropriate to include some case histories: Klein's "The Importance of Symbol-Formation in the Development of the Ego" (1988, 219–32), largely a case history of a child analysis, and parts of Marion Milner's account of an analysis of a schizophrenic woman, *The Hands of the Living God: An Account of Psycho-Analytic Treatment* (1988 [1969]). These could be set against Freud's Dora.

There are two problems with this syllabus. Though it traces the contours of object relations, it is in some ways even more abstract than the course I began by describing. Bion's sense, in the epigraph to this essay, that no theory will attract him unless it reminds him of the real life he lives, might well be shared by student readers of this syllabus. The way these theories might enter into literary analysis is not immediately evident. Yousef's originality in seizing on the possibilities of the dyad of analyst and analysand is one way of responding to this work. But the texts I mention cannot be explored in the same way as the earlier syllabus allowed, as in Ellmann's volume, which is in many ways the culminating example of the phallic tradition of literary criticism. Thus in the last part of this essay I move to an alternative way of teaching psychoanalysis.

What do students want? Unsystematic perspectives?

This second method intersperses the students' core texts and the works of criticism associated with them with any psychoanalytic text that seems relevant to these texts. It does not presuppose previous knowledge of psychoanalytic texts and methodologies but assumes that the single text enables a grasp of structure and method that is sufficiently powerful. I give three examples of this practice. Two are autobiographical, one is a wish.

The first was a supervision of an MA essay on a one-to-one basis. The student was writing an essay on dolls and toys in the nineteenth century. She was beginning with Jane's doll in *Jane Eyre*, and continuing with the Doll's Dressmaker in *Our Mutual Friend*, but she found it difficult to generate material and was falling into a simple descriptive account of what was going on. She had discovered historical material on dolls, but nothing was emerging for her. I was puzzled for a bit, but then remembered Luce Irigaray's (1989) essay, "The Gesture in Psychoanalysis." This girl had never read any psychoanalytic text. She would not have grasped many of the references, particularly to Dora and to Schreber at the end of the discussion. But she did learn some of the essentials of analysis through the essay itself. I pointed her specifically to the passage on the doll (1989, 132–35). There Irigaray offers a non phallic alternative to the representation of loss in the little boy, Ernst's, fort-da game. She argues that "In the absence of her mother, a girl's gestures are not the same. She does not play with a string and a reel symbolizing her mother, for her mother's sex is the same as hers and the mother cannot have the objective status of a reel. The mother's identity as a subject is the same as hers" (1989, 132). The mother cannot be externalized in a symbol whose very function as a symbol represents separation because mother and girl are in identity with one another: instead the girl child's response to maternal deprivation is, firstly, utter loss, and loss of the will to live – "she neither speaks nor eats." Then she invents through the doll not a fully objectified entity, not a split-off symbol, but a form of "quasi-*subject*" (1989, 132; my emphasis). The doll is a form of herself and the mother fused, because they occupy the same subject position. The negotiation of absence is created through *space* rather than through the object. In order to organize a "symbolic space" (1989, 132), the girl uses her own body as the symbol of absence, dancing, opening herself to "cosmic space," creating relational "territory" that organizes the gap between herself and the lost mother. Indeed space is crucial to Irigaray's reading. The girl thinks through her loss territorially, inscribing herself within a circle, setting spatial boundaries and limits to her identity.

The mother can never be replaced by a symbol. "Human beings must love something," Jane, the narrator of the novel, says of her doll, a doll she nurses by the fire and takes to bed – "I could not sleep unless it was folded in my night-gown" (Brontë 2006, 35). This doll, "a faded graven image," lay "safe and warm" in the child's night clothes. There was enough in these brief paragraphs for my student to mine despite her lack of a context in psychoanalytical thinking. She experimented with seeing the doll as a "quasi-subject" rather than an object, an analogue of Jane herself, who comes into being here as a mother, belonging to the same subject position as the mother, and mothering herself, even giving birth to herself, a re-birth into warmth – "folded in my night-gown." This is neither an anthropomorphic projection nor a retreat to the womb, but a more powerful and troubled attempt to re-create the self from loss. Jane's subdued movements, certainly not dancing, from stair-head to nursery, a sort of ritual boundary-making, also came to be seen as part of a total situation of mourning, situating the doll in a ceremony of loss. That Jane lacks the vitality ascribed to the gestures of the mourning girl by Irigaray led to an understanding of the depths of psychic illness Jane is threatened with and indeed suffers. Her attempts at symbol-making through the doll are attempts to integrate herself, a strategy we see throughout the novel.

A grasp of one element of Irigaray's work led to further understanding of others. The lack of context did not seem to matter here. What my student did was to infer and make connections through close reading of the psychoanalytical text and the novel. But to do this she had to understand phallic theories of gender and their contestation.

The second case of psychoanalytical reading took place as a class epiphany, in a graduate class in the United States, which was struggling to read Tennyson's *Maud* (1855). The course was on nineteenth-century poetry and the emotions, "Victorian Lyric Poetry and the Passions." We began by reading poems against nineteenth-century psychological and medical texts, followed by Stanley Cavell's (2005, 155–91) reading and critique of Austin's "perlocutionary" category of emotion. Thereafter each session was arranged round a cluster of poems constellated with a range of prose texts, nineteenth-century and modern – philosophical, psychological, historical, medical, psychoanalytical. The aim was to give the students multiple methodologies and languages for thinking about emotions. There were two consecutive sessions that included *Maud* and other poems. The first session included, as constellated prose texts among others, Goethe's *The Sorrows of Young Werther* (1774), Benjamin Richardson's *Diseases of Modern Life* (1876), passages from the work of Maudsley, and Freud's "Mourning and Melancholia" essay. The second session included, among other texts, Thomas J. Graham's *On the Diseases of Females* (1871) and Freud's "The Aetiology of Hysteria" (1896; 1953–74, 3:186–221).

In the second session, we were getting nowhere, puzzling over the violence of the disorganized, paratactic logic of the first poem in *Maud*, and speculating on the strange hallucinatory nature of Section VII, in which the hero thinks he remembers the two fathers, Maud's and his own, arranging a marriage between himself and the yet unborn child – "Well, if it prove a girl ..." (Tennyson 1988, l. 291). Then one of the students suddenly referred to two points in Freud's hysteria essay: "Whatever the case and whatever symptom we take as our point of departure, *in the end we infallibly come to the field of sexual experience*" (1953–74, 3:199); "children cannot find their way to acts of sexual aggression unless they have been seduced previously. The foundation for a neurosis would accordingly always be laid in childhood by adults, and the children themselves would transfer to one another the disposition to fall ill of hysteria later" (1953–74, 3:208). What would happen if we posited that the "hero" of *Maud* had been abused by his father? This essay was written before the literal seduction of the child was called into question (later by Freud himself), but I do not think this mattered for our subsequent discussion. We had agreed in a general way that the speaker was hysterical. But this prompt from Freud enabled us to read the poem, not as a desperate *expression* of hysteria, but as a poem *about* a person driven to illness and suffering by an early trauma, with consequences for his whole way of experiencing the world and his language for it. I stress that this was not a narrative release so much as an analytical liberation. Reading the poem as an expressive text meant that we were locked into the violence of the speaker's mental life and could only re-describe it. Reading the poem through the analytical prompt meant that we could read it over and above the speaker's anguish through Freud's two metaphors of discovery, the archeological uncovering of buried remains, and the pursuit of chains of "associatively connected" memories (1953–74, 3:198).

Freud's prompt suggested an adult seducer: the father, or fathers, of the speaker and of Maud. We began to read the erotic implications of line 71 of the first poem – "Maud with her sweet purse-mouth when my father dangled the grapes." Maud's mouth took us back to the "lips" of the "dreadful hollow" in the very first stanza, where "blood" moves from metaphor – the "blood-red heath" (l. 2), to the literal – "a silent horror of blood" (l. 3). The lips recur in the final stanza – "Or an underlip, you may call it a little too ripe, too full" (l. 85). Perverse orifices or hollows recur: the "old man" who ruined the speaker's father "Dropt off gorged from a scheme that has left us flaccid and drained" (l. 20); "Pickpockets, each hand lusting for all that is not its own" (l. 22), endorse the erotics of illicit theft from a pocket, a longstanding sexual innuendo; "centre-bits," robbers' tools for making holes, "Grind on the wakeful ear in the hush of the moonless nights" (l. 42), another erotic allusion; "Must *I* too creep to the hollow ..." (l. 53). These are predominantly vaginal images, but in this analysis we did not make the obvious symbolic equations because these images are assigned both feminine and masculine significations: the speaker is hyperconscious of the blurring of gender markers when, dangerously, gender markers disappear – "When the poor are hovelled and hustled together, each sex, like swine" (l. 33). It's as if his reading of sexuality is polymorphous, as if abuse has rendered him feminine as well as masculine. And this hystericizing of sexuality has its repercussions in his account of class and class oppression.

Section VII, an enigmatic four-stanza poem where the two fathers speak of a possible marriage even before Maud's birth, overheard, or possibly fantasized by the speaker, is a magnificent evocation of uncertain traumatic memory, the tricks the unconscious can play. Did he just dream the episode a moment ago, or was it a long-ago occurrence? Did he confect the memory from the oriental fiction of the *Arabian Nights*? The boy child would be 6 or 7, the Oedipal moment, at this time.

(The narrator is 25 to Maud's 17, eight years older than she, but we must remember the agreement is prior to her birth.) What is fascinating about this poem is the conjuring of mnemic uncertainty. It may even be that the poem represents a screen memory overlaying a more disturbing episode of abuse. The two fathers agree to bind him, after all. Again, the literal occurrence of these events is not the objective here, but a structural understanding of the poem and its language. What emerges is first of all a series of deranged images whose logic is only available when their origin in traumatic memory is disclosed, and secondly, a disintegrated syntax that breaks rather than makes connections, as if the narrator's linguistic coherence has been radically impaired. The need to image social violence through the taking in of dangerous substances – vitriol, alum, poison, in stanzas X and XI – is an example of the first form of distortion, where these murderous stimulants suggest what Freud, in "The Aetiology of Hysteria," terms, in his eloquent criticism of abuse, a "premature" arousal, at the "mercy" of an "arbitrary will." Arbitrariness, indeed, characterizes the second form of incoherence. The narrator strings together chains of events and arguments through the dominant paratactic connective, "And," as if they are causal when in fact the connections are the result of a kind of persecutory associationism. To return to stanza X, the connection between the "vitriol" madness of domestic violence and the preceding stanza IX, is not logical, but based on the intoxicant affinities of adulterated wine and vitriol. "Peace in her vineyard – yes! – but a company forges the wine." Adulterated wine calls forth the verb, "forges." The narrator's world is predicated on being cheated, deprived, with a corresponding social critique that becomes a projection of his own fears and fantasy.

We did not read any of the work of Bion in this class, but had we done so we might have described this rhetoric as an attack on linking, that destructive process whereby there is nowhere to put hatred, no symbolic form in which it can be projected and investigated: "Feelings of hatred are thereupon directed against all emotions including hate itself, and against external reality which stimulates them" (1984, 107). The speaker of *Maud* uses words like missiles, split off parts of himself that attack a feared attacker.

It is with Bion that my final example is concerned, a single line of poetry drawn from the ending of Browning's "Childe Roland to the Dark Tower Came" (1855): "Dauntless the slug-horn to my lips I set / And blew. *'Childe Roland to the Dark Tower came'*" (2007, l. 204). The metrical pattern of the final line is disrupted by the huge caesura following

"And blew." All that follows is simply the title of the poem itself. Everyone speculates about the ending of *Childe Roland* and its "meaning." Students rightly ponder the endless hermeneutic possibilities of this last line and what its phallic act of desperation signifies. Here psychoanalysis can help us not simply with content but with form. In a hypothetical teaching situation I would want to concentrate on the function of this massive pause. "There is much more continuity between intra-uterine life and earliest infancy than the impressive caesura of the act of birth allows us to believe," Bion (1977, 37) wrote, in his paper *Caesura*, following Freud's image of the caesura of birth. Interestingly, psychoanalysis borrows from poetics with a technical term. Can poetics borrow from psychoanalysis? In other work – I would want students to read *Four Discussions with W.R. Bion* (1978) as a comparatively contained way of coming at the nature of his thinking – Bion saw the function of the pause or the gap as a kind of hole that resists meaning. It is a generative space or void but our impulse, so strong is our dislike of the gap, is to fill it with "bogus ideas, paramnesias" (1978, 39). The "itch of the patient to fill the gap" (1978, 22) is comparable to the "itch" for closing down critical interpretation.

How could we think of the caesura in Browning's poem? For Lacan the move would be to the "unconscious," "that chapter in my history that is marked by a blank or occupied by a falsehood" (1977, 50). In an impressive recent reading, Cornelia Pearsall (2012) has interpreted the poem through trauma, noting the heavy ictus on "blew," with its resonance as a "blow." The verb has a double resonance as expiration, and a wound. One could read the caesura as a wound in the text, or a death, as the breath literally expires after the verb. This break or severance might have many possibilities. But here it seems like a break in the self's history of the self. It is a pause after which the poem re-inscribes its own title in italic, in a new form. This is a return to the point of no return, as John Ashbery wrote in "Wet Casements." The chasm in the text suggests that the "new" poem, *Childe Roland* in italics, begins again after the break, as in Joyce's *Finnegans Wake*, and concurrently interpretation begins again. The gap here is a seismic epistemephilic gap, the blank that both excites and destroys curiosity. Perhaps the gap here signifies that pause in which the poem's totality needs to "seep," as Bion put it, "from conscious rational levels to other levels of mind" (1978, 34), there to be creatively assimilated in the deepest ways. Alternatively, perhaps the pause after the blowing of the horn (which can enunciate nothing in language, can only make sound) registers psychic damage, what Bion describes as "a revival of thalamic fear – the fear which is so powerful that it makes thinking impossible" (1978, 45). This is a fear that has been building throughout the poem. No caesura is alike. Each pause will create different possibilities in different poems – every pause is unique.

***

The deep structures explored in psychoanalysis become ways of opening up thinking. In this essay I have asked, in the context of teaching, what Freud, Lacan, and Freud's Dora want. I have asked what the teacher and what the student want of psychoanalysis. On balance I prefer the third way of teaching, the use of a constellation of theoretical texts round a core literary text. It is a method that relies on serendipity, but the insights are often dramatic. We know of course that the epiphanies and inspirations of teaching are always unpredictable. But they will never come about unless the students feel that psychoanalysis reminds them, in Bion's words, of "real life."

Notes

1 Of the large volume of criticism on *Dora*, the most useful were McCaffrey (1984), Bernheimer and Kehane (1990), and Lakoff and Coyne (1993).

2 These phases are: rehearsal of the determining structure of castration for male and female subjects and the problematic nature of the phallic phase for women (Lacan 1982, 75–77); the phallus as primordial signifier on analogy with language, and the signifier/signified split that entails the "passion" of division and the repression undergone in the conscious/ unconscious split (78–79); the consequent "speaking" of the signifier in the unconscious (the Other) and the formative structure of need, demand, and desire that ensures there is always a residue of desire and lack in both male and female (i.e. this follows the patterns of castration) (79–81); the need to veil lack (82–83); sexual difference organized round having (male) and being (female) the phallus (83–85).

References

Armstrong, Isobel. 1989. "Teaching Women's Writing and Feminist Theory: Diary of a Two-Term Seminar." In *Teaching Women: Feminism and English Studies*, ed. Ann Thompson and Helen Wilcox, 88–95. Manchester: Manchester University Press.

Armstrong, Isobel. 2001. "Dreams by Day and Night: Kant, Freud and Ella Freeman Sharpe." *Women: A Cultural Review*, 12: 71–83.

Bernheimer, Charles, and Claire Kehane, eds. 1990 *In Dora's Case: Freud – Hysteria – Feminism*, 2nd edn. New York: Columbia University Press.

Bion, Wilfred. 1977. *Caesura*. London: Karnac Books.

Bion, Wilfred. 1978. *Four Discussions*. Perthshire: Clunie Press. Reprinted in *Clinical Seminars and Other Works*. 1994. London: Karnac Books.

Bion, Wilfred. 1984. *Second Thoughts: Selected Papers on Psychoanalysis*. London: Karnac Books.

Bollas, Christopher. 1987. *The Shadow of the Object: Psychoanalysis of the Unthought Known*. London: Free Association Books.

Brontë, Charlotte. 2006. *Jane Eyre*, ed. Stevie Davies. London: Penguin.

Browning, Robert. 2007. *The Poems of Robert Browning*, vol. 3, ed. John Woolford, Daniel Karlin, and Joseph Phelan. London: Longman.

Butler, Judith. 1990. *Gender Trouble: Feminism and the Subversion of Identity*. New York: Routledge.

Cavell, Stanley. 2005. *Philosophy the Day After Tomorrow*. Cambridge, MA: Belknap Press.

de Beauvoir, Simone. 1997. *The Second Sex*, ed. H.M. Parshley. London: Vintage.

Ellmann, Maud, ed. 1984. *Psychoanalytic Literary Criticism*. London: Longman.

Freud, Sigmund. 1953–74. *The Standard Edition of the Complete Psychological Works of Sigmund Freud*, 24 vols., ed. James Strachey, with the assistance of Anna Freud, Alix Strachey, and Alan Tyson, trans. James Strachey. London: Hogarth Press.

Freud, Sigmund. 1963. *Dora: An Analysis of a Case of Hysteria*, ed. Philip Rieff. New York: Macmillan.

Freud, Sigmund. 1977. *On Sexuality: Three Essays on the Theory of Sexuality and Other Works*, ed. Angela Richards, trans. James Strachey. Penguin Freud Library 7. Harmondsworth: Penguin.

Irigaray, Luce. 1985. *Speculum of the Other Woman*, trans. Gillian G. Gill. Ithaca, N.Y.: Cornell University Press.

Irigaray, Luce. 1989. "The Gesture in Psychoanalysis." In *Between Feminism and Psychoanalysis*, ed. Teresa Brennan, 127–38. London: Routledge.

Klein, Melanie. 1988. *Love, Guilt and Reparation, and Other Works, 1921–1945*. London: Virago.

Kristeva, Julia. 1982. *Powers of Horror: An Essay on Abjection*, trans. Leon S. Roudiez. New York: Columbia University Press.

Kristeva, Julia. 1986. "Stabat Mater." In *The Kristeva Reader*, ed. Toril Moi, 160–86. Oxford: Blackwell.

Lacan, Jacques. 1977. *Écrits: A Selection*. London: Tavistock.

Lacan, Jacques. 1982. "The Meaning of the Phallus." In *Feminine Sexuality: Jacques Lacan and the École Freudienne*, ed. Juliet Mitchell and Jacqueline Rose, trans. Jacqueline Rose, 74–85. London: Macmillan.

Lacan, Jacques. 1990. "Intervention on Transference." In *In Dora's Case: Freud – Hysteria – Feminism*, 2nd edn., ed. Charles Bernheimer and Claire Kehane, 92–104. New York: Columbia University Press.

Lakoff, Robin Tolmach, and James C. Coyne. 1993. *Father Knows Best: The Use and Abuse of Power in Freud's Case of Dora*. New York: Teachers College Press.

Laplanche, Jean. 1985. *Life and Death in Psychoanalysis*, trans. Jeffrey Mehlman. Baltimore: Johns Hopkins University Press.

McCaffrey, Phillip. 1984. *Freud and Dora: The Artful Dream*. New Brunswick: Rutgers University Press.

Milner, Marion. 1988 [1969]. *The Hands of the Living God: An Account of Psycho-Analytic Treatment*. London: Hogarth Press.

Pearsall, Cornelia. 2012. "Seeming Dead Indeed: The Trauma of the Dramatic Monologue." Lecture presented at "Re-Assessing the Dramatic Monologue in the 19th and 20th Centuries: Browning, Before, Beyond" conference, Royal Holloway College, London, June.

Sharpe, Ella Freeman. 1950. "Metaphor." In *Collected Papers on Psychoanalysis*, ed. Marjorie Brierley, 155–58. London: Institute of Psychoanalysis.

Tennyson, Alfred. 1988. *Maud*. In *The Poems of Tennyson*, 2nd edn., ed. Christopher Ricks. London: Longman.

Winnicott, D.W. 1971. *Playing and Reality*. Harmondsworth: Penguin.

Yousef, Nancy. 2010. "Romanticism, Psychoanalysis and the Interpretation of Silence." *European Romantic Review*, 21: 653–72.

Chapter 22

Touching and Not Touching

Naomi Segal

Most human beings have five senses, more or less. Everyday experience is "multisensual" (Rodaway 1997, 4) and "the senses are not merely passive receptors of particular kinds of environmental stimuli but are actively involved in the structuring of that information." I say more or less five, for the history and geography of the senses show that while that total is traditional, it is often disputed not only for the sake of precision but because of a general feeling that there must be something else.

We have five senses in which we glory and which we recognize and celebrate, senses that constitute the sensible world for us. But there are other senses – secret senses, sixth senses, if you will – equally vital, but unrecognized, and unlauded. These senses, unconscious, automatic, had to be discovered. Historically, indeed, their discovery came late: what the Victorians vaguely called "muscle sense" – the awareness of the relative position of trunk and limbs, derived from receptors in the joints and tendons – was only really defined (and named "proprioception") in the 1890s. And the complex mechanisms and controls by which our bodies are properly aligned and balanced in space – these have only been defined in our own century and still hold many mysteries (Sacks 1986, 68).

One suggestion lists ten basic senses, including four varieties of touch plus two of orientation (Gold, in Rodaway 1997, 28). Others searching

A Concise Companion to Psychoanalysis, Literature, and Culture, First Edition.
Edited by Laura Marcus and Ankhi Mukherjee.

for the proverbial sixth sense cite extrasensory perception (Howes 1991, 258, 290), desire (Serres 1985, 57–60), proprioception defined as "our totally intuitive sense of our own bodies" (Josipovici 1996, 110), or more rarefied abilities like that of the skilled wine-taster. Different cultures have more or fewer senses, or lay stress on different aspects. Of three non-literate societies cited by Constance Classen, "each has a very distinct way of making sense of the world: the Tzotzil accord primacy to heat in their cosmology, the Ongee to odor, and the Desana to color" (Howes 2005, 148). Words for sensing are also variable, and often clustered: "the Hausa have one word for hearing, smelling, tasting and touching, understanding and emotional feeling" (Ritchie, in Howes 1991, 194); French too, of course, uses one word (*sentir*) for smelling and for both physical and emotional feeling.

However many senses we wish to number, it is interesting that, until recently, they were discussed only in order to be distinguished and separated. Since Aristotle, the senses have been placed in a hierarchical order, dependent either on proximity to the thing sensed or on the difference between human and animal. Thus "touch (and thereby taste) was found in all animals and so became the lowliest sense ... [Aristotle] posed a hierarchical order of the senses, from most to least valuable: vision-hearing-smell-taste-touch" (Stewart, in Howes 2005, 61). Even if animals showed more skills than us with certain senses, theirs were intrinsically the inferior ones. This hierarchy slides into the other, for the last three of these are the "proximity" or "intimate senses" (Rodaway 1997, 26), devalued because they are deemed the furthest from thought, imagination, and memory. As I have remarked elsewhere, these three senses are also the ones in which the nuances of active and passive perception are linguistically the least differentiated. While for sight and hearing we have three verbs:

> I look at the picture, I see the moon, I look tired
> I listen to the music, I hear thunder, I sound interested

for smell, taste, and touch, one verb has to stand in for all these functions:

> I smell a rose, I smell burning, I smell funny
> I taste the soup, I taste a trace of cinnamon, it tastes bitter
> I feel the velvet, I feel the sun on my face, I feel pretty

But this could be a reason for suggesting that, far from being more blunt, the words we use for the proximate senses "do more work, convey more variation, carry more weight" (Segal 2001, 18).

However undifferentiated language seems to think them, recent theory has turned back to these less favored senses because, actually, they are better at imagining (Baudelaire), remembering (Proust), and of course loving.

Contemporary theory sees the senses as a multiplicity – hence the use of terms like "sensorium ... sense ratio" (McLuhan, in Howes 2005, 43–51) or "sensotypes" (Wober, in Howes 1991, 33). To McLuhan sensing is a kaleidoscope (in Howes 1991, 167), to Serres a knot or an island (Serres 1985, 51–52), to Howes synesthesia, the latter defined as a way of "short-circuiting the five sense model" (Howes 2005, 292). It is the meeting of senses and sensations that most preoccupies current thinking: the "pluri-sensorial" (Howes 1991, 6), "combinatory" (Howes 1991, 167), "multidirectional ... intersensoriality" (Howes 2005, 12). And, as the rest of this essay will explore, the multiplicity of the senses is most richly focused in the sense of touch.

Curiously, whichever way one looks at the lists of senses, touch is almost always found at one end.

> In the evolution of the senses the sense of touch was undoubtedly the first to come into being. Touch is the parent of our eyes, ears, nose, and mouth. It is the sense which became differentiated into the others, a fact that seems to be recognized in the age-old evaluation of touch as "the mother of the senses".
>
> (Montagu 1986, 3)

Among the three histories of feral children discussed by Constance Classen, Victor's faculties were ranked thus: "'The sense of smell is first and most perfected; taste is second, or rather these senses are but one; vision occupies the position of third importance, hearing the fourth, and touch the last'" (Bonnaterre, in Howes 1991, 49), whereas Kaspar Hauser "had an almost supernatural sense of touch. The touch of humans and animals gave him a sensation of heat or cold, at times so strong that he felt as if he had received a blow" (1991, 54). More generally, "the senses of *Homo sapiens* develop in a definite sequence, as (1) tactile, (2) auditory, and (3) visual. As the child approaches adolescence the order of precedence becomes reversed, as (1) visual, (2) auditory, and (3) tactile" (Montagu 1986, 314–15). Indeed in infant development, of humans as well as animals, the stimulation of this sense is so crucial that "when the need for touch remains unsatisfied, abnormal behaviour will result" (Montagu 1986, 46) – "children need touch for survival" (Field 2003, 5).

For "the human sensorium … never exists in a natural state. Humans are social beings, and just as human nature itself is a product of culture, so is the human sensorium" (Howes 2005, 3). In infants, the first version of this social interaction is the whole complex of holding, massage, breastfeeding understood as "reciprocal interstimulation" (Montagu 1986, 43) provided by the mother or primary caregiver. This is never only one-sided: among the Wolof of Senegal, "when a visitor arrives, male or female, often before any word is exchanged, he or she is handed a baby. This gesture is intended to 'mediate' the relation between adults" (Howes 1991, 184). Touch is "a kind of communication between person and world, a corporeal situation rather than a cognitive positioning … Touch is direct and intimate, and perhaps the most truthful sense" (Rodaway 1997, 44); it is the sense we use to test the material reality of a thing by direct bodily perception (Josipovici 1996, 2, 29). If, then, "the history of the senses has been, essentially, the history of their objectification" (Mazzio, in Howes 2005, 85), the "history of touch is, essentially, a history of resisting objectification" (in Howes 2005, 86).

What does psychoanalytic theory have to say about the senses? However much – at least in Freud – it depends on the existence of the psyche "in" a lived body, the body as physically sentient seems to play a very minimal part. Laplanche and Pontalis's index lists "sense of guilt" and "sense of inferiority" but nothing on "the senses." In Freud, the infant's body as a network of erotogenic fields has sensation but not senses. Yet the sense of touch is implicit in the importance he gives to the skin as a way of understanding the ego, situated between a psychical "inside" and a psychical "outside." In *Das Ich und das Es* (*The Ego and the Id*) (1923), he describes the ego as "first and foremost a bodily ego; it is not merely a surface entity, but is itself the projection of a surface" (Freud 1984, 364): "a mental projection of the surface of the body" (1984, 364–65n.).

I start from the principle that the body is not simply a lived object in space but an emissary: through its ability to touch it communicates something of the self to something of other selves. Of course, as Drew Leder (1990) observes, we know little of the "lives" of even our own internal organs, let alone the biographies of our feelings or the feelings of others. But we live this ignorance in a dramatic way, and that drama is mediated through our organ of touch, the skin.

Freud's image of the "body-ego" (Freud 1984, 366) was perhaps the first of the key influences on Anzieu's theory of the skin-ego; others include ethologists Harlow and Bowlby and psychoanalysts Abraham and Torok, Bicks, Bion, Meltzer, Tustin, and Winnicott. Anzieu first published an article on the topic in 1974 but his fullest account, *Le Moi-peau* (*The Skin-ego*) was published in 1985 and expanded in 1995. In Freud's time "what was repressed was sex" (Anzieu 1995, 43); in the 1980s the ignored and problematic issue was the body. Since Lacan, the stress on language had meant that the body was not being psychoanalytically theorized; yet "every psychic activity leans on a biological function" (1995, 61). Anzieu's aim was to fill this gap. "Psychic space and physical space constitute each other in reciprocal metaphors; the Skin-ego is one of these metaphors" (Anzieu 1990, 58).

In the late twentieth century, with a world flowing out of control – and how little has changed since then – the typical patient is no longer a neurotic suffering from hysteria or obsessions but a borderline case whose problem is a lack of limits. Maths, biology, and neurophysiology have all become sciences of interfaces, membranes, and borders, and embryology has shown that the ectoderm forms both the brain and the skin; thus "the centre is situated at the periphery" (Anzieu 1995, 31). Like any shell or peel, the skin has a double surface – "a protective one on the outside and, underneath it or in its orifices, the other, which collects information and filters exchanges" – and it is this complex structure of surfaces, rather than the old image of thought penetrating through into a truth-core, that can help us understand our physical, psychical, and intellectual worlds in a different way.

The skin appears on the embryo before the other sense systems; its outward look varies enough to give off signs of age, sex, ethnicity, and personality, it consists of no fewer than five kinds of tissue and it is the site of endless paradoxes:

> The skin is permeable and impermeable. It is superficial and profound. It is truthful and deceptive. It regenerates, yet is permanently drying out. ... It provokes libidinal investments as often narcissistic as sexual. It is the seat of well-being and seduction. It supplies us as much with pain as pleasure. ... In its thinness and vulnerability, it stands for our native helplessness, greater than that of any other species, but at the same time our evolutionary adaptiveness. It separates and unites the various senses. In all these dimensions that I have incompletely listed, it has the status of an intermediary, an in-between, a transitional thing.
>
> (1995, 39)

Under its mother's care, an infant receives both stimulation and communication, and thus

> the establishment of the Skin-ego responds to the need for a narcissistic envelope and creates, for the psychic apparatus, the assurance of a constant, certain, basic well-being. ... By "Skin-ego" I am referring to a configuration used by the child's ego during its early stages of development to represent itself as an ego containing psychic contents, based on its experience of the surface of the body.
>
> (1995, 61)

Babies have a "bodily pre-ego" which helps them to develop as individuals, and this is based on reliable feedback from a "twinned" (1995, 81) other of a kind that will be echoed later in love relationships. As we have seen, touch is the first sense-faculty to develop embryonically and thus "the skin is the basic reference point for all the various sense data" (1995, 83); and because touch is the only reflexive sense it gives rise gradually to the reflexivity of thought. The baby develops the phantasy of a "skin common to the mother and the child, an interface with the mother on one side and the child on the other" (1995, 85) – again an illusion of reciprocal inclusion that "is revived in the experience of [sexual] love, in which each, holding the other in their arms, envelops the other while being enveloped by them." But just as love can fail, the common skin can appear too tight, too loose, or violently torn away, leading to pathologies of the skin-ego.

Anzieu goes on to list eight main "functions" of the skin-ego, each having its potential pathology. They are: holding (*maintenance*); handling or containing (*contenance*); protection against stimuli (*pare-excitation*; in Freud, *Reizschutz*); individuation (*individuation*); consensuality or intersensoriality (*consensualité*); sexualization (*soutien de l'excitation sexuelle*); libidinal recharging (*recharge libidinale*); and inscription or signification (*inscription des traces*). And there is an extra, ninth function which, like the last fairy at the christening, crowns the positive with a negative: the skin's capacity for self-destruction or toxicity (*activité toxique*).

As we have seen, the term "consensuality" is used by Anzieu for the fifth function of the skin-ego, which brings together the perception of all the senses in one place – all our senses are sited somewhere on our skin – and thus stands for the coherence, coincidence, or co-presence of perceptions (Anzieu 1995, 127). The qualities of the sense of touch serve as "the ground or backcloth on which other sense qualities stand out as figures" (Anzieu 1994, 35).

The word was borrowed from Donald Meltzer, who observes of a child's imaginative play: "we are envisaging attention as the strings which hold the senses together in consensuality" (Meltzer et al. 1975, 12–13). It is from him that Anzieu takes the term for what can go wrong with this function: the consensual convergence may, as Meltzer puts it, be passively "dismantled" by an autistic child when, "somewhat akin to allowing a brick wall to fall to pieces by the action of the weather, moss, fungi and insects" (1975, 12), the senses are made to attach singly and separately to the internal or external object that is "the most stimulating at that moment." But when consensuality works well and the skin-ego is in place, it can lead towards an ability to "seek out concordances and convergence" (Anzieu 1994, 104) and forms of thought that emphasize analogy, the microcosm, and "systems of correspondence between words, things and thoughts."

Of course the most obvious meaning of the term – in both French and English – is to do with consensus and consent. Etymologically, as Anzieu notes, the idea of consensus derives from the "mutual agreement of the senses" (1994, 35) and the idea of a "common sense" brings the body together with the mind to create a basis for thought:

> The word "sense" has a double meaning. "Sense" means "signification", which finds its most extensive organization in language. "The senses" are the body organs by which the human being makes contact with its surroundings and in the first place with its mother. The work by which the infant creates its psychic apparatus, and by which the patient and analyst create interpretation, consists of articulating "sense" with "the senses". Words have value and bear meaning through their weight of flesh. The unconscious is not language; it is the body … the intelligence of the body.
> (Anzieu 2000, 268)

If the intelligence of the body is the basis of both sense and consent, the question of consensuality is also to do with human relations based on the sense of touch, most particularly the mother – child couple and the relation of desire. As Merleau-Ponty argues in *Le Visible et l'invisible*, every touch is double: it involves both an active and a passive experience; I feel myself feeling and felt. Thus, when I touch a sculpture or a piano, I am also dwelling on the surface of the body of the other. If pleasure is a tactical, tangential experience, is it also contagion? What are the limits of consent between bodies? Is love ever mutual?

*

In the last section of this essay I will look at some literary representations of the spatial modalities of desire as it moves towards the body of the other. What we find, particularly in French Romantic male-authored poetry, is a motion that never arrives. Instead it starts by zooming and ends not in a caress but a gliding-above, a frozen hovering. Zooming and hovering are, perhaps surprisingly, parts of a single gesture, the motion-above that is flight. One example is Baudelaire's poem "Élévation," in which, in a series of vivid images of movement, the poet imagines his "spirit" leaping up away from the earth and forging "avec une indicible et mâle volupté" ("with an ineffable, virile delight") towards "les champs lumineux et sereins" ("light, serene fields"). But in the last two lines, motion is replaced by another spatial relation. Happy is he

> – Qui plane sur la vie et comprend sans effort
> Le langage des fleurs et des choses muettes!
>
> – Who hovers over life and understands with ease
> The language of flowers and silent things!
> (Baudelaire 1968, 46)

Birds and other flying things are a central passion of Romantic poets: Hugo's verses are full of swans, doves, butterflies, eagles, and other avatars of the poetic "songeur ailé" ("winged dreamer") or his loved ones (Hugo 1969, 339). In Baudelaire they are part of a fascination with claustrophobia that focuses on the lowering skies and tide of roofs of 1850s Paris. And yet, as we see in all these poems, flying never reaches a goal. Vast skies are framed in the city by windows or balconies and swans paddle in dust; over the ocean, albatrosses soar only to be snared and mocked; even the last voyage of death cannot be imagined except as anticlimax: "La toile était levée et j'attendais encore" ("the curtain had gone up, and I was still waiting") ("Le Rêve d'un curieux," Baudelaire 1968, 122).

The excitement of the poem is, rather, in the repetition of take-off – what Leo Bersani calls "a kind of vertical leap of consciousness" (Bersani 1977, 24) – that is rehearsed in a cluster of prepositions or verbs of sudden movement. Zooming as a fantasy cannot be separated from the moment of departing from the ground. Birds take off by generating enough airflow to create lift or by dropping on to an existing gust of wind. Aeroplanes build up speed by taxiing, again relying on headwind or high-lift devices to set up the first upward motion. Dumbo proves he is no ordinary elephant by becoming the staple of drunken imaginings. Freud identifies the dream or fantasy of flying as a typical phenomenon, especially in children:

> why do so many people dream of being able to fly? The answer that psychoanalysis gives is that to fly or be a bird is only a disguise for another wish, ... a longing to be capable of sexual performance. ... Whenever

> children feel in the course of their sexual researches that in the province which is so mysterious but nevertheless so important there is something wonderful of which adults are capable but which they are forbidden to know of and do, they are filled with a violent wish to be able to do it, and they dream of it in the form of flying, or they prepare this disguise of their wish to be used in later flying dreams. Thus aviation, too, which in our days at last achieving its aim, has infantile erotic roots.
>
> (Freud 1985, 219–20)

And Kafka's "Wunsch, Indianer zu werden" ("Wishing to be a Red Indian") (1913; Kafka 2001) traces in a single breathless if-only sentence a centaur-like zooming that loses spurs, reins, ground, and, by the fifth line, even the horse. Something of the same fantasy surely underlies Anzieu's 1992 description of himself: "I have formed with my superego a couple united in the way a horseman is with his mount – and I don't know exactly which of us was the man and which the horse" (Parot and Richelle 1992, 257). As in Kafka, the imagined unity of two such different creatures out of their more complex interdependence as master and servant effectively means that one of the two must disappear. There is here a defiant endorsement of the castration complex that I shall return to.

In *Le Corps de l'œuvre* (1981), Anzieu identifies creativity as "the illusion of lightness" (Anzieu 1981, 12) and "take-off" or "lift-off" (*décollage*) as its essential first stage: this is what transforms creativity, a predisposition, into creation, an activity: "Most creative individuals are never creators; what makes the difference, as Proust says of Bergotte, is the take-off" (1981, 17–18).

The fantasy of flying is gratuitous, purposeless, either an act of sheer undirected joy or the premise for something else. To soar like Superman is a simple phallic image – but take-off is a rather more complicated one. As the metaphors from Baudelaire, Kafka, and Anzieu suggest, the desire to fly forth is a wish to gain by losing. It is all about positive separation, but – as the aviational terms *décollage* and "unstick speed" show – it is also a risk of ungluing or unscrewing, of removing, of being separated. If what can fly is the phallus rather than the man, who is he when he is no longer anything but his desire to desire? The boyish bravado – "I'm youth, I'm joy ... I'm a little bird that has broken out of the egg," cries Peter Pan when challenged by Hook (Barrie 1988, 135) – that dreams of sexuality in the form of flying is dealing with the fear of castration by a kind of preemption; but then what becomes of the self that feared?

It explains, I think, the Baudelairean insistence that "les vrais voyageurs sont ceux-là seuls qui partent / Pour partir" ("the only true travelers are those who leave for the sake of leaving") ("Le Voyage," Baudelaire

1968, 123): the fantasy of soaring or zooming is simply the fantasy of taking off without any next stage. Or rather, what it leads to is a corollary that is also almost directly its obverse. Let us now examine the second fantasy of sexual desire: that of hovering. If we return to the ending of "Élévation" where the poet, once on high, uses his position to drift overhead understanding the language of silent things, we find that Baudelaire's term is *planer*, to hover or glide. Anzieu's term, borrowed from Proust, is *survoler*: to fly above. Both images describe a relationship of stable superiority, a God's-eye view, conferring knowledge rather than pleasure, an ability that Baudelaire suggests is something like hearing the unvoiced speech of the inanimate (flowers as *bijoux indiscrets* born to blush unseen?) but which Victor Hugo and others would present as reading the world as book – even though as writers they have created the thing they read.

As fantasies, authorship and hovering are closely allied, then. They both confer a divine privilege – but over something that is only *fantasized* to have preexisted the leap. In a letter of 1852, after all, Flaubert defines the presence of the author in the text as being "like God in the universe: everywhere present and nowhere visible" (Flaubert 1980, 16). Of course, our image of what it might be like to be God is drastically conditioned by our position "from below," and it is this tyranny of invisibility that the aspiring author longs to assume.

In fact, of course, the ones who actually are immortal (since they have never lived) are the characters: Flaubert's compulsion to ironize stupid Emma or Charles is surely an expedient based on envy. These infants of his wishful mastery are actually the easiest things in the world to master – impossible not to master. But they are also attempts at mastering readership (Emma embodies this, since she lives and dies by reading), and readers are much harder to control. The wish to be immortal, which the children of our imagination do not even have to form, so inconceivable is it for them to die, is something that only flesh-and-blood people can have, and they have it by seeking virtual readers who will, like corpse-brides, agree to make them virtual writers. Nothing could, perhaps, seem further from the body that makes it possible to have desires at all. But that would be misleading.

Like Anzieu, Sartre uses the term *survol* in describing how Flaubert in fantasy rises up above the rest of the human race who have made him feel abjectly despised: after climbing in fantasy to the top of a high tower from which giant-like position he can despise everyone, there is a sort of rush of motion and "whether he has been snatched up from the earth or the futile planet has dropped by itself into the abysses of space-time infinity, the fact is that he finds himself *in the air*" (Sartre 1971, 1185). Or again, "all of a sudden, panting and sacred, he rises up above his torturers, above Nero himself: how small they look, these instruments of his glory. He hovers and looks down, from the ether, at the rag he has left behind in their hands" (1971, 1177). The rag, like the skin of flayed Marsyas, is the bodily thing left after the fantasy has disembodied him. But we should not forget that it is the bodily thing that produces the fantasies.

Here is another, less human but also less agonized, version of hovering. Leconte de Lisle (1818–94), whose poems are suffused with a fulsome remembrance of Réunion, the Indian Ocean island where he spent his youth, writes of jungle scenes in which the apparent peace of sleep contains the coiled menace of animal violence: far-off lions or elephants slumber in the noonday heat, a tiger "falls asleep, its belly in the air, and dilates its claws" (Leconte de Lisle 1976, 175); and the jaguar dreams, a proper Freudian *avant la lettre*, that it is plunging "its streaming nails / Into the flesh of terrified, bellowing bulls" (1976, 185). His birds are nobler: his albatross, unlike Coleridge's or Baudelaire's (and contrast the vulnerable swans of Mallarmé or Rilke: some poets like their zoology classically uncomplicated), does not plunge to earth but "tranquil amidst the terror" of a violent storm on high, "approaches, passes and disappears majestically" (Leconte de Lisle 1977, 67). It is in "Le Sommeil du condor" ("The Sleep of the Condor"), however, that the full fantasy of hovering – the coexistence of extreme power with extreme stillness – is clearest.

The condor is a member of the vulture family. It is supposed to have various peculiarities: to be able to go for long periods without feeding and to flush pink when emotional; but the aspect that has made most impact, and was noted by Darwin, is its ability to hover for long periods without apparently flapping its wings. Leconte de Lisle's poem begins, like Baudelaire's with vivid prepositions of flight, and then observes "Le vaste Oiseau, tout plein d'une morne indolence" ("The vast Bird, filled with gloomy indolence") (Leconte de Lisle 1977, 166) gazing down upon the map-like panorama of America. As night rolls in like a tide from the east, it waits "comme un spectre, seul, au front du pic altier" ("alone, like a ghost, atop the lofty peak"), until at last the darkness covers it. Then,

> Il râle son plaisir, il agite sa plume,
> Il érige son cou musculeux et pelé,
> Il s'élève en fouettant l'âpre neige des Andes,

Dans un cri rauque il monte où n'atteint pas le vent,
Et, loin du globe noir, loin de l'astre vivant,
Il dort dans l'air glacé, les ailes toutes grandes.

He groans out his pleasure, shakes his plumage,
erects his muscular, hairless neck,
and soars up, whipping the acrid snow of the Andes;
with a hoarse cry, he rises to where the wind cannot reach
and, far above the black globe, high above the living star,
he sleeps in the icy air, his great wings outstretched.
(Leconte de Lisle 1977, 167)

This is, of course, a fantasy of phallic absoluteness: permanently tense, permanently relaxed – the ballet of male desire. But, as we have already observed, the ideal relies on failure: not simply on the logical impossibility of this fusion of extremes, but also on a different, psychic impossibility. In relation to Baudelaire's sudden switch from zooming to hovering, Leo Bersani observes:

> The emergence of an erotic esthetic will also involve the eroticizing of knowledge. But in early poems such as "Élévation" and "La Beauté", the sexual imagery is merely juxtaposed with the epistemological claims. In "Élévation", the description of the poet's spirit plunging beyond the confines of the "starry spheres" suggests sexual penetration ... but this erotic "rising up" seems to have no effect on the nature of the poet's comprehension of "the language of flowers and of silent things". An effortless serene understanding is unaffected by the erotic energy of the leap into understanding.
>
> (Bersani 1977, 25)

My own view is that these contraries are disconnected in a rather different way. The erotics of the flying fantasy is threefold. If we trace it in reverse, the end-point of hovering stands both for the *survol* of superior knowledge, control from on high, and for the erectile tension that has become a sort of immortality or grace. Before this, the effort of desire is expressed in the fantasy of zooming, reaching-towards. Before even this, the initial movement is a taking-off, the initiative of excitement that lifts. Each one of these actions is, separately and together, a tracking-forth of the excitement of castration. Like "escape velocity," the most extreme and deathly version, or Vincent's aimless aim of going into space, they are all fantasies of distance.

In Anzieu's citation from Proust, the relation of take-off to hovering that represents Bergotte's creativity is a sort of zigzag: "In order to travel in the air, it is not the most powerful automobile that is needed but one which is capable, by sheer ascensional force, of ceasing to run on the ground and cutting across the line of its horizontal speed with the vertical" (Proust 1954, 554). Bergotte's talent may be nothing very special in itself, despised by family friends in Rolls Royces, but it has this capacity: "from inside his modest machine which had at last "taken off", he hovered above them [*les survolait*]" (1954, 555; Anzieu 1981, 17). Carefully examined, the first motion is horizontal, the second vertical, the third again horizontal, but no longer moving forward, for the relation of superiority is not directional but static. It is all about separation. This knowledge is, *pace* Bersani, still erotic, but an erotics of distance, coolness born out of heat.

The whole point of this fantasy is its inability to touch. The fact that it must not come to an end means that it is, effectively, all end. It is castratory because, ultimately, the machine hovers alone, isolated from its origin. The obvious corollary of the condor – that patient predator – is the modern bomber-plane. Its association with death may be suicidal, like that of Yeats's Irish airman in 1919, driven on high by "a lonely impulse of delight," very similar to that of Saint-Exupéry's heroes experiencing "the mysterious labor of a living flesh" (Saint-Exupéry 1931, 23); or it may be homicidal like that of Marinetti, who writes in *The Battle of Tripoli* (1912) of the pleasure of bombing without needing to dirty his hands. But ultimately it goes out beyond the flesh, representing the extreme "clean" violence of the *survol*: brains without bodies. In 1921, with remarkable prescience, Marinetti wrote of the possibility – like Kafka's Red Indian fantasy – of the violence of hovering imagined at the furthest extreme from bodily presence:

> Phantom-aeroplanes laden with bombs and without pilots, remote-controlled by a "shepherd" aeroplane. Phantom-planes without pilots which will explode with their bombs, which can also be guided from the ground by an electric control-panel. We will have aerial torpedoes. One day we will have electric war.
>
> (Marinetti 1985, 121)

Anticipating the tactics of today's aerial bombardment, and the very reverse of our contemporary suicide bombers, these masculine fantasies of desire are both self-separation and separation from the other. Consummation, it seems, is neither sought nor achieved; but there is no loss either, because the "other" – land viewed from above, flowers and other mute things – is actually much too far away to be heard, seen, or touched.

References

Anzieu, Didier. 1981. *Le Corps de l'œuvre*. Paris: Gallimard.

Anzieu, Didier. 1990. *L'Épiderme nomade et la peau psychique*. Paris: Éditions du Collège de psychanalyse groupale et familiale.

Anzieu, Didier. 1994. *Le Penser*. Paris: Dunod.

Anzieu, Didier. 1995 [1985]. *Le Moi-peau*. Paris: Dunod. Trans. Chris Turner as *The Skin Ego*. New Haven: Yale University Press, 1981.

Anzieu, Didier. 2000. *Psychanalyser*. Paris: Dunod.

Barrie, J.M. 1988 [1911]. *Peter Pan and Wendy*. London: Pavilion.

Baudelaire, Charles. 1968 [1857]. *Les Fleurs du mal*, in *Œuvres complètes*, ed. Marcel Ruff, 40–131. Paris: Seuil.

Bersani, Leo. 1977. *Baudelaire and Freud*. Berkeley: University of California Press.

Field, Tiffany. 2003 [2001]. *Touch*. Cambridge, MA: MIT Press.

Flaubert, Gustave. 1980 [1853]. *Correspondance II*, ed. J. Bruneau. Paris: Gallimard.

Freud, Sigmund. 1984 [1923]. *The Ego and the Id*, trans. James Strachey, 339–407. Pelican Freud Library 11. Harmondsworth: Penguin.

Freud, Sigmund. 1985 [1910]. *Leonardo da Vinci and a Memory of His Childhood*, trans. James Strachey, 143–231. Pelican Freud Library 14. Harmondsworth: Penguin.

Howes, David, ed. 1991. *The Varieties of Sensory Experience*. Toronto: University of Toronto Press.

Howes, David, ed. 2005. *Empire of the Senses: The Sensual Culture Reader*. Oxford: Berg.

Hugo, Victor. 1969 [1856]. *Les Contemplations*, ed. Léon Cellier. Paris: Garnier.

Josipovici, Gabriel. 1996. *Touch*. New Haven: Yale University Press.

Kafka, Franz. 2001 [1924]. *Die Erzählungen*. Frankfurt: Fischer.

Leconte de Lisle, Charles-Marie-René. 1976 [1889]. *Œuvres*, vol. 2: *Poèmes barbares*, ed. Edgard Pich. Paris: Société d'édition "Les belles lettres".

Leconte de Lisle, Charles-Marie-René. 1977 [1884, 1886]. *Œuvres*, vol. 3: *Poèmes tragiques; derniers poèmes*, ed. Edgard Pich. Paris: Société d'édition "Les belles lettres".

Leder, Drew. 1990. *The Absent Body*. Chicago: University of Chicago Press.

Marinetti, Filippo Tommaso. 1985 [1921]. *L'Alcova di acciaio*. Milan: Serra e Riva.

Meltzer, Donald, et al. 1975. *Explorations in Autism*. Strath Tay: Clunie.

Montagu, Ashley. 1986 [1971]. *Touching: The Human Significance of the Skin*. New York: Harper & Row.

Parot, Françoise, and Richelle, Marc, eds. 1992. *Psychologues de langue française*. Paris: Presses Universitaires de France.

Proust, Marcel. 1954 [1918]. *A la recherche du temps perdu*, vol. 1: *A l'ombre des jeunes filles en fleurs*, ed. Pierre Clarac and André Ferré, 431–990. Paris: Gallimard.

Rodaway, Paul. 1997. *Sensuous Geographies*. London: Routledge.
Sacks, Oliver. 1986 [1985]. *The Man Who Mistook His Wife for a Hat*. London: Picador.
Saint-Exupéry, Antoine de. 1931. *Vol de nuit*. Paris: Gallimard.
Sartre, Jean-Paul. 1971. *L'Idiot de la famille: Gustave Flaubert de 1821 à 1857*, vol 2. Paris: Gallimard.
Segal, Naomi. 2001 "'L'Échange de deux fantaisies et le contact de deux épidermes': Skin and Desire." In *Sensual Reading*, ed. Michael Syrotinski and Ian Maclachlan, 17–38. Lewisburg: Associated University Presses.
Serres, Michel. 1985. *Les Cinq Sens*. Paris: Grasset.

Index

A Concise Companion to Psychoanalysis, Literature, and Culture, First Edition.
Edited by Laura Marcus and Ankhi Mukherjee.

Printed and bound by CPI Group (UK) Ltd, Croydon, CR0 4YY

24/03/2025

14645547-0001